THE UNIVERSITY OF
WINCHESTER

Martial Rose Library
Tel: 01962 827306

To be returned on or before the day marked above, subject to recall.

A Quiet Word

A Quiet Word

Lobbying, Crony Capitalism and
Broken Politics in Britain

TAMASIN CAVE and ANDY ROWELL

THE BODLEY HEAD
LONDON

Published by The Bodley Head 2014

2 4 6 8 10 9 7 5 3 1

First published in Great Britain in 2014 by
The Bodley Head
Random House, 20 Vauxhall Bridge Road,
London SW1V 2SA
www.bodleyhead.co.uk
www.vintage-books.co.uk

Addresses for companies within The Random House Group Limited can be found at:
www.randomhouse.co.uk/offices.htm

The Random House Group Limited Reg. No. 954009
A CIP catalogue record for this book
is available from the British Library

ISBN 9781847922328

The Random House Group Limited supports the Forest Stewardship Council® (FSC®),
the leading international forest-certification organisation. Our books carrying the FSC
label are printed on FSC®-certified paper. FSC is the only forest-certification scheme
supported by the leading environmental organisations, including Greenpeace. Our
paper procurement policy can be found at www.randomhouse.co.uk/environment

Typeset in Dante MT Std 11.5/14 pt
by Palimpsest Book Production Limited, Falkirk, Stirlingshire

Printed and bound in Great Britain by Clays Ltd, St Ives plc

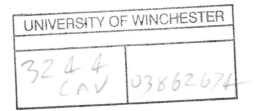

For the kids

Contents

Preface

'I expect my right to privacy to be upheld. Does this mean I have something to hide? Of course not. It just means I don't see why my business is Tamasin Cave's business.'

This has been a common response among lobbyists as we have probed into their affairs. Why should they reveal their activities to 'self-appointed' transparency campaigners like us? It is a fair point. We have no more right to know what lobbyists are up to than anyone else. That is just the point. None of us have the right to know.

We disagree with the prevailing view among lobbyists that they should be able to influence our politicians in the interests of whoever is paying without public scrutiny. Their lobbying shapes Britain and our lives. We think the public has a right to know.

For the past eight years, with colleagues at Spinwatch, a not-for-profit organisation that examines the players shaping the public agenda, and many others concerned about the hidden influence of lobbyists (see acknowledgements on page 365), we have been asking government for rules that would force lobbyists to operate in the open.

The way to do this is with a simple register. It would require lobbyists to publicly declare who is lobbying whom, what they are seeking to influence and how much money they are spending doing it. As lobbyists, we would be on it. As would company X lobbying for NHS contracts, company Y lobbying against proposals for a living wage and company Z pushing for corporate tax breaks. When we can see who is influencing our politicians, we can begin to hold them to account.

Lobbying in the face of the commercial influence industry, we have witnessed and been on the receiving end of many of their tactics. We have observed the two faces of the lobbying industry. One is professional. These people know politics and its processes inside out and how best to present their case to government. This is lobbying as seen by politicians, courteous and respectful. But there is another, darker side to the business. One that involves a selective approach to the truth, media manipulation, the undermining of opponents and other dubious practices.

Take this by way of a small illustration. We kicked off our call for a register of lobbyists to coincide with an investigation into lobbying by MPs. They took evidence from lobbyists who presented their professional, public face as expected. We sat in the gallery as a pharmaceutical lobbyist described the industry's lobbying of government and the NHS. The picture created was of a harmonious relationship based on 'trust' and 'straightforward dialogue'. They were, he said, 'all working to the same end'. No mention of the protection of profits in this account of why pharmaceutical companies lobby government.

The MPs, however, had in front of them a lobbying 'battle plan' drafted by the pharmaceutical industry. Strategies to influence government included 'deploying ground troops' in the form of patient front groups, which it hoped would 'have the effect of weakening political, ideological and professional defences'. The industry's plan was then to 'follow through with high-level precision strikes' on regulators and politicians. Straightforward dialogue, absolutely.

What emerges is a picture of an industry at odds with itself. Its purpose, in theory at least, is proper: it is right that government should listen to outside interests. Its methods are sometimes not. On an individual level, lobbyists are not generally out to cause harm. Collectively, Britain's £2bn commercial lobbying industry is capable of causing significant damage to our country.

Yet the threat to the influence industry of being regulated in the way we are advocating, itself a tiny step towards making government more accountable, is small. The appetite among politicians to force lobbying into the open is weak, despite promises and pressure to act.

We have seen a series of lobbying scandals unfold in the press. They have involved more than one current Cabinet member, former ministers, Lords and ex-generals; defence interests, energy firms, private health companies and, of course, the Murdoch empire. These are not rogue operators, bad apples or isolated cases. They are the establishment. The barrel is rotten.

This book, therefore, is an attempt to reveal something of the whole: the commercial influence industry that is embedded in British politics, operating year round and across government, but which only rarely finds itself in the spotlight. Our aim is to reveal its ways of working and show how influence is crafted, very deliberately, using a set of tools. There is nothing mysterious about what lobbyists do. It is simply hidden. It is our aim that by the end of this book you will be as familiar with this box of tricks as lobbyists are.

Lobbyists are a bit like Borrowers: they leave their footprints all over government policy, we just never get to see them at work. The best lobbying is that which goes unnoticed, and it follows that the majority of it does. For the most part, this book presents only the most visible of their activities, which is to omit a large part of the day-to-day work of lobbyists.

Much of this involves the dry, but crucial, monitoring of government and gathering of political intelligence. Then there is the constant technical reworking of laws and regulations, which may affect very few outside of those lobbying, but which can bring millions of pounds' worth of benefits to a company. This aspect of lobbying is also under-represented here.

For the purpose of a book on *how* lobbyists go about influencing government, the interaction between company CEOs and policymakers is also omitted to a large extent. That major corporate chiefs have access to lobby ministers on a regular basis is widely known. Some even have their own dedicated hotlines to government.

Outside of a few cases, we have also steered clear of lobbying in Brussels. Given its significance to policymaking in this country, this is a serious omission, but one that can be justified on the grounds that it would be a book in itself. The steady growth in power in Brussels has been mirrored by an upswing in lobbying activity, most of which goes unreported and unnoticed by EU citizens.

Finally, there are inevitably some influential lobbyists missing. Pharmaceutical companies, for example, are significant players in UK politics. Anecdotally, from talking to professional lobbyists with experience of the pharmaceutical lobby, it also has one of the worst reputations in the business. Their influence needs greater scrutiny than we give it here.

We readily acknowledge the limits to what we can know from the outside of the industry looking in. To get a definitive, warts-and-all guide to the practices of lobbyists would require one of them to write it.

Given their collective reluctance to allow even the slightest public scrutiny of their activities, we decided not to wait for that day.

1

Lobby: Introducing the Influence Industry

A lobbyist attempts to influence the decisions of government.
  Definition of a lobbyist

'We're in it for money.'
  Peter Gummer, aka Lord Chadlington, lobbyist, 2012[1]

Lobbying is a serious, hidden feature of British politics. Commercial lobbyists, that is the thousands of people whose paid job it is to influence the decisions taken by our politicians, operate without scrutiny. They are invisible. Lobbying is best done, is most effective, when no one is watching.

Only very seldom do we get to glimpse who is doing it, how they are doing it and what impact their actions have on the way this country operates. Towards the end of 2011 we were given a brief window into this world, one of these rare chances to see the influencers at work, thanks to the phone-hacking scandal plaguing Rupert Murdoch's News Corporation.

The inquiry by Lord Justice Leveson primarily sought to get to the bottom of what was happening in our news media. It uncovered industrial-scale phone hacking, examined the corruption of officials and police, and exposed a culture within parts of the British media that used bullying, intimidation and possible blackmail to get its story. It was not a pretty sight.

But Leveson was also charged with examining the relationships between the press and Britain's politicians. It was in this frame that we saw – in forensic detail – the lobbying onslaught by a major multinational company to bend government to its will.

Rupert Murdoch, as one of the most influential figures in British politics, has a knack of getting his own way. He likes to endorse, beat up and sway politicians through his newspapers. He also uses them to promote his own political views. Few of Britain's leaders have stood up to him. Many have helped him. Some, like Tony Blair, have become his friend (Blair was chosen as godparent to Murdoch's child). For decades he has entered Downing Street by the back door and the subtle deals that have been struck have only served to increase his power. He, alone, is one of Britain's fiercest lobbyists.

This, though, is not a book about Murdoch's considerable influence. His lobbying might is both understandable and understood. He has also been a useful lightning rod for our worries over the power wielded by a business elite in British politics. But while Murdoch is an extreme case, he is not exceptional.

Instead, this is an attempt to examine everyone else. The influencers that we usually cannot see. The countless others who are having a quiet word, a private dinner, or an undisclosed meeting with our political leaders. News Corp and the hacking scandal, however, provide a first opportunity to examine how influence in government is quietly, day-by-day, deliberately constructed and retained by the people with the skills, contacts, money and clout: lobbyists.

One of the things that Leveson did was to put politicians, media chiefs and their lobbyists on the stand and hundreds of pages of their emails, texts, records of phone calls and meetings in the public domain. These provide a detailed record of many of the tactics and techniques regularly used by commercial lobbyists. If we can become familiar with these tools, we should be able to begin picking out the features of the others in the gloom.

★

In the summer of 2010, Rupert Murdoch announced his intention to expand his media empire. He wanted full control of the UK's biggest subscription TV company, BSkyB. A bid went in just shy of £8bn for the 60 per cent of the company he did not already own. A merger with BSkyB would have effectively allowed News Corp to double in size.[2] It would have become the most powerful media group Britain has ever seen.

Determined that nothing should stand in its way, News Corp unleashed its lobbyists. The operation was, in the words of Leveson, 'formidable and relentless'.[3] It was also covert.

Corporations, like News Corp, lobby government for one of two reasons: government represents either a threat to the company's business, or an opportunity. Murdoch was faced with a mounting threat.

Inevitably, as MPs and police probed further into who knew what about the illegal activity inside the company, the issue was raised of whether Murdoch was a 'fit and proper person' to wield such power. It was also questioned, not for the first time, whether it was in the interests of the British public that so much media control should be concentrated in the hands of just one billionaire. The government was minded to look into it. The man charged with the job was the Liberal Democrat Business Secretary, Vince Cable.

Cable himself presented a major hurdle. He was no fan of Murdoch, and News Corp knew it. He was described in correspondence as 'highly independent-minded'. This was just as well. The task before him was to look at the evidence and, with a clear mind, make an unbiased judgement on whether the public interest would be served by such a concentration of media power.[4] This was when we learnt what a 'quasi-judicial' process was. Cable was not 'persuadable'.

It is worth pointing out from the start that a proper public debate to determine the best outcome was out of the question. What the British people thought about concentrations of power and influence in the British media, and in particular the impact on the country from Murdoch controlling more of it, was not given a thought. Instead, the decision rested with the Business Secretary and on weak laws designed to protect media plurality.

Much to the frustration of News Corp, Cable heard its case in favour of the BSkyB deal, but refused to respond to its lobbying. It also understood that to push him aggressively would be counter-productive. Undeterred, News Corp's lobbyists conjured up lobbying strategies to win him round.

First, they used the tried and tested method of getting others to do their lobbying for them. Using influential third parties to front a campaign is a common tactic among lobbyists. News Corp figured if they could not get to Cable, they could get to his people, who would, in turn, make the case for the merger.

They sought to harness the influence of Cable's senior party colleagues, including his confidant, Matthew (Lord) Oakeshott, the former Liberal Democrat Treasury spokesman. Like any good lobbyist, they first got to know their target. Oakeshott was deemed a 'difficult character' who, unfortunately for them, 'hates lobbying'. They decided on a 'very soft approach'. The plan was to set Oakeshott up with a useful meeting with the editor of one of their papers, *The Times*. News Corp's lobbyist would then 'pop in' unannounced to surreptitiously lobby Oakeshott. 'Do we think it's ok?' wrote News Corp's lobbyist of his crafty plan.[5]

News Corp also knew that it needed to sell the BSkyB deal as benefiting something other than Murdoch's bank balance. This is a key skill of lobbyists: reframing a narrow, commercial interest as synonymous with the national interest. The pitch had to appeal to the Business Secretary, which meant it had to be sold as being good for the British economy.

An unnamed former Murdoch employee turned Liberal Democrat MP, who had Sky call centres in his constituency, was enlisted to push the economic benefits from the bid's approval, 'especially in times of austerity', noted the lobbyist.[6] A yes from Cable, they argued, would secure jobs in Liberal Democrat seats.

They were, though, getting nowhere fast with Cable. So, they went for the nuclear option. James Murdoch warned the government, via the media, that a block on the bid could lead to Britain losing out on jobs. Cable was to hear a threat and an ultimatum. Other countries, Murdoch said, were more welcoming of News Corp's money. The government must decide whether it wanted to risk 'jeopardising an £8bn investment in the UK' with a prolonged media plurality investigation.[7]

This is another one of the oldest tricks in the book. It boils down to this: give us what we want or we will leave the country. It is bullying. And it is a surprisingly common tactic by large multi-nationals to have their way with government.

The playground tactics did not end there. News Corp's lobbyist also argued that a positive decision on the bid was an opportunity for the

Business Secretary to show the 'maturity' of his party, the Liberal Democrats being the junior partner in government. Were they really suggesting Cable should grow up?

None of this was relevant to an evidence-based judgement on media plurality. But News Corp was nothing if not determined. It also had one final hand to play. Its wild card. News Corp's lobbyists could leverage the power they held through their newspapers to curry favour, or worse. It was proposed that Cable and Liberal Democrat leader Nick Clegg should be helped with supportive coverage on tricky political issues in the Murdoch press.[8] However, Cable's party colleagues were also unsettled and alarmed that the affair would 'lead to retribution' against the party if he took the wrong course. A hammering in the *Sun* was something to be feared.

Cable was incensed by the lobbying onslaught, which he described as like 'being under siege from a well organised operation'.[9] But, in an ill-advised move, he expressed his feelings to two undercover *Telegraph* journalists. He had, he said, 'declared war on Mr Murdoch'. It did not take long for the recorded comments to hit the front pages, exposing Cable's bias against the proposed merger. He was swiftly removed of the responsibility. In his war with Murdoch, Cable had just shot himself.

The Prime Minister handed the decision in late December 2010 to Cable's cabinet colleague, the Conservative Culture Secretary, Jeremy Hunt. This was Christmas come early for News Corp. Hunt was its chief advocate in government and openly supportive of the deal. No doubt there was rejoicing when it 'briefly' came up over a festive dinner just days later, hosted by the former editor of the *Sun*, Rebekah Brooks, and attended by both James Murdoch and the Prime Minister.[10]

David Cameron's close relationship with the Murdochs and in particular his friendship with Brooks were probed by Leveson, as best he could. As was their contact with the Chancellor, George Osborne. Both men were in regular, social contact with the Murdoch clan. However, both appeared to recall little of their conversations regarding News Corp's £8bn bid for BSkyB, the biggest in UK media history.

Under pressure, Cameron claimed to have had a couple of conversations with News Corp, but none that were 'inappropriate'. Oh, except for that brief chat about the bid with James Murdoch over Christmas dinner. Osborne also struggled to remember if it had come up during any of his many encounters with News Corp, including a weekend spent socialising at his country house and a private dinner with Brooks. She confirmed that, at the latter, it did.[11]

News Corp's lobbyist, the man in charge of the day-to-day charm offensive with government, was Fred Michel. From the evidence presented, he went about his job with an obsessive zeal. However, after the fiasco with Cable, Hunt was careful in his new role as judge on the bid to follow correct procedure and ceased all informal contact with News Corp. He left the door ajar, though, in the form of his special adviser, Adam Smith. Special advisers are often key routes of access and influence for lobbyists. The relationship that developed between the News Corp lobbyist Michel and Hunt's proxy, Smith, became what Leveson called the 'serious hidden problem' in the bid process.

Michel's methods are worth studying in some detail to get a picture of a lobbyist at full tilt. Smith was crucial to Michel. He was Michel's inside track on the bid's progress, the government's thinking and even the tactics of the merger's opponents. Smith was also a channel for News Corp's views to Hunt. Once the company's fate passed into Hunt's hands, Michel courted Smith with an intensity that might lead others to take out a court order.

The sheer number of texts, calls and emails speaks volumes, with Michel initiating the vast majority of them. In the course of the bid's progress – just over a year – Michel and Smith exchanged nearly 800 texts.[12] All but a handful were dated after the bid moved to Hunt. There were also over 150 emails and nearly 200 phone calls. As is often the case with lobbying, most of this contact was informal and beyond public scrutiny.

But it was not just the bombardment, it was the manner in which Michel went about securing influence. He employed flattery to soften his target, as lobbyists often do: 'Jeremy is superb,' he texted following one key Parliamentary appearance by Hunt. He used hospitality, another common tactic, to cement a personal and social relationship with Smith, inviting him to a Take That concert with Michel and his wife. The intimacy is often deliberate. The right friend inside government is a valuable commodity to a lobbyist.

Michel's language also drew Smith into a relationship of common cause with News Corp. They talked of shared victories and common enemies. Michel joked about opponents and discussed with Smith the need to 'knock [them] down'. He criticised the Conservatives' political opponents as a sign of his loyalty. Only occasionally did Michel get heavy, at one point calling for the government to 'show some backbone' in its support for the bid. The conspiratorial language is another attempt to cement ties.

Smith, for his part, did nothing to deter Michel's lobbying. They were the normal advances of a lobbyist, even if they were intense in this high-stakes bid. Quite the opposite. Smith seems to have gone out of his way to further News Corp's cause, at one stage reassuring Michel that he was 'causing a lot of chaos and moaning' in the department on News Corp's behalf.[13]

Smith fed information on the government's progress to the lobbyist, even to the point where on one occasion Michel thought, wrongly, that Smith was acting illegally. Finally, as the phone-hacking scandal erupted, it was most likely Smith who leaked confidential information on the government's approach to investigating the scandal to News Corp, the company under investigation.[14] Michel's tight squeeze on Smith was paying off.

But, if all was going to plan inside government, events surrounding the bid were increasingly out of control. By the summer of 2011, the scandal surrounding News Corp had its own momentum. The *News of the World* had been implicated in the hacking of the phones of the murdered child Milly Dowler and other victims of crime. Politicians were now expressing their revulsion. Murdoch moved to lance the boil with the closure of the *News of the World*, but the damage was done. Amid the barrage of headlines and shouts from Parliament, Murdoch withdrew his bid for BSkyB.

These were exceptional circumstances in which News Corp found itself. Take away the phone-hacking scandal, however, and what is left is an everyday case of corporate lobbying for commercial ends of a kind that happens a lot: 'One just has to learn to recognise it for what it is,' Cable told Leveson. 'Mr Michel was an example of a lobbyist at work . . . That is commercial lobbying.'[15]

★

Commercial lobbying, the business of influencing government, is ubiquitous in Britain

We have the third-biggest lobbying industry in the world after Washington and Brussels. A best guess values the business in the UK at around £2bn, although no firm figures exist for the numbers employed or the true scale of the investment. One estimate suggests that the industry has doubled in size in the last thirty years.[16]

A more helpful way of understanding the reach of the UK's influence industry is to come at it from the other direction: how significant a role do lobbyists play in the way Britain is governed? Let us look at just one central function of government: the writing and passing of laws.

'Lobbying is absolutely fundamental to the way we legislate in the UK, right across the board,' said Tim (Lord) Razzall, a politician of forty years' experience, at the 2011 Liberal Democrat Conference. 'The lobbying organisations do your . . .' He corrected himself: '. . . a lot of the work for you.' Legislators are 'inundated' with appeals from lobbyists whenever laws are being crafted. 'Very often' the way to get changes to proposed laws is simply to email them over. Do politicians actually take any notice of the overtures of lobbyists? 'Absolutely,' said Razzall. The government takes a 'huge amount' of notice.[17]

This is one of the truths of the influence industry in Britain: lobbyists are central to the process of government. To see lobbyists as separate and external to the system is a mistake. Rather than being parasitical, lobbyists should more accurately be viewed as essential to it, subsidising it even. As lobbying activity has increased, so our government has become ever more dependent on lobbyists to function. 'Our vaunted constitution is really a framework of lobbying', Austin Mitchell MP remarked twenty years ago.[18]

Today, politicians rely to a great extent on lobbyists to do their job. Politicians require information, expertise and advice from the outside world to inform their decisions. Coming up with good, workable policy is also a costly process that requires research and detailed knowledge, time-consuming activities that the civil service is increasingly hard pushed to provide, but in which lobbyists willingly invest. Contributions from respected lobbyists, such as the drafting of amendments to laws, are welcome. Government policies also need buy-in and support if they are to be successful. In this, too, lobbyists can provide a ready-made volunteer army to help government achieve its aims.

Lobbying, seen from this angle, looks positively public-spirited. More than that, it appears as an essential factor of good governance. Politicians cannot know what is in the best interests of those affected by its decisions. They will not anticipate every unintended consequence or potential benefit their actions might have. They need help.

But the value of lobbying is much more than merely practical. Lobbying is central to our idea of democratic government. We still have a lingering expectation that our politicians will listen to the people that they serve, and that their decisions take our wishes into account even if they do not act on them. If you have ever written to your MP, or petitioned government, you are lobbying. You are attempting to influence the decisions of politicians. Lobbying, seen in this light, is central to a healthy democratic system that is open to the interests and concerns of citizens.

So why then is there concern around lobbying? Or, as the question was put to us recently by one Conservative MP: 'How is democracy being harmed by the current situation? That is not a rhetorical question. It is an absolutely straight question. What is the problem?'[19]

This is a recurring question. Many political insiders simply cannot fathom why there is a stench around lobbying. What is the problem?

In theory, lobbying is benign. It leads to better government. It gives people a voice. And, in a liberal democracy, everyone rightly has the ability to lobby their representatives. The problem lies in what happens in practice.

The problem, as we will show, stems from lobbying within the context of the sophisticated, commercial influence industry as it exists in the UK. Commercial lobbyists acting for particular, narrow interests bend our system of government to their will to such an extent that it can be said to no longer serve the interests of the wider public. Certain players in society, through their paid lobbyists, are drowning out everyone else. Viewed from this angle, lobbying appears as a corrupting force that undermines democracy.

Money is central to the problem. But it is important to state from the outset the role that money does not play in British politics. Lobbying, at least on the national level, is not a tale of cash in brown envelopes and shady backroom deals. Those days are gone. Or largely gone.

The cash-for-questions scandal in the mid-nineties was a lesson for commercial lobbyists. It involved the most successful operator of the day, Ian Greer, who famously advised his client, Harrods' owner, Mohamed Al Fayed: 'You need to rent an MP just like you rent a London taxi.'[20] A number of Members of Parliament, including the Conservative Neil Hamilton, put themselves up for hire and pocketed tens of thousands of pounds for their services. When they were found out, the ensuing outcry brought down Greer's business, led to Hamilton's disgraced exit from politics and bankruptcy, forced the Prime Minister into an unprecedented examination of standards in public life and required the lobbying industry to clean up its act.

Few commercial lobbying firms of the type run by Greer now take such risks, or even require the paid services of MPs, although members of the House of Lords are another matter. The practice of MPs acting as paid lobbyists has not ceased altogether though. Twenty years on from Hamilton's disgrace, another Conservative MP, Patrick Mercer, was caught by undercover journalists posing as lobbyists offering his services in exchange for cash.[21] What is clear from this is that a culture still exists inside Westminster where this is considered, if not usual, then not overly risky behaviour. Today, however, these 'cabs-for-hire' are bit players in the lobbying game.

Nor is this a story of seriously big money in politics. Britain is not the United States. We are not plagued by the problem Americans face, where US politicians are required to fundraise more than they legislate merely to retain their seat. Washington's lobbyists play a central role in funnelling campaign contributions from commercial interests to law makers.[22] The amount of money spent on lobbying in the US is also off the scale compared to the UK. Which is not to say that we have a cottage industry here.

No, the key money problem is much more mundane. Lobbying, as practised by those with any influence in the country, costs money. As lobbyist Tim (Lord) Bell says, 'A labourer should be paid for his labours.'[23] This book explores how that money is spent.

It is easy to think of exceptions to this. The under-funded but nimble campaign group with a powerful cause that succeeds in changing government policy is one. It is also true, or partly true, that money spent on lobbying does not equate to influence or success. Politics is not nearly that straightforward. Just ask News Corp. But to be a player, to have influence, almost always requires deep pockets. To simply get to the table involves an outlay. Lobbying of the kind that can make a difference is an investment that relatively few can afford.

Most of those that make the investment do so for commercial reasons. Put simply, lobbying pays. It delivers a financial return. And the payback can be significant. Various attempts have been made to quantify the rate of return, mainly based on figures from the US, where lobbyists must disclose their lobbying budgets.

A study by the libertarian Cato Institute estimates that from a US corporate lobbying spend of roughly $3.5bn a year, the value of the resulting corporate subsidies alone secured through lobbying is about $90bn a year. For every dollar spent on lobbying for tax benefits in the US, another study found a return of between 6 and 21.[24] Another puts the figure at nearer 1:100.[25] Others, depending on the issue, put the figure significantly higher.

Given the rewards, it is not surprising that the share value of firms that lobby 'significantly outperforms' those that do not.[26] An index based on the amount of lobbying that American companies undertake confirms this. According to The Economist, this index has outperformed the market, producing 'stunning' results comparable to the returns of 'the most blistering hedge fund'. 'It seems remarkable that companies would do anything but lobby,' it noted.[27]

This return on investment goes a long way to explaining why the lobbying industry has experienced such growth. It is another way of making money. Whether facing down a threat to profits, from say a corporate tax hike, or pushing for opportunities to profit, like government privatisations, lobbying pays. This is an important frame through which to see the influence industry. It is a view that is often obscured.

It follows then that those with the deep pockets, willing to make a tactical investment for commercial gain, and whose purpose is profit-making, dominate the industry. Business spends substantially more on lobbying than any other group in society.

By way of example, here is the client list of one of London's leading lobbying firms, Portland, headed by a former spinner for Tony Blair. It also employs Alastair Campbell. Their services do not come cheap.

Portland is, or has recently been, paid lobbyist to: in food and drink, Coca-Cola, McDonald's, Nestlé, Tesco and AB-InBev, the UK's largest brewer; in tech and telecoms, Apple, Google, Cable and Wireless, and Vodafone; it is employed by six energy businesses; four finance companies;

four trade bodies; three professional-services firms; two clients in air travel; one payday loan company; and Britain's largest defence company, BAE Systems. Non-corporate interests include the governments of Russia and Kazakhstan and the tax haven of Jersey, none of them short of a few quid. It counts just two other non-commercial clients: the NSPCC and the Scout Association.[28]

Businesses lobby for as many different reasons as there are government decisions. How much they spend will often depend on the size of the opportunity or threat. If government is looking to put curbs on the sale of a particular product – cigarettes are an obvious example, as increasingly is alcohol – the lobbying effort will be scaled to the size of the potential market loss. Similarly, the value of a potential market gain will determine the intensity of lobbying by companies seeking to enter it. The opening up of the £100bn NHS budget to private sector health companies might be a good example. It follows that the greater the prize, the harder the fight.

As profit-making entities, it is entirely rational for companies to lobby. And there is nothing inherently wrong in it. Companies should seek to be heard by government. However, they have been allowed to become dominant. Their collective lobbying budget and the associated influence of their lobbyists has bought them a structural advantage.

This is where the answer lies to the question 'What is the problem?' The concern is that the business of influencing government – commercial lobbying – is dominated by narrow, corporate interests. They have the loudest voice.

But what about trade unions and consumer organisations, charities and pressure groups? They are lobbyists too. This is a common refrain from corporate lobbyists. And it is true. Trade unions are explicit in their role as lobbyists. They attempt to sway government in the interests of their members, whether it is over wages, pensions or working conditions. When quiet negotiation and bargaining prove fruitless, they will also often go public and organise vocal lobbying campaigns and demonstrations, the aim of which is the same.

Many non-governmental organisations (NGOs) exist purely to influence government, unlike their business counterparts. Some are also big players, spending significant resources and mobilising armies of supporters to put pressure on politicians to act in a certain way. The bigger charities, like the National Trust or Liberty, are regularly consulted by government. But, while they may get an audience with politicians, their influence is often limited. 'These groups have little effect on policy, despite this access', says one lobbyist. Often they are simply 'an easy source of information' for government.[29]

We make no judgement on the moral equivalence between a corporation lobbying to protect its profits and, say, a consumer group lobbying against price rises. Or between a car company that provides jobs and clean-air campaigners. That depends on where you stand and your political leanings.

But when business lobbyists point to these competing voices, the impression given is that they are, somehow, in balance. That equal weight is given to both sides of an argument. That politicians listen to the voices of all interested parties in any decision – 'stakeholders' in corporate speak – with the same level of concentration.

Based on the evidence before us, this is manifestly not the case. The influence of those who advocate for better private sector wages is no match for the employers lobby. Consumer groups who campaign for lower profits and fairer fuel bills enjoy far less influence than the energy firms. Those seeking to protect the environment consistently lose to the chemical, oil and biotech lobbies.

When it was revealed that bankers faced with increased regulation were putting pressure on politicians to water down the rules, this was the response from its trade body, the British Bankers' Association: 'It is important that there is a dialogue between industry and the government, just as consumer groups and trade unions quite properly speak to government officials on a regular basis.'[30] The impression this gives is that there are equivalent and equal lobbies.

There are, though, whole areas of policy where the only voices heard are private, commercial interests. This is especially true for the banking sector. It is a fearsome and influential player in British politics. But there has been no coherent lobby to counter it either before or since the financial crisis. Instead, what we see are activists: people who voice their concerns by spending their Saturdays occupying a branch of Barclays, or who are prepared to sleep in a tent at the foot of St Paul's Cathedral.

The tents give us a clue as to the public's position in the influence game. We have largely been evicted from decision-making.

There is a palpable sense among many that government now works, in large part, for the benefit of large corporations and the finance sector rather than in the interests of citizens. Polls consistently show that the majority of British people feel they have no voice in government. The opinions of the public are something to be managed rather than sought. Meanwhile government is ever more attentive to the needs of capital.[31]

This is the perception. We aim to show that it is a valid one. It is the case that sharp-elbowed lobbying by corporate interests has forced the people out of government. An easy way to grasp this is to look at where Britain might be heading.

American politics is a bust system. Just 9 per cent of Americans have confidence in their legislators.[32] British politicians fare slightly better, but the numbers are still small.

People in Washington talk openly of the United States not as a democracy, but a corporatocracy. That is, a political system controlled by and serving the interests of corporations. Barack Obama ran for President on the ticket of changing this broken system so that it instead served the American people.

In speech after speech he talked of 'fundamentally changing the way that Washington works'. He was explicit that that meant tackling the influence of lobbyists. 'For far too long Washington has allowed Wall Street to use lobbyists and campaign contributions to rig the system and get its way, no matter what it costs ordinary Americans,' he repeatedly said.[33]

Lobbying is by no means the most significant challenge facing the American government, or Britain's. But Obama understood that unless he tackled the influence industry, he had no hope of tackling the big issues facing the country. 'Unless we're willing to challenge the broken system, and stop letting lobbyists use their clout to get their way, nothing else is going to change.'[34]

Lobbying is the 'gateway' problem.

Think of any number of issues facing the country and then ask this: how likely is it that this government, or any government, is going to take the necessary steps to tackle it, in the wider public interest? Energy security and climate change; public health problems; dwindling tax receipts and the resulting pressure on public services; the rising cost of living and the fall in real terms in pay; a stable banking sector that serves the economy and not itself. The lobbies that dominate these areas of policy – the oil and energy companies, the sugar-heavy-drinks industry, the tax haven crowd, the employers lobby and the banks – benefit from the status quo.

Undeniably, the American system is more corrupted by campaign finance and big-money lobbyists than ours. On party funding there is no comparison. Commercial lobbying as a mechanism for corrupting democracy, however, is one we share. What is more there is a worrying complacency in the British political class. There is an unwillingness to admit our vulnerability to such a corruption.[35] Our lawmakers might look across at America's big-money politics, and Washington's K-Street, and experience relief. But back home in Westminster they still ask: 'What is the problem?'

One British politician, however, has followed Obama's cue. David Cameron. In the final months of his general election campaign, the incoming Prime Minister delivered a speech on lobbying. To put it in context, it came just days before another headline-grabbing lobbying scandal, involving politicians-for-hire.

Cameron made a pledge to 'sort it out'.

We all know how it works. The lunches, the hospitality, the quiet word in your ear, the ex-ministers and ex-advisers for hire, helping big business find the right way to get its way.

We don't know who is meeting whom. We don't know whether any favours are being exchanged. We don't know which outside interests are wielding unhealthy influence. This isn't a minor issue with minor consequences.

I believe that secret corporate lobbying . . . goes to the heart of why people are so fed up with politics. It arouses people's worst fears and suspicions about how our political system works, with money buying power, power fishing for money and a cosy club at the top making decisions in their own interest.

It is increasingly clear that lobbying in this country is getting out of control. We can't go on like this.[36]

Yet it has gone on. In the event, Obama did not change Washington. And Cameron has done nothing to challenge the influence of lobbyists in Britain.

Concerns have been raised about Britain's influence industry for over sixty years. The first calls for rules for lobbyists came in 1969.

The last thirty years have seen unprecedented growth in the reach of
the industry and its penetration into government. The amount of
money involved increases year on year. It is not a case of it 'getting'
out of control. Yet we know as little today about their activities as
they did back in the fifties.

*

There is nothing mysterious about what lobbyists do, it is just hidden.
Deliberately. As one lobbyist notes: 'The influence of lobbyists
increases when . . . it goes largely unnoticed by the public.'[37]

Influence is constructed, consciously, using particular skills and a
set of tools. Imagine it like building a bridge: it takes specialist knowledge and expertise; it requires planning and the organisation of the
right people to build it; you need to put effort in and persevere; and
you need money to fund it. Depending on whether it is a stream or
a sea you are trying to span, it could take a month or years. It is the
same with the construction of influence.

This book is an attempt to map lobbying. The aim is that by the
end you will be as familiar with the ways that they construct influence
as lobbyists are. Lobbying, when exposed, loses much of its potency.
We see the special interests at work. And when we can do that, we
can begin to hold our politicians to account.

But before lobbyists can set to work influencing the system, they
need access to it. An open door to government. Chapter 2 explores
what this looks like.

Access can be bought. It is not a cash deal, though. No money
changes hands. Funding political parties might be described as a cash
deal if a donor buys access to the Prime Minister.

Lobbying does not operate in an exchange economy like this. There
is seldom a straight quid pro quo between lawmaker and lobbyist.
Rather an investment is made in the relationship. Lobbyists build trust,
offer help and accept favour.

Lobbyists can help lawmakers in many ways: they might simply
supply useful information or political intelligence (unlike politicians,
lobbyists are free to roam Westminster); they can help secure
support for policies or provide opportunities to promote them; they
can make valuable introductions, or know of opportunities for

post-politics employment. They may even throw in the occasional dinner.

The lobbyist speaks the same language as the lawmaker, is interesting and attentive, and over time the lawmaker may come to see the lobbyist as a friend. Think back to News Corp's Fred Michel and his courting of the special adviser Adam Smith. The lobbyist meanwhile will be seeking to influence the lawmaker. And while there is no obligation – the politician does not owe the lobbyist anything – he or she becomes someone the lawmaker can help out.[38] Lobbying operates in this type of gift economy. It is not corrupt, but it is corrupting.

What these friendships are not, however, is accidental. Relationships with politicians and officials are the stock-in-trade of lobbyists. They have also worked out a way to shortcut this process of relationship-building. They hire the lawmaker's actual friends in the form of ex-employees or colleagues, people whom politicians have already taken counsel from. Lobbying is packed with former special advisers, ex-government officials and retired politicians. It is a dominant feature of the influence industry. Lobbyists are insiders.

Lobbyists today, though, do far more than seek ear-time with government. Politicians and officials do not make decisions in a vacuum. They are influenced by what the media says, the views of influential others – business leaders, think tanks, commentators – and sometimes public opinion. The game thus played by the influence industry is to control the intellectual space in which officials make policy decisions. They have developed a number of sophisticated techniques to achieve this audacious aim.

One of the primary ways to dominate the so-called information environment of politicians is to simply feed the media with the information and comment that the lobbyist wants them to hear. The public's enthusiasm for a daily paper might be waning, but politicians generally have a voracious appetite when it comes to consuming the media. And as we explore in Chapter 3, lobbyists have adopted many of the techniques employed by their colleagues in public relations to control and shape the media. The UK has one of the most sophisticated PR industries in the world.[39]

Lobbyists like to distance themselves from public relations, although the distinction is largely one of semantics. Both professions have at their core the need to: shape the message that they want their audience to hear, decision-makers in the case of lobbyists; work out how best to target their audience; and then execute a plan to make sure that the message reaches them. It could be that quietly buttonholing the official at a drinks party is the best way to get the point across. Or the lobbyist might invite them to a seminar organised for the purpose. Or it could be that a TV appearance, the equivalent of grabbing a megaphone, is what is required. It is the lobbyist's job to identify the audience, hone the message and work out which strategy is likely to spur action.

Of course, it does not help if it is only the corporation lobbying that is making the case to government. That looks like special pleading. A case of 'Well, they would say that.' Lobbyists need other people, influential third parties to carry their message to government. That way it looks like a cause with widespread support. This can be engineered.

Putting their words in someone else's mouth is a key tactic of lobbyists, as we show in Chapter 4. It can take many forms, some quite legitimate, like the use of opinion polling to provide 'proof' of wider support. However, the deceptive use of third parties is widespread. Lobbyists engineer third parties that have the credibility of looking independent, seeming to be motivated by something other than self-interest and profit, and therefore have a much greater chance of being believed. From the creation of front groups to the grooming of academics, it is a pervasive tactic of the industry.

Many of the UK's so-called 'independent' think tanks are paid to provide third party endorsement. 'Wonk whores' is how they have been described by someone in the business. Often the policy ideas that they promote originate in the lobbying strategies of large corporations seeking the credibility, and crucially distance, of a seemingly independent, expert organisation. The UK's think tanks do not have to say who is paying them, although some do. They can promote policies without ever having to reveal which vested interest is seeking to benefit. The tactic of hiring think tanks to provide third party endorsement is an open secret in lobbying.

These are some of the ways that lobbyists make sure that politicians hear their case. Pushing their message out by any and all means necessary. But there are some lobbyists who also perform a secondary role. And that is to make sure that politicians hear their case only. Their job is to deal with the opposition.

High profile, or particularly contentious, issues attract dissent. The plan for a high-speed rail link through parts of the country is a good example. HS2, as it is known, has drawn widespread opposition in communities that will be affected by it. These people, many of whom will lose their homes or whose quality of life will be adversely affected by the development, have been referred to by lobbyists as the 'antis'. Lobbyists hired to push through such a development are often charged with neutralising the threat the antis pose to its proceeding.

Chapter 5 explores some of the sophisticated techniques developed over decades to deal with the opposition. This could be an organised campaign group like a charity, a looser activist network – environmentalists have long been the bane of commercial lobbyists – or just a group of concerned residents. Often the common thread running through opposition groups is that they lack the opportunity to be heard through other, more official channels.

Lobbyists talk of being engaged in 'guerrilla warfare' with their opponents, many of whom are armed with nothing more than a critical blog. Lobbyists are fond of their military and intelligence metaphors. Tactics deployed to counter the threat include monitoring opponents. One seasoned lobbyist describes the 'listening posts' developed to pick up the online warning signals of activist activity. In the lobbyists' arsenal are also tactics developed to 'divide and rule' critics, pitting one against another. Then there are the more serious activities used primarily when big-money commercial interests are threatened: the infiltration of opposition groups, otherwise known as spying, the use of smear campaigns and intimidation.

Not all lobbying battles are so obviously aggressive. Chapter 6 looks at a less confrontational technique used today by lobbyists to head off opposition: the public consultation. It is now the method-of-choice for developers dealing with a threat at a local community level. What looks like progress – consultation as a means of giving people an active role in determining what happens in their neighbourhood or country – is often anything but.

Locally, the job of soliciting public views has been outsourced to lobbyists. Consultation in their hands is a means of flushing out community opposition and providing a managed channel through which would-be opponents can voice concerns. Opportunities to change the outcome, whether it is preventing an out-of-town supermarket or protecting local health services, are almost always nil. Instead, the public is presented with marginal choices or the semblance of choice. You might get to change the colour of the bricks.

National governments have similarly embraced consultation as a way to secure a mandate for unpopular policies. We explore the collusion between government and lobbyists to rig these public consultations and the methods used by commercial lobbyists to circumvent the process.

Local community activists can provide lobbyists with a headache. But some corporations face a much wider threat to their business. Chapter 7 explores some of the ways in which key global industries – sugar, alcohol and oil – have lobbied to delay the threat of government action to curb consumption of their product. And they learnt how to do it from one industry: tobacco.

The tobacco industry has lobbied for six decades to protect its profits by delaying legislative restrictions on cigarettes. For years its primary method was to deny the science on smoking's links to disease, the explicit aim being to sow doubt in people's minds. It has been responsible for setting up front groups and paying scientists to question and undermine the evidence. And it has vilified its critics. At the same time, it has sought to push responsibility for harm from its products onto individuals. These are all delaying tactics to stave off government intervention.

The campaign, still being fought today, has been crafted and honed over decades by lobbyists. The sugar, alcohol and oil industries employ many of the same tactics. They have the same goal: to delay action by governments and protect their products and profits. They sometimes even use the same lobbyists to do it.

Government has the power to seriously dent a company's balance sheet. It can put whole industries out of business. But if politicians can pose a threat, they can also offer substantial commercial opportunities. For particular sectors, like defence, government is by far the biggest customer. The pharmaceutical industry is another that is reliant on government. The latter sets the rules (with Brussels) and through the NHS provides a huge market. The IT industry has also blossomed with government assistance.

Chapter 8 looks at the business opportunities provided by government privatisation and public sector reform. It focuses on the future of the publicly funded school system. We look at some of the lobby groups pushing for reform and some of the corportations – technology and media giants, for example, including Murdoch's News Corp – seeking to profit from the potential growth in digital learning. Many of these companies are intent on taking education out of public control. We examine the reach of these players inside government and some of the lobbying methods they use to achieve their aims. The lobbyists for school reform, however, have gone about it quietly.

Increased private sector involvement in education has sparked little attention in the UK. Particularly when compared to recent moves by the government to open up more of the NHS to private companies. Mainstream public debate over school privatisation has been muted. Cross the Atlantic, however, where they are experiencing similar reforms and where education reform lobbyists are more visible, and the airways are full of it. The implications of this for public debate are clear. If we cannot see the lobbyists, if we do not grasp their agenda, we are barred from participating in crucial discussions on issues that affect our lives.

Even with its bloated influence industry, the UK's politicians have never been in favour of lobbyists operating in plain sight. It is unsuited to the way our government operates. As one senior lobbyist remarked: 'Most dealings with the system are settled by quiet negotiation.'[40]

Britain's current Prime Minister, however, has promised to open up 'secret corporate lobbying'. Lobbyists from now on are to be subject to transparency rules, in the form of a compulsory register of lobbyists. Done properly, this smallest of measures would allow us to see who is lobbying whom, what they are seeking to influence, and how much money is being spent in the process. A register will not prevent commercial lobbying. The information it contains merely gives us a window on the interaction between lobbyists and our politicians. It is another means of holding our politicians to account. America has had transparency rules for lobbyists since the forties, and effective ones since the nineties. Canada has operated a register for twenty-five years.[41]

Chapter 9 is a case study. It describes the progress of our campaign for a lobbying register and how the lobbyists have applied their skills to thwarting it. More than that, it is an illustration of how much of government operates today: the privileged access afforded to some; the lengths it will go to hide its dealings with commercial lobbyists; the disdain it has for proper participation; and its attempts to mislead the public. The resulting policy – the register as proposed – is a fake. It is not what it claims to be. It will not open up lobbying.

This is not a case, however, of being sore because we did not get what we wanted in this particular instance. It is not our aim to debate the rights and wrongs of particular government decisions or certain policies. Whether we agree or disagree with the direction of government is largely irrelevant. Our politics, while present here, are not important.

Lobbying – felt as undue influence – offends people who lean right and left. The focus on corporate lobbying in this book is based on the fact that commercial interests dominate the influence business. For this reason it has typically been of most concern to those on the left of politics, like trade unionists and environmentalists. However, it should be of equal concern to those on the right. Lobbying, huge PR efforts, the hiring of political insiders and the constant schmoozing of politicians are all signs of market failure. They are ways of openly gaming the system. It is also true that declining industries have much more to gain from lobbying than expanding industries. The result is that losers lobby harder.[42] Lobbyists are used to build and sustain power and to keep competition out.

This is not a book about specific government decisions or policies. It is about how these policies are shaped and by whom.

There are always competing interests in any government decision: should you protect the people living under a proposed flight path or the convenience of the travelling class; should small businesses be relieved of regulations, or employee rights protected; should the IT contract go to X or Y company or none at all? These are decisions government has to take. But you would hope the decision was a rational one. That it was based on accurate information. And that it was taken in the interests of the many not the few and with a responsible attitude to the public coffers.

It is about government making good decisions. That this does not always appear to be the case can, in large part, be attributed to lobbying.

2

Defend: Lobbyists versus Democracy

'The case for capitalism needs to be re-made.'
Steve Hilton

Lobbying is an old profession, but perhaps not as old as lobbyists would have you believe. Their preferred history places lobbying at the birth of democracy: 'The forums of Greece and Rome were frequented by ancient lobbyists,' writes a lobbyist, Lionel Zetter, in his book *Lobbying: The Art of Political Persuasion*. 'The courts of kings and princes were thronged with courtiers . . . the lobbyists of their day.'

Zetter, who has more than twenty years' experience in the influence business, warms to his theme. 'If the barons had not lobbied King John, he would not have signed the Magna Carta at Runnymede and democracy in Britain might have evolved very differently.'[1]

This is a grandiose claim: lobbyists as the radical instigators of democracy to whom we are indebted. And yet there is a grain of truth to it. Lobbying has long been a feature of the British system of government. Petitioning government is central to our idea of democracy. But there is a distinction to be drawn between lobbying – the activity – and the multi-billion-pound commercial industry as it exists today. This grew not from the debating forums of ancient Greece but from much more recent events.

The root of the modern, commercial lobbying business is much closer to the reality of the Magna Carta than to its legacy (that being parliamentary democracy and equality under the law). When the radical barons stood up to the king it was in defence of their interests. According to the British Library, keepers of two of the four surviving documents of 1215, the Magna Carta was in the main 'a practical solution to a political crisis which primarily served the interests of the highest ranks of feudal society'.[2] It was lobbying by narrow, private interests to defend their advantage.

It is uncontroversial to say that, in today's world, the highest ranks are those with the greatest economic power, largely corporations and some extraordinarily wealthy individuals. And it is they who are pushing their agenda, not on a despotic king, but on democratic governments. The activity of lobbying may be ancient, but the lineage of the commercial influence industry dates back to the crises experienced by capitalists just a century ago. It has largely been a fight to protect and further their interests ever since.

*

Britain's nascent lobbying industry developed in parallel to that in the US, and for the same core reason. To remove the risk posed by democracy to industrialists.

A hundred years ago ordinary people in their numbers got the vote. Suddenly the issues that affected their lives started to dominate politics. People were organising for social change. There was hope that now it was possible that government might respond to the will of a majority.

Looked at through the eyes of wealthy industrialists, this meant government could no longer be relied on to defend their narrow interests. The business elite needed to find ways to stay on top regardless of who was in power.[3]

In the 1920s a 'crusade for capitalism' was launched from a building mid-way between Parliament and London's Victoria Station. Number 25 Victoria Street is now an anonymous corner office block with a couple of ostentatious pillars surrounded by the vast, concrete bureaucracy of government departments.

But, back in the early twenties it was the base for a huddle of business-backed lobbyists with a decidedly anti-democratic agenda. Coordinating them was one of the UK's first business lobby groups, National

Propaganda, or as it was soon after to be known, the Economic League. It led the self-proclaimed crusade.[4]

'What is required is some years of propaganda for capitalism as the finest system that human ingenuity can devise,' argued material sent to the League's members.[5] British society at the time was unstable. It had high unemployment, the government was unsteady and anxious to avoid any repeat of the Russian Revolution over here. Democratic reforms passed in 1918 had just tripled the electorate.[6] And the union-backed Labour Party had arrived as a major national political force.

The socialists posed a serious threat to the crusaders. Labour's 1918 election manifesto pledged taxes on capital, increased rights for workers and the nationalisation and democratic control of public services. It was explicit in its promise to take on some of the most powerful, vested interests in Britain.[7]

It was in this context that Britain's organised business lobby was born.

Coordinated by the Economic League, the emerging lobby began pushing out its 'propaganda for capitalism'. It placed articles in newspapers and paid journalists to write them. It also took the industrialists' message direct to the people by funding a network of speakers who would talk to the public about economics in simple terms. These were people who could make themselves heard. They could also handle any violent opposition they might encounter. They were 'big men in every sense of the word,' wrote the League. 'Tough and well able to look after themselves.'[8]

National Propaganda, however, was more than a platform for bigging up capitalist views, however robustly. It had a second purpose. This was, according to the League, to 'fight subversion relentlessly and ruthlessly'.[9]

Business financed a network of groups associated with National Propaganda. These undertook a range of activities to thwart their opponents. They disrupted meetings of pacifists and other progressive organisations. They broke into their offices, stole documents and acted as agents provocateurs. They were also given access to intelligence on left-wing activists.[10] Business interests have long been adept at dealing with Britain's intelligence services.[11] By the time of the General Strike in 1926, the League had grown to between 150 and 200 corporate members and had its own intelligence operation, described as 'considerably more diverse and sophisticated . . . than the state's own'.[12]

The aim of this machine was twofold: to defeat those that challenged their power and replace their ideas with 'constructive thoughts' on the benefits of capitalism.[13]

An identical campaign was being waged on the other side of the Atlantic. If Britain's business elite felt threatened, corporate America in the following decade was under siege. In 1929 America suffered the biggest stock market crash the country had ever seen. The Great Depression that followed was viewed as truly system-endangering. For America's businessmen and their sympathetic politicians, the period was catastrophic and disorientating.[14]

The public blamed them, angrily. People mobilised against businesses and not just workers. Consumer groups turned militant, one example being the vocal opposition to the growth of big business chain stores.[15] People had not just turned against the business class, they were rejecting the ideas that supported their rule. And this was translating into politics. Reforming politicians, with new ideas, posed the biggest threat. President Franklin D. Roosevelt, who believed in involving the public in determining the future of the country, was intent on diminishing the power of business.[16]

America's leading businessmen saw the need to organise collectively against the threat, as in Britain. The call to arms went up. One of the driving forces was the business lobby group the National Association of Manufacturers (NAM).[17] Its biggest weapon was what we would now call public relations.

With an annual budget in the thirties of $1m NAM went about trying to shape public opinion by re-selling business to America's middle class.[18] The focal message was that big government and unions were the people's enemy. Instead, they were to identify business with 'every cherished value'. The central task, as explained in a NAM conference in 1939, was to 'link free enterprise . . . with free speech, free press and free religion as integral parts of democracy'.[19] This was its crusade: to redefine what people thought of as democracy by plonking capitalism right at its heart. Its intent was to tell the people what government by the people meant.

The most famous of the PR pioneers from this period is Edward Bernays. The American began his long career in the twenties working mainly for large corporations. Like many at the time, Bernays did not hold the public in high esteem. He shared the fear, common among many intellectuals and industry, of what the irrational masses might do given half the chance. The public's judgement could not be relied on. Without reason they could vote for the wrong person, or hold the wrong ideas, unless directed otherwise from above. Democracy, he thought, needed to be managed by an 'invisible' elite.[20]

Bernays' thinking and approach were influenced by his uncle, Sigmund Freud, the father of psychoanalysis. Bernays took Freud's ideas that people were driven by unconscious desires and applied them to shaping public opinion. If people were guided by emotion over reason, he figured, you could tap in to that emotion and get people to do what you wanted them to do.

There is now a $10bn global public relations industry built on the ideas of Bernays and other early pioneers.[21] Bernays, for example, was the first to recognise the power of getting someone else to say what you want to say – the third party endorsement – an understanding that lies at the heart of public relations. 'Most of the things we do today were identified by Bernays 80 years ago,' noted Harold Burson, founder of one of the world's biggest PR agencies, Burson-Marsteller. 'He had brilliant ideas.'[22]

As with the lobby in Britain, America's business leaders in the thirties were not just concerned with selling capitalism. They were also bent on bringing down their opponents. NAM was determinedly anti-union. And in the same way that it pioneered the emerging techniques of PR, it also helped develop tactics for defeating the newly empowered workers. Tactics included: discrediting union leaders in the eyes of the public; making strikes a law and order issue, so that the often brutal force of the police and legal system could be brought in; and secretly masterminding 'back to work' movements to divide and demoralise workers. It is a formula that has been used over the decades on both sides of the pond.

The publicity effort in these strike-breaking campaigns was handed over to America's emerging PR industry, among them John Hill of the newly formed Hill & Knowlton, whose UK offices today sit on London's fashionable Soho Square. The PR men developed ways to turn public opinion against the workers; they pioneered the technique of astroturfing by setting up and funding fake 'citizen committees' to look like grassroots public opposition; manipulated the local press; and paid journalists to put forward the industry's perspective without their backing ever being revealed. Again, these are tactics that would be honed over the coming decades.

In the nearly hundred years that followed, these two methods – persuasion and coercion – have been employed in tandem by an 'invisible' influencing elite to protect the interests of capital.

★

Forties Britain saw a new wave of activity by these influencers. After the war, the business lobby was faced with a government intent on introducing social welfare reforms and key industries were earmarked for public ownership. A new lobby group was established to fight back.

Aims of Industry was backed by, among others, the chair of the Ford Motor Company, ICI, Tate & Lyle, British American Tobacco, the head of one of the largest property businesses in Britain, the owner of a food conglomerate, and the man behind the Rank film group. It established an effective PR operation to battle nationalisation plans.

Its material was placed into British newspapers and magazines and it was a regular feature on the BBC. By 1949, its listeners could catch at least one Aims of Industry spokesperson a week. Causes included working with the sugar industry, Tate & Lyle in particular, against nationalisation. 'Tate not State!' and 'Take the S out of State' were both slogans featured on leaflets that were handed out in their millions by shopkeepers to their customers.[23] They fought and won in 1950 and sugar stayed in private hands. More were to follow. Aims of Industry was proud of its record of being able to get its message across to 'not only the worker, but his wife'.[24]

The PR tactics of Aims of Industry, which developed a relationship with the Economic League, followed the line of its predecessors. The 1950s, however, marked a new development in Britain's growing business lobby: the birth of the commercial lobbying industry.

The British Establishment, the club at the top of society united by common backgrounds and unspoken understandings, remained intact. But increasingly ways were being developed to buy access to this club.

MPs, who have always held jobs outside of Parliament (they only received a salary in 1911), had regularly acted as a bridge between commerce and politics. From the mid-fifties, however, they were increasingly being sought out by PR companies to help with lobbying.

For the first time in any numbers, PR companies began to act as intermediaries between politicians and the agencies' corporate clients.

In 1957 it was known that eighteen MPs were working for PR firms. By 1965 this had jumped to at least fifty. There was little or no public disclosure of the practice. MPs occupied what one described as the 'grey zone' where lobbying ties were not formalised and 'need not become generally known'.[25] One MP critical of this coming together of public relations with political influence remarked: 'The door is wide open for a new form of political corruption.'[26]

The trend coincided with the arrival of the big American PR firms in Britain. Hill & Knowlton was the first into Europe in the mid-fifties. Rival Burson-Marsteller set up shop in London shortly after. They were following their American clients as they looked for opportunities overseas. Hill & Knowlton was also the first company to formally combine lobbying services with PR aimed squarely at influencing government.

This was now a commercial proposition: corporations could buy access and influence. A new breed of lobbyist, with PR skills, was stepping up to provide a private channel to politicians for a fee. The activity of these lobbyists was all under the radar.

While business was enjoying these new privileges, however, the electorate was again losing faith with the political system. The sixties in Britain and across much of the West saw a sharp rise in progressive, social movements. Some, though not all, had a pro-democratic or anti-business agenda, like the green and pacifist groups. Britain by the seventies was in crisis economically, but it was also socially bewildering for many business leaders. They were on the defensive. Strikes and protest rallies were a common feature up and down the country. People in their numbers were tuning out from corporate messaging. So once again Britain's business leaders chose to organise against the threat. They needed people to tune back in.

'The End of Freedom in Britain' shouted the headline of one Aims of Industry advert placed in *The Times* in 1973. This was in the midst of widespread industrial action. It was accompanied by an image of the average British family bound up. Remembering Bernays, NAM and others it read: 'If our free economy is destroyed, our liberties will also be destroyed.'[27]

The same year, Aims of Industry warned its member businesses of a new phenomenon: organised political pressure groups. These were militants, it said. They wanted companies to change their ways to conform with 'extreme political beliefs'. Demands cited by Aims included the withdrawal of foreign investment from apartheid South Africa, that women and minority groups were included on boards of directors, and action by companies on environmental issues. 'And what next?' it asked.[28]

These concerns were shared by corporate America, which was facing its own, not dissimilar, set of economic and social challenges. Understanding of the changes taking place and what it meant for business, however, appears more advanced in the US.

'We are not dealing with sporadic or isolated attacks from a relatively few extremists or even from the minority socialist cadre . . . The most disquieting voices joining the chorus of criticism come from perfectly respectable elements of society.' This is from a confidential memo to the US Chamber of Commerce in 1971 written by a lawyer and Philip Morris board member, Lewis Powell. It was used to outline the 'Dimensions of the Attack' and to offer a plan for countering it. Business was warned that this was about their very survival.[29]

Corporate America needed more political power. That was Powell's message. It needed to work hard to cultivate that power. And when necessary, this power must be used 'aggressively and with determination' to fight for corporate interests. In short, business was just not lobbying hard enough. The message got through.

On both sides of the Atlantic business rallied. As part of its campaign it invested heavily in a new breed of business lobby groups: free market think tanks. Via these, business set about making its core requirements 'acceptable in society'.[30] The list of demands included reduced regulations; cuts to the state and reduced funding for social services; and privatisation. Once again, it went on the offensive with ideas.

The Heritage Foundation, one of the most important of the US business lobby groups, was established two years later with a budget of a quarter of a million dollars from the ultra-conservative Coors brewing family, which has been a generous source of funding for US business lobby groups for decades.[31] Today Heritage operates on an annual budget of around $80m (£53m).[32]

In Britain the more modestly funded Centre for Policy Studies was set up the following year, with ties to the Heritage Foundation. Its task included influencing government and shaping the climate of opinion in the name of free market capitalism. Despite being called a think tank, it was less interested in extending the boundaries of knowledge. Its job was explicitly to prepare the British public for specific policies: privatisation, trade union reform, deregulation, NHS and education reform and more.[33] The CPS, like many other think tanks, still refuses to say who funds it. Its president was Margaret Thatcher.

Many of the ideas promoted by the CPS came from its near neighbour in Westminster, the Institute of Economic Affairs (IEA). This is the oldest of Britain's many free market think tanks.[34] It does not publish its backers either. It was formed in the fifties to work against what was dubbed the 'tide of collectivism sweeping across Europe'. The IEA was Britain's base for what was then a tiny minority strand of economic thought, economic liberalism, later to be known as neoliberalism. At its core was this belief in the overwhelming superiority of free markets, with it a loathing of all things socialist.

The CPS took the IEA's radical ideas and popularised them. Thatcher was grateful to it. Both organisations were helped significantly by willing partners in the British press, particularly in later decades in the Murdoch press, with the IEA lobbying to further Murdoch's reach, for example into television, and Murdoch making popular the ideas of the IEA that he then benefited from.[35] Murdoch is said to have funded and participated in think tanks possibly more than any other corporate player.[36]

But it was not just the business lobby groups that were emboldened by the arrival of Margaret Thatcher. Her government provided a world of opportunities for Britain's growing lobbying industry. Privatisation – the selling off of publicly owned industries – was particularly lucrative for commercial lobbyists. From 1984 to 1990 the government sold off more than forty-two businesses, employing nearly a million workers.[37] The opportunities for those that could act as the bridge between companies seeking to profit and government were huge. Privatisation was a 'lobbyists' paradise'.[38]

One of those to spot the opening was the lobbyist Tim Bell. His trade was in information. A former advertising man, who is said to have worked for Murdoch virtually all his life,[39] Bell was part of Thatcher's inner circle of advisers, credited with helping her win three elections. Midway through the eighties, Bell also began providing communications advice to corporate chiefs, although he saw himself as more than a PR man, who he once described as a 'bunch of wankers who went out to lunch a lot'.[40] Bell was quick to recognise that he could sell his services to both government and corporate clients. It was a golden era for lobbyists like him who openly flaunted their contacts and influence on government. 'The Thatcher government was much more open and prepared to talk to outside people,' said Bell. 'It did not have this ridiculous suspicion that anyone who dares to speak to a government minister must be a criminal or trying to do something wicked', he added.[41]

In the thirty years since Margaret Thatcher, the culture in which Bell's industry operates may have altered, but surprisingly little has changed of the activities of commercial lobbyists. Compare the following two lobbying campaigns, thirty years apart, each concerned with the privatisation of the National Health Service.

Then, as now, the shift from public to private – privatisation – and the awarding of contracts was more than a process of tendering. It was an intensely political operation. Extensive lobbying and PR campaigns were needed to overcome public opposition and resistance among public sector workers. Little has changed over the years.

In the early eighties the government was pressing ahead with its plans to contract out parts of the NHS, including the cleaning of hospitals. Many companies were circling for the contracts and they organised collectively to push the policy shift. A greater number of local health officials, however, opposed the move.

The cleaning firms had strong advocates inside Parliament. Some MPs lobbied government to outsource more while being paid consultants to would-be contractors. One Conservative MP, Michael Forsyth, ran a lobbying firm that was hired by the industry to force the policy through. Their strategy included regular briefings, receptions in the House of Commons and private lunches with politicians.[42]

On one occasion Forsyth's firm organised a lunch between the then Health Minister and his cleaning clients. The contractors voiced their anxieties about problem local health commissioners who were holding out against privatisation. The suggestion of an investigation into their recalcitrant ways was outlined at the meeting. The resulting inquiry by the Department of Health was a reprimand to these rebellious local bureaucrats.[43] Government was watching what they were up to.

They must contract out to the private sector. The warning came about as a result of lobbying by companies looking to profit from their contracts.

Fast forward to the current NHS privatisation programme. In 2010, as the Coalition government embarked on its reforms, private health-care companies keen to win local NHS contracts were anxious about what they called 'maverick behaviours' by local health commissioners who were intent on keeping the health service public. Like the cleaning firms, they had also long joined forces. The private healthcare lobby group, the NHS Partners Network, which represents giants like Capita, Care UK, Virgin Care and the US health insurer, United Health, put its shoulder to the door.

Its chief lobbyist, David Worskett, met with the Health Minister, Frederick Curzon, known as Earl Howe, to discuss their concerns. The idea was floated of an inquiry into the behaviours of these 'maverick' local commissioners. According to the lobbyist, Howe promised to look into it as a matter of urgency.[44] Howe did not publicly disclose the meeting. (He apparently regards the NHS Partners Network, not as an external lobby group, but as part of the NHS family, demonstrating the value of a carefully positioned lobby organisation.)[45]

The lobbyist, meanwhile, set about making the inquiry happen.[46] Worskett wrote to a senior Department of Health official to propose that the department instruct the independent NHS regulator, the Co-operation and Competition Panel (CCP), to undertake an investigation. The letter went off to the official, but not before Worskett had checked it with the head of the regulator. 'What do you think?' he wrote. 'Looks good to me,' was the reply. Worskett asked that details of the letter be kept secret until he 'pressed the go button', adding: 'I would prefer to keep it fairly tight'.[47]

Two months – and a £250-a-head seat at a gala dinner for the regulator – later, the inquiry was given the go-ahead. The CCP, an organisation committed to using fair and transparent processes in its job of advising government on anti-competitive practices,[48] went away and investigated. It came back with what private healthcare needed. Evidence of commissioners 'unreasonably restricting patients' choice'. Its report even claimed that their tactics were leading to people dying.[49] The report led the BBC's *Today* programme. The mavericks had been severely warned.

Lobbyists then, as now, opened the door to government. Relationships with politicians remain crucial. PR skills are still used to influence and persuade. What is as clear now as thirty years ago is the ease with which companies circling the NHS, with the aid of lobbyists, can pull strings.

It is worth taking a moment to note too the number of parliamentarians over the years who have become a bridge between government and companies looking to benefit from privatisation. In Thatcher's day, many MPs became consultants, directors and shareholders in the companies seeking contracts in the NHS.[50] Other public servants also cashed in by setting up or joining companies to take advantage of her policies. Some became millionaires.

As the Coalition government progressed with its shake-up of the NHS in 2010, research by the Social Investigations website claimed that 142 Lords have recent or current financial connections to individuals and companies involved in healthcare: that goes up to around one in four when looking at just Conservative peers. 'At best this represents a conflict of interest,' says the site's Andrew Robertson, 'and at worst institutional corruption.'[51]

What has changed significantly in the intervening years, however, is the scale of Britain's commercial lobbying industry: it is estimated to have doubled in size since the early 1990s.[52] Tim (Lord) Bell's PR and lobbying agency, Bell Pottinger, brought in £63m in fees in 2012. This is more than double what it made a decade earlier. Most of this continues to come from business.

Today, however, this corporate income is being supplemented by a secondary source. One that brings clarity to the undemocratic nature of the industry. London's lobbyists lead the world in the business of massaging the reputations of overseas governments, some with dreadful human rights records. What these governments are buying is a good Western image.[53] London's influencers are being paid to help them persuade mainly Western audiences that they are not undemocratic.[54] 'It's laundering,' says one seasoned business commentator.[55]

This is now where the really big money comes from, where multi-million-pound PR campaigns can be written off as 'a negligible rounding error in their national budgets', writes a former *Financial Times* journalist, Tim Burt.[56] The industry is, understandably, touchy about the latest charge that is being levelled at it. The immediate response from one agency boss to an innocuous inquiry about his clients was: 'We don't have any dodgy governments. Well, we have two governments, but they're both democratic'.[57] The same cannot be said of some of the clients taken on in recent years by the UK's lobbyists.

Governments who currently or have recently hired the capital's expertise include: Sri Lanka (Bell Pottinger); Saudi Arabia (Burson-Marsteller);[58] Maldives (Hill & Knowlton); Kazakhstan (Portland Communications); and Russia (Portland Communications).[59] The list of abuses brought about by such governments on their own people is long and worthy of its own book.

Some high-profile foreign despots are considered out of bounds, although the choice appears arbitrary. 'The only client I ever turned down was Gaddafi,' says former Burson-Marsteller CEO Bob Leaf.[60] However, Burson-Marsteller was hired after the military coup in Argentina to massage the country's international image, and worked with Indonesia when it was accused of genocide in East Timor.[61]

Bell Pottinger is a similar case. 'We had a call from Zimbabwe asking us to advise Zimbabwe,' said a former Bell Pottinger lobbyist, Peter Bingle. 'We said, "Thank you very much, but no." That would have been a very malign campaign if somebody had run it.'[62] Bell Pottinger has, though, worked for the Pinochet Foundation, which defended the brutal Chilean dictator Augusto Pinochet,[63] and for the last dictatorship in Europe,[64] Alyaksandr Lukashenka of Belarus.[65] Bell Pottinger was also recently hired by the Bahraini government to handle its public relations during the Arab Spring. It is with a certain irony that it was a survey conducted by Burson-Marsteller which revealed that the single greatest priority for young people in the Middle East is living in a democratic country.[66]

Lobbyists like Tim Bell argue that their motivations are pro-democratic, helping dictators on the road to better governance. For example, when Bell was hired by Belarus' Lukashenka to help it secure the lifting of EU sanctions, Bell advised the dictator of the measures he needed to adopt, like the release of political prisoners, if change was to come.[67] The sanctions were an attempt by Brussels to push Lukashenka to implement reforms.[68]

Bell Pottinger, through employees such as Sir David Richmond,[69] a former top-ranking Foreign Office official, facilitated conversations between Belarus and governments in London, Brussels and Washington.[70]

At the same time, Bell's people were busy courting the media with the message that 'Belarus is embarking on a journey of democratic change'.

All was going well until Belarus 'reneged on its promises', in the words of Bell, and the sanctions were reinstated.[71] This is what democratic change by PR looks like.

London has attracted this business for a number of reasons. Besides the advantages of language, geography and a certain global perspective, London's lobbyists are helped by the UK's lack of transparency. London's reputation managers, unlike rivals in New York and Washington, have no legal requirement to declare their clients.

Lobbying firms working in the US for foreign governments are required to register their activities under the Foreign Agents Registration Act (although some do not). The rules are to make sure that the US government and the American people are in a position to assess what they are up to as 'foreign agents'.[72] By comparison, London's launderers operate totally in the dark. 'It is all under the radar,' says industry watcher Danny Rogers, editor-in-chief of PR Week: 'It's only anecdotally that you can find out what's going on. That's what makes it so powerful, of course, but it is also what can give it its shadowy reputation.'[73]

This is what London is selling today. A sophisticated, global approach to PR and lobbying, with added secrecy. And it happens that, at the moment, a lot of the big money to be made is from overseas governments often intent on crushing popular democracy at home.

Lobbyists in defence of their industry will often cite the many 'good' causes that they promote to policy-makers. And there are many. Portland's Oliver Pauley names its campaign for the Scouts Association. Their huts were being threatened by a proposed hike in water tariffs. Pauley's work to save them was his 'best' case of lobbying.[74] However, it is probably safe to say that Putin's money – Portland lobbies for the Russian government – goes further in supporting the business than the Scouts.

And it is this fact – that there is money to be made from lobbying, whether it is corporates profiting from policy or governments benefiting from better international reputations – that has fuelled the growth of Britain's commercial lobbying industry.

*

Alongside this booming industry, the business lobby's crusade for capitalism continues in Britain. It also remains characteristically anti-democratic.

We live in a golden age of think tanks according to the lobbyist Alex Deane. Their importance has never been greater in terms of their influence on government. Many of these think tanks are direct descendants of National Propaganda. Like Aims of Industry, often they are set up as 'educational charities',[75] but the purpose of many, defined by their output, is to come up with persuasive ways of selling capitalism 'as the finest system that human ingenuity can devise'. The message, however, has had to be refined.

'The case for capitalism needs to be re-made,' wrote Steve Hilton in 2001. Hilton was one of the central Tory modernisers in opposition, and became policy guru to the Prime Minister, David Cameron, in 2010. 'Labour and business are united in developing a considered and intelligent response to the growing strength of the anti-capitalist movement,' he lamented. His party was 'stuck in the simplistic certainties of the great guru of free markets, Milton Friedman'. With the Conservative Party's apparent inability to make a socially acceptable case for capitalism, it was in danger of being left behind.[76]

Hilton articulated this intelligent response to anti-business sentiment as 'corporate social responsibility' (CSR). This is a form of corporate self-regulation, where companies monitor their own compliance with the spirit of laws and ethical standards. Voluntary, selective and often driven by PR rather than corporate policy, CSR has had decidedly mixed results. A fluffy, conscience-salving form of global paternalism is how one Conservative minister described it.[77] CSR gives companies something good to talk about while invariably altering little of their core profit-making activity. Edward Bernays was a great advocate for business presenting itself as a public good, delivering more than just profit and shareholder returns.[78]

These and other ideas were promoted by business-funded think tanks close to the New Labour project: the Social Market Foundation, which, with its long list of corporate funders, attempted to meld social justice and neoliberal economics; the Institute for Public Policy Research, started with seed money from a Labour donor, Clive Hollick, later managing director of the private equity giant KKR; Demos, another which began with largely corporate funds;

and The Policy Network[79] bankrolled by City veteran Evelyn de Rothschild.[80]

'What New Labour did was to suit people who exert power in society not through the political system, or not through the democratic political system,' said Derek Draper. As the assistant to Peter Mandelson, one of New Labour's architects, Draper was the near equivalent of Hilton, right at the heart of the project. 'It suited big business, entrenched interests and the status quo, the things that Labour is supposed to be a counterforce to. What that means is big business get to carry on exerting their power behind the scenes, getting their way because there's no countervailing pressure.'[81]

With the arrival of New Labour, the Conservative Party found itself in unfamiliar territory, competing for business support. It needed a new way to sell itself – and capitalism – to the country. It settled on 'compassionate conservatism'. Think tanks the Policy Exchange, Reform, the Centre for Social Justice and ResPublica were all created in the 2000s to sell the proposition of a modern Conservative Party in touch with issues that the majority actually cared about, like health, education and social justice. Underpinning this, however, was a universal belief in the market's role in delivering solutions in the form of private sector provision of services. Government, in other words, could still be relied on to protect corporate interests. The business lobby, and in this we include wealthy individuals with a pro-business agenda, was an enthusiastic donor.

These think tanks are very good at getting their messages across. Their spokespeople are the equivalent of the 'big men' that the Economic League sent out to spread the word, capable of explaining economic problems in simple terms. They still need to be tough and know how to handle themselves. Not in a physical fight with the opposition, but in the sparring that goes on in the media. Their ability to make themselves heard today comes from their close relations with politicians and the press. 'Think tanks are changing minds at the heart of our national debate,' says Deane. This is their primary purpose.

To find today's influential huddle of lobby groups descended from National Propaganda, you just need to nip round the corner from 25 Victoria Street. Meetings for the think tanks and campaign groups leading the crusade are held within the offices of the campaign group

The TaxPayers' Alliance (TPA) at number 55 Tufton Street, in Parliament's shadow.

The TaxPayers' Alliance is worth looking at in some detail. Its influence is rightly noted by Deane: 'Not only am I pleased to see that my comrades in arms at The TaxPayers' Alliance continue to exert remarkable influence on the tax debate, but also I note that they recently provided the firepower for the No campaign in the recent Alternative Vote referendum.'[82] If ever there was an example of the anti-democratic nature of the business lobby, it is these two campaigns.

The TPA neither declares its annual budget, thought to be in the region of £1m, or its source. A 'monster' is how it has been described, by people on the right of politics, mainly for its aggressive national and local press operation.[83] In 2009 the *Daily Mail* quoted the TPA in 517 articles, with the *Sun* over 300 times.[84] In one seven-week period in 2010 the TPA scored thirteen front pages and more than 150 articles in the *Daily Express*.[85] It is adept at making itself heard.

The TPA's stated purpose is to force politicians to listen to ordinary taxpayers, a laudable democratic aim.[86] Its output, however, is something else entirely. After a shaky start, the TPA reportedly found its feet when the modernised Conservative Party decided not to campaign to lower taxes in Britain. Focus groups revealed that the majority of ordinary taxpayers were opposed to tax cuts that led to reductions in public services, affecting hospitals and schools. At the time tax cuts were not a priority for the majority.

What resulted from the Tory modernisers' lack of focus on lowering taxes was that an increasing number of businesses and donors intent on reducing their tax bills flocked to the one organisation that promised to keep the tax debate alive. The TPA was explicit in its aim of 'challenging the consensus' to create a low-tax Britain. 'That will not happen overnight,' warned the TPA's campaign director, James Frayne. 'It will take years . . . decades perhaps.'[87] The lobby group was committed and it had secured the funds.

Since then the TPA's influence on the tax debate has included lobbying against the top rate of tax for the highest earners. 'New 50p tax rate will stifle the economy,' ran just one headline in the *Telegraph*, based on a 2009 TPA report.[88] It claimed that keeping the 50p tax rate for those earning over £150,000 could have 'dire unintended consequences' for the nation. The campaign was widespread, drawing in others, including the lobbying agency Westbourne Communications, where Frayne has also worked. Yet opinion polling showed the majority of people stubbornly in favour of the tax, with fewer than a quarter opposed.[89] Despite this public support, the tax was binned in the 2012 Budget.

The TPA's campaigning skills were also used to great effect in the NOtoAV referendum campaign that Deane refers to. It was led by the TPA's founder, Matthew Elliott. AV, or the Alternative Vote, was the compromise proposed by the Liberal Democrats to reform Britain's first-past-the-post voting system. Under the current system an MP can be elected with less than a third of the vote. With AV an MP has to have the support of more than half of voters. 'AV forces politicians to work harder to earn and keep their support,' explains Peter Facey of Unlock Democracy, who was involved in the pro-AV campaign.[90] AV was not perfect, and it took some explaining, but it was an improvement in democratic terms. The public were asked to vote on it.

The No campaign wasted no time in setting the terms of the debate: switching to a new system would cost taxpayers £250m they said, although this figure was a fiction, both voting systems costing roughly the same amount.[91] Following the time-honoured PR traditions of presenting false choices and using babies to move people, it ran billboards with a picture of a sick baby in an incubator with the caption: 'She needs a new cardiac facility, not an alternative voting system.'[92] The Yes camp lost the referendum 2 to 1.[93]

The two campaigns in which the TPA was involved – one overtly promoting a tax change that would largely benefit the business elite, the other opposing democratic reform – are a neat illustration of the nature of the modern, organised business lobby in Britain.

Also revealed is the intricate revolving door between business-backed campaign groups, the commercial lobbying industry and politics. James Frayne moved from the TPA to work at two lobbying agencies, Portland and Westbourne Communications. He was then invited by the Education Secretary, Michael Gove, to help him communicate his schools' reforms. Alex Deane was David Cameron's first chief of staff. He then set up a TPA offshoot. He moved next to the Bell Pottinger agency before crossing the road to its rival Weber Shandwick.[94] Meanwhile the former political director at the TPA, Susie Squire, went on to become David Cameron's official Press Secretary.[95]

But the campaigns also give us insight into the approach of lobbyists today, an approach that dates back nearly a hundred years to Bernays. Rather than participating in rational public debate, what these lobbyists seek to do is tap into people's emotions in order to control debate.

In 2013, James Frayne, the ex-TPA lobbyist, penned an article on 'The power of emotion in political campaigns' for the influential website ConservativeHome. 'People make political decisions based primarily on emotion rather than reason,' he wrote.[96]

Frayne is reputed to be one of the best Tory-leaning media strategists in politics today.[97] He has been described as a strategic thinker of immense insight. He does, however, prefer to keep a low profile.[98] He has been dubbed 'London's best kept secret'.[99]

Giving advice to his Conservative allies, Frayne argued there was a need for election campaigns to develop greater expertise in the science of persuasion and influence. Campaigns needed to take in neuroscience and psychology. Party strategists, Frayne argued, should 'investigate the process by which people make political decisions, and how they can intervene in that process to make them vote for a particular party'.

Frayne's thinking has been influenced by US politics, which is far more professionalised than in the UK, and where the influence of PR is more apparent.[100] Frayne has sought to encourage more US-style political campaigning into the UK. His previous blog, CampaignWarRoom, for example, offered daily insight on campaigns on both sides of the Atlantic. He also gained experience helping out on Mitt Romney's failed presidential campaign in 2012.[101]

Frayne's advice to Britain's politicians is to take a much more self-consciously emotional approach to winning popular support. To achieve this, Frayne was moved to predict that they will soon start working with experts on how the mind works. 'Messages that touch people on an emotional level,' wrote Frayne, 'cause a physical reaction in the brain that makes such messages more likely to be stored in our long-term memory, and therefore more likely to affect our political outlook.'

Frayne has advised business to follow suit. In a 2013 book, he urges companies to learn from political-campaign techniques and apply them to corporate PR to 'become experts in public persuasion'. Business needs to start leading the public conversation again, he says.[102] They should ditch the 'backroom lobbyists' and replace them with campaigners who will generate public conversations on the issues that matter to business. This 'permanent', emotionally driven PR assault on the public is the way to secure influence today, he says.

Political and corporate leaders have long understood the power of emotion. What has changed from Bernays' time to Frayne's is our scientific knowledge of how the brain functions. Frayne has the modern advantage of a CAT scanner, perhaps. But the ideas and the motivation are the same: the use of emotional messages, displacing rational thought and debate, to shape public opinion.

In precisely the same way as early pioneers like Bernays, what Frayne proposes is anti-democratic. Politics demands that people engage in rational debate about what is best for themselves, their families, often their community and perhaps the country. It demands that people are treated with respect about their rational ability to understand the issues and what needs to be done. People will disagree as to the solutions, but that is as it should be. The desire by lobbyists to bypass rational debate in favour of 'touching people on an emotional level' shows a shared contempt with Bernays for our ability to do this. But, like Bernays, commercial lobbyists are not working in the interests of ordinary people or for the health of our democracy.

Their interest lies not in debating, as in the forums of ancient Greece, but in manipulating.

3

Access: A Business of Insiders

'I've been working with people like Steve Hilton, David Cameron, George Osborne for 20 years-plus. There is not a problem getting the messages through.'
  Tim Collins, lobbyist, 2011[1]

The veteran lobbyist Tim Bell has always enjoyed access to government. He has been helped in this by occasionally seconding his consultants to departments and paying their salary. 'It is one of his techniques,' says his unofficial biographer, Mark Hollingsworth.[2]

When Margaret Thatcher's Trade and Industry Secretary, David (Lord) Young, was in need of an adviser in 1987, Bell, an aide to Thatcher as well as chair of Bell Pottinger, lent him one of his staff, Peter Luff. Then a director of another of Bell's lobbying outfits, Good Relations, Luff was officially seconded to Young's department, where he stayed for two years. He remained on Bell's payroll.[3]

Bell and Young were close, with the lobbyist said to be impressed that Young could have all that power and influence 'without being troubled by the electorate'.[4] From reports at the time, it seems the electorate barely noticed Luff's appointment. The *Guardian*'s Andrew Rawnsley was almost a lone commentator when he noted that Lord Young and Tim Bell appeared to be reorganising Whitehall as 'their own club'.[5]

When asked what was in it for him, Bell replied: 'Nothing. You either make a commitment towards your society or you don't.' Today, he describes the practice as a form of career development, it was 'all part of the training' for politics, he said.[6] There is no evidence that Bell or his clients benefited from the relationship, or that Luff gave them privileged access to the minister. Although quite how the public is served by a corporately funded inside man, accountable to no one but his backers, is a mystery. And, as Hollingsworth documents in his biography of Bell, it was not without controversy inside government.

'It was disgraceful,' said a former official who worked closely with Luff. Here was a lobbyist working at the highest level, with access to all the inside information of a senior cabinet minister's office, while at the same time being a commercial lobbyist. 'There was a clear conflict of interest.'[7]

At least it was public, though. Since then we have had nearly three decades of lobbying scandals, and demands for more transparency and greater government accountability. Yet despite this clamour it is clear we have far less of a clue who has the inside track to government than before.

The discovery of a man called Adam Werritty inside the Ministry of Defence dominated headlines for nearly a month in the autumn of 2011. It transpired that Werritty was acting as an unofficial adviser to the Defence Secretary at the time, Liam Fox. Werritty had business cards embossed with the official Parliamentary Portcullis, but was not employed by the state. He regularly visited Fox inside the Ministry of Defence, but had not been security vetted. He met up with Fox on eighteen overseas trips in fifteen months to, among other places, Dubai, Bahrain, the US, Israel and Sri Lanka, sometimes sitting in on discussions with foreign officials and dignitaries. Many assumed that he was the minister's official aide, but he was not. He was a good friend of Fox and best man at his wedding.

When his presence was discovered, the questions came thick and fast: who was paying for Werritty's first-class lifestyle if not the taxpayer? Whose interests was he representing? And what on earth was he doing for them?

It was a complicated saga. The official inquiry into the affair barely scratched the surface. The network of donors supporting Werritty was dense and opaque. The money we could see came from Tory benefactors, Israeli supporters and American neocons, among others. Some, though not all, had links to the defence industry. There were connections too with lobbying agencies and a private intelligence firm. Werritty also had 'defence-related business interests'.[8] As the BBC's Nick Robinson commented at the time: 'No official adviser would be allowed to have any such conflict of interest.'[9] Not nowadays anyway.

Werritty was connected to a number of entities. He was paid by Atlantic Bridge, an 'educational and research' charity with links to the US, but which was described by the head of its American sister organisation as a 'shell game'.[10] It was wound up after an investigation by the charities watchdog. However, a month before it was damned by the Charity Commission, a not-for-profit company called Pargav was set up,[11] which took on the job of supporting Werritty. A third mysterious organisation was the Sri Lanka Development Trust. It was registered by a private intelligence and risk firm. Werritty was its contact.[12]

It is important not to get distracted by the complexity of the set up though. Whatever else Werritty was – part of a shadow foreign policy operation is one explanation put forward – he was a way in. He was described as the 'go-to-guy' for defence lobbyists seeking access to the Defence Secretary.[13] Werritty himself was 'not a lobbyist' according to the official inquiry into the saga, which did not probe his business affairs, but he had the basic requirement any lobbyist needs in spades. Access.

Before any lobbyist can get down to the business of influencing, he or she needs access. This is step one on the way to influence. Having access to government is no guarantee of influence, but without access there can be no influence.

Werritty was a way in to the Defence Secretary. On one occasion he was used by a lobbying firm, Tetra Strategy, as a conduit to Fox. The client was a Dubai-based private equity boss who did business with the Ministry of Defence.[14] The financier paid Tetra Strategy £10,000 a month for help that included briefing Werritty, whom the lobbyists believed to be an official adviser,[15] and brokering a meeting with Fox. Werritty was seen by the firm as 'a useful ally . . . on a number of different fronts'.[16]

Bell Pottinger, which until 2012 was part of the same group as Good Relations, was the only other lobbying agency known to have rubbed shoulders with Werritty, although any connection between the lobbyists and Werritty is emphatically denied. Tim Bell, who has had a thirty-year friendship with Liam Fox and who has long lobbied for defence interests, is reported as saying that Werritty attended meetings his firm held with the Sri Lankan government, a client of Bell Pottinger's until the end of 2010. Bell also told the *Guardian* that he had known Werritty 'for a number of years', although he told us he thought he had met him 'only once'. The media, he said, 'knew nothing about what was going on.' He dismissed the saga as a 'whole lot of noise about nothing'.[18]

Bell, though, did concede being 'distantly' linked to the debacle. 'Adam Werritty worked for Michael Hintze, at CQ CQ [sic] hedge fund, and, errm, Michael Hintze was a client of mine' said Bell.[19] Hintze, the billionaire founder of hedge fund CQS and former Goldman Sachs banker who has donated £1.5m to the Tories in the past decade, was at the centre of the saga. He had funded Atlantic Bridge, had provided Werritty with desk space, and one of Hintze's employees was the sole director of Pargav.[20] One of the 'many issues' Bell advised Hintze on was how to kill the story. He was present when Hintze handed over Pargav's accounts to *The Times*. This was a move designed to clear Hintze by revealing that he had not funded it. But the accounts did disclose the network of donors that had. That did it for Fox. He resigned as Defence Secretary the same day.[21]

For nearly a month the story sent the British press into a frenzy, and not just those after the Defence Secretary's scalp. Investigative journalists too put their best efforts into finding out the truth. The pack had caught the scent of a good lobbying story. One weary government press officer even noted the number of journalists on Werritty's trail phoning up with the hilarious opener: 'Hi, I'm Fox hunting.'

It was an intriguing tale. Werritty's set up was unusual in its complexity, its conspiracy thriller-like cast, and his remarkable bond with the Secretary of State. It also displayed one essential feature of the influence industry. The whole set up depended on, was created around, Werritty's relationship with Fox. Without that it was meaningless. What he had going for him was access.

*

Effective lobbyists tend to be well connected. Contacts give them a way in. Access is step one. A long-time lobbyist, Steve John, now at

Bupa,[22] argues that 'Access structures the success or failure of the lobbyist, all of which comes after the access is achieved.'[23] Having access to government does not equate to having influence in government. It is just that without access, influence is, if not impossible, then limited. You can only cook up deals once you are in the kitchen. The rest of us, incidentally, only ever see front of house.

Access is a big deal in the influence business. This is why lobbyists are forever boasting about their contacts.

'I've been working with people like Steve Hilton, David Cameron, George Osborne, for twenty years plus,' Tim Collins, chief lobbyist at Bell Pottinger, told undercover journalists in one of many sting operations. 'There is not a problem getting the messages through,' he added.[24] The lobbyist is making it clear he has high-level access. He is out to impress.

Another caught displaying her contacts was Sarah Southern, a former aide to David Cameron turned lobbyist. 'I am friends with all the people who are now [David Cameron's] closest advisers. I'm friends with the people who are chiefs of staff to members of the cabinet. I'm also friends with a number of people in the cabinet,' she told undercover reporters in 2012.[25] One of those that Southern was able to provide access to was Conservative party treasurer Peter Cruddas, whose position allowed him, in turn, to legitimately offer access to David Cameron and other senior party figures.[26]

When undercover reporters posing as contractors targeted some of the military's top brass, they were not immune to showing off their contacts. Lieutenant-General Richard Applegate confided that he used a lobbying agency (as a 'firebreak') that could gain access 'from the Prime Minister down'. Lord Stirrup, the former head of the armed forces, was said to be able to call on 'powerful contacts' to help in a lobbying campaign (though he did not suggest breaking any rules and indeed was cleared of breaching the House's rules).[27] Lieutenant-General Sir John Kiszely boasted that four years after retirement his military connections were still 'current', before dropping in that the Armed Forces Minister and his wife were staying with him over Christmas. (Kiszely later changed his story and said he had no plans to host the Minister.)[28]

It was the same a decade ago when Derek Draper, then a lobbyist, famously informed Greg Palast, an undercover reporter for the

Observer: 'There are 17 people [in government] who count, and to say I am intimate with every one of them is the understatement of the century.'[29] Palast asked for proof. Draper rose to the challenge, literally, says Palast: 'He stood up from his chair, took a pager from his belt and read off one phone message after the other from the powerful and near-to-power. "Ed Miliband – call me; Dave Miliband – please call; Paul Hackett . . . that's [John] Prescott's office . . ."[30] It was an impressive list.'

Almost without fail the government's response to these claims of privileged access is to deny them. The lobbyist is dismissed as a show-off, or, worse, a deluded, Walter Mitty type. The *Telegraph* was briefed that Adam Werritty 'pretended he was something he wasn't', always 'hanging around and trying to be part of a group'.[31] It even went with the Walter Mitty headline. Fred Michel, the News Corp lobbyist who revealed to the Leveson Inquiry the extraordinary access he had to Jeremy Hunt's office, was a man 'showing off to his boss'.[32] Bell Pottinger's claims of access, which Bell maintains are true,[33] were dismissed by Downing Street as 'a load of rubbish'.[34]

The reaction from lobbyists is more enlightening. They rightly point out that their value extends beyond their political connections. They are, they say, much more than walking rolodexes. 'If you build your success on a contact book then you are destined to fail,' says one.[35] There is truth to this. If you know nothing of the institutions of Parliament and government, how policy is made, the process of legislation, are ignorant of the politics at work at any given time, you are indeed going to be a useless lobbyist. A good lobbyist will understand the inner workings of government: spotting opportunities to intervene and knowing when not to; understanding which strategy to use when; being aware of the current preoccupations of politicians; and having a handle on their personalities, tastes and how best to approach them.

Peter Luff, the former Good Relations lobbyist who became MP for Worcester and eventually minister in charge of the MoD's multi-billion pound equipment budget,[36] explains how it works: 'If someone I know and who knows my way of thinking rings me up and presents a good case, I am more likely to meet that person than if I get a cold letter which does not make a good case. The person has bought access in a sense . . . He has known what levers to pull.'[37]

Contacts are therefore key. It is a reality of life that people tend to be more influenced by those they know. So getting to know politicians is vital. This gives lobbyists their access. Recent attempts to put a value on lobbyists' contacts inside government show that direct access to influential cabinet ministers could be worth in excess of £100,000.[38] The better connected, the more valuable the lobbyist.

Lobbyists, however, also need to have an insider's knowledge. They need to know the politician. What politicians like, how they think, their prejudices and quirks. And that too comes from having contacts and access. This kind of knowledge cannot be acquired from reading about government. Intelligence and information on policy and politicians are picked up from having access to such intelligence and information. Lobbyists need to have an inside knowledge of government.

Which is why the influence business is a business of insiders.

*

Westminster is a breeding ground for the lobbying industry. Parliament and the political parties are where many lobbyists begin their careers. This is where they build their contacts and pick up their insider knowledge. The commercial lobbying industry is often a natural next step for ambitious politicos.

The people who staff the political parties are regular intakes to the influence business. Particularly those who have a communications role. Their fortunes, though, are generally tied to the electoral success of their party. This is the nature of the business. When a Conservative victory looked likely ahead of the 2010 general election, anyone who had worked within the same building as David Cameron saw their premium rise. Typical is someone like Sophie Pim, Cameron's former operations manager. She was hired by the lobbying agency Fleishman-Hillard in 2007 for her 'first hand experience of the inner workings of the Cameron team'.[39]

In the same way when the Liberal Democrats formed a government with the Conservatives, lobbyists were quick to make their introductions with Liberal Democrat staffers. 'They are suddenly much in demand,' wrote Peter Bingle, an ex-Bell Pottinger lobbyist, 'after years of being locked away in the cupboard and only being let out for birthdays, weddings, funerals and Southwark council's planning committee.' Bingle, like many in the industry, went out of his way to court these former nobodies, sponsoring a reception for Liberal Democrat party workers.[40] Likewise, as businesses looking for influence have woken up to the possibility of a Labour victory in 2015, Labour staff are seeing their value rise.[41]

The many advisers to the political parties can also be valuable as lobbyists, in particular special advisers to ministers, so-called SpAds. There are currently around eighty inside government. Officially they are temporary civil servants, but uniquely they work in the overlap between government and party politics. Special advisers are often at the heart of policy-making. The frequency and speed with which they are snapped up by the industry are evidence of their worth. The case of Bill Morgan provides just one, very good, example.

Morgan started as an adviser to the Conservative Party in opposition. His job was to help the shadow Health Secretary, Andrew Lansley, who was developing his controversial changes to the NHS. After two years in post he then moved into the influence business, joining the specialist health team at the lobbying agency Mandate Communications. In 2010 Morgan returned to Lansley's side, the moment he took up the reins as Health Secretary. Together they set about making their plans for the NHS a reality.

As Morgan joined the new government, a former colleague at Mandate (rebranded MHP Communications) described how its clients had 'obviously benefited' from Morgan's inside knowledge of where health policy was heading. More than that, with Morgan's new job in government, he wrote, they can 'look forward to continuing to be at the heart of the major policy debates'. Morgan would remain 'a good friend', the lobbyists assured.[42] Put another way, the agencies' healthcare clients, of which there are many, could enjoy an inside track to government.

When Lansley was reshuffled out of government in 2012, Morgan returned to MHP. His influence perhaps diminished by Lansley's departure, he was still, MHP told clients, in a position to assist them on how best to influence change in the new NHS.[43] MHP is one of the most sought-after lobbying agencies in London today.

Morgan is someone who has shared his time between helping to author the changes that will allow unprecedented private sector involvement in the NHS, and working for commercial healthcare companies seeking to influence health policy. He is an insider through and through. There are similar cases across many areas of government policy, including education reform (see Chapter 8).

Parliament is another source of talent for the lobbying industry. Politicians, depending on their political leanings and connections, can be of far greater value than someone who did the future Prime Minister's photocopying, or who advised a short-lived, unpopular minister.

Before looking at parliamentarians, however, there is another category of lobbyist worth noting to whom they are connected. Those with close personal, often familial, ties to Westminster. Whether it is a shared interest in politics, the long hours, or the relatively small size of the village in SW1, a surprising number of lobbyists are personally attached to politicians. In this, it feels akin to farming.

One firm, for example, specialises in employing the sons of influential officials. Others are tied by marriage although potential conflicts of interests appear to be carefully managed. Nick Clegg withdrew from overseeing new lobbying rules because of the potential conflict presented by his wife Miriam Gonzalez Durantez's job in a lobbying law firm. Former Health Secretary Andrew Lansley's wife, Sally Low, provides 'policy advice' to companies, although denies lobbying government directly and says clients with an interest in health would be 'inappropriate'.[44] James Lundie, the partner of Schools Minister David Laws, was until recently a top lobbyist at global PR and lobbying firm Edelman. However, when Laws became a minister, Lundie announced he was switching jobs to avoid a potential conflict of interest.[45]

Edelman used to employ another political spouse, Heather Rogers Hutton, married to the former Work and Pensions Secretary, John Hutton. At the start of New Labour's third term, Edelman was paid by a private contractor to fix up meetings with Hutton's department. In its sights were lucrative contracts to run programmes to deal with long-term unemployment.

A strategy drawn up by Edelman identified 'targets' in the department, selected from its 'political contact list, as appropriate'. The *Sunday Times*, which covered the story, claimed that it was initially told by a source at Edelman that the contractor was 'Heather's client'. It was then told that Rogers never worked on the account. The department also said that Hutton had not been involved in the decision to award the contract. The subsequent success of the client in winning bids, however, was enough to prompt Hutton's Conservative shadow to demand an investigation into the relationships between client, lobbyist and department.[46]

John Hutton, now a Labour peer, leads us on to the legislators proper. He is one of a large number of peers with links to the lobbying industry. Hutton has a few outside jobs: chair of the UK's nuclear lobby group; adviser to the US's largest construction and engineering company; and special adviser to the accountancy giant PwC.[47]

He is also connected to the global lobbying firm APCO, although this is not declared in his official register of interests. Hutton sits on APCO's board of senior advisers, which helps clients with, among other things, political intelligence, government relations, reputation management and policymaking processes. It singles out its expert counsel on government systems for defence, communication and public service reform.[48]

APCO lobbies for, among others, ATOS, the multinational IT firm. This company has picked up an astonishing £3bn worth of public sector outsourcing contracts in recent years. This includes work for the Department for Work and Pensions,[49] for whom it conducts controversial medical assessments for benefit claims. ATOS' methods have led to a nationwide campaign against the firm by disability activists. It is not known how APCO has helped ATOS lobby government. Hutton told us he could not contribute to this book as he 'doesn't concentrate on' the areas listed above. He declined to say why he had not declared the interest.

If Hutton is quiet about his lobbying ties, Tim Bell, the best-known of the lobbying Lords, is less so. Bell is one of a number of peers who began in the industry, only later becoming legislators well into their PR and lobbying careers. Another is fellow Conservative Peter Gummer, or Lord Chadlington. He is head of a communications group, which like Bell's business operates a number of lobbying agencies.

A lifelong supporter of the Tory party, Gummer is among other things the Prime Minister's neighbour. David Cameron bought a bit of Gummer's drive in 2011 for the price of a small house.[50] Gummer, who is head of the PM's local constituency association, has also for years been a generous donor to the Conservative Party. He helped bankroll Cameron's 2005 Conservative leadership campaign, and has donated a further £60,000 since.[51] Here is a man with contacts.

On the Liberal Democrat bench is Tim (Lord) Clement-Jones, who is with the global law and lobbying firm DLA Piper. Today Clement-Jones registers that he is a partner in the firm, but he was previously listed as the 'key contact' of DLA's lobbying arm. One other notable peer is Peter Mandelson. Since 2010 he has run a consultancy called Global Counsel. While there is no evidence he has lobbied per se, Mandelson, as one of the architects of New Labour and a former European trade commissioner, has some of the best connections in the business. He is someone who could earn a lot of money from his rolodex. He is also, like many, coy about who he works for. When new rules were introduced to force peers to reveal their clients, Mandelson was one who chose to use a loophole that allows him to keep his hidden.[52]

Aside from current parliamentarians, many former politicians have found lucrative work in lobbying, both ex-ministers and backbench MPs. Besides their contacts, one advantage to lobbyists of having a former MP on the staff is that they can pass in and out of Parliament with the ease of sitting politicians. They are pass holders. Everyone else has to queue.

Conservatively, twenty-five of the 200 pass-holding former MPs in 2010 were connected to the lobbying business, giving them easy access to work their former colleagues in the tea rooms of Parliament.[53] Getting this figure took two and a half years. There was, let us say, a reluctance by the authorities to reveal who has access to the House. In the time it took to prise the names of these pass-holding ex-MPs from the House of Commons under freedom of information laws, five on the list had died.[54]

The number of MPs joining the influence industry was expected to balloon in the wake of the expenses scandal, as MPs were ejected en masse.[55] Andrew MacKay MP was one. A former aide to David Cameron as leader of the Conservative Party, MacKay signed up to work for the PR and lobbying giant Burson-Marsteller. This was not long after he had been called a 'thieving toad' by constituents in Bracknell for inappropriately claiming over £30,000 in second home and cleaning expenses.[56]

It is worth briefly noting the traffic flowing the other way. Of the new MPs that flushed out the duck-housing, moat-cleaning MPs, nearly 15 per cent elected in May 2010 came straight from lobbying backgrounds.[57] Many sought to play down their links. Priti Patel, now MP for Whitham, campaigned for her seat on a ticket of supporting small businesses. Prior to that, she helped promote the interests of the UK's largest tobacco company, an alcohol multinational and a group lobbying on behalf of Britain's banking sector.[58]

Many former ministers have also found work in the influence business. Take just ex-health ministers. The list includes Conservative health minister in the 1990s, Julia (Baroness) Cumberlege, who runs her own consultancy advising, among others, the pharmaceutical industry, on understanding government and how to influence it.[59]

Tom Sackville is another ex-Tory health minister from the 1990s, who until recently chaired the pharmaceutical-funded health 'think tank' 2020Health, described by former Health Secretary Andrew Lansley as 'providing valuable impact on future policy'. Sackville is also chief executive of the International Federation of Health Plans, which represents 100 private health insurance companies. He has been described as a 'global lobbyist for the insurance industry'.[60]

His former colleague ex-health minister John Bowis became an advisor to lobbying firm Hanover in 2010, which lobbies for, among others, pharmaceutical company MSD. Bowis is also an advisor to pharma giant GSK.[61]

Ex-Labour health minister Melanie Johnson became an adviser to the UK pharmaceutical industry's main lobby group, the Association of the British Pharmaceutical Industry. An influential figure in the NHS, Norman (Lord) Warner is another who has taken on a number of jobs since he was health minister, including giving advice on policy development to DLA Piper. Many more retired health ministers have taken up paid jobs as advisers to private healthcare companies.

There are clear advantages to having an ex-minister on the payroll. When the then MP for South Thanet in Kent, Stephen Ladyman, was abruptly sacked by the incoming Prime Minister, Gordon Brown, in 2007, the former Transport Minister accepted a £1,000-a-month position as a consultant to a traffic management company, ITIS Holdings. Ladyman already knew the firm. It had major contracts with Ladyman's former department measuring traffic jams.[62]

Ladyman was banned from lobbying for the company for a year by the official body that oversees the revolving door. This did not stop Ladyman tabling Parliamentary questions pertinent to ITIS during this period. He also made contact with former colleagues on ITIS' behalf: 'I'm not allowed to lobby until one year after I left office,' he wrote to the Highways Agency. 'After that date, I'd really like to bring some of my ITIS colleagues along to chat with you.'[63] The rules designed to prevent former ministers from exploiting their contacts in government to further commercial interests have little impact.

Ladyman lobbied using his House of Commons email account, Parliament's address, and taxpayer-funded facilities. His sideline was run from his constituency office.[64] When he wrote to lobby London's transport officials to pitch for a role for ITIS during the Olympics,[65] he opened with: 'You may remember me from my time as Minister of State for Transport.' They replied: 'I do indeed and am delighted to hear from you . . . we would be interested to hear your proposals.'[66] This is the value of paying an insider to lobby on your behalf.

These are some of the most visible insiders that make up the lobbying industry. Those who take the path from Westminster into lobbying, like former ministers, are easy to spot. The political connections and experience of these players give us a feel for their access and insider knowledge, both of which are vital to effective lobbying. This starts to give us a picture of who is influencing government and to grasp the depth of the lobbyists' reach into government.

At the same time, we also need to get a clear picture of the breadth of the lobbying industry; the size of the pitch and the numbers of players involved. We need to be familiar with the places that those who enjoy privileged access to our politicians operate from and the diversity of the interests that they represent. To do this we need to go on a lobbying tour around central London.

*

The most visible side of the commercial lobbying industry is the lobbyists-for-hire who sell their services to clients who are mainly for-profit corporations. Although this does not represent the whole for-hire lobbying industry, just shy of eighty firms are registered with the industry body.[67] Together, they represent nearly 2,000 clients. Approximately 85 per cent of these are commercial, for-profit organisations.[68] All the big name companies are represented, from Goldman Sachs to Google, Microsoft to McDonald's, as well as a large number few will recognise. Foreign government clients currently include Kazakhstan and Bahrain and the tax havens of the Isle of Man and Bermuda. Some agencies do also lobby for charities, although at roughly 7 per cent of the total declared client list, they appear more as a fig leaf than a serious source of income.

Many of the big-name lobbying agencies sit along an artery that runs east from the ropey end of Oxford Street to the edge of the Square Mile. It is unlikely that the blocks in between will ever become synonymous with lobbying in the same way that 'K Street' has become a common way of referring to Washington's lobbyists, but this twenty-minute walk is where many of the big players have set up shop. One reason why is clear from a map of this part of central London: they sit equidistant between Westminster and the City, the bridge between politics and money.

The offices of lobbyists can be a good indication of the type of service on offer. Weber Shandwick's huge HQ in Holborn, just down the road from ITN's studios, houses a full-service, global-communications agency. The London office of the world's largest independent global PR and lobbying firm, Edelman, occupies a 38,000 sq. ft office block just down the road from the Department for Business. Edelman is proud of its 'independence'. London visitors wait in reception to the sound of The Smiths.[69] Its New York office contains a chunk of the Berlin Wall.

Quiller Consultants is a different kind of firm. It is all about discretion and offers a more selective offering focused on lobbying and managing the reputations of its clients. It is tucked away six doors down from Buckingham Palace. Tim Bell has his office in Mayfair, next door to the Saudi Embassy. Still others are clustered with the think tanks around St James' on top of Parliament. And those whose primary job is public relations for finance sit within the borders of the Square Mile. Compare this to the charity sector lobbyists, who predominate in the relatively cheap seats in north and east London.

But many of the big commercial lobbying agencies extend along this strip from the West End's eastern side. The majority are subsidiaries of multinational PR giants, which are themselves part of global communications businesses offering marketing, advertising, branding, product placement and crisis management alongside PR and lobbying. One of the Big Four global groups is Omnicom, which feels like it is trying to sound sinister: it represents 5,000 clients in more than 100 countries with revenues in 2011 of nearly $14bn.[70] The others are Publicis, which is on track to merge with Omnicom, Interpublic and WPP run by the British advertising tycoon, Martin Sorrell.[71]

Let us start the tour at the Oxford Street end. Here in Soho Square is the Hill & Knowlton agency, part of WPP. A couple of blocks west is Grayling, one of Peter Gummer's lobbying firms. Walk east and look up and you will see the offices of the UK's central business lobby group, the Confederation of British Industry, looming over the strip from the incongruous Centre Point tower.

If you were to head south down Charing Cross Road towards Covent Garden, you would reach Omnicom's FleishmanHillard above the tube station. Independent giant APCO is just further up the road. Instead, continue east for 500 metres and you will reach WPP's Burson-Marsteller. At the end of High Holborn and tucked in a smart alleyway is Lexington Communications, an independent agency.

Dogleg south a block from here to arrive at Omnicom's Fishburn Hedges; cut through past Holborn tube station to Lincoln's Inn Fields, and in one of the Regency townhouses is Brunswick; negotiate your way round the Inns of Court to Chancery Lane, home of Bell Pottinger, until 2012 part owned by WPP; cross over the lights and just off Gray's Inn Road is Weber Shandwick, part of Interpublic. At the north end of the street is the independent Hanover.

Besides this strip, there are a number of other agencies dotted along a parallel artery, Fleet Street. Portland, an influential lobby shop of the moment, is tucked off a side street. Hume Brophy and Luther Pendragon are another two here. It is perhaps fitting that PR and lobbying agencies now occupy the street that was once a byword for British journalism. As the press corps have dispersed and their numbers dwindled, PR's ranks have swelled. The ratio today stands at roughly one journalist reporting the news for every four PRs trying to shape what they write.[72]

Today, though, these big lobbying agencies have competition in the influence business. As we explored in the previous chapter, some think tanks are effectively operating like commercial lobbying agencies. Many of these nestle in offices a stone's throw away from Parliament. Like the agencies, think tanks will approach clients with a package of measures designed to influence government: a report, an event, ear-time with politicians. 'The exact same services that a lobbying agency would provide,' says one agency lobbyist. 'They're just more expensive.'[73]

Think tanks can provide clients with unrivalled access to politicians. 'The think tank route is a very good one,' said the former minister Patricia Hewitt to undercover reporters seeking lobbying advice in March 2010. Identifying the right think tank, she counselled, was key: 'Does that think tank already have a relationship with minister X? Can we invite minister X to give a seminar? Your client would then sponsor the seminar. You do it via the think tank. And that's very useful, because what you get for your sponsorship is basically you sit next to the minister.'[74] Corporations pay think tanks for this kind of access to politicians.

Law firms also provide lobbying advice to their clients. The practice is commonplace in the US. While there are fewer players in the UK, those law firms that do give such advice, have influence. DLA Piper is one with a significant lobbying practice in Britain.[75] Beachcroft, another international law firm, says that it offers advice on public policy to private sector healthcare clients and hosts private client events with policymakers. It employs two former senior cabinet ministers. In a brochure advertising its health advisory services, Beachcroft boasts of them having 'unrivalled knowledge of the workings of Westminster'. One of its ex-ministers, the Tory peer David Hunt, led the first Parliamentary debate on the recent NHS changes in the House of Lords. He reminded his fellow peers of his relevant interest in the law firm, as the rules require.[76]

As well as lawyers, competition to agencies is coming from other professionals. Management consultants and accountants are also in corporate boardrooms giving lobbying advice to clients.[77] We will return to them. What is notable is that the activities of these professionals are far less visible than their PR counterparts.

Such lobbyists-for-hire are powerful players, whether in PR agencies, law firms or think tanks. They all employ insiders with access to government, and the vast majority of their clients are corporations. But their numbers are dwarfed by lobbyists working directly for businesses or industry trade bodies. There are four in-house lobbyists for every hired gun. The corporate players in the lobbying business are often far better connected.

Let us start with the corporate chiefs and one elite group in particular: the Multinational Chairman's Group. This tiny, privileged lobby group consists of the bosses of major multi-national businesses, typically based in Britain although not always for tax purposes. BP, Shell, HSBC, British American Tobacco, GlaxoSmithKline, the drinks giant Diageo, Unilever and Vodafone are all said to be members. They are invited to Downing Street to tell the Prime Minister how they believe government policies, taxes in particular, are affecting international corporations.

The discreet club, for example, helped persuade the Blair government to drop what they saw as a punitive tax on the pensions of the country's very top earners. Gordon Brown, then Chancellor, had proposed the tax and was refusing to back down, so the group went over his head and appealed directly to Blair, claiming the plans would lead to an exodus of the rich from Britain. The tax rate was subsequently reduced and delayed to give them more time to rearrange their finances.[78]

Dialogue between senior politicians and multinational bosses is to be expected. Their access, through groups like this, however, can lead to influence over areas of policy in which they should arguably have no place. BAT, for example, used a No. 10 breakfast meeting of the Chairman's Group to buttonhole New Labour's Trade Secretary, Stephen Byers. At the time Byers was intent on holding a potentially damaging inquiry into allegations that BAT was colluding in cigarette smuggling on a massive scale. He had been avoiding BAT. Following the intervention – and a sustained lobbying effort – an inquiry went ahead, but it was conducted in secret, buried and quietly forgotten. A BAT lobbyist was able to dismiss it as 'a distraction' and 'not a problem'.[79] The threat had been averted.

The next notable and no less influential group with unfettered access to government are the bankers. In Britain, these City figures are often indistinguishable from the politicians and regulators who are charged with protecting the public interest. The UK comes second only to Switzerland for the number of people moving through the revolving door between the finance sector and government. The access and insider knowledge they have is unrivalled.

Take Sebastian Grigg, ex-Goldman Sachs, now an investment banker at Credit Suisse. Grigg was a significant government adviser to Gordon Brown on the bank bailout strategy. With a team from Credit Suisse, he reportedly set up camp in one of the Treasury's corridors to work through the problems in Britain's failing banks. Grigg's political allegiance, however, is to the Conservative Party. He is also a long-standing friend of David Cameron. They were at Eton together and at Oxford, where both were members of its notorious Bullingdon Club.[80]

Chancellor George Osborne is said to be friendly with Richard Sharp, ex-Chairman of Goldman Sachs and another influential Tory figure. The Conservative Mayor of London, Boris Johnson, is close to, among many others in banking, Goldman Sachs' Michael Sherwood. Worth around £225m, 'Woody' is a former classmate of the Deputy Prime Minister, Nick Clegg. He is also Boris' ping pong buddy. 'When is our next ping pong challenge?' Johnson wrote to Sherwood in the summer of 2010, joking that he was looking forward to the chance to educate Sherwood at 'pingers'. He probably would have lost. Sherwood reportedly plays for an hour a week with his close friend Matthew Syed, the former England champion.[81] This is somehow indicative of the power imbalance between politicians and bankers.

This cheery exchange of emails with London's Mayor occurred as Sherwood's firm was facing a barrage of criticism. Not many months earlier, Goldman Sachs had famously been dubbed a 'great vampire squid wrapped around the face of humanity, relentlessly jamming its blood funnel into anything that smells like money'. It had also just been accused by US officials of defrauding investors.[82] Still, London's Mayor was desperate to reassure the investment bank that he was committed to defending their interests against the twin threats of tax rises and EU regulations. Johnson wrote to Goldman's CEO, Lloyd Blankfein: 'I know that recent hasty and ill-thought-out changes to taxation and other public policies have led some to cast doubt on London's future competitive position.' He urged Goldman not to take 'precipitate action' and leave the capital. Johnson pledged to 'strongly defend' London's financial services industry. 'I will do my utmost,' he assured them.[83]

Just days later, Johnson took Sherwood to lunch with the then shadow Chancellor, George Osborne. The purpose of the lunch was for a 'select group of senior bankers' to discuss these 'threats' to London's financial sector. In his invitation to Sherwood, London's Mayor was again at pains to reassure the banker of his commitment to defending the bank's position.[84] Which meant lobbying to keep taxes low and regulation light.

Goldman Sachs' London HQ sits on Fleet Street, on the border of

Westminster and the City. A number of other corporate giants also surround Parliament. Follow the bend in the Thames from the Palace of Westminster and just off the Strand is BAT's HQ. The windows of the Shell building at Waterloo overlook the Whitehall departments that line the opposite bank. BP and BAE Systems sit behind the offices of Whitehall near the private clubs of Pall Mall. This, incidentally, is where the Institute of Directors is based, another of the many dedicated business lobby groups. Returning to the Westminster HQs: the offices of the outsourcing giant Capita are on Victoria Street, an artery running from Parliament, which is home to the Department for Business. Boeing, Rolls-Royce, Microsoft and a host of others are nearby.

For the time being at least, Google has its corporate headquarters at the top of this strip. Or Google's version of a corporate HQ with yurts, sharing cubes and 'huddles'. Like all multinationals, Google employs a lobbying agency, Portland Communications. This has its own roster of insiders, including Alastair Campbell, Tony Blair's former spin doctor, and it is run by Campbell's old deputy in No. 10, Tim Allan.[85] It also counts two other ex-heads of communications, one to Gordon Brown, the other to the Coalition government. David Cameron's former director of policy, who co-authored the Coalition's programme for government, is also on the staff. As is the man who wanted David Cameron's job, Michael Portillo. Portland is currently one of the best connected in the business.

The collective political nous of Portland, however, only supplements the tech firm's well-connected in-house lobbying operation. In recent years Google has become a major lobbyist. So much so that it could be more accurately described, as one commentator put it, as 'a political organisation with a legacy tech business attached'.[86]

In the US, Google is throwing money at lobbying. It spent over $5m in just the first three months of 2012,[87] when it had Congress and privacy watchdogs breathing down its neck. In 2011–12 a mainly successful two-year assault to head off an anti-trust investigation into the firm clocked up a lobbying bill of around $25m.[88] Google also has a significant Brussels lobbying operation, who are part of the estimated 15,000–30,000 lobbyists operating in the EU capital.[89] In 2013, it was among a number of US tech firms that launched one of the fiercest lobbying offensives ever seen over the prospect of new data privacy laws.[90] These figures, though, do not do justice to its influence.

Google has courted the great and the good in politics with determination. In recent years the Google party was the hot ticket at the
World Economic Forum, the elite networking event in Davos.[91]
Google's strictly invitation-only annual Zeitgeist conference is another
flame that draws the big names. For two days every year politicians,
along with royalty, press barons, bankers and the occasional pop star
descend on the Grove hotel in Hertfordshire, primarily to network.[92]
Imagine a list of a couple of hundred guests that includes David
Cameron, Bill Clinton, Jim O'Neill, formerly of Goldman Sachs, WPP's
Martin Sorrell, Gwyneth Paltrow and Arsène Wenger and you get a
feel for it.[93]

Google is useful to illustrate the second-tier lobbyists inside large
companies that sit below corporate bosses. The internet giant's
communications and lobbying is headed up by Rachel Whetstone. She
has Conservative politics in her blood. Her grandfather helped found
the free market think tank the Institute of Economic Affairs, where
her mother is still a director.[94] Both she and her partner, David
Cameron's former chief strategist, Steve Hilton, were for a long time
part of Cameron and George Osborne's inner circle. They went horse-
trekking together.

Hilton quit Britain for California in 2012 to join Whetstone, who is
based in Google's US headquarters. He is now a fellow at the Hoover
Institution, a key conservative, part-corporate-funded think tank based
at Stanford University. In 2011, Google welcomed another of David
Cameron's closest aides to its West Coast 'Googleplex': Tim Chatwin,
who used to work alongside Hilton in No. 10.[95] Google has sucked up
people from the other party in government too, the Liberal Democrats.
The party leader, Nick Clegg, lost his political adviser Verity Harding
to Google's UK-based lobbying team in 2013.[96] There she joined Naomi
Gummer, daughter of Cameron's neighbour, Peter Gummer, one of
the lobbying Lords. Gummer Jnr was before that a political adviser to
Jeremy Hunt, at the time Culture Secretary and in charge of internet
regulation.[97]

Google is one of the better-connected multinationals operating in
Britain, but it is not exceptional. Tesco, for example, has its insiders.
Its chief lobbyist, David North, is a former private secretary to Tony
Blair. Until 2012, Tesco's 'eyes and ears in the corridors of power'[98]
was Lucy Neville-Rolfe, now elevated to the Lords. She previously

held a number of senior government positions, including in No. 10's policy unit.[99] In 2011, Tesco also hired Victoria Gould, one of Tony Blair's closest aides since leaving government.[100]

This pattern of identifying and hiring insiders to lobby for narrow, corporate interests is the norm. London's corporate offices are peopled with lobbyists whose eyes are trained on Westminster and the decisions taken within it. These are lobbyists with insider knowledge of how decisions are taken and the people taking them. They know, because they used to work there.

*

We now have an idea of the insiders who work in lobbying and their reach within government. We have an understanding of the scope of the lobbying business that encircles the Westminster village. In order to get a more complete picture of the influence industry we need to get a feel for the social world that they operate in. Socialising is an important part of the job. It builds contacts, increases access and opportunities to lobby.

It is sometimes assumed that lobbying is a battle for influence. Both the industry and transparency campaigners are guilty of perpetuating this image, slipping into the language of conflict. We talk of lobbying 'assaults' on politicians. Lobbyists use phrases like 'deploying ground troops' and 'weakening political defences'. But when you get the two sides together – lobbyist and official, both insiders – relations are normally far from hostile. The industry is very amiable, most of the time.

Lobbyists can often be at pains to demonstrate their social connections with politicians. Shortly after Boris Johnson took the reins in City Hall, for instance, he was contacted by Simon Walker, then chief lobbyist for the private equity industry. Walker wrote to congratulate the new Mayor, expressing his particular delight on his victory 'as a canvasser, cyclist and a Balliol man,' referring to their shared political affiliations, mode of transport and the Oxford college both attended. On another occasion, Walker praised an 'epic oration' delivered by Johnson at a Policy Exchange event: 'It's good that someone is defending the citadels of capitalism'. In another letter, he commented on a 'splendid' TV programme Johnson presented. 'This is not mere flattery,' he wrote, 'I also have a request on behalf of my members . . .', reminding us that there is purpose to his epic schmoozing. Walker wanted Johnson to join him and some investors for dinner.'⁰¹

Lobbying is a sociable business. Lobbyists are relentless networkers. And there is no better introduction to them at it en masse than at the party conferences. Or 'Oktober Fest-style orgies of drunken favour', as the *Daily Mail*'s Quentin Letts called them.[102] With all those politicians in one place, this is when lobbyists really ramp up the schmoozing.

From one perspective, the Liberal Democrats' autumn conference we attended in 2012 was a bit of a washout. Brighton's seafront was lashed by gale force winds. Nick Clegg was battered in the polls. On the busiest night of conference, a small number of Liberal Democrat activists drifted around the vast concrete conference centre looking for things to do. This did not feel like democratic participation at its best.

Next door, however, the luxurious, Victorian Grand Hotel was alive with the buzz of lobbyists. To outsiders they can seem all of a type, indistinguishable from each other and from the party apparatchiks with whom they are drinking. Overwhelmingly male, young to middle-aged, white, self-assured and well-dressed. Like many of our politicians.

A few were easy to spot in the heaving hotel bar. Tesco's then chief lobbyist, Lucy Neville-Rolfe, diminutive and with a blue Mallen streak, and Ian Wright of the drinks giant Diageo (with his pink laptop). The smart set from the business lobby group the Institute of Directors were knocking against the TheCityUK finance lobby group. The airport expansion lobby was crammed in a corner. The smokers' lobby shouldered their way through, seemingly friendless.

And in among them were the hired guns. The agency lobbyists. Michael Burrell of the global lobbying giant APCO, short and tanned with the debating style of a Jack Russell. Charles Lewington, the head of the Hanover agency, is his opposite. Tall, suave and once described as the 'flouncing afghan hound' to Alastair Campbell's Rottweiler when Lewington was his Conservative opposite number.[103] The lobbying law firms were there in Eben Black of DLA Piper. An ex-*News of the World* political editor, he resembles a more steely Tom Watson MP.

It is a long drink-fuelled evening. This pack would go on past three in the morning. Earlier on, discreet drinks parties in private suites have been arranged for lobbyists to get valuable 'ear-time' with politicians.

Think tanks have organised 'intimate discussions over dinner' for their corporate sponsors to sit down with a minister. Monday night was also Clegg's formal, not-so-intimate fundraising dinner. One lobbyist skipped pudding. 'Too many people there,' he said.[104] This is a time for introductions, bonding, exchanging gossip and refreshing friendships with their political counterparts. This is mingling with a purpose.

Party conferences are the one time that lobbyists' schmoozing breaks cover. But the wining and dining and relentless networking are constant features of the influence business. Even if, the rest of the time, it is hidden from public view.

Compared with twenty years ago, lobbying is a far less showy affair today. The hospitality budgets have been cut and the parties are smaller. There is also a greater focus on professionalism in the industry, with less importance attached to personal connections developed through a lively but closed social scene.

The social side of lobbying has not disappeared, however, it is just more discreet. You will still find lobbyists in London's private dining rooms, at events where business people and politicians can talk without interference. The former *Financial Times* journalist turned Brunswick lobbyist Tim Burt writes of 'the old club nature' of the influence business, with its 'relentless networking, aversion to outside scrutiny, appetite for parties and the dinner-table pursuit of clients'. It sounds a bit like the old British Establishment.

The timeless practice of 'gastronomic pimping', as the late Nye Bevan MP referred to it, is alive and well. Hospitality has long been used by lobbyists to curry favour, deepen relationships and influence, or extract information from politicians and officials. Some of London's best restaurants do well out of it.

The man formerly in charge of Britain's tax system, Dave Hartnett, famously became known as Whitehall's most wined and dined civil servant. On 107 occasions in two years he accepted the hospitality of some of the UK's biggest banks, law firms and accountancy firms.[105] Hartnett was a pivotal figure in the recent 'sweetheart' tax deals with large corporations agreed to by the Revenue.[106]

The nuclear industry has also been generous with its hospitality at particular moments. Throughout the government's 2007 public consultation on the future of nuclear power, mandarins charged with carrying out the exercise were entertained at London's top spots by organisations with a vested interest in new power stations. No office meetings for this lot. The lobbyists were out to impress. Venues included the Ritz, Goring and Royal Lancaster hotels. This is another case of civil servants accepting hospitality from a group they should have kept at arm's length.[107]

The nuclear lobbyists are still going. In the first half of the Coalition government's term, three senior officials from the Office of Nuclear Development enjoyed the hospitality of nuclear companies or those with a stake in nuclear new build over fifty times. The occasions included breakfast at the exclusive Cinnamon Club, lunch at the historic Reform Club, drinks at Whitehall's Royal Horse Guards Hotel and dinner at Knightsbridge's Michelin-starred Berkeley hotel.[108]

This is the other life led by some of Britain's top officials, spent in some of London's finest eateries. The lobbyist is buying dinner and privileged access. Through disclosure laws, we can sometimes know the venues they select for this lobbying but never what was discussed. This is the quietest side of the influence business. There are no officials present to take notes and no oversight of any agreements made. More often, though, this lobbying activity remains entirely hidden.

In 2011, the Communities Secretary, Eric Pickles, was lavishly dined by Bell Pottinger. Pickles claimed it was in a 'private capacity', which he felt meant he did not have to declare it under the current rules governing ministers' behaviour. Also present at the dinner was the boss of a regional airport, who was awaiting a decision by Pickles' department on a planning application to almost double the capacity of the airport. Pickles denied speaking to the airport operator at the event.

The dinner was held in a private dining room at the Savoy, famed for its 'particular grandness and opulence'.[109] It only came to light when Bell Pottinger's then chief lobbyist, Peter Bingle, boasted about it on his blog: 'Pickles' attendance at the dinner in the Savoy's Gondoliers Room. The discussion must remain private, but I can reveal that the guests were more than just impressed.'[110] But not with the surroundings. The lobbyist is providing direct access to the minister on whom a client's commercial fate rests. The lunch is thrown in for the minister.

Although this kind of public bragging is unusual in lobbying circles, the practice of private client dinners with politicians appears common. Charles Lewington's firm, Hanover, says it regularly hosts such private lunches. Portland is rumoured to host monthly dinners between clients and officials, including at the 'extortionately expensive' Haymarket Hotel off Trafalgar Square.[111] Education Minister, David Laws, was one recent guest at a dinner with Portland's 'clients and friends'.

The financial sector lobby group TheCityUK are frequent and generous hosts. Among the group's guests in 2012 was the incoming banking regulator, Andrew Bailey. Also invited to the dinner, held in the private dining room of the global law firm Linklaters, were representatives of Clifford Chance, Deloitte, DLA Piper, JP Morgan, Morgan Stanley and RBS.[112] Bailey declined an invitation to an 'informal gathering' of bankers and policymakers a fortnight later on what TheCityUK's Chris Cummings hoped would be the 'sun-drenched rooftop terrace' at the offices of the law firm SJ Berwin.[113]

The doyen of the dinner party lobbyists is said to be Roland Rudd, one of the most influential players in the industry.[114] Rudd is founder of Finsbury PR, the City-based financial PR and lobbying firm. He counts among his clients some of the biggest names in finance, from Deutsche Bank and RBS to the private equity giants KKR and Blackstone.[115]

Both Rudd and his rival in the City, Alan Parker, head of the Brunswick agency, have made a business from being the best-connected men in town. Just a brief glimpse at their top-tier political friends is enough. Parker, who reportedly has three secretaries, two for business, one for social events,[116] has holidayed with David Cameron. Rudd has had him over to dinner.[117] Parker was friends with Gordon Brown, who is godfather to one of Parker's children. Rudd is close to Peter Mandelson. Tony Blair's son did work experience at Finsbury.

Rudd regularly assembles a table of big-name guests at his grand Kensington house. Dinners are reputedly relaxed, informal occasions. The guest list is drawn from Rudd's corporate and banking clients, alongside political heavyweights and their other halves.[118] Tony Blair dined there when he was Prime Minister. 'It's great fun,' says Rudd.[119]

As is the case for all lobbyists' hospitality, these are not social occasions. They are an opportunity to build contacts, lobby and learn. In his first week as London Mayor, Boris Johnson received an invitation from Rudd to have dinner with him and guests at Rudd's home.[120] These included nineteen chairmen and CEOs who were keen to hear

Johnson's plans for London.[121] On the evening of the dinner in early 2009, the Mayor cycled off to Rudd's home, arriving, we know from freedom of information disclosures, for a 'meet & greet' at 19.35 p.m. The first course was then served at 20.05 p.m. The main course promptly at 20.25 p.m. Boris was back on his bike by 22.30 p.m. The intervening three hours are private. Who was there, the names of the corporate chiefs, and what they discussed with London's newly elected Mayor are a secret.

London's private clubs provide yet another discreet base for lobbyists. These are exclusive places thanks to either a membership fee or a vetting procedure. The most elite and oldest of the Conservative clubs is the Carlton Club just off Pall Mall. It is referred to as one of the homes of the Conservative Party. Liam Fox and Adam Werritty were both club members. As was Ian Greer, the doyen of lobbyists during the eighties, until his fall from grace with the 'cash for questions' affair in the mid-nineties.[122]

London's theatre district is home to the gentlemen-only Garrick Club, one of the few to exclude women from becoming members, but which has a warm welcome for lobbyists. Just down the road, The Club at The Ivy, the private members' club next door to the glitterati's favourite restaurant, has also been favoured by lobbyists. Not long ago, Brunswick lobbyists described it as a regular haunt and one where they anticipated seeing the government minister, Gordon Brown's chief of strategy and former Brunswick CEO, Stephen Carter.

Central London is littered with dark places where business and government can quietly interact. These private places provide space for socialising without interference. The socialising provides lobbyists with extended access and opportunities to lobby beyond the offices of Westminster and Whitehall. Relaxed, out-of-hours and outside the rules of disclosure, lobbying in these circumstances can be particularly effective.

The influence industry and its access to government should be starting to come into view. We can understand the importance of lobbyists as insiders. We can start to see the map of the industry and the range of interests enjoying access. And we can grasp how the social side of the business amplifies lobbyists' access and influence while keeping them private.

This is not the whole picture, however. There is an even less visible part of the business. To get a complete view of the influence industry, we need to look inside government itself, into the departments and ministries in Whitehall.

*

For nearly a hundred years, concerns have been expressed about the 'revolving door' between Whitehall and industry. As early as 1925 instances were noted of 'persons holding responsible positions under the State, resigning their appointments and accepting lucrative positions in private undertakings with which they have been in contact during their official careers on behalf of the public'. Then, as now, the problem was an issue of public confidence, which it was said at the time could be 'gravely affected'.

Government offices are a breeding ground for the influence business, as much as Westminster and the political parties. Former civil servants, though, can be even more useful as lobbyists than those with connections to the parties and Parliament. They too supply access and inside information, but officials also bring first-hand experience of how government processes, like procurement, work. This knowledge is clearly valuable to those who do business with government.

Communication between officials and businesses, it must be noted, is a good thing. There should be a healthy exchange of information between a sponsor department, the industries it is responsible for and its contractors. Government should be accessible. Open channels of communication are necessary and encouraged. A fast-moving revolving door from the civil service into business can, however, lead to poor decisions being made, particularly in government purchasing.

When David Cameron expressed concerns that 'lobbying in this country is getting out of control', 'cronyism' was one danger he warned of: 'This isn't a minor issue with minor consequences,' he said. 'Commercial interests – not to mention government contracts worth hundreds of billions of pounds are potentially at stake.'[123]

The selling of insider knowledge and access by ex-civil servants privileges those able to afford the fee. These are typically large corporations, which only serves to increase their influence further. But perhaps of equal concern is the influence that the prospect of future employment can have on the decisions taken by officials while in government. Civil servants with one eye on their next career move might be inclined to favour the wishes of their new employer over the public interest.

One department that has seen more movement through the revolving door than any other is the Ministry of Defence. Since 1996, officials and military officers have taken up more than 3,500 jobs in arms and defence related companies. Two hundred and thirty-one jobs were secured in 2011/12 alone.[124]

A decade ago the government committee charged with monitoring this movement to the private sector, the Advisory Committee on Business Appointments (ACOBA), expressed muted concern. The high numbers, it said, amounted to 'traffic' from the ministry to the defence contractors.[125] It also hinted at the danger this presented to decision-making, again in its typically understated way: 'It might be supposed that such officers (and their civilian counterparts) might enter their final postings with a hope or expectation of post-retirement employment with companies with which they would be dealing officially.'[126]

Government is the arms industry's biggest customer. And the Ministry of Defence's closeness to its suppliers is widely known. It is also gaining a reputation for its disastrously expensive contracts that deliver poor value for taxpayers and often poor performance for the military. More than one commentator has asked whether the two are connected. It is almost impossible to show cause and effect. It is, however, a valid question.

The Italian defence company Finmeccanica, whose offices are tucked behind Parliament Square, has in recent years hired two prominent MoD civil servants: Kevin Tebbit and William (Lord) Bach. Tebbit ran the ministry. Bach, as Procurement Minister, was in charge of how it spent its equipment budget.

Tebbit left the MoD in late 2005. Eighteen months later he was officially working for Finmeccanica UK. Bach became a director of the company in early 2007, just under two years after leaving his MoD ministerial job. Tebbit immediately introduced himself to the then Defence Secretary in his 'new capacity' at Finmeccanica. 'I am looking forward to working with you,' he said. The Defence Minister wrote to tell Tebbit that he was glad Finmeccanica had appointed someone 'with such a strong knowledge of the MoD'.[127] Tebbit was clearly of great value. Finmeccanica had bought itself two insiders with unrivalled knowledge of the ministry, a big customer.

Both men were in post during negotiations in the mid-2000s on a billion-pound defence contract with Finmeccanica. Its subsidiary AgustaWestland was to build seventy Future Lynx helicopters to be deployed in Afghanistan. There has been persistent criticism of the AgustaWestland contract. According to Colonel Stuart Tootal, former commander of 3 Para who resigned from the army in 2008 after having been deployed in Afghanistan, other types of helicopters were much better suited to the Army's needs.[128] Alternatives were also likely to have come in cheaper. Many are still perplexed as to why the MoD chose these particular helicopters over others.

There is no evidence in this case that the two facts – the revolving door and the successful but controversial bid – are connected. However, it is fair to comment that the revolving door can lead to a perception that decisions taken in government could be influenced by the reward of future employment. And when significant numbers of civil servants are passing through, the perception, at least, will only strengthen.

The top rung of the Department of Health is another to experience 'traffic' to the private sector. In recent years, civil servants instrumental in driving through the market reforms of the NHS have moved into positions with companies that are seeking contracts created by the changes.

Ian Dalton, a senior health official, quit the department in 2013 to head BT's expanding health business. BT, for example, is a major player in the UK's nascent 'telehealth' market, where technology is used to deliver healthcare services remotely. The telecoms giant noted Dalton's wealth of experience in the NHS and England's 'evolving healthcare market'.[129] Dalton's civil service colleague Jim Easton made the move to a private healthcare firm, Care UK, a couple of months earlier.[130] It is also well-placed to benefit from the opening up of the NHS to the private sector.

Another to make the jump was Mark Britnell, former head of commissioning in the Department of Health. Commissioning is the system that determines how the NHS spends its £100bn budget, which has seen a radical overhaul. Britnell left in 2009 to join KPMG. The accountancy giant is one of the companies cashing in on the new commissioning system in the NHS.

Dalton's colleague Gary Belfield took over from Dalton at the department. He stayed in post less than a year before himself moving to KPMG.[131] Not long after, KPMG was awarded one of the first private sector contracts under the new system. The win was announced by Belfield on behalf of his new employer.

The valid concern here is that those who set the rules of engagement, in privatising the public sector, and the companies who now pay their substantially higher wages, are the ones who are going to directly benefit from them.[132] The perception, at least, is that the wider public interest has been shut out by narrow, commercial interests.

The main conclusion we should draw is not that the system is corrupt. The chief concern is that it is captured. Those who make decisions in government and those who seek to influence those decisions, mainly corporations, think the same way. They see their interests as mutual and interchangeable. Mark Britnell, confidently and without remorse, said that the NHS will be 'shown no mercy' under the current reforms. This was one of the key officials charged with looking after it.[133]

The values of the market have been infused into all areas of government. And private sector thinking, alongside expertise, has been drawn into whole areas of policy. Margaret Thatcher kicked it off in 1979 when she sought to 'deprivilege' the civil service. New Labour then set the benchmark for involving business in decision-making. The current government has flung the doors wide open to business playing an active role in deciding how this country operates.

The government draws its talent from a small pool shot through with vested interests. Recent hirings into key government positions include John Nash, a private equity education investor, appointed Education Minister in 2013;[134] Ian Livingston, outgoing boss of and multimillion-pound shareholder in BT and from 2013 the UK's new Trade Minister; Livingston replaces Stephen (Lord) Green, who was also an adviser to the government on banking reform. Green ran HSBC when the bank facilitated criminal money laundering.[135]

A tiny number of private corporations also dominate advisory roles. McKinsey, the American global management consultancy, whose London HQ sits just north of Whitehall, is one to have successfully penetrated government. Under New Labour it gained significant power over government policy, health policy in particular. The

Department of Health's thinking has been guided by the firm ever since. McKinsey is a believer in markets, private sector provision of services and reducing the role of the public sector. This helps to understand why the NHS is where it is today and where it is most likely to be heading.

The latest NHS shakeup, possibly the final one, saw McKinsey advising at every level, from the top of the Department of Health and the health regulator, Monitor, which is run by two ex-McKinsey consultants, right down to the ground and the new commissioning groups where McKinsey is also bidding for contracts.

McKinsey does not just advise governments, though. Most of its $7bn revenue comes from helping corporations. The firm's response to suggestions that it faces a conflict of interest from its work helping to reform public services while at the same time working for businesses that might stand to gain from such reforms, is typically to keep its head down. McKinsey is notoriously secretive about its clients: 'We just don't talk about our client work,' is the standard response to inquiries. This said, they include health insurers, private hospital groups, pharmaceutical companies and financial sector investors.

As the Coalition was embarking on its changes to the NHS, McKinsey was already talking to its private sector clients. An email from McKinsey to the head of Monitor reads: 'We have been gathering our thinking on the implications of the new Government programme for the NHS [and] have started to share this with clients . . . Would you like to meet to discuss it?'[136] McKinsey's insider status has great commercial value to its clients.

McKinsey appears also to act as broker between corporations and the public sector. Internal emails show McKinsey connecting the Department of Health and senior NHS officials in London with one of Germany's largest private hospital chains, Helios. The focus of the discussions was on 'potential opportunities' in London.

In this instance, McKinsey also appears to advise officials on how to minimise public resistance to the takeover of London's NHS hospitals by private providers. In one exchange, McKinsey warns the Department not to bundle off all the hospitals to the private sector at once. Instead it should start 'from a mindset [of] one at a time'. Officials should be mindful of the various 'political constraints' associated with privatisation, it cautioned.[137]

Management consultancies like McKinsey are not the only companies that occupy this influential position as advisers to both government and corporations. The Big Four accountancy firms are in the business too, selling advice and at the same time benefiting from reform.

Take changes to the education system and the move to convert schools to independently run academies. PwC, the biggest of the Big Four, with offices round the back of Whitehall, has been assisting the Department for Education on its academy school programme. At the same time it has developed a service to partner with groups of newly created academies to provide back-office functions, which it calls a 'schools solution for sharing'.[139] Unlike public sector 'sharing solutions', however, this service would be provided on a for-profit basis. 'PwC isn't spending all this money for the hell of it,' said the PwC rep to a group of school reformers regarding the investment the firm had made in developing the service: 'We see this as a great opportunity.'[140]

It is the position that the Big Four accountancy firms play in influencing Britain's tax system, however, that carries the most significance.

The Big Four are at the heart of the tax avoidance industry. They stand accused of manufacturing tax-avoiding schemes on an industrial scale,[141] yet their employees are regularly invited into government to help shape tax policy. It is even the case that the same employees that have helped write policy have then returned to their firms and used their insider knowledge to advise their corporate clients on how to use those same laws to avoid tax. A case of 'poacher, turned gamekeeper, turned poacher again', as a group of MPs put it.[142]

The firms are quick to insist that their involvement in tax policy is limited to providing 'technical insight'. They are adamant that they do not write legislation or make policy decisions. That is a matter for government, they say.[143] The accountants are clearly capable of influencing tax laws, though, as evidenced by the fact that some of them specifically offer it as a service. Ernst & Young, for example, whose offices face the Houses of Parliament across the river, has a team that is dedicated to lobbying for tax changes for corporate clients.

Ernst & Young's Tax Policy Development team is led by its global head of tax policy, Chris Sanger. Another team member until late 2012 was a partner, Vincent Oratore. Both Sanger and Oratore are advisers to the government. They are inside the tent. In July 2010, just weeks after the Coalition government was formed, they were appointed to

HM Treasury's newly created Tax Professionals Forum. This body looks at how the government can improve the way it develops tax policy.[144]

In the meantime, Ernst & Young's lobbying team is being paid by clients to reduce their taxes. It does this in one of two ways. First, it can find opportunities to minimise a company's tax bill within the existing tax structure. Or it can come up with proposals to put to government for changes to the tax system, so that a company's tax liability will be reduced in the future.[145]

'Unlike a traditional lobbying service,' the pitch reads, Ernst & Young's team will work with its clients to develop 'technical policy options in a form that is used inside Government today'. Put simply, this means it uses its knowledge of policy-making to help clients lobby for tax changes. This, it says, reduces delay, anticipates any policy-makers' concerns and gives the proposed tax break 'the maximum chance of adoption'. The insider status of Ernst & Young is of obvious benefit to its clients.

The advantage to clients lobbying for tax policy changes, as opposed to avoiding tax, are clearly stated in Ernst & Young's pitch: 'In an era where the government is focusing on actively identifying and countering tax avoidance, and where there has been considerable media coverage on particular "tax avoiders", policy development offers a low risk alternative.' In other words, lobbying for tax breaks is a less risky way for corporate clients to reduce their tax bill. It will not damage their reputation, because no one will know.

So, while the two Ernst & Young tax specialists are advising the government on a more business-friendly approach to writing tax law, they are at the same time part of a team that is paid to lobby for changes to the tax system for particular private interests. Ernst & Young, however, denies exerting undue influence on government or misusing information.

The Coalition government has gone further than any in actively and openly seeking advice from large corporations that stand to gain from policy changes. It has even given the very biggest companies their own hotline to the corresponding minister. The scheme launched in 2011 and saw key companies in oil, telecoms, pharmaceuticals and others paired with ministers to provide a seamless 'one-stop' service in their dealings with Whitehall.[146]

Many of these already privileged corporations have also been invited in to help shape Britain's tax system. This included changes to policy, which are 'self-evidently very generous moves that encourage tax haven activity', as tax inspector turned journalist Richard Brooks put it.[147]

The advisers that helped to develop these policies, which favour large corporations over any other part of society, were drawn from firms that stand to substantially benefit from the changes. These included the tax directors of BP, AstraZeneca, International Power, RSA (Royal Sun Alliance) and HSBC. The government's wider corporate tax reforms have been overseen by, among other beneficiaries, Vodafone, Diageo, GlaxoSmithKline, Rolls-Royce and Shell.

To talk about lobbying in a scenario like this seems futile. This advice has been openly solicited by government. Again, they think the same way. You cannot get a cigarette paper between the beliefs of many government ministers and multi-national CEOs. Both express a belief in the need for Britain to have a so-called 'competitive' tax system. But arriving at a tax system that privileges large, international companies does not come about by accident. 'It's the result of ten years' hard work,'[148] says John Bartlett, group head of tax at BP. Lobbying has, in fact, played a major part in embedding this thinking in government.

Corporate advisers to government are an insidious feature of Whitehall. But they are, by nature, occasional. Others are fully employed in the departments in Whitehall. These secondees, often but not always on the payroll of their corporate employers, are a more permanent feature of government.

The energy industry has been generous with its people. At least fifty employees from EDF Energy, npower, Shell and others have been embedded in government to work on energy issues in the four years to 2011. Thirty-six of these were inside the Department of Energy and Climate Change.[149] Thirteen were working in the environment department (DEFRA).[150] Shell was also inside the Foreign Office.[151] The nuclear power industry had a further fifteen of its people seconded to work alongside civil servants. A Rolls-Royce employee became 'head of new nuclear capabilities and removing barriers'. Two from EDF were inside the nuclear regulator.[152]

The alcohol industry has its insiders too. When the Scots sought to tackle their problem with alcohol consumption, a senior Diageo executive was seconded as programme director to the Scottish government's alcohol misuse team. The move was criticised by health professionals for its blatant conflict of interest. Diageo was also criticised for having 'privileged access' to policy-making.[153] This was denied despite Diageo's stated aim to be the 'preferred partner with government in the creation of public policy'.[154]

The accountancy giants also regularly loan people to government, including their tax experts to the Treasury, as we have seen. At least fifty people have been seconded from the Big Four to government departments in the last three years, including fifteen to the Cabinet Office and ten to the Department for Business. They also famously donate hundreds of thousands of pounds in staff time to political parties every year.[155]

This more permanent presence inside government has its clear advantages beyond currying favour. They are the same advantages sought by lobbyists: access to government and insider knowledge. It also presents the same key concern as direct lobbying. It is a route only open to those organisations that can afford to loan their staff. It privileges large corporations, which are already advantaged.

★

When you stand back and look at the reach of lobbyists inside government and the easy access to decision-makers they enjoy; at the scale of the industry that surrounds Westminster and the social world it shares with politicians; when you start to build a picture of the way that lobbyists have become embedded in our government, and have bent our government to their will – you could be led to ask one question: Why the media frenzy and weeks of headlines, why the enormous efforts to uncover the truth, why all the fuss over just one man with access, Adam Werritty?

4

Distort: Lobbyists Manipulate the Media

'We have evolved a system which is highly accomplished at spinning the press.'
  James Frayne, lobbyist[1]

The *Telegraph* party is normally one of the highlights of the Conservative Party conference. 2012's annual shindig, however, was a little less sparkling than previous years. The Prime Minister was a no-show. 'Snubbed' is how one journalist at Britain's bestselling broadsheet put it. Instead, the guest of honour, so prominently and deliberately displayed that you were required to step around him on the way in, was the Chancellor, George Osborne. Given how easy it was to gatecrash, this seemed a lapse in security.

Inside was a marketplace of gossip. The room heaved with people, everyone just talking: clustered or off in corners, loud and back-slapping, or ear-to-ear and conspiratorial. The free champagne bar kept throats from being parched. No one touched the buffet. This is where politics, money and the media bond.

The gathering brought together politicians and journalists from across the British press, with a smattering of party donors who had bought themselves a pass. Filling in the gaps were commercial lobbyists. Lots of them. It felt like walking in on the Westminster after-show party. It felt like we should not be there (partly a consequence of not having a ticket). It felt like a clique.

The political commentator for the *Telegraph*, Peter Oborne, noted more than a decade ago that politics and journalism 'have effectively ceased to be discrete disciplines', with journalists collaborating with politicians to an extent that they no longer report political events in a 'detached and fastidious' way.[2] 'Like babies in a high chair, waiting to be spoon-fed their stories,' is how Nick Davies put it in *Flat Earth News*. Uncritical of the lines they are given, many political reporters show an astonishing lack of interest in explaining what is actually going on in British politics. The friendships in this room help to explain why.

But it is not just politicians and their spinners who are having their way with our media, supplying it with the stories and messages that they want us to absorb. The journalists in this room also serve as very useful tools for lobbyists. They too court and collaborate with reporters, feeding our media with the information that serves their mainly corporate clients. The collective output of commercial lobbyists permeates our press, giving us an even more distorted view of the world around us.

Someone like George Pascoe-Watson is typical of the crowd at the *Telegraph* bash. Pascoe-Watson was previously one of the most powerful people in journalism as political editor of the *Sun*. Today he works alongside Alastair Campbell and Campbell's old deputy in Tony Blair's office, Tim Allan, in Portland. This lobbying firm is hired to help ensure that their clients' interests – be it Tesco, Vodafone, McDonald's or the arms company BAE Systems – are served by government. One of the central ways that they do this is to make sure that their clients' interests are also served by the British media.

This is where the corporate superclass conspires with the political class. What is clear from the party is that the *Telegraph* and others have become all too willing hosts.

★

Politicians do not make decisions in a vacuum. They are influenced by all manner of sources. But the information and opinion that they glean from the media, in particular, has a significant impact on the way they think and act. Politicians are avid media consumers. So lobbyists use the press to speak to politicians, loudly.

The media is a central means of influencing government. Lobbyists use it to raise issues with politicians, influence public opinion, demonstrate support, attack opponents and issue threats. 'A cabinet minister who reads a page lead – generated by your campaign – in the *Financial Times* over his breakfast cornflakes, is more likely to give that campaign serious consideration,' says a lobbyist from the Association of British Insurers.[3]

To a lobbyist, the media is less a source of information than a tool to be used. Unlike the rest of us, who to a large extent have to rely on journalists to be our eyes and ears in Westminster and Whitehall, lobbyists get their detailed knowledge from specialist services that monitor daily what is happening in politics. Lobbyists instead see the media as something to be used for their own ends. But it is a double-edged sword. The skill is in knowing when and how to use it, but also crucially when to avoid it.

The influence of lobbyists increases when lobbying happens quietly. The more noise there is around an issue, the less control lobbyists have over it. News Corp's bid for BSkyB is a case in point. To begin with, the most effective lobbying occurs way before anyone else has picked up on an issue. It pays to be quiet at this stage. Politicians have more freedom to negotiate with lobbyists when their actions are not being scrutinised by the press. A lobbyist who goes blabbing to a journalist when they could have made their point in private is going to be resented by officials. Keeping a low profile and avoiding the press is often a deliberate strategy by lobbyists.

Policy-making by quiet negotiation is also a way to avoid drawing opposition. No lobbyist is going to want to alert potential critics just to have them organise against them. NGOs invariably take their concerns to the press. Their interest is in rousing the public and stirring debate. They sometimes have little choice, enjoying fewer opportunities to influence through official channels. Lobbyists seek to avoid this scenario.

Take the case of a campaign run by the lobbyists Hill & Knowlton and held up for praise in the industry's 'excellence awards'. The client was the Crop Protection Association, otherwise known as the pesticides industry. The big chemical firms were facing the threat of a tax to try and reduce the use of pesticides. They responded with a lobbying strategy that included 'avoiding national press coverage . . . as this would attract a strong response from the environmental NGOs'.[4] At the time, the government and public had hardened their stance on pesticides, even *The Archers* had taken a stand. So the public were to be kept out of the tax debate with a national news blackout. The lobbyists did, however, target one useful constituency: farmers. Seeding stories in the farming press they were able to drum up opposition to the tax. It was a winning strategy: the idea for a tax on pesticides was dropped.[5]

There are, though, many occasions when either a quiet word in the government's ear is not sufficient to persuade it to take action, or public debate cannot be avoided. This is when lobbyists will draw on the skills of their colleagues in public relations and start playing with the media.

The game might involve seeding the press with information that lobbyists want politicians to hear. They may want to raise the profile of an issue they wish the government to act on, or set out their side of a particular story, or feed the press with opinions that serve the lobbyists' interests. This will involve plying journalists with information that supports their case, with various degrees of subtlety. The recurring coverage supporting the case for the expansion of Heathrow is one of the more obvious recent campaigns, which is as constant in London's *Evening Standard* newspaper as the drone of planes is at five in the morning for many West Londoners.

The army of commentators in the media gives lobbyists another opportunity to influence government. These can be used to reinforce the impression that a narrow interest has the support of influential others. This is at heart what PR is about: getting someone else to say what it is you want them to say (unlike advertising, which is all about blowing your own trumpet). Support can be orchestrated and lobbyists regularly court and brief journalists to make sure they are onside.[6] 'Decision-making . . . is increasingly driven by opinion,' says the lobbying firm Westbourne Communications. 'What the media is reporting; what influential third parties are saying; and, sometimes, what the public is thinking.' Politicians listen to what these commentators say. Only sometimes do they take into account public opinion.

Take one tiny example concerning the campaign to axe the 50p top rate of tax for Britain's top earners. Westbourne Communications promoted a briefing for media pundits. The document laid out rebuttal points for commentators, challenging the most common 'myths' put forward by the tax's supporters. It even included the names of the left-leaning pundits most likely to be putting forward these views, complete with mug shots.[7] The Scrap the Tax campaign did little to sway public opinion, but it did inform influential voices in the press calling for it to be axed. Following a concerted and wide-ranging lobbying campaign, of which this was a tiny part, Osborne had the support he needed. He scrapped the tax.

The use of third parties, like the commentariat, to front campaigns is rife in the industry. The reason for it is simple. Corporations, in the main, have something of a credibility problem to overcome with the public and parts of the media. The views of a company are far less likely to be accepted by the public than those of a seemingly independent third party, without a commercial interest in a particular policy or position. So, lobbyists pay or persuade others with credibility to do the leg work for them. Bell Pottinger offers clients 'relationship building with opinion formers and academics who influence the media and can be independent voices on behalf of' their clients.[8]

Alternatively, lobbyists' game with the press might involve the antithesis of all this press activity: making sure that potentially damaging information never reaches the ears of government. As well as delivering their message onto the politician's breakfast table, lobbyists will not want the newspaper to reveal anything that will damage their interests or reputation. This is the less well-publicised side of the business. How lobbyists use PR tactics to minimise hostile coverage is not something they talk about, but it is often where they get paid a premium.[9] Companies will hire PR and lobbying agencies, sometimes in conjunction with law firms, seeking not to promote themselves, but to try and limit coverage.[10] Research suggests that for every story fed into the news factory by the PR industry, there is one being carefully kept out.[11] Half or more of the time spent by PRs in some organisations is taken up lowering their employer's profile.[12]

Beyond these two distortion tactics – using third parties and keeping things quiet – lobbyists might need a more concerted effort to really shift opinion and government policy. They may wish to move a whole conversation that has turned against them. What they need is to be playing on ground on which they can win.

Lobbyists trying to secure political support will often start by making sure that a debate is framed in such a way that they have a strong chance of success, away from discussions they are sure to lose (in this they are similar to politicians). Consequently, lobbyists work hard to 'control the ground'. This has the effect of determining what can acceptably be discussed, pushing everything else to the fringe. The acceptable ways of describing the world, crafted by lobbyists, are then vigorously promoted. And many, very valid and crucial debates that ordinary people want to have are subtly shifted or ignored. This deliberate reframing through the media not only frustrates debate, but has the power to limit our ability to think clearly about issues that are of public concern.

What follows are some of the techniques that lobbyists use in their game with the British media, remembering that our politicians are as susceptible as anyone to being influenced by their work.

★

In the previous chapter we looked at the significance of having a Westminster insider on your lobbying team for the contacts and knowledge he or she brings. Corporations in the same way need people who are familiar with the insides of the media to help them speak to and influence the press. Lobbyists with a background in journalism understand the way that news is produced and what journalists need to make a story.

Someone like George Pascoe-Watson, as former political editor of the *Sun*, not only offers clients insight and contacts in the media, but also an insider's understanding of politics built up on the paper. Another that stands at this intersection of politics and the press is Robert Watts, former *Sunday Telegraph* deputy political editor who joined the British Bankers' Association to help it with its 'positive campaigning'.[13] The *Telegraph*'s public policy editor, Andrew Porter, recently moved to Brunswick. There are very many more.

Lobbying agencies and companies reward ex-hacks generously for their insider knowledge, with salaries normally far in excess of what they earned as journalists. Lobbyists are equally generous to those they need to write their stories. Hospitality is used to court journalists as well as politicians and the natural sociability of the former is exploited to build relationships.

The financial services industry has the cash to be more generous than most. It also has one of the biggest tasks on its hands, repairing its reputation in the midst of an economic crisis it largely caused. The sector's central lobby group, TheCityUK, has been on a determined charm offensive.

For example, in 2012 it played host to a well-known BBC senior reporter at 'London's Country Estate', the Grove hotel in Hertford-shire.[14] The bank lobbyists also targeted an influential ITV journalist, inviting them to be a guest at the PR dinner of TheCityUK's 'strategy' group.

The purpose of such events, according to the lobbyists, is to brief senior journalists on the economic and social value of financial services. This is what you would expect a finance sector lobbyist to do. But journalists were also invited to provide the lobbyists with their views on 'how the industry might go about changing perceptions'. They were also open to guidance on how TheCityUK might help the jour-nalist go about this job – their job – of rehabilitating bankers' reputa-tions.[15] This feels like collusion.

Journalists are carefully profiled by lobbyists and hospitality provided to suit their interests. Databases are kept on their tastes. Are they into football or cricket, heavy rock or opera? It is not in lobbyists' interests to spend money taking journalists to see Robbie Williams if they prefer Vaughan Williams.

The central purpose of such generosity is to build relationships. Equally journalists need to cultivate sources of information, and why not couple it with a day at Ascot courtesy of Ladbrokes? The rela-tionship, though, is rarely one of equals. Outside of the big names, hacks can be at the mercy of influential PR people. Annoy them with a story detrimental to a client and journalists can find themselves cold-shouldered. When it is a firm like Alan Parker's financial PR firm Brunswick, which at times represents over a quarter of the FTSE Top 100 companies, a snubbed business journalist might also find him or herself out of a job. Still, Parker is said to call journalists 'boss'. Tim Bell is reported to open calls with journalists with 'Hello, my love', regardless of gender.[16] 'Chummy familiarity and false deference,' is how one ex-hack turned flack puts it.

Pascoe-Watson's old boss, the former editor of the *Sun* Rebekah Brooks, is described by one Murdoch insider as having a 'craven rela-tionship' with PR people. Scores, if not hundreds, of front page stories are alleged to have been written by PR men.[17] This is the goal of lobbyists. To feed their information into the media and have it presented as news. The astonishing extent to which this happens across our media, not just the tabloids, is documented in journalist Nick Davies' book *Flat Earth News*.

According to research commissioned by Davies, only 12 per cent of stories in the broadsheets and the *Daily Mail* were generated by the journalists themselves. Eighty per cent of news stories in the quality papers consists mainly or has clear elements of PR material or agency wire copy (these are the news agencies that feed the national media with stories. They too are stocked with material generated by the PR business). Much of this activity seeks to influence our shopping habits, lifestyle choices or viewing tastes. But a significant amount is directed at influencing the decisions of our government. As the ex-Portland lobbyist James Frayne said of the lobbying business: 'We have evolved a system which is highly accomplished at spinning the press.'[18]

As a source of truth, information derived from PRs and lobbyists, whether news or comment, is unreliable for the simple fact that it is designed to serve an interest. And yet, still to a very large extent we rely on our media to deliver an account of what is happening in Britain, the real decisions we face as a nation and an accurate reflection of people's views. That a significant proportion of this is generated by the PR and lobbying industry is disturbing. That most of the time it goes unnoticed is even more worrying.

There is an inherent danger in lobbyists telling out-and-out lies. Much of what they do relies on their credibility and the threat of being found out looms large. It is difficult to get someone in the business to admit to telling whoppers, but it does happen, particularly for reasons of commercial confidentiality. Fabrication and distortion on the other hand are almost built into the job.

Lobbyists commonly use tactics that, while not lying, are deceitful. Exaggeration, for example, is an overused technique by lobbyists to push their case. The bankers have been particularly prone to it in recent years. For example, when the government threatened a windfall tax on their bonuses, and was holding out against a reduction in the top rate of tax, lobbyists presented an exodus to low-tax Switzerland as fact. Nine thousand City high-flyers would decamp they warned, leaving the UK worse off. As is very often the case, the predictions did not come true. Figures for the following year for Britons applying to work in the Swiss financial services sector actually fell.[19] The predicted exodus was hyperbole designed to scare politicians.

When 'non-domiciled' hedge fund managers were faced with changes to their tax-exempt status in 2007, threats were used as part of a vigorous lobbying campaign to defend the status quo. The industry body claimed such a move would pose a 'serious threat' to the British economy.[20] At the time this had a certain irony. The collapse of two Bear Stearns hedge funds the same year marked the start of the credit crunch, the wider, global financial crisis and all that came next for Britain's economy.

The financial meltdown did not, however, cause the City to change tack. Hedge funds and the systemic risk they posed to the financial system were now firmly in the sights of European regulators. Facing this threat, the industry came over all doomsday, again. It publicly warned that schools, hospitals, shopping centres, small businesses, peoples' pension contributions, all would take a hit from the proposed regulation of hedge funds. It would drive lucrative business out of Europe, according to the British Private Equity and Venture Capital Association.[21] The new regulations would result in 'very negative social consequences across Europe', the hedge fund lobby group, the Alternative Investment Management Association, said as a final, dark warning.[22]

'It's not arbitrage to thwart [regulation],' said the chair and CEO of Goldman Sachs, Lloyd Blankfein, after issuing a clear warning that the bank could exit certain countries and its operations 'moved globally' if rules became too onerous. 'It's about a need to compete with rivals.'[23] It is warnings like this that prompt politicians like Boris Johnson to pledge to do their 'utmost' to ward off regulation.

The same tactic was used to great effect in the campaign to reduce Britain's 50p top rate of tax. In 2011, for example, Diageo's outgoing boss, Paul Walsh, threatened that Britain would lose out if it was not scrapped: 'At the moment, if I am going to create jobs I am not going to create them in the UK because it's a high cost environment,' he said.[24] If the country's tax regime became so egregious, he saw 'no option' but to look at other alternatives.[25] It would lead, he said, to 'long-term damage' to Britain's competitive edge.

The threat, however, is based on a central myth that higher taxes harm a country's real economic competitiveness. This is not true. Of the four most competitive countries in the world, according to the World Economic Forum, two are among the highest-taxed countries. Dramatic differences in taxes as a share of the economy – from 29 per cent in Japan to over 55 per cent in Denmark – have no obvious impact on growth. As the *FT*'s Martin Wolf concludes: 'Such a spread seems to have no effect on economic performance.'[26] Countries do compete, but mainly on things like infrastructure, a healthy and educated workforce, and technological readiness – all things that rely on taxes being paid. Companies are also not nearly as mobile as they claim to be.

Awareness of the many tactics used by the influence industry to persuade and push their agenda is growing, thanks in part to books like Davies'. Underpinning them all is that lobbyists understand what the media needs. It is the lobbyist's job, in the service of his or her employer, to provide it. Journalists need events to cover, so the industry fabricates events. Newspapers need pictures, preferably of celebrities, so lobbyists get them to endorse their cause. The media likes human interest stories, so lobbyists produce real-life case studies to back up their case. Experts bring authority to a story, lobbyists will supply them. Evidence is needed to support a case. Lobbyists create it.[27] This is what constitutes much of what passes as news.

Campaign groups are masters at some of these tactics, particularly the staged event. The six Greenpeace women who scaled the Shard in the summer of 2013 provided a genuine spectacle for London's office workers, a live feed for thousands online, and press coverage that stretched as far as New Zealand and Japan.[28] It also drew attention to Greenpeace's Save the Arctic campaign.

How lasting and how much political impact these impressive stunts deliver, though, is arguable. Campaign groups make the most of their resources – and Greenpeace has enough to invest all the gear required to shin up the Shard, including cameras on helmets, a media team and online campaign – but they are limited. Sustaining the media's attention and, crucially, getting this attention to translate into political action are significant challenges (not to mention dangerous, as the arrest by Russia of 30 Greenpeace activists in 2013 showed). Who remembers Greenpeace's fake polar bear that chained the pumps of a petrol station together during the Davos World Economic Forum to protest about drilling in the Arctic?[29] Or, the 'polar bears' that climbed onto an oil rig owned by Statoil, which was heading off to drill in the Arctic?[30]

Contrast this with a recent lobbying campaign by Statoil that, alongside its antics in the Arctic, is Europe's second-biggest retailer of natural gas. It reportedly spent £2m on a marketing campaign in the UK to target an 'informed elite' of business, ministers and government officials as they drew up the UK's energy plans.[31] This included paying for a series of articles in the *Telegraph*, in which it made the case for gas as a lower-carbon energy source and presented itself as a moderate, responsible and green supplier of it.

The resources of corporations like Statoil significantly outgun Greenpeace's. But the company is also advantaged by fitting with the values that run through much of the media. Campaigners occupy fringe positions in a discussion that has in part been shaped that way by lobbyists (we will go on to explore how they do this). The values and views of companies sit safely, acceptably and largely unchallenged in the middle of the debate. This shared value system – as well as close relations – can bring obvious advantages to a lobbyist trying to get a message across in the press.

Take the case of a media campaign instigated by the private healthcare industry with the help of a free market think tank to warn the government not to let up on NHS privatisation. The industry lobby group, the NHS Partners Network, was aware of the enormous public hostility to the government's plans. In response, it wanted to 'up' the profile on particular issues without 'inflaming the debate'. In this instance a 'whole sequence' of articles and opinion pieces appeared in the *Telegraph* which served that purpose. This 'is something I have been orchestrating and working with [the think tank] Reform to bring about,' wrote the head of the lobby group, David Worskett. He was clear, however, that this did not in any way imply 'orchestration' with the *Telegraph*.[32]

No one is going to say that news is an accurate reflection of reality. It is at best a selection of stories about important things that are happening, which are of interest to a lot of people. The problem is journalists, for many reasons, have become uncritical of the information they receive from lobbyists. Worse, some of them have become willing collaborators in the deliberate distortion of news.

★

If we are slowly coming to realise that much of what we read in the papers has flown straight from the desks of PRs and lobbyists, we are perhaps less aware of their efforts to prevent stories from being reported. Lobbyists are employed by corporations, wealthy individuals and governments to make sure that the bad news never reaches the ears of politicians, investors and the wider public.

Lobbyist Tim Bell is said to be a master at killing stories. Now in his seventies, Bell has been weaving his magic with the British media for the best part of four decades. As chair of Bell Pottinger, Bell is still hands on for his big clients, the foreign governments and corporate executives. The more exciting, or controversial the client, the bigger the money, the more he is going to get involved. He has been described as an adrenaline junkie.

'Bell is a classic fast-talking, charming guy who can persuade you to do things that you don't want to do,' says Mark Hollingsworth, Bell's unofficial biographer.[33] First is to use this charm to persuade a reporter to run the story he wants them to write. The second is in persuading journalists not to run stories. 'If an [offending] story about the client is spiked, the journalist is handed an even better exclusive about someone else. If the article is published, future co-operation is withdrawn,' Hollingsworth explains.[34]

Bell's reputation for making unwanted press attention go away led one company to seek out his services. The client, whom next to no one had heard of in Britain, had a big problem it needed to disappear. In 2006, it had arranged the illegal dumping of 500 tons of highly toxic waste in a very poor country, Ivory Coast. Thousands of its residents subsequently became ill and filed for compensation.[35] More worryingly for the client, journalists were picking up the story. The client, the oil trader Trafigura, has since become a case study in how not to make a problem vanish.[36] It was not Bell's finest hour, but it serves to give further insight into lobbyists' practices.

After the toxic waste had been dumped, Trafigura set out to push its version of events with a cover story. It used Bell Pottinger working in concert with leading libel specialists Carter-Ruck to force their account, partial and misleading though it was, on the media.[37]

The *Guardian* was one of a number of papers to pursue the story in 2009. Its editor, Alan Rusbridger, explained what happened when it published a truer account of events: 'Bell Pottinger sent a threatening message . . . which ended: "Please note that in view of the gravity of these matters and of the allegations which have been published, I am copying Trafigura's solicitors, Carter-Ruck, into this email."[38] Other journalists at BBC *Newsnight*, the Norwegian state broadcaster and a Dutch newspaper had identical threats. But they did not stop there. The BBC received a libel writ. And, crucially, a judge was persuaded to slap an injunction on journalists reporting a confidential internal document they had in their possession. Even publishing the fact that the company had obtained an injunction was banned.

The step too far was the super-injunction. Paul Farrelly MP tabled a question on the injunction and the document using Parliamentary privilege. Journalists were then barred from reporting comments made to Parliament, without being allowed to report why. What Carter-Ruck and Co. had not accounted for, though, was public curiosity and Twitter. Once the MP's question was found, it took less than a day, with the help of Stephen Fry's re-tweets, for enough of an outraged public to make Trafigura trend on Twitter.[39] Shortly after, the gag was lifted.

Bell claims no responsibility for what he refers to as the Trafigura 'ruckus'. 'I don't tell clients to try and injunct stories,' he said. However, he does admit to killing stories on behalf of clients and indeed delights in being called a master of it, 'if what that means is that I get hold of a journalist who is about to write some untruths and give him some truths to write instead,' he said. 'I am afraid the world is run by idiots', who are far too interested in 'scandal' and 'sensationalisation'. 'There is,' he added, 'a role for people like us who try our level best to get as much accurate information in front of the public as we possibly can.'[40]

The unholy alliance of PRs and lawyers who pressurise and intimidate journalists to protect corporate clients is one of the least explored aspects of the lobbying business.

Carter-Ruck is one of two big legal beasts, the other being Schillings, in the lucrative business of protecting reputations, whether celebrity or corporate. It was Schillings who pioneered celebrity privacy injunctions.[41] Like the Trafigura case, Schillings' work for footballer Ryan Giggs had the opposite effect of killing the story. But most of their work naturally remains under the radar and without publicity. Schillings says it uses the law to protect its clients' reputations 'without drawing attention to the issue'.[42]

The lawyers will often work in tandem with PR companies to kill stories.[43] This might simply involve a phone call to the editor, when the lawyers can provide some 'muscle in terms of reminding the news organisation of its responsibilities', as Alasdair Pepper at Carter-Ruck puts it. This does the job most of the time, he says.[44] If not, they might advise clients take the 'nuclear options' of suing for libel or seeking an injunction.[45]

Some of this activity will be warranted. Journalists get stories wrong. But some of it is what is known in the PR trade as reputation management. 'Instead of dealing with problems, the reputation management team is more concerned in dealing in image,' says one of Britain's foremost media lawyers, Louis Charalambous.[46] 'Sometimes this is at the expense of the truth.' This obsessive focus on managing the message, the tail wagging the dog, means little or no action is taken to deal with the initial criticism.[47]

The combination of legal muscle and softer, but no less potent, PR techniques is aimed squarely at preventing certain stories from reaching our ears.

Tom Giles, editor of the BBC's *Panorama* programme talks of increasingly experiencing the threat of a mass outbreak of legal action. He also points to a growing amount of PR activity aimed at neutralising stories. Attacks on Twitter are becoming more common.[48] This will see an outbreak of people tweeting certain views to support a particular company during transmission. 'That is invariably set up by a PR organisation,' Giles says.

Channel 4 journalists have experienced similar operations that couple libel actions and PR activity: complaints will be made to journalists' bosses, stories against them leaked to newspapers and the broadcasters' regulator, Ofcom, drawn in. Channel 4's head of news, Dorothy Byrne, described how stories critical of their Sri Lankan investigation into war crimes appeared 'all over the world, in a highly organised way, the internet is full of them. They appear to be normal stories and they are not. They are obviously coming from somewhere.' There was even a demonstration outside Channel 4, which she claimed had been organised by the Sri Lankan Ministry of Defence. 'I think it's not just us that needs to be aware of the PR industry, it's the whole of society that needs to be aware of it,' she said.[49]

Obviously, finding evidence of something that does not exist, news that never makes the news, can be problematic. We can, however, look to the lobbying industry for clues. One firm in the reputation management business is Quiller Consultants, which is part of Peter Gummer's communications empire. It promises to help defend the names of clients who find themselves 'in the eye of a media and political storm'.[50]

In the autumn of 2011, Quiller was hired by the Corporation of London, the City's local authority and lobbyists, to help it contain the fallout from the Occupy protest. The 'high-profile, intensive crisis/reputation management'[51] brief Quiller was handed was to minimise the damage to the Corporation's reputation from the campers outside St Paul's Cathedral.

The Corporation was in the frame as it was behind the legal action to remove the camp from St Paul's. But, more significantly, Occupy London was calling for democratic changes to the Corporation. On 7 November 2011, protesters issued a statement asking for the Corporation to be subject to the Freedom of Information Act, to publish its accounts and for the end of City businesses voting in elections.[52] Many of its demands reflected long-held concerns. Occupy was trying to bring them to the fore. The camp was attracting a lot of media attention and the same week it issued the statement, the movement was gaining real momentum too. On 9 November, thousands of protesting students marched past St Paul's steps in solidarity.[53]

This was the point at which the Corporation picked up the phone to Quiller. Forty-eight hours later, three of its spinners arrived at the West Wing of the Corporation's HQ Guildhall. They were George Bridges, a friend to the Chancellor, George Osborne, who helped run the Tories' 2010 general election campaign; Alasdair Murray, a former Times and Mail on Sunday journalist; and another ex-hack, John Eisenhammer, Quiller's co-founder and its man for 'handling of difficult and sensitive issues'.[54]

Every day for the next week Quiller was invited to meetings at the Corporation.[55] We have no information on what they actually did. They might have been sitting on their hands for all we know. Quiller did, however, produce a document, 'City of London Corporation: The "Occupy" Protests', which summarises the fallout, or lack of, for the Corporation.

According to analysis of coverage of the Occupy protest commissioned by Quiller, only 10 per cent of stories were unfavourable to the

City of London Corporation, despite it being a central focus of the protest. This dropped to 6 per cent without the *Guardian*, which was the major exception to the overall tone of the coverage. The stories that did negatively focus on the Corporation, it noted, did not get followed up by others. They also reflected the 'well-established views' of the Corporation's critics. What is implied is that as long as it stayed that way, and the views of critics did not bleed into the pages of, for example, the *Telegraph*, the situation was contained. Quiller advised that a sense of perspective about the coverage was needed. There had been no harm done to the Corporation's reputation. What role was played by Quiller in achieving this is not known.

*

So far, we have touched on the role of lobbyists in relation to traditional, mainstream media. This is safe terrain for them. They are used to dealing with a more or less limited set of outlets and journalists with whom they are familiar. Today, though, we access our information online and from a far more diverse set of sources. This makes the job of a PR much harder, to the extent that today 'media management' seems a contradiction in terms. The big challenge they face is how to deal with digital and social networks.[56] According to lobbyist Peter Gummer the industry has to make the digital space its own. 'There's no reason why we shouldn't,' he adds. 'This is our moment.'[57]

The organising power of the web is a major concern to corporations. Witness the comment from the head of Unilever that if social media could bring down the government of Egypt, what could it do to his company?[58] Unilever values its reputation at £2bn.[59]

The number of people creating material online and the speed with which it is shared via Twitter and other social media are increasingly unmanageable for PRs. Couple this with the nature of most bloggers or Twitter users: unlike some journalists they have no interest in trading information for future tip-offs. There are no deals to be done. How are lobbyists to protect reputations in this ever-expanding online world?

'It gets more difficult,' one experienced corporate-crisis handler told fellow PRs attending a conference across the road from Parliament. His point was eloquently made by events across town in the City. As

he spoke, Occupy protests were creating headlines around the world. It had spread to dozens of countries, across continents and was calling for a worldwide demonstration, all via the web. Social media sites such as Facebook and Twitter were central to the spread of information.

The world-weary PR speaking was Mike Seymour, international director of crisis and issues management at global PR and lobbying giant Edelman. Seymour is an expert in limiting negative coverage when a company finds itself in the news for the wrong reasons. His first job was handling the communications fallout from the world's worst offshore oil disaster, the 1988 North Sea Piper Alpha fire, in which 167 men died. 'Compared to the world we live in now there was a gentle rhythm to what we had to deal with [then],' said Seymour.

Seymour illustrated his point with a slide that 'gave him a headache': a dense overlapping diagram showing the new media landscape in which PRs now try and control the information that reaches our ears. This is the brave new world of social media, internet chat rooms, the blogosphere, citizen journalism – which is described as a major irritant by one lobbyist[60] – and an explosion of online media sources in which the PR industry finds itself. It is not a world the reputation managers are comfortable with. Used to going through a manageable number of intermediaries, namely journalists, suddenly they are being forced to deal with a fluid online and unpredictable space and directly with . . . the public.

Even so, PRs have risen to the challenge. They have developed methods to try and control information in the digital space. It starts with surveillance.

'To think of them [the public] as a lump is dangerous,' said a more animated Seymour: 'We have to be careful to analyse who they are and how they're likely to behave . . . We have to look on them as influencers, especially if they are gatherers of people against us.' The 'us' is the client in crisis whose reputation Edelman is hired to protect. Following the closure of the *News of the World*, having abandoned his bid for BSkyB and with the phone-hacking scandal showing no signs of let-up, Murdoch called in Edelman to try and contain the crisis at News Corporation.[61]

Edelman's first job for a company in crisis is to find out what people are saying about it, what Seymour calls the concept of 360 [degrees] monitoring: companies and their lobbyists are investing in ever more sophisticated monitoring systems to defend their reputations online. Peter Gummer describes his companies' monitoring system as 'a vast analytical test' which tracks clients' reputations daily.[62] This is something they consider necessary. It means that if you bad-mouth a big corporation in 140 characters, chances are they will find it.

The task then is to sift through the noise and find out who among them are the 'influencers'. 'The person making a lot of noise is probably not the influential one, you've got to find the influential one,' said a now quite paranoid-sounding Seymour. 'Then, of course, you've got to have those listening posts out there so they can pick up the first warning signals,' he said, coming over a bit Cold War.

Once they know what they are up against, PRs can set to work. It turns out it is surprisingly easy to apply some tried-and-tested PR techniques to the internet's trillion or so web pages, from doctoring web content and drowning out negative coverage so that it is harder to find, to intimidating opponents.

The first course of action is an obvious one. The doctoring of Wikipedia. Journalists know, but few will readily admit, that its contents have found their way into many a news story. The online encyclopedia also receives an impressive 400 million unique readers a month. It is perhaps not surprising then that companies and their PR advisers are keen to give their clients' profiles a scrub.

Brewer AB InBev's lobbyists, Portland Communications, tried to remove all 'wife beater' references from the Stella Artois Wikipedia entry (the beer is so called because of its strength and perceived connection with violent behaviour).[63] The controversial loan firm Wonga – typical APR 4,000 per cent[64] – also appears to have tried to doctor its image. A computer in their offices deleted references to 'usury' from its entry.[65] Wonga argued that an 'unauthorised junior employee' had been responsible.

Less subtle and more serious cases have also come to light. A computer registered to the American multinational Dow Chemical repeatedly tried to remove a large section from the company's Wikipedia page detailing 'controversies'.[66] This included information on the Bhopal disaster, widely seen as the world's worst industrial disaster. Dow bought the company responsible for the disaster, Union Carbide, but refuses to adequately compensate victims. Its doctored Wikipedia entry was viewed nearly a quarter of a million times in

2012.[67] In early 2013, another company exposed for manipulating Wikipedia was BP. It was estimated that the oil giant had rewritten just shy of half of its page, including sections on its environmental record and allegations that it had greenwashed its image.[68]

None of this editing breaks Wikipedia's rules, although people and companies are encouraged not to alter their own profiles. But how to deal with paid editing is 'the next big thing' according to Richard Symonds of the UK arm of Wikipedia. One firm which is already testing its patience is the wiki-cleansing website Wikiexperts. This claims to be the first comprehensive service for businesses, offering article writing and a 24/7 monitoring and repair service to protect a company's Wikipedia presence.

One firm of lobbyists that has been busier than most on Wikipedia is Bell Pottinger. It has a team which 'sorts' negative coverage for clients.[69] Up to nineteen active Wikipedia accounts, ten of which had over 100 edits each, have been traced back to Bell Pottinger's offices.

Accounts associated with Bell Pottinger have doctored the entries of arms manufacturer and client The Paramount Group; the London-based Russian oligarch Boris Berezovsky; the profile of Rupiah Banda, the former President of Zambia; at least two large financial firms; the Central Bank of Sri Lanka, also a client; and the founder of Carter-Ruck.[70]

One of the most prolific of the accounts connected to Bell Pottinger went under the name Biggleswiki and some of the most frantic editing concerned illegal logging in Malaysia. In April 2011, Biggleswiki inserted 'citation needed' to many of the critical sentences on the profile of Abdul Taib Mahmud, the Chief Minister of the Malaysian state of Sarawak. Mahmud, who is understood to control the granting of logging licences, has been dogged by allegations of corruption and abuse of public office.[71]

Biggleswiki then deleted some of the material and added a 'Disputed Section' on the profile. Any subsequent reader would think that the negative criticism of Mahmud was unsubstantiated. Biggleswiki also removed important material from the profile, claiming it was 'unreferenced' and therefore unsubstantiated.[72] Once the extent of its activity was discovered, Wikipedia froze ten accounts that it believed were associated with computers owned by Bell Pottinger.[73] Tim Bell does not see anything wrong or unusual in this work.[74] He describes

Wikipedia as a 'ridiculous organisation . . . created by a bunch of nerds'.[75]

Wikipedia is an important, but single, source of information and people are mostly aware of its limitations. It is not relied on to provide an accurate and full account. We have, though, become dependent to a large extent on another company, Google, for delivering information. Here, too, lobbyists have developed a method to keep damaging material from the public.

There are now hundreds of companies offering to manipulate Google searches to make finding critical content all but impossible. Many of these reputation washers are anonymous web specialists and technologists.[76] A promotional video for one such company, Reputation Changer, promises to make negative content 'disappear'.[77] This is done by driving negative content down the Google rankings, relying on the fact that few of us regularly click beyond the first page of results. They will create new, positive content that fools the search engines into pushing the 'dummy' content above the negative, hiding the articles they do not want you to read.[78]

BP is one firm to have been found manipulating Google in the wake of the disastrous spill in the Gulf of Mexico. What BP appears to have been attempting was to get its message, which was 'Learn more about how BP is helping', at the top of Google searches relating to the spill. NGOs and other critics with much smaller pockets and without the capacity have consequently been blocked from getting their message across.[79]

Lobbying agencies are in the business too. In one company document, Bell Pottinger outlines how it uses a number of reputation management techniques to control the search results of key search engines. It boasts of creating and maintaining third party blogs that are used to seed positive content designed to rank highly in Google search results.[80] Lobbyists, the document suggests, are creating phoney content to manipulate Google and hide bad news.

Bell Pottinger works for the Kingdom of Bahrain, a country that has a poor human rights record. In 2009 the lobbyists were hired to promote the Kingdom, an account understood to be worth a seven-figure sum annually.[81] In February 2011, as the Arab Spring took hold in Bahrain and pro-democracy demonstrators gathered in the capital, Manama, Bell Pottinger took on the extra responsibility of handling media inquiries about the protests and the authorities' bloody reaction to it.[82]

The previous year, Bell Pottinger had also brought in a major Washington PR and lobbying firm, Qorvis, to undertake some of its work for Bahrain.[83] Qorvis was later paid $40,000 a month directly by the Bahraini government.[84] Far more is known about Qorvis' work for the Bahrainis than Bell Pottinger's. US lobbying firms are required to make public the PR and lobbying they do for foreign governments. The UK does not have such a law.

Qorvis declared that it was being paid to monitor media coverage, conduct press activities for government officials, and draft and distribute fact sheets, opinion pieces, speeches and news articles. This is a straight PR brief. The aim in this case was to position Bahrain as a 'committed player in the war on terror, an agent of peace in the Middle East' and other unspecified issues pertinent to the Kingdom.[85]

The reality may be a little less benign. Allegations have been made of Qorvis' online manipulation to protect its government client from negative coverage.[86] One former Qorvis insider described the methods used by the firm to spin clients' reputations online as 'black arts', which included creating blogs and websites that link back to positive content 'to make sure that no one comes across the bad stuff online'.[87]

Favourable content promoted by Qorvis includes spinning the US government's position on the Bahraini government's behaviour. A month into the protests, the US Secretary of State, Hillary Clinton, demanded that Bahrain show restraint with demonstrators and condemned the use of force against them. Bahrain was 'on the wrong track', she said, calling the situation 'alarming'.[88] The *Guardian* reported Clinton's statement as 'a sharp rebuke' to the Bahraini authorities.[89]

This is Qorvis' press release put out three days later on behalf of the Bahraini government. It began: 'US Secretary of State Hillary Rodham Clinton today emphasised the commitment of the United States toward Bahrain and her hope for the success of the National Dialogue in the island kingdom.'[90] No mention was made of them being on the wrong track.[91]

'Such releases are not aimed directly at public opinion so much as at Google and other search engines,' says the US investigative reporter Ken Silverstein. 'A steady stream of press releases serves to push news stories lower in search engine returns. When it comes to Qorvis' clients, the news is almost invariably bad so burying it makes sense.' One lobbyist told Silverstein: 'Qorvis' releases are pure propaganda and it doesn't even bother flogging them to journalists. They just trot the stuff out so there's something else to read on Google when one of their clients fucks up.'[92] 'Of course we do it as well,' says Bell of search engine optimisation. 'Everybody wants the best information to appear at the top of the page.'[93]

★

This should give us a picture of how lobbyists use their PR skills to promote their message in the traditional media and online, plus their efforts to make sure that damaging information never reaches our ears. We need now to stand back from this day-to-day interaction with the media and look at how lobbyists use it to shape whole areas of public debate.

Lobbyists are not simply concerned with making sure that politicians and the public absorb the 'right' information through the press, or ignore the bad. Some are also determined to narrow public debate to fit their aims, dictating what is acceptable to discuss and what is not. This has clear implications for our democracy. By consciously limiting debate and our ability to think clearly about issues that are of public concern, they are helping to determine what is politically possible.

How lobbyists do this is by owning the terms of a debate. The framing of it. Attention is shifted away from discussions where the outcome is unlikely to serve their interests and onto debate where they are almost guaranteed to win. Once the terms have been fixed and a narrowly framed conversation becomes dominant, dissenting voices appear marginal and often irrelevant.

Campaigns succeed by 'controlling the ground in which the debate is discussed'.[94] This was the central lesson of a 2012 masterclass on lobbying, attended by, among others, the man who led the campaign against the proposal for an alternative voting system, Matthew Elliott, co-founder of the Taxpayers Alliance, and lobbyists from the agency Westbourne Communications.

How lobbyists go about owning a debate is by using PR techniques. First is identifying the ground on which they can win. If lobbyists are going to lose an argument on the grounds of the cost to the environment, can they win it by steering the debate towards often hypothetical benefits, such as economic growth and jobs? Next is to create an effective story around this which will capture and dominate the public's attention. The message needs to be kept simple and given a human face to carry well. This line is then pushed relentlessly and as one. All players need to be singing from the same hymn sheet. Contradictory or confusing messages only weaken a campaign. These rules, as we will show, have been applied across industries for years.

Here is an example of how to get it right. In the run-up to the referendum on whether Britain should switch to an alternative voting system, the anti-campaigners, NOtoAV, were first out of the blocks to set the parameters of debate. 'We were very quick off the mark,' said Dylan Sharpe of the TaxPayers' Alliance. The importance of getting in early and framing the question was 'massive'.

AV is a much fairer, more democratic way of electing MPs than the current first-past-the-post system. This was the reason it was proposed. It was also ground on which the No campaign could not win. It did not want to debate the dubious merits of first-past-the-post. So the No camp framed the debate around terms that would lead to AV's defeat. It focused the message on cost. Switching to AV, it said, would cost taxpayers a lot of money, a fact widely disputed. They kept the message simple and gave it a human face, pitting the money spent on the switch to AV against the needs of soldiers for equipment and babies for hospital treatment. This framing was central to AV being trounced in the referendum.

This is how to get it wrong. High Speed 2, or HS2, the proposed rail link between initially London and the West Midlands, was badly sold by the government, according to the lobbyist James Bethell of Westbourne Communications. The framing and messaging were weak. 'What's in a name?' said Bethell, who was subsequently drafted in by the government and the HS2 steering body to counter vocal public opposition.[95] 'The biggest infrastructure investment for an entire generation was sold on the basis of cutting a few minutes off a train journey.'[96] This contributed to HS2's opponents being allowed to dominate the debate. Communities whose homes would be affected by the line were winning. They were actual, human faces.

Projects get vital popular support only if they spell out the real benefits for normal people, according to Bethell. Westbourne's HS2 strategy was, therefore, to shift the debate away from the costs and benefits of reduced journey times for a few commuters, and on to a wider national debate about job creation and the potential gains to Britain's Northern cities. The messaging focused on a fiction that pitted wealthy people in the Chilterns worried about their hunting rights against the economic benefits to the North. It was about 'posh people standing in the way of working class people getting jobs', Bethell explained.[97] This, they figured, was ground on which they could win popular support.

This deliberate reframing, however, has also largely failed as the facts of HS2 have come to light. A report by the government's own auditors found little evidence to prove that HS2 will help boost regional economic growth in Britain's North. It also found that claims of job creation may have been overstated, the government not knowing how many jobs would be created without the investment.[98] The auditors also found that data on which the economic case for the £43bn rail project was built was out of date and occasionally wrong.[99]

In the case of HS2 the lobbyists had little to back the messages they pumped into the press. Lobbyists are often less concerned with facts. It was all about reframing. Discussions on HS2 were no longer to be about commuting and speed, but about jobs and economic growth. The crucial thing was to be in a fight they could win, and then getting this message out to a sceptical public, wavering commentators and increasingly nervous Parliamentarians.

The deliberate reframing of debates by lobbyists to achieve a favourable outcome can be swift, as with HS2, or it can be a process lasting years. The campaign to shift the conversation on nuclear power in the UK, for example, has involved a sustained lobbying effort over more than a decade.

Opposition to nuclear power ten years ago was national and widespread, included many in the political class, and was founded on two major and seemingly intractable problems: it was expensive and dirty. This was the feeling of the Labour government in its 2003 White Paper: 'Current economics make new nuclear build an unattractive option . . . whilst important issues of nuclear waste still need to be resolved.'[100] This was a debate that the nuclear industry realised it could not win.

Today, neither of these conditions has changed. Nuclear power is still very expensive and we have yet to resolve what to do with the hazardous waste. If anything these twin problems have become more pronounced. But what has happened in the last decade is that the lobbyists have repositioned nuclear power, very deliberately, as the solution to climate change. Almost as the ink dried on the government's damning 2003 position paper, a sustained lobbying campaign to reframe the debate over nuclear power began. It started with a simple banner advert on the Nuclear Industry Association's website with the message: 'Nuclear: climate friendly energy'.[101]

The following year the PR and lobbying giant Weber Shandwick was paid by the nuclear power company British Nuclear Fuels (BNFL) to come up with a communications plan for Nuclear New Build in the UK. Weber Shandwick wrote a strategy document called 'The Case for Nuclear Energy' to underpin BNFL's lobbying effort. This outlined its main selling points. Number two on the list was: nuclear power is essential in combating CO_2 emissions.[102]

This was a deliberate reworking of the nuclear power debate. Government was increasingly concerned about climate change. If government was to tackle the problem, the industry and its lobbyists asserted, nuclear power had to play a central role in providing the UK's energy. Cost and waste concerns were sidelined. The case for cleaner, cheaper alternatives to nuclear power in the form of renewables and energy efficiency was pushed to the edge of the debate. The message was vigorously promoted by BNFL and others.

With the frame set, BNFL engaged another PR company, Strategic Awareness, to hone the 'sell'. It produced a series of nuclear energy 'racecards' that contained the core messages senior BNFL staff were to use to push the line in the media. For example, the cards simply say on climate: CO_2 emissions = climate change = irreversible damage to our environment. The messages were designed to make the debate 'personal' and 'real', using 'simple, straightforward language', while 'emphasising how nuclear protects values'.

The coordinated and determined lobbying campaign by the nuclear industry paid off. The Labour government pledged its support for new nuclear power stations. By 2007 Tony Blair was parroting the line: 'If we want to have secure energy supplies and reduce CO_2 emissions, we have got to put the issue of nuclear power on the agenda,' he said.[103] Not without some considerable effort, nuclear had successfully steered the debate away from its sizeable problems and on to nuclear power as central to solving climate change.

Then, on 11 March 2011, one of the most powerful earthquakes on record hit north-east Japan. The resulting tsunami killed almost 20,000 people and caused a meltdown at the Fukushima Daiichi nuclear plant, triggering the most serious nuclear crisis since Chernobyl.[104] The issue of nuclear safety was once again at the front of people's minds. The messaging from the industry needed to be robust and sustained to deal with the threat. In the hot seat for the UK nuclear industry was John McNamara, an ex-journalist turned nuclear spinner.[105]

McNamara led the Nuclear Industry Association's communications strategy in the aftermath of Fukushima. The industry's lobbyists were also at the heart of the government's response. Two days after the disaster the Department for Business was firing off emails to the industry to discuss 'messaging'. 'HM Government and Industry need to work closely with this,' read one email. 'We do not want to lose ground to anti-nuclear views.'[106] Not after all the work that had been done.

Another memo reinforced the need for everyone to be singing from the same hymn sheet. 'We should all work together . . . to be robust,' wrote one official.[107] The government's Office for Nuclear Development met with the industry's lobbyists to discuss a joint communications and engagement strategy aimed squarely at making sure the British public remained on board with a new generation of nuclear power stations.[108] Politicians also needed reassurance that their previous support for nuclear was well placed, said McNamara. The industry had to start re-engaging. On top of a campaign targeting journalists and politicians, the strategy included using social media to 'reinforce our key messaging that nuclear should be at the heart of our low-carbon economy'.[109] They were sticking with the line.

The man more responsible than anyone else for changing government's mind on nuclear power and getting it back on track is John (Lord) Hutton, the ex-Barrow and Furness MP. Hutton is head of the lobby group, the Nuclear Industry Association. He recently co-wrote the foreword to the current Coalition government's new nuclear strategy alongside the Energy Secretary, Ed Davey.[110] Years earlier, Davey had been the architect of the Liberal Democrats' anti-nuclear policy. Davey had said: 'In addition to posing safety and environmental risks, nuclear power will only be possible with vast taxpayer subsidies or a rigged market . . . the alternatives are cleaner, safer, greener and better for the environment and the taxpayer.'[111] In 2013, by contrast, Davey wrote that the UK can 'look back on nearly sixty years of successful and, above all, safe exploitation of low-carbon nuclear power'.[112]

The success of the nuclear industry to turn its fortunes around in this way has led others in the energy business, with decidedly more chutzpah, to adopt a similar strategy. Gas, a fossil fuel, was officially repositioned as a solution to climate change in spring 2012. After eighteen months of intensive lobbying by the industry,[113] politicians in Brussels declared energy from gas a low-carbon source of power. Shoehorned into an EU document showing the enormous cuts in emissions needed to tackle climate change are positive mentions of gas as a low-carbon energy technology. A multi-billion European fund for R&D on clean technology now includes funding for gas projects. The repositioning has succeeded in potentially diverting billions of taxpayer euros earmarked for new renewable technologies to a mature, fossil fuel industry.[114] The debate on what constitutes 'good' for the climate had been shifted.

Following on from successes in nuclear and gas, shale gas has also positioned itself as green. This is the controversial fossil fuel extracted from hydraulic fracturing using a mixture of chemicals, water and pressure, a process known as 'fracking'. In May 2011 a UK climate sceptic lobby group, the Global Warming Policy Foundation led by Margaret Thatcher's former Chancellor Nigel Lawson, published a report on fracking. 'If Europe and the wider world are bent on cutting carbon emissions, they would be foolish to ignore the claims of shale gas,' it stated.[115]

Much of the rest of the heavy lifting to sell shale gas and fracking has been done by the government, the lobbying agency Bell Pottinger[116] and the 'independent voices' of 'opinion formers', as Bell Pottinger describes them, particularly in the *Telegraph*. 'Glorious news for humanity,' is how Boris Johnson described fracking in his typically understated way in one column in the paper.[117] 'An answer to the nation's prayers,' as opposed to 'wave power, solar power, biomass – their collective oomph wouldn't pull the skin off a rice pudding,' he wrote.

Later that month, another *Telegraph* commentator predicted that 'there will be lucky Lancastrians', where shale gas has been found, 'on their knees and praying in Morecambe, saying all hail to the shale'.[118] The grateful people of Morecambe might do well to look beyond the bay to the US, where shale gas has been widely exploited and resistance is fierce due to health concerns and its impact on climate.[119]

Opponents to fracking have also come under attack in the press, with third parties accusing them of, among other things, ignoring the needs of the poor for cheaper fuel bills. This claim is not only hypothetical, but also – like HS2 – homes in on a divisive fiction that anti-fracking protestors in Balcombe, West Sussex, are wealthy and selfish.[120] Communities protesting in the less affluent Morecambe, who do not fit this framing, have received little attention. Instead, the Prime Minister visited Lancashire to talk up the jobs and economic benefits that fracking will bring to the county.[121] The lessons appear to have been learnt from HS2.

The campaign in the *Telegraph* and other parts of the media appears to be about heading off opposition and calming Parliamentarians. The government is on board. It gave fracking the green light in the UK in December 2012: 'Shale gas represents a promising new potential energy resource for the UK . . . as we move to a low carbon economy,' the Energy Secretary, Ed Davey, said. While the debate was largely framed around energy security and the benefits to the national economy, shale represents another successful reframing of a dirty energy source as a solution to climate change.

Perhaps the most audacious repositioning of them all, though, is that of the dirty Canadian tar sands. The country sits on the second largest oil reserves in the world behind Saudi Arabia. Whereas Saudi oil is light crude, Canadian oil has to be essentially boiled out of sand, hence it is known as the oil or tar sands. To get it out of the ground uses far more energy and water than conventional oil. The average emissions of greenhouse gases for the tar sands are estimated to be up to 4.5 times as intensive per barrel compared to conventional crude oil produced in the United States.[122] CO_2 is not the only problem though. Research has revealed that tar sands are leaving a legacy of carcinogenic chemicals.[123] It is highly polluting stuff.

The Canadians geared up to export their tar sands oil to the world. However, this coincided with the European Union announcing that it wanted to lead the world in climate-protecting legislation. One piece of EU climate legislation in particular would have led to restricted sales of Canada's dirty oil.

The Canadians went on the counter-attack, developing a lobbying strategy targeted at the US and key European capitals, including Brussels and London. Its Pan-European Oil Sands Advocacy Plan had a twin purpose: first, to make sure that the tar sands oil was not discriminated against in European markets; second, to defend Canada's image as a responsible energy producer. This clearly meant countering the prevailing view that tar sands are one of the dirtiest fossil fuels of all time,[124] with messages that Canada is exporting clean energy.

The line was pushed to MPs, Members of the European Parliament, journalists and friendly NGOs who were flown on tours of the tar sands. The Canadian regional government of Alberta, home to the oil, employed the lobbying agency Hanover to push the pro-tar sands green line. The lobbying was off the scale. In little over eighteen months to April 2011 in excess of 100 lobbying events were organised by the Canadians and Albertans. The result was a delay in the EU legislation. 'I always feel it's a lot harder to undo legislation than to take action before it becomes law,' said Alberta's Energy Minister.[125]

The collective efforts of the fossil fuel and nuclear industries have shifted thinking on where our energy is to come from. Nuclear power, without being framed in the context of the urgent need to address climate change, drew widespread opposition. Reframe it and pump the low-carbon line, however, and many people move to a position of reluctant acceptance. The nature of nuclear power has not changed: it is still dirty and expensive. It is also a lower carbon source of energy than fossil fuels. But because it produces electricity and provides no answer to our main fossil fuel problems, which are heating and transport, nuclear power will not 'solve' climate change, as promised. What has shifted is the way we have been invited to think about nuclear power. The other fuels have succeeded to a greater or lesser extent in positioning themselves within this 'low-carbon' frame too.

This is not the book in which to discuss the merits of various energy sources, or the best approach to tackling climate change. Instead, it merely shows that the way we think about where our energy is to come from has been informed by constructed stories placed in the media explicitly designed to reshape public debate in a way that serves the commercial interests of those doing it.

This is equally true of the campaign to prevent system-wide reform of the financial services sector in the wake of the recent crisis. Efforts to think about and discuss what a socially useful financial sector would look like have been thwarted by a lobbying machine bent on preventing such a debate. The media has played a key role in this.

'Seeing the British establishment struggle with the financial sector is like watching an alcoholic who still resists the idea that something drastic needs to happen for him to turn his life around,' wrote Joris Luyendijk, anthropologist and banking blogger.[126] The system after the crisis, even patched and tweaked by recent regulations, remains highly dysfunctional.

What was obvious to many in 2008, as banks collapsed and the economy tanked, was that radical change was needed, not just reform. 'Never again' was the cry not just from citizens, but from moderate commentators in sections of the press. A broad section of the political class also recognised the need for change. Crucially, though, they were unable to articulate the fundamental overhaul necessary in the immediate aftermath of the crisis. Likewise, few journalists found the space or courage, or overcame the complexity of the problem, to turn this belief into a coherent and compelling story. The fact that banking has clothed itself in a certain mystique has also thwarted debate. Discussions appear open only to specialists. To many, it is intimidating.

As people struggled with imagining a financial system that served the needs of society from the vast money-making, risk-taking machine that was now partly exposed, the City was already regaining control of the public debate. Public anger at the industry – banker basher – was still intense, but it was beginning to be tempered by a competing and compelling message. The City was 'a vital national asset' to Britain. We may hate them, this said, but we need them.

This was the line to deflect calls for fundamental change. It counted the benefits from the City, some of them concentrated on the very few, and discounted the enormous losses and disadvantages from having such a dominant financial sector. It is a line that has been pushed since with vigour.

The campaign to control the debate around the future of the City took off with two reports, one commissioned by the Treasury,[127] the other by the Mayor of London, Boris Johnson.[128] Both were focused on making sure that London retained its position as a powerful international financial centre. Both were by City insiders: Win Bischoff, chairman of the bailed-out Lloyds Banking Group, and Bob Wigley, a former Merrill Lynch banker, which also indirectly received a bailout, who advised Johnson on City matters. They also only included the views of City insiders.

Not surprisingly, both told a good-news story of the City in terms of its contribution to Britain in tax, jobs and creating wealth. Implicit in this was a warning that if the City was tamed, the whole country, not just those in the Square Mile, would lose out. From this an organisation was born to coordinate and promote the message, TheCityUK. 'The financial services industry needs one trade body shouting off one hymn sheet,' said Nick Anstee, the head of the City of London Corporation.[129] In 2011 TheCityUK, which is housed in a squat building behind the Corporation's more impressive, fifteenth-century Guildhall, had a budget of over £3m.[130] One of its central tasks was to make the interests of the City if not synonymous with, then relevant to, ordinary people around the country.

'TheCityUK's purpose is to help restore the reputation of the financial services sector within the UK,' explained TheCityUK's lobbying agency, the financial sector specialists Cicero, to the UK Trade Minister and former chair of HSBC, Stephen Green: 'This is not just about highlighting the vitality of financial services in key cities . . . but also about casting the UK's financial services sector as a vital national asset. One of the ways we're doing this is by promoting key messages such as the nationwide benefits arising from the sector . . . We want to emphasise the industry's position as a major contributor to UK economic growth and job creation.'[131]

This is the financial services industry promoting a message that almost directly contradicts what most people would understand as reality.[132] The UK's weak economy, with all the implications that has for jobs, is in part thanks to the excesses of the few in the City. In the sector itself, the tens of thousands of jobs that have been culled have less affected 'London's Cristal-swigging investment bankers than employees at branches and call centres across Britain,' as one *Financial Times* commentator succinctly put it.[133]

While the industry has reached out to the public with this campaign, it has targeted politicians and others with messages designed to hold back regulation. There was a 'big job to do' to improve the image of the sector with policymakers, said Iain Anderson, head of Cicero, acknowledging the 'loud political question' of bankers' bonuses while the rest of the country faced cutbacks in services.[134] The agency targeted Westminster and Brussels politicians on behalf of TheCityUK.[135]

The bankers' strategy for fending off regulation, reflected in the press, began with laying low followed by denial: reform was unnecessary. It then moved to a position of reluctantly acknowledging that reform was needed, but only if rules could be agreed to globally. This was a cleverer approach given that international consensus on regulation would be difficult to reach and, if it were, would be set so low as to be ineffective. Bank lobbyists then followed this argument with a warning that too much prudence too soon would hit Britain's economy. This strategy, says Robert Jenkins, a member of the Bank of England's Financial Policy Committee, is 'intellectually dishonest . . . because it is untrue'.[136]

Jenkins has described the debate promoted by banking lobbyists as 'framed by fallacies':[137] a series of false choices advanced by lobbyists and accepted as given. The myths include a phony choice between having a safe banking system and one that generates growth. Another is that governments must choose between stability and having an internationally competitive financial centre. Does society have to choose? No, argues Jenkins.

The result of governments and regulators operating according to these myths and false choices is 'suboptimal' regulation. It also makes global coordination on banking reform more difficult. 'Remove these myths and one might more quickly agree than one fears,' said Jenkins. 'Perhaps that was precisely the worry of those who advanced the myths to begin with,' he added.[138]

However, in Britain at least, debates about what we want from our banks (remembering that some are part-owned by the public) have been dominated by the City's framing. With a well-coordinated and well-rehearsed campaign, it has succeeded in controlling the ground. It has monopolised the speaking parts over regulation, sold the line to politicians and consequently inhibited real change. The extent to which we have taken on their messages has so far restricted our collective ability to think through alternatives.[139]

There are times though when lobbyists' messaging fails. When the carefully crafted stories in the news get disrupted by contradictory messages and when the imposed frame of a debate starts to crack. This is when public debate can find some space.

When the Coalition government announced its recent changes to the NHS, it did so within a carefully constructed frame. The reforms were vital to the survival of the NHS. Britain's ageing population, the increasing costs of new technology in healthcare, and the national economic crisis all meant that change was essential. The threat to the NHS was clear. The government's reforms were pitched as the only solution to this perceived crisis. They were also sold as empowering patients, through greater choice, and putting power into the hands of GPs, one of the most widely trusted professions. This was ground on which the government figured it could win.

The Conservatives had done much to de-toxify the NHS as an issue for the party. Labour's line that 'You can't trust the Tories with the NHS' had for years had resonance with large sections of the British public. The Conservative Party had long been accused of wanting to run down and privatise the service (a process in fact greatly accelerated by Labour). However, a concerted, pre-election Tory campaign promising not to disrupt and reorganise the service, coupled with a firm commitment on spending, had shifted opinion. As early as 2006 half the country thought that the Tories believed in the principles of the NHS and wanted to improve it.

Mid-reform, however, the cracks in the narrative started appearing. The private sector, which had been circling the £100bn NHS market for many years, had started eyeing the commercial opportunities from the current reforms. General Healthcare Group, the UK's largest private hospital operator, talked to investors in 2010 of the 'clear opportunities' for the firm. The then head of GHG, Adrian Fawcett, announced: 'We are entering a new, exciting era, driven by the forthcoming healthcare reform that will ultimately change, to our benefit, the landscape in which we operate.'[140]

Another private operator, the outsourcing firm Tribal, struck a similar note. Its director of business development at the time, Kingsley Manning, predicted that the reforms 'could amount to the denationalisation of healthcare services in England'. He foresaw 'the biggest transfer of employment out of the public sector since the significant reforms seen in 1980s' and 'the transfer of billions of tax-payers' assets to employee-controlled businesses'. 'The old certainties are gone: the NHS cannot be protected from economic reality any longer,' he said.[141]

Details then emerged of a speech given by a former senior Department of Health official, Mark Britnell, who was named as an adviser to David Cameron. He was speaking to a New York conference of hedge fund managers in October 2010, six months into the reform process. The NHS was in the process of moving to be a 'state insurer, not a state deliverer of care', he said. The reforms would present 'a big opportunity for those companies that can facilitate the process'. The NHS would be shown 'no mercy', Britnell said, 'and the best time to take advantage of this will be in the next couple of years'.[142]

The hedge-funders had been assembled by Apax Partners, one of many private equity groups looking for the most advantageous places in the world to place their capital. One corporate adviser explained how the countries that will attract the most investment will be those that offer the best rate of return.[143]

Cumulatively, to many newly trusting of the Tories, these messages rang truer than the government's assurances that it was not about to privatise the NHS. The values displayed by these private companies also appeared at odds with widely held views of the NHS as a public, non-profit-making service. The Health Secretary Andrew Lansley's much-repeated messages of empowering GPs and patients sounded increasingly like fiction. Or, as lobbyists would have it, a narrative.

By spring 2011 the private health industry was facing what it described as considerable threats. Government had been forced to pause its controversial reforms because of widespread public opposition. The industry noted a return to levels of hostility towards the independent sector not seen or heard for some years.[144]

Its response was typical of lobbyists. One of the key private health-care lobby groups, the NHS Partners Network, outlined its strategy. It honed its messages, which were then 'cleared' by No. 10. It used 'common hymn sheets' on key issues, to make sure it was speaking as one. And it orchestrated a media campaign with the help of the think tank Reform, a vocal champion of greater private sector involvement in the NHS. This resulted in a sequence of articles and editorials in the *Telegraph*, on the importance of the government not going soft on public service reform.

The message promoted was the danger posed by the NHS turning its back on competition. Change was necessary, the lobbyists argued, to help the service adapt and respond to the huge demographic and financial challenges it faced in the coming decades, the same justifications the government had put to the electorate. The industry had caught up with the story being sold to the public. It was about the survival of the NHS in straitened times. For goodness' sake do not mention the bumper profits.

To an extent the strategy worked. The day the reforms passed into law, the tagline across the bottom of BBC news broadcasts read: 'Bill which gives power to GPs passes'. The government's message had stuck.[145] But, more importantly, the framing of the debate within the mainstream media had remained intact. Discussions on private sector involvement in the NHS – ground on which both officials and companies were reluctant to debate – were marginalised. The government and private sector lobbyists, through their access to the press, owned the terms of the debate.

The British people, however, seemed on this occasion unconvinced. Half of the country were opposed to the reforms and wanted the government to abandon them. Only 19 per cent were in favour.[146] Doctors and other NHS leaders were calling for the plans to be dropped. Nurses passed a vote of no confidence in the Health Secretary. Lansley was also attacked by the government, but for different reasons. One Downing Street source suggested he should be 'taken out and shot' for failing to properly communicate his plans.[147]

What the public was denied though was a genuine, informed discussion on the changes being introduced to the NHS, including the role of the private sector in providing healthcare. The government's attempts to control the debate through simple and misleading messages meant that there was insufficient information and little room to participate. The private healthcare industry protected its interests by aligning its messages with the government's, while at the same time lobbying politicians quietly and in private. This is when lobbyists are their most effective, out of the spotlight. But even when the framing started to give way and a limited debate emerged – unhelpfully polarised and antagonistic as it was – both government and lobbyists were able to marshal the support of influential third parties and their friends in the media to regain control. There is no conspiracy here. They merely, often, share the same views and values and, as we have seen, the same world.

This is not an attack on journalists. Some engage in what is known as 'blowjob' journalism. Many do not. To ignore the messages handed to them by PRs is to wilfully create more work for themselves. The pressure on reporters to fill newspapers today is immense. Many journalists are starved of time and desperate for stories and the incentives for questioning the majority view are weak. To deviate from the accepted parameters of debate takes a certain courage. A career in journalism is rarely helped by being the crank hack with unconventional views.

The responsibility instead lies with us. We know that the media does not provide an accurate picture of the world. We therefore need to be aware how and to what extent they are used by lobbyists to further their reach. It means becoming more questioning of the source and recognising the purpose of the information we receive in the press, seeking out the stories that are omitted and accessing our news from more diverse sources. We understand that the internet is an unreliable source of information. We similarly need to grasp how it is being manipulated by lobbyists to serve certain interests and be more diligent in getting past their attempts to hide information.

We can feel excluded from debates in which our views appear either irrelevant, marginal or extreme. In which case, we need to acknowledge that this is a deliberate tactic to shut down real public debate and seek out other, more active ways to participate in politics.

As a society, these discussions are vital to us: Where is our energy to come from? What do we want from our banks? Who do we want looking after us when we are sick? We should realise that it may not be wise to rely so heavily on our media to provide the venue for such debates.

5

Conceal: Hiding behind Third Parties

'Put your words in someone else's mouth.'
Merrill Rose, US lobbyist[1]

In early 2012 you may have noticed that the cigarette counters of large supermarkets acquired shutters. Fairly nondescript, normally grey, with the word 'tobacco' on them, they could be described as a minor alteration to retail furniture. Or, as a non-smoking, non-lottery-playing shopper, you may not have noticed them at all.

Who would have guessed that these inconspicuous grey shutters have been the subject of an all-out lobbying war that has raged for years, costing millions of pounds? Why did the cigarette companies fight them so hard?

In late 2009 a law passed by the Labour government introduced a point-of-sale display (PoSD) ban on cigarettes. Hence the shutters. The reasoning behind the new law goes that if kids cannot see cigarettes, they are less likely to start smoking. The Health Secretary at the time, Alan Johnson, was impressed with evidence from other countries such as Iceland and Canada where smoking among young people has fallen by up to 10 per cent since display bans were introduced. England's then Chief Medical Officer, Professor Liam Donaldson, described the move as another step on the road to victory over tobacco-related illness.[2] It follows that for the cigarette-makers this meant potential loss of sales.

The tobacco industry launched an immense lobbying campaign to fight the shutters. It was fronted, in large part, by people other than the tobacco firms. The industry got third parties, in this case shop-keepers, to lobby for them. They wanted politicians and the public to see not the hidden hand of the western world's largest cigarette-maker, Philip Morris International, but the friendly face of their local corner shop struggling against excessive government regulation.

This technique of using third parties to lobby is all about putting your words in someone else's mouth.[3] The rationale is obvious: the third party has the credibility of looking independent; seems to be motivated by something other than self-interest and profit; and there-fore has a much greater chance of being believed. Credibility, authen-ticity and the impression of independence are key. It is about separating the message from the self-interested source.

The use of seemingly independent third parties is endemic in the influence business. Lobbyists employ them to support any number of interests. It is a common technique within the pharmaceutical industry, for example, where patients and doctors are financed to lobby for commercial interests. Some scientists are also prominent third party lobbyists, being paid by industry to oppose everything from environ-mental regulations to public health measures. Some academics are similarly funded for their expertise and supposed independence.

Influential think tanks also make useful third party lobbyists, having both the ear of government and no requirement to disclose their funders. The mission of the conservative Centre for Policy Studies, for example, is to 'get at the fairly small number of people' who influ-ence political thinking; its board is a well-connected band of party donors, peers, senior financiers and media players; and yet it has never published its backers.

In addition, whole groups are created from scratch, and quietly backed by corporations, to provide a front for industry views. The 45-year-old British Nutrition Foundation, for instance, is a charity that promotes itself as a source of impartial information on healthy living. Many of its 'sustaining members', however, are in the sugar and processed food industries, including Coca-Cola, PepsiCo, Tate & Lyle and Nestlé. In 1985, a former head of the charity was quoted in a *World in Action* documentary as saying that during the period he was there, 'the foundation was solely taken up with defence actions for the industry'. It had been engaged, he said, in frustrating government committees that were trying to recommend reductions in sugars, salt, and fats in foods.[4]

Third parties are crucial for relaying messages to government and the public through the media. They enjoy a credibility that corporations do not. 'For the media and the public, the corporation will be one of the least credible sources of information,' said a lobbyist from Burson-Marsteller. 'Both these audiences will turn to other experts . . . to get an objective viewpoint.'[5]

Some third party activity will be legitimate and their views objective. It is perfectly right that a corporation should be able to call on expertise to back its case. The sympathetic opinions of influential others, whether a politician or NGO, are valid ways to demonstrate a campaign has wider support. Opinion polling is a common way of getting third party endorsement for an issue.

The use of others to carry a message to government can also be a deeply deceptive tactic in the hands of lobbyists. The power of third parties lies in their independence. Lobbyists, however, will create, train and finance third parties for the purpose of lobbying. Sometimes strenuous efforts are made to conceal their hand and all traces of lobbyists' involvement are hidden. At other times the funding source is selectively and quietly disclosed. This limits the fallout from being found out. It also relies on the fact that the overwhelming majority of people – politicians and public – will remain ignorant of who is pulling the strings. Our media is full of people who are not what they appear to be. We hear only their voices advocating a position while their backers stay hidden. Their voices fill politicians' heads.

The tobacco industry, a pioneer in the influence business, has used third parties for decades. It has covertly funded think tanks, retailers, scientists, academics and even journalists to do its lobbying for it (see Chapter 7).[6] And it used one of its favoured tactics to fight the display ban. 'Project Clarity', as the campaign was known internally, was designed by the tobacco giant Philip Morris International (PMI) to try and derail or, failing that, delay the new law. (Philip Morris was split back in 2008 into a domestic division and PMI, operating outside the US.)

The run-up to the 2010 general election was its opportunity to leverage political support for the cause. It wanted to 'create a post-election political environment that allows government decision-makers to mitigate . . .

the effects of the ban'.[7] In short, it was planning to create a false grass-roots campaign using shopkeepers that would give politicians the excuse to ditch the legislation.[8]

PMI called in the assistance of two lobbying firms to work on the campaign. The first, Gardant Communications, rebranded Meade Hall & Associates in 2012, with offices tucked behind Tate Britain, is a ten-minute walk from Parliament. It is run by a colourful Old Etonian, Paddy Gillford, now known as the Earl of Clanwilliam. Friends with David Cameron, Gillford has a reputation for 'high jinks':[9] he rides a Harley Davidson with the flag of another close friend, the King of Bahrain, emblazoned on its side. He also shot one of his own fingers off at a stag party.[10] Gardant Communications worked alongside another lobbying firm, iNHouse Communications, ten minutes the other way from Parliament just off Trafalgar Square, which also has strong links to the Conservatives. It claims to be on first-name terms with many members of Her Majesty's Government.[11]

Despite the coterie of lobbyists, however, it would be the shop-keepers in the public eye. PMI wanted the retailers to front its lobbying and PR campaign, as well as a potential legal challenge by the companies against the government. Leaked PMI documents reveal that retailers were essential to the campaign's success, 'so must be parties to the lawsuit and must take the lead in the communications effort'.[12] Once any lawsuit was filed, larger business lobbying organisations such as the British Retail Consortium and Confederation of British Industry were also to be brought in for support.

Key to Project Clarity was the lobby group for Britain's newsagents, the National Federation of Retail Newsagents (NFRN). It would co-ordinate PR and lobbying efforts. Its spokespeople, including the chief lobbyist, Niki Haywood, would be trained and supported by a media consultant that PMI proposed to hire for the campaign. Shopkeepers were to feature in a promotional video against the ban.

The tobacco giant's plan was to go after MPs seeking votes, with the newsagents' representative, Haywood, lobbying Parliamentary candidates in the run-up to the 2010 general election. Regional rallies for prospective candidates were planned around the country that Haywood and PMI would work on together. Would-be MPs would then be asked to sign up to a 'pledge' to oppose the ban, which the lobbyists could then hold them to should they be elected.

One of the lines being pushed on politicians by the anti-shutter campaign was the boost it would give to tobacco smuggling. This was presumably to motivate prospective MPs, who could then be seen to be tackling crime and boosting tax revenues by opposing the ban. Had they dug around a bit, though, they would have discovered that all the major western tobacco companies have facilitated the smuggling of their own products. Why would a company smuggle its own products? The benefits are clear: they still make a sale; they can use smuggling to gain access to closed country markets; and by selling to smugglers, they avoid duty and keep prices down.[13] Eventually the companies were found out. Facing EU litigation, PMI, for example, had to sign an agreement with the EU for an estimated $1.25bn in 2004 to settle claims on cigarette smuggling.[14] Despite this, PMI saw stories about the illicit trade as an issue to sway opinion. Here again, it sought to recruit influential third parties to give the argument credibility. PMI identified former police and customs officers who could carry the message.

The campaign paid off. Just days before the election, the Conservative shadow Health Minister, Mike Penning, jumped on the potential legal challenge as a reason to oppose the ban. He told the newsagents' lobby group that although he was not a lawyer, he had always been concerned whether the government's legislation was legal. If elected, he said, the Conservatives would bring the proposals back before Parliament.[15] The news caused great excitement among PMI and its lobbyists. The afternoon Penning's comments were reported, an internal PMI note called it hugely important and 'directly attributable to the grassroots efforts'. This was confirmation that Conservative Party policy had been swayed by a fake grassroots campaign orchestrated by a tobacco giant.

True to their word, when the Conservatives came to power they delayed the ban, by two years in the case of smaller shops. Newsagents could still display their cigarettes until 2015, nearly six years after the law was passed.

But PMI had not won and it is not one to give up. It returned to grassroots campaigning with the aim of securing a retreat of the law.[16] This time, the plan was to recruit 100 active and supportive sitting MPs to heap political pressure on the government. PMI enlisted the Leicestershire Asian Business Association (LABA) to act as its mouthpiece.

The plan was to direct-mail LABA members with the details, who would then mail out to all MPs inviting them to join the campaign.

Important politicians, like the Health Secretary, Andrew Lansley, and his minister, Anne Milton, were singled out for special attention. They would receive letters from LABA, as well as a postcard campaign from the Association of Convenience Stores and the newsagents' lobby. It was also expanded to include approaches to other ministers, government advisers and regulation committees.

Other third parties were to be roped in to lobby for tobacco too, including the London Chamber of Commerce, the Federation of Small Businesses and the campaign groups the TaxPayers' Alliance, Big Brother Watch and the Freedom Association. More scaremongering in the press was planned, with the shutters linked to shoplifting, retailer safety – 'women in small businesses' – and job losses from, for example, petrol station closures, as well as the illicit trade in cigarettes.[17]

This was a concerted lobbying campaign aimed at heaping pressure on the government to remove the ban. It combined a media campaign designed to alarm, with third party lobbying, including a determined 'grassroots' effort, aimed at demonstrating widespread opposition. The latter was specifically created, in the words of PMI, so that shopkeepers could talk directly to their MPs, for their commercial arguments to outweigh all other issues, and for the MPs to see benefit, local and national, in siding with their local corner store.[18] PMI's methods, like the postcard campaign, directly aped the techniques of NGO grassroots campaigning. The fundamental difference being that the hand of the cigarette firm was hidden.

The NFRN, which is nearly 100 years old, is understandably coy about being seen as a front for tobacco. While it admitted that it had received funding for its anti-display ban campaign from the tobacco industry, when asked by the *Guardian* to identify the companies involved, it refused to do so as it would breach 'perfectly reasonable confidentiality'. It turns out, it was not just PMI.

BAT at first categorically denied that it had funded the group, and stressed its high standards of behaviour and integrity. 'To accuse us of underhand tactics and the funding of an independent retailer organisation (the NFRN) . . . is untrue,' it said in a statement.[19] The U-turn took just twenty-four hours, when the company chairman, Richard Burrows, confirmed the tobacco group had funded the newsagents' group and had met them and yet another lobbying firm, Hume Brophy, to discuss the campaign.[20]

The admission led Colin Finch, the NFRN's past president, to call the Federation a puppet of the tobacco companies. He accused the industry of using retailers to legitimise their campaign.[21] And that is exactly what the third party technique is all about.

It is a technique that has been copied, honed and expanded over years by the business lobby, ever since the PR pioneer Edward Bernays realised its potential in the thirties. But as with all good tactics, the role of the lobbyist is rarely seen. Campaigns might seek to exploit a dormant constituency who may share their stance, spurring these allies into action and through funding giving them prominence with politicians and the media. Or, if allies are hard to come by, lobbyists will create them from nothing, hiring people and forming groups tailored to the task of promoting their cause and their message to government. Sometimes with a certain ingenuity.

Tobacco has been fighting on a number of fronts in Britain, not just over the shutters. The next public health proposition made by the government was plain or standardised packaging. This anti-smoking measure is not quite as it sounds. It removes the branding from cigarettes, and replaces it with large graphic health warnings, branding being seen as a key factor in why young people start to smoke. In Australia, the first country to try it, cigarettes are now also packaged in a drab olive green, which is distinctly less appealing than traditional cigarette packets.

To fight their campaign against plain packaging, the tobacco companies once again enlisted the help of third parties. However, this time they got a little more creative.

Shopkeepers were still part of the mix. In Australia, BAT financed the Alliance for Australian Retailers' campaign. In the UK, BAT funded a body representing rural shops and an organisation of Scottish wholesalers.

Another third party that the industry turned to was Forest, the so-called smokers' rights group. This is a front for the tobacco giants, funded by BAT, Imperial and Japan Tobacco. When the government signalled it was going to consult on the issue of plain packaging, Forest announced it was setting up a campaign called Hands Off Our Packs, which is essentially a tobacco industry front-front organisation.

The industry also turned to less obvious third parties to again target MPs. PMI hired another PR and lobbying company, Luther Pendragon, with offices at the other end of Fleet Street to Hume Brophy. In turn, they started to approach trading standards officers and local authorities from the north-east to the south-west.

The text of one leaked letter outlined how the lobbyists were working for PMI on the government's proposals to introduce plain packaging and 'the effects that this might have on local businesses and communities'. The lobbyists wanted to meet trading standards officers or council representatives.[22] The trading standards officer was then urged to write to their local MP suggesting a delay on plain packaging.[23] Tobacco was getting council officers to lobby for it.

Despite the outreach effort, Luther Pendragon refused to talk about its work for PMI. It put the phone down on us. It did draw public criticism, though, including in a letter published in the prestigious medical journal The Lancet.[24] As a result, the UK's pharmaceutical lobby group, the Association of the British Pharmaceutical Industry, severed its ties with the lobbying firm.[25] Within a week of The Lancet letter, Luther Pendragon dropped the PMI account.[26]

Yet another third party group that the tobacco firms employed to oppose plain packaging were ex-police officers. PMI hired a former Special Branch detective, Will O'Reilly, to investigate the illicit tobacco trade. O'Reilly's name appears in the press warning of the supposed growing problem with smuggling.[27] He is quoted as saying that plain packaging would make it worse,[28] a claim heavily disputed.[29] A further two ex-police officers were also cited as expert witnesses by the tobacco companies in their submissions to the government over plain packaging and EU legislation. The two former policemen, Peter Sheridan and Roy Ramm, are members of a campaign group called the Common Sense Alliance, which is funded by BAT. Again, the links to the tobacco companies were hidden.[30]

A small army of specialists were brought in to supplement these and other third party messengers such as business associations, anti-counterfeiting groups, researchers, and think tanks, like the Institute of Economic Affairs and the TaxPayers' Alliance. The PR company Finsbury helped PMI on key campaign decisions; the law firm DLA Piper was tasked with working up national stories, exclusives, op-eds and 'thought-provoking pieces'; the advertising company Pepper Media targeted its audience with regional stories about illicit trade. The specialist broadcast PR company Markettiers4dc was also roped in as consultants on the campaign. Also laid out was which broadcast and national and regional print media to target. Papers like the *Financial Times*, *Daily Mail* and *Telegraph* were in. The *Guardian* and the *Independent* were out.

The messages promoted, which were revealed in leaked PMI documents, included: that Britain would be inundated with illegal cigarettes; that there was no evidence plain packaging would work; there were 'legal implications' if it was introduced; and that the government should 'wait and see what happens in Australia before walking into the unknown'.

Once again, MPs were to be hit with these messages, along with civil servants and the 'business elite'. An internal PMI spreadsheet detailed how more than 100 MPs were targeted.[31] An 'Influencers' map was drawn up that identified which politicians, think tanks, business groups and government departments were in favour and which were against the health measure.

The documents reveal that the tobacco industry also sought to rig the government's public consultation on plain packaging in its favour, again by using third parties. PMI, they show, had the 'potential' to flood the government's consultation with over 18,000 responses, including 6,000 from its recruited group of smokers, 950 from industry, 10,050 from its 'retail group', 40 from think tanks and 1,000 from a trade union. They were not alone. BAT was 'shooting' for a massive 200,000–300,000 individual submissions, primarily via websites such as Forest, and a direct retailer and consumer 'engagement force'. Japan Tobacco International was submitting evidence to the government via 'business, retail, and other associations'. Imperial was said to be following a similar approach.[32]

The documents also talk about how there was a need to develop a 'consumer website', which appears to have been the origins of the Know-more.co.uk website that appeared a year later. This described itself as 'the community for Britain's smokers'. One message inserted into a cigarette packet read: 'Plain packaging is the latest in a stream of proposals targeting smokers. Other excessive schemes have been suggested. Know-more by learning the issues, then say no more to the government by joining our community and speaking out.'[33]

Smokers, to whom the effect of a move to plain packaging is arguably negligible, were being enlisted to defend the commercial interests of PMI.

The website they were being directed to is registered to a major US lobbying firm, Democracy Data & Communications (DDC). This firm, which has links to America's Tea Party, has a history of setting up fake grassroots websites and front groups. DDC's founder used to work for one such group, Citizens for a Sound Economy, which has longstanding ties to the tobacco industry.[34]

When the government announced its legislative plans in the 2013 Queen's Speech, plain packaging was not included. It looked like the industry's efforts had paid off. The measure had been dropped. The morning of the Speech, Simon Clark of the tobacco industry front organisation Forest blogged that it was time to 'get the party started'.[35]

Two months later the government formally announced that it was going to wait and see whether plain-packaging legislation in Australia cut youth smoking rates before proceeding with it in the UK. This 'wait and see' delaying tactic had been the central message employed by the tobacco lobbyists Luther Pendragon, and PMI's media strategy.[36] Interviewed by Andrew Marr on the BBC, Cameron also suggested that there was not enough evidence and too much legal uncertainty to proceed.[37] The words could have come straight from PMI. The third party campaign had indeed paid off, for now at least.

The decision infuriated public health groups and many politicians of all parties.[38] Coming in the week the government also shelved plans for public health measures on alcohol, the Conservative MP and ex-GP Dr Sarah Wollaston tweeted: 'RIP public health. A day of shame for this government; the only winners big tobacco, big alcohol and big undertakers.'[39] Tobacco lobbyists spun it rather differently. Angela Harbutt from the industry front-front organisation, Hands Off Our Packs, claimed the decision meant 'Ministers have listened to ordinary people.'[40]

*

Fake grassroots campaigning, or astroturfing as it's known, of the type used by PMI is endemic in US politics. It is spreading to the UK.

Corporations and lobbyists create and fund groups that are explicitly made to look like a grassroots group.[41] It works as a technique precisely because it serves up constituents in a way that mimics genuine campaigns for causes that do have popular support. Fake versions have the same impact for as long as the recipient remains ignorant of the organising force behind the campaign. In the case of the display ban and plain packaging, the tobacco industry cloaked its interests and MPs heard only the concerns of small business constituents and the hypothetical impact it would have on their local economy and jobs.

One of the self-professed pioneers of the use of grassroots 'people power' campaigns for businesses in the UK is the lobbyist James Frayne. A strong advocate of US political campaign techniques, Frayne has honed his skills in Britain working in commercial lobbying agencies, in a think tank and on a number of high-profile third party lobbying campaigns. He declined to be interviewed for this book.

Frayne was campaigns director at 'Britain's independent grassroots campaign for lower taxes', as the TaxPayers' Alliance dubs itself.[42] However, the Alliance does not reveal the names of its backers, which while not proof it is a front for vested interests, is typical of front groups. It is known, though, that a large part of its funding comes from wealthy individuals, many of whom are prominent donors to the Conservative Party, and on the Eurosceptic wing of the party.[43] It also networks with US groups accused of engaging in astroturf campaigns, like Americans for Prosperity,[44] funded by the oil billionaire David Koch.[45]

Frayne also worked for the big-name agency Portland as head of its campaigns unit in the three years running up to the 2010 general election, although it is not known what activity he was involved in.[46] He then moved to a young, bullish agency, Westbourne Communications, started by another ex-Portland lobbyist. 'We know how to mobilise public voices behind our clients to change opinion,' Westbourne claims.[47]

Frayne's rationale for mimicking grassroots campaigning is down to what he sees as a radical shift in the balance of power in Britain towards 'communities'. The explosion in internet access, coupled with the slow decline in power of the mainstream media and political class, he argues, have contributed towards this shift. Frayne thinks these trends should be tapped into by businesses. He claims to have success-fully lobbied against government plans to increase taxes and regulation on businesses by 'positioning ordinary people against elites'.[48]

In the previous chapter, we described Westbourne's work to reposition the campaign for Britain's new high-speed rail line, HS2. It was paid £100,000 by 'businesses and rail unions' to drum up support for the project and change public perception. The opposition were dominating the media debate, it needed to create a pro-HS2 camp. The PR team targeted a range of third parties to people this, including economists, trade unionists, MPs, celebrities and members of the public. Twelve thousand people, for instance, responded to a postcard campaign instigated by HS2's lobbyists.

The campaign was directed at changing public opinion, so the PRs seeded the media with supportive third parties. Thirty economists were recruited to sign a letter to the *Financial Times* supporting the project; one hundred businesses were persuaded to endorse a letter published in the *Telegraph* showing their backing.[49] This is Westbourne's forte: mobilising voices behind its clients to change opinion.[50]

Westbourne also worked, alongside the TaxPayers' Alliance, on the campaign to scrap the top rate of tax for the highest earners. This also used third parties in the media to persuade politicians. Nowhere does it say who was funding Westbourne's '50p tax campaign'.

Ahead of the Chancellor's annual Budget announcement in early 2012, third party letters appeared in newspapers calling on Osborne to ditch the tax. The one in the *Financial Times* was this time signed by twenty economists. Another was again published in the *Telegraph* from the bosses of 573 small and medium-sized firms, described as the 'bedrock' of British industry. A quick look at the list, though, revealed it included five managers from the Switzerland-based banking giant Credit Suisse.[51]

The letter was accompanied by an editorial from the *Telegraph*'s political editor, Robert Winnett. It was headlined: '50p tax rate is damaging economy and delaying recovery from recession, warn 500 business leaders'. According to Winnett the intervention was likely to alarm government ministers. This was, he asserted, the first time that ordinary British business owners had set out the damage caused by the 50p levy. Until that letter, public criticism of the 50p rate had been largely limited to those with clear vested interests in seeing it scrapped: heads of multi-national businesses and international entrepreneurs, not ordinary Brits.[52]

Few reading the *Telegraph* letter would have clocked the role played by a lobbying firm in recruiting supporters, seeing instead the concerns of British businesses struggling to survive. This has obvious echoes with the approach taken by PMI. Even fewer people know who paid for the intervention. But the aim was clear: to sway public opinion. As Westbourne says on its website: 'getting the right message out through the national media is still one of the most effective ways of changing opinion'.[53]

How effective it was in this case is questionable. Over half of the British public was in favour of keeping the top rate of tax.[54] Surveys were also regularly showing a lingering distrust of the Conservatives as the party of the rich rather than ordinary people.[55] With the media filled with supportive third parties, however, George Osborne gambled that there was a brief window of opportunity to get rid of the tax before the next election.[56]

Frayne's assertion that he pioneered the use of grassroots mobilisation on behalf of business is hard to prove. But he has clearly brought to the UK some of the lessons from America, where astroturfing is commonplace. Like many lobbying techniques, astroturfing really took off in the US from the eighties onwards, mirroring the growth in genuine grassroots movements, many of them environmental.

One of the early proponents of the idea was Ron Arnold, an established right-wing activist. He, like Frayne, argues that pro-industry citizen groups can do things an industry by itself cannot. For example, they can 'turn the public against your enemies,' Arnold once said.[57] One of his notable successes is America's so-called Wise Use movement, which uses astroturf and disinformation campaigns to oppose environmental laws.[58] At one stage, for example, it sought to eliminate the Endangered Species Act. Ron Arnold vowed to wipe out environmental groups, replacing them with pro-corporate Wise Use groups.[59]

Astroturfing is an entrenched part of American politics today. Front operations backed by corporate funds are used to promote countless industry agendas. Efforts have been directed at some of the highest-stakes issues facing the country, such as energy policy and healthcare reform. Spotting the fake campaigns, however, can be tricky. It should be possible to just follow the money. From Exxon through the American Petroleum Institute to the Energy Citizens 'grassroots' group, say, or from billionaire David Koch, through front group Americans for Prosperity to Patients United Now, a lobbying campaign opposing US healthcare reform. Following the money, though, is exactly what these groups do not want Americans to do.

Astroturf work is expensive. Manufacturing a constituency to support a business agenda requires significant investment. Campaigns using populist and often misleading messages will involve extensive advertising campaigns, phone banks and direct mailouts to urge the general public to lobby Congress for corporate-friendly laws. None of the money at the moment is disclosed, unlike funds involved in the direct lobbying of officials, which in the US must be declared. The total direct lobbying spend in 2012 was $3.3bn.[60] Spending on astroturf campaigns is estimated to be two to three times this.[61]

Invariably, these fake groups adopt populist-sounding names, invoking words like 'citizens' and 'choice'. The Coalition for Vehicle Choice, for instance, was set up by large manufacturers in the US to oppose fuel efficiency standards. Citizens for Sensible Control of Acid Rain was largely absent of sensible citizens, just consisting of the large electricity companies.[62] The Coalition for Health Insurance Choices was a front for insurance giants to fight healthcare reform.[63]

The approach taken by these groups is often to pit ordinary people against elites. Frayne appears to be following their lead. Take one group, called the 21st Century Energy Project, run by Ed Gillespie, a lobbyist and senior adviser to Mitt Romney in 2012 (Frayne also worked on the Romney campaign). In the early noughties, the group ran television and print adverts attacking 'liberal elites' who were opposed to President George Bush's energy plans. After it had been said that the group was funded by ten member organisations, eight of whom denied it, it transpired that it was funded entirely by Gillespie's lobbying clients.[64] These included Enron, which funnelled its funding through another organisation, Americans for Tax Reform, a low-tax advocate that allies itself with the tobacco industry;[65] and Daimler-Chrysler, which routed its money through the industry-funded 'consumer group', Citizens for a Sound Economy. This routing of money through other front groups makes tracing corporate financing of astroturf campaigns near to impossible. The only entity that a politician or public will hear is the astroturf group. This is their power.

The significant impact that these groups have on public debate in America, and on the actions they spur in Washington, should be a warning to Britain. Astroturfing 'is very popular in the States, it is starting to happen over here', the lobbyist and ex-head of the Chartered Institute of Public Relations Lionel Zetter told MPs in 2009.[66] But the apparent novelty of astroturfing in Britain means that we are not as awake to its tactics and impact as citizens Stateside.

Some of their tactics, personnel and corporate funders are the same, however, even if it is sometimes difficult to untangle the threads to them. Just take the tobacco industry.

Americans for Prosperity is a front group for corporate interests that campaigns for, among other things, low taxes. It has links to the UK TaxPayers' Alliance.[67] Americans for Prosperity was one of two organisations in the US that has mobilised opposition to tobacco taxes and smoke-free laws, particularly through the American Tea Party movement, which the TPA has been likened to. The movement itself also has connections with tobacco dating back to the eighties. The precursor to Americans for Prosperity was an organisation called Citizens for a Sound Economy. It used to employ the founder of the PR company behind PMI's latest astroturf campaign in the UK, which encouraged smokers to lobby the government against plain packaging.[68]

One of the leading US proponents of astroturfing is Jack Bonner. At one stage his Washington office contained 300 phone lines, which his young, articulate workforce would hammer to build phony grassroots support.[69] The firm has been accused of underhand tactics, such as forging letterheads and making up signatories of supposed grassroots supporters on letters sent to Congress.[70] Campaign recruiters also appear to have been instructed to lie to community organisations to seek their support.[71] In response to these accusations a Bonner spokesperson said that such incidents were 'isolated' and that the company was bringing in a 'no forgeries' policy.[72]

In the mid-nineties, Bonner was hired by Philip Morris to build opposition to a smoking ban in the workplace, which was the threat to its bottom line at the time. Bonner was paid around $1.5m by Philip Morris to solicit 7,000 letters from small businesses, criticising the proposals. This is not a million miles from what PMI has been up to in the UK twenty years on to fight the cigarette display ban.

In 2012 lobbyists for the tobacco industry were also caught trying to fake and deceptively solicit third party support for its campaign against plain packaging regulation in Britain. The industry argued that some half a million ordinary people were opposed to the measure, evidenced by the signing of petitions, online forms and postcards or by writing directly to the Department of Health.[73]

Except they faked an unknown number of them. In June 2012 a civil servant, who happened to be the Tobacco Programme Manager in the Department of Health, was leaving London's busy Waterloo Station when he saw two men wearing Hands Off Our Packs campaign T-shirts. This was the campaign run by the tobacco front group Forest. The official watched as one of the Hands Off Our Packs canvassers filled in a number of responses to a petition against the measure, forging one signature after another. The civil servant challenged him. The man refused to say what he was doing.[74]

The Department of Health received other complaints about their tactics. One person was told by friends who were canvassing that they would not get paid if they did not collect enough signatures. Feeling sorry for them he signed a false name and address.[75] Another person said that they had been told by Hands Off Our Packs canvassers that the government was changing tobacco packaging to plain brown and removing the smoking warning on the packs, when the opposite was true. The canvassers had been targeting parents in a children's playground.[76]

Another person having spoken to a Hands Off Our Packs canvasser was 'clearly under the impression that the consultation on standardised packaging was a consultation to ban cigarettes'.[77] Forest, which employed a firm called Tribe Marketing to conduct the work, argued that it was disturbed to hear of the reports,[78] but later conceded that some signatures had been forged, and that Tribe had indeed incentivised signature collectors based on volume. It was eventually forced to admit that hundreds of people – some 639 people to be precise – had been employed by Tribe in over thirty locations to garner signatures.[79] Tribe subsequently investigated the matter, with Forest condemning what they called this 'inappropriate behaviour' maintaining these were isolated events.[80]

As the tobacco industry celebrated its initial success over plain packaging, the Forest lobbyist Simon Clark turned his attention to a new tobacco front group he had just created called Action on Consumer Choice. This has been set up to defend not just the interests of tobacco companies, but also food and alcohol producers in the UK.

It is modelled on a US front group, the Center for Consumer Freedom, run by a long-term tobacco lobbyist, Rick Berman. The idea behind the American group was to broaden the campaign beyond smoking to win the support of a broader coalition of interests in the hospitality industry. What is kept quiet is tobacco's hand in it.[81] This could well be Clark's intention in the UK.

*

Lobbyists have developed many ways to separate the message from the self-interested source, some more effective than others. One of the most successful and therefore practised ways is to fund think tanks. These are the organisations, many of whom cluster around Parliament, that seed politics and the media with policy ideas. That many of these ideas have very often come from the lobbying strategies of corporations is an open secret in the influence business. Few of the influential think tanks disclose their funders.

'Wonk whores' is how some think tanks have been described. John Blundell, one-time head of the big daddy of think tanks, the Institute of Economic Affairs, has criticised the practice of global companies buying up think tanks 'left, right and centre'. Their large cheques, he lamented, came attached to particular policy recommendations, with senior company executives sitting on committees ready to 'candle-snuff' dangerous ideas.[82]

Think tanks are used by corporations to put policy ideas to government and put distance between themselves and the message going out. Think tanks provide the cover. Take the example of the free market think tank Reform.

One of a number of organisations to grow up under David Cameron's Conservative Party, Reform has been an ardent and effective advocate of more private sector involvement in the delivery of public services, or privatisation, particularly in the area of health. Modelled on Washington's Heritage Foundation, it was launched in 2002 by Nick Herbert, the Conservative MP and ex-Policing Minister, and Andrew Haldenby, formerly of the CBI, the Centre for Policy Studies think tank and the Conservative Party.[83] Both men previously worked on an anti-Euro campaign alongside James Frayne. Reform describes itself as determinedly independent and states that none of its research is funded by either companies or individuals.[84]

Reform's financial backers include major names in the business lobby: CBI, City of London Corporation, the big four accountancy firms, the banks Barclays and Lloyds, private equity interests, government outsourcing giants G4S and Capita, as well as lobbying firms. It has also accepted funds from the UK's largest private hospital group, General Healthcare Group, and the private health insurer PruHealth.

In the mid-noughties, a lobbyist for Standard Life Healthcare, which is now part of PruHealth, grumbled about the communication challenge facing the private healthcare industry. When money for health services is tight, how to get more British people to buy private health insurance, without being seen to undermine the NHS, was proving difficult. 'The problem we will always have is that we'll get accused of "Well you would say that, wouldn't you?"' he told a conference on the Future of Healthcare.

His proposed way of getting around this challenge was to use third parties: 'It's actually not us who needs to be saying it; we need other people to do so.'[85] The lobbyist confirmed that the private health insurance industry was working to 'get some of the think tanks to say it, so it's not just us calling for reform, it's professionals, it's outside commentators . . . it does need others to help us take the debate forward'.[86]

This is confirmation of the role played by think tanks in third party lobbying. They can be persuaded, through funding – and shared values – to promote a corporate agenda.

The insurers did indeed turn to the think tanks, including Reform. It has led much of the debate on how the NHS should be funded in future, calling on government to 'grasp the nettle' and introduce radical changes, such as user charges for health services and a bigger role for private health insurance. In 2009, for example, as the country prepared for a general election, it produced a report on the 'Future of Health'. This advocated a greater use of 'insurance-based private funding' in Britain's health service. It was co-sponsored by PruHealth.[87] The Association of British Insurers has also been a Reform corporate partner.

A public debate on the NHS is one that we should all be demanding. If there is not enough money to support the service – the desperate crisis in funding is disputed – we need to have a discussion on how we are to fund and access healthcare. Politicians are inclined to avoid leading this debate. But, in their absence, it is being dominated by private health companies who are putting their words in the mouths of seemingly independent bodies whose political influence and media reach give them an advantage over alternative, non-profit-driven views.

Worse, some who wish to see certain outcomes, namely greater private involvement in both the funding and the provision of services, appear to be engaged in more deceitful tactics, suggesting that it is not an open debate that they seek. These tactics suggest that they are out to manipulate debate to serve commercial ends.

In the spring of 2011 the conversation over the government's proposed NHS reforms intensified. The medical professions had just called on the government to scrap its radical plans and health workers were taking to the streets in protest.

On 16 March, the day after the British Medical Association urged a halt on the top-down reforms, BBC Radio 2's popular lunchtime show welcomed two guests on to discuss the changes. Around five million people tune in to the Jeremy Vine talk show every day to hear him deftly navigate topics from bin collections to bereavement. It is a potentially huge platform for lobbyists.

Vine announced his guests as Helen Evans, a health expert from a group called Nurses for Reform, and Dr Paul Charlson, a GP in Hull and chair of an organisation called Conservative Health. In the ten minutes that followed, Evans told listeners that Britain's NHS service had been failing people for over sixty years. Her remedy was more competition in the NHS and private or 'independent' hospitals providing the nation's care. This went beyond the government's stated proposals, but was broadly in line. Charlson told his audience that the controversial changes to the NHS were a very good idea.[88] What was not revealed to the five million listeners eating their lunch was who was backing Evans and Charlson.

Nurses for Reform, which Evans runs, is a front group. Like most, it does not disclose who funds it. It calls itself a growing network of nurses campaigning for consumer-led reform of the NHS. But, by its own admission, the actual number of nurses that are signed up to the campaign amounts to only a couple of hundred.[89] Given the paltry number of members, out of a total NHS workforce dwarfed only by the Chinese Army, Walmart and a couple of others – the NHS is roughly fifth on the list of the world's largest employers – Nurses for Reform has a surprisingly high profile.

David Cameron gave Evans an hour of his time towards the end of 2009, just weeks before the PM-in-waiting launched a nationwide, pre-election advertising campaign promising to 'cut the deficit, not the NHS'. This blitz was designed to reassure voters that the NHS was safe in his hands. Evans used her meeting with Cameron to outline her ideas on the future of health policy, including an end to state-run hospitals, the introduction of market reforms like widespread health advertising and doing away with national collective pay bargaining for nurses and doctors.

Needless to say, Evans is not a fan of nationalised health services. She has called the NHS 'a Stalinist abhorrence' and 'a 60-year mistake'.[90] Given the immense pre-election work done by the Conservatives to detoxify their image over the NHS, the headlines which Cameron woke to on New Year's Day 2010 were a disaster. One read: 'Cam's plan to pan NHS'. More than one commentator was prompted to ask why he was meeting 'this unedifying bunch of ideologues who want the wholesale privatisation of the NHS?'[91]

The ideologues behind Nurses for Reform are to a large extent hidden. As is often the case, it has ties to many free market, pro-privatisation think tanks.[92] Nurses for Reform's advisory board has at various times included: Eamonn Butler, co-founder of the free market think tank the Adam Smith Institute, where Evans is also a fellow. This also lobbies for the wholesale privatisation of the health service. Another adviser to Nurses for Reform was the economist Ruth Lea, who is connected to many similar free market think tanks, like the Centre for Policy Studies. This too promotes the privatisation of health. Another is Shane Frith, who is linked to a number of pro-privatisation think tanks.[93] Frith was also behind the Doctors Alliance, a group described as a movement of reform-minded doctors involved in 'influencing the debate on the need for market-oriented health system reform across Europe'.[94] None of these groups discloses its funding.[95] Frith was also communications manager at the think tank Reform, which does publish its backers.

Nurses for Reform also has commercial connections to the private healthcare sector. Its company secretary is Evans' husband, Tim Evans, a lobbyist who in the past has worked for the trade body representing private hospitals. The couple also ran a lobbying consultancy together specialising in health, which it marketed to, among others, private hospital firms and pharmaceutical companies.[96]

Vine's other NHS reform champion was of a similar ilk. It is true to say that Dr Paul Charlson is a GP. He also runs a private centre which specialises in cosmetic anti-ageing treatments (Botox), atypical of the average doctor. And he is head of the lobby group Conservative Health. But Charlson was also spokesperson for a lobby group called Doctors for Reform, which claimed an unverifiable membership of 1,000 medics. It was funded from private donations, and did not reveal from whom, but was known to be supported by the think tank Reform.

The launch of Doctors for Reform was managed by James Frayne, the UK's pioneer of grassroots 'people power' campaigns for businesses. Frayne was at the time communications manager at Reform.[97] He argued that the remit for Doctors for Reform was to mobilise hundreds of senior NHS doctors in favour of a reformed health service. Changes advocated by the group included introducing 'an insurance element' into the NHS in addition to state funding, and a system of top-up payments.[98] Both proposals undermine the foundation of the NHS as a universal, free at the point of use healthcare system. Both would benefit the private health insurance industry. Prudential, the insurance giant behind PruHealth, was Reform's most generous sponsor in 2012, investing £67,500 in the think tank.

Evans and Charlson make good third party lobbyists. As medical professionals – Evans is a former nurse – they are credible and carry authority. Doctors and nurses are also among the most trusted professions. Despite their tiny memberships, and undisclosed backers, both Charlson and Evans were given air time on the second most listened to current affairs programme on the BBC. Had their sponsors been invited to appear, which is a lot less likely, listeners would have at least been aware of their agenda.

This is the value of the third party technique. When Adrian Fawcett, CEO of General Healthcare Group, which funds Reform, called the government's changes to the NHS 'a new, exciting era that will ultimately change, to our benefit, the landscape in which we operate,' we hear 'Ka-ching'! But when Dr Charlson, who was supported by Reform, calls for policy changes that will ultimately benefit private hospital companies, we hear something different.[99]

★

These efforts are indicative of a widespread problem. Lobbyists go to enormous lengths to populate politics with seemingly independent voices, while hiding or at least not openly declaring their commercial backers, with third parties carefully created or selected to suit particular circumstances. The scale of it is hard to quantify. But the range of the third parties engaged in lobbying campaigns that have come to light suggests it is a central means of influencing public and political opinion.

Charities make an effective and persuasive front for corporate interests. One example is a charity that successfully lobbied for Parliamentary action on the issue of obesity. The Obesity Awareness and Solutions Trust claimed to be 'completely independent' and to derive its income from individual donations and membership fees. It recruited a large number of MPs and Lords to the cause on this basis. However, it was almost entirely funded by a weight loss company called LighterLife. It never declared its financial dependence on the company. MPs were 'pretty cheesed off' at having been deceived, but the company had successfully got the attention of politicians.[100]

Third parties can also be mobilised for more direct commercial ends. Take the case of Microsoft, which in 2007 was faced with the threat of its rival Google expanding through the acquisition of DoubleClick. It needed to rally people with authority and clout to try and obstruct it. A lobbying firm with which Microsoft had strong links, Burson-Marsteller, approached board members of a number of top UK businesses and urged them to raise the issue of Google's dominance with politicians, regulators and the media. Burson-Marsteller did not disclose to the executives who it was representing, who in turn would have relayed the message to politicians unaware of the ultimate client.[101] The lobbyists also asked companies to join a new organisation, the Initiative for a Competitive Online Marketplace, that had a similar agenda. This was a group set up by the lobbyists and backed by Microsoft.

When a whole industry faces a threat, competitors will come together and create a front to fight a common enemy. So when Brussels proposed new rules on data privacy, an organisation was set up to oppose them. The European Privacy Association sounds like it might be a supporter of citizens' rights to data privacy. In fact it is part of a formidable tech industry offensive to weaken the new rules and avoid restrictions on the commercial use of private data. It initially did not disclose its corporate backers. Only after pressure did it reveal that they included Microsoft and Google.[102]

As well as threats, commercial opportunities also spur companies to set up front organisations. Pharmaceutical company, Roche, for example, employed the lobbying agency Weber Shandwick to run a campaign to increase government expenditure on cancer drugs. The group, Cancer United, promoted the argument that patient survival is linked to the amount spent on drugs by governments, which was based on a heavily disputed Roche-funded report. Cancer United claimed to represent a coalition of doctors, nurses and patients calling for equal access to cancer care across Europe. When the group went about recruiting board members and reached out to the press and clinicians, there was no mention of it being entirely funded by Roche.[103]

Opportunity is another reason corporations will band together under one umbrella organisation. Roche was among a number of pharmaceutical companies funding a vigorous lobbying campaign that successfully won extra government funding for cancer drugs in the UK. The campaign was helped by a lobbyist, Bill Morgan, who went on to became an adviser in the Department of Health during the period when the new funds were secured. This time Roche's funding for the Rarer Cancers Foundation charity, which ran the campaign, was disclosed. Roche said it was 'disappointed by interpretations that cast aspersions on our good intentions and the independence of any patient and professional group that we support'.[104]

The need to cloak corporate interests in a non-commercial guise is what lies behind many corporate front groups. The pharmaceutical industry has long used patient groups, for instance, to front campaigns. These people have a clear interest in lobbying for medical advances, some of which can be provided by pharmaceuticals, but their illnesses have arguably at times been exploited for commercial ends.

In the late nineties the European Parliament was gearing up to vote on legislation that would allow drug companies to patent genes developed in their research. It was dubbed a fight over the right to patent life and a powerful campaign that included environmental and religious groups was launched against the industry. Britain's Chief Rabbi accused the firms of trying to play God.

The pro-patent pharmaceutical industry was forced to fight this organised, vocal lobby on uncomfortable ground. It needed to transform its commercial interest into a moral case. It turned to a British lobbyist, Paul Adamson, to try and swing the vote. Adamson persuaded thirty terminally ill, wheelchair-bound patients, who might benefit from biotechnology research, to lobby Members of the European Parliament. Wearing yellow T-shirts with the slogan 'Patents for Life', they shouted: 'No patents, no cure!' Their lobbying won out. In the summer of 1998 the legislation was voted through 432 to 78 in favour.[105]

Industry will often require a trusted, human face to front a campaign. The nuclear industry is no different. It has always had an image problem with a section of the population, particularly on the issue of nuclear waste. When a proposal was put forward for a nuclear dump at British Nuclear Fuels' Sellafield site in Cumbria, the nuclear waste organisation Nirex used trade unions to front its lobbying. British Nuclear Fuels, which was a major shareholder in Nirex at the time, had a 'difficult history and few friends' in the area. So the lobbyists hid behind the unions, which were seen as a powerful force in the local community.[106]

Union promotional literature used to sell the dump, while seen by Nirex as flawed, was powerful in winning local hearts and minds. This was down to the fact it came from an 'independent third party' that was well respected in the community and crucially for its credibility, one that had been antagonistic towards the company in the past.[107] The workers' campaign, part funded by the nuclear industry,[108] went under the banner of 'Trust Us'.

Trusted sources come in many guises. Scientists, seen as objective and therefore untainted, are regularly used to front corporate lobbying. As the government was reviewing Britain's energy strategy in the mid noughties, British Nuclear Fuels and the lobby group the Nuclear Industry Association were training people to speak on nuclear energy's behalf. Academics were considered important third party recruits. British Nuclear Fuels noted the government 'does put store by what independent bodies/experts have to say'.[109] Recruits were invited to attend a media training workshop run by the global PR giant and long-time lobbyists for nuclear Weber Shandwick. The industry was preparing its PR campaign.[110] These hand-picked, industry-trained academics were what the public and politicians would hear over the radio. The following year the government u-turned and gave the green light for a generation of new nuclear power plants.

There is a constant hum of corporate-backed expertise in public debate. A number of front organisations exist to promote what is dubbed 'sound science'. These groups commonly talk in populist terms, using words like 'rational' or 'common sense' to describe their approach to science. Invariably they have been set up by lobbyists or corporations to oppose environmental and public health regulations.

The Scientific Alliance, for example, was formed in 2001 to offer a 'rational scientific approach' to the environmental debate in response to what it saw as 'the growing concern that the debate on the environment has been distorted by extreme pressure groups'.[111] It was set up by the lobbying agency Foresight Communications[112] and quarryman Robert Durward, the director of the British Aggregates Association. It did not publish its funding sources, but at least to begin with it shared a contact telephone with both the trade body and Durward's quarry in Lanarkshire. The government had been causing difficulties for the aggregates industry. A landfill tax was introduced in 1996, designed to encourage more recycling of construction materials, and a specific tax on aggregates was introduced the year after the Scientific Alliance was founded.[113]

The Alliance, however, has spoken out over a breadth of environmental issues, including taking a sceptical approach to the science of climate change.[114] For example, it attacked government plans to send Al Gore's film on climate change to schools. It advocated instead that children should see *The Great Global Warming Swindle*, a heavily criticised sceptical film. A legal challenge was mounted to the government's plans by a member of the New Party, a political group described by one Tory MP as 'fascist and undemocratic'. Durward was its chair, Foresight was its lobbying agency.[115] The day after the legal challenge became news, a spokesperson for the Alliance was interviewed on Radio 4's *The World at One*. The Scientific Alliance was announced as it refers to itself, as an organisation that 'campaigns to improve the quality of debate about science'.[116]

This is the value of third party lobbying. Chosen by people who understand the workings of the media, third parties are planted into public debates without scrutiny. Knowing the limitations on politicians' time, seemingly independent people are able to carry messages to government while their financial backers stay hidden. Not all set out to deliberately deceive, though some do, but the layers created between the messenger and the source are put in place to manipulate rather than encourage open debate.

As a nuclear lobbyist admitted in 2006, at the height of the industry's campaign to force the government's hand, it was spreading messages 'via third party opinion because the public would be suspicious if we started ramming pro-nuclear messages down their throats'.[117]

That is it in a nutshell.

6

Attack: Outwitting the Opposition

'Shit them up.'
James Bethell, Westbourne Communications[1]

'It's not funny any more,' whined the lobbyist. 'They're not the usual anarchists. Among them are articulate middle-class people. Who are voters.'[2] The normally bullish Jack Irvine, an ex-hack for the *Mirror* and News International and now lobbyist for the Cayman Islands, was addressing a packed room of suits from the tax haven community. Also present were lawyers, accountants, fellow lobbyists, officials flown in from Bermuda, Jersey, Guernsey and the Cayman Islands, and representatives of Her Majesty's government.

Less than a week earlier, in October 2011, the first tents had pitched up outside St Paul's Cathedral. The view from the cathedral steps looked more like a scene from Glastonbury rather than picture post-card London. Nearly four years after the financial crisis hit, the Occupy movement had arrived in the capital, inspired by Americans who had targeted the financial titans of Wall Street. They came to highlight the massive inequalities caused by the crisis, including demanding an end to global tax injustice.[3] 'Last night I infiltrated the anti-capitalists camping at St Paul's,' continued Irvine, a straight-talking Glaswegian.[4] De-suited and disguised in a T-shirt, jeans and leather jacket, he had been collecting intelligence. He started to read from an Occupy leaflet: 'I'll just read the punch line: "We need to take back the power".' The assembled audience laughed. 'And we need to do it now.' Although the audience laughed again, Irvine insisted it was not funny any more.

What was putting the wind up Irvine and this crowd was that politicians were beginning to sit up and not just notice public concern over tax avoidance, but were starting to adopt the language of critics. Campaigners from the tax justice movement, a collection of reform-minded accountants, tax advisers and economists, church groups, development charities and activists, had successfully stirred up public debate. They had alerted ordinary taxpayers to the levels of abuse in the tax system. Politicians were now responding to a surge of public anger about the use of tax havens and financial wizardry by wealthy individuals and companies to legally avoid paying their taxes. And the issue was becoming very, very intense, said Irvine.

The tax avoidance racket was finally out in the open and for the havens, bankers, accountants, lawyers, consultants and their lobbyists who made their living from it, this was a problem that needed sorting.

The gathering that autumn was the brainchild of the lobbying firm Cicero, whose discreet offices sit on the tip of Soho's Golden Square, and its client, the International Financial Centres Forum. This group was set up to 'contribute to the public conversation' on tax havenry.[5] Behind it are a handful of law firms few people have heard of. These are the members of the so-called offshore magic circle who operate in tax havens, firms like Appleby, Maples and Calder, Mourant Ozannes, Ogier and Walkers.[6]

The purpose of the conference was to talk strategy. How was the avoidance industry to get on the front foot, deal with its critics in the tax justice crowd and win the public over? Dishing out advice with Irvine was the Cicero lobbyist Mark Twigg, a former adviser to the Labour Party and the City.[7] Four months earlier Twigg, whose firm lobbies for Barclays, HSBC, Morgan Stanley and Merrill Lynch, as well as the financial sector lobby group, TheCityUK, had declared that the time for banker bashing was over.[8] It was now time to defend the tax havens.

Dealing with the tax justice movement, and the wider 'existentialist rage against capitalism' was proving problematic, said Twigg, whose firm, Cicero, also represents the Swiss Bankers' Association, the lobby group located in what is seen as the world's number one problematic tax haven.[9] 'The fact that they take fresh deliveries from Ocado every day and seem to spend most of their time drinking lattes in Starbucks,' he added, 'these people are not seen to be down-at-heel, woolly leftwing social justice campaigners that we used to have in the good old days.'[10]

The obvious 'ordinariness' of the protesters was seen as troublesome by the lobbyists. The British people might identify with them and have sympathy for their cause. But it was also turned on its head and used to try and discredit them. The apparent hypocrisy of protesters drinking Starbucks lattes featured prominently in coverage of the camp, especially in certain sections of the press. Both the *Daily Mail*,[11] and the *Sun* ran stories on the theme.[12] The protestors' supposed love of lattes was even highlighted on the BBC's satirical quiz show *Have I Got News for You* by the then Conservative MP, Louise Mensch, leading Ian Hislop, editor of *Private Eye*, to retort: 'You don't have to want to return to a barter system in the Stone Age to complain about the way the financial crisis affected large numbers of people in the world.'[13]

Twigg offered up a few golden rules for the assembled tax haven crowd on dealing with what he called this broad, diverse and loosely organised protest. First was to stay positive and not get sucked into negative campaigning. 'That's what a lot of the NGOs would like us to do. We have to stay on positive territory and sell the story we want to sell.'

Second was to avoid talking to campaign groups 'on the fringes', referring to activist groups like UKUncut and Occupy and long-time campaigners the Tax Justice Network, a particular bête noire of Irvine's. The point was expanded on by another of the Forum's advisers, the lawyer Richard Hay. The strategy was to expend energy on the 'more moderate' NGOs. 'If we can show that their comments are wrong or unfair, then they feel uncomfortable about that,' he said.[14]

This strategy of dividing critics into 'moderates' that can be engaged in debate and the isolation of 'extremists', or those on the fringes, is a tried and tested tactic of lobbyists. At its core is the truth that a common enemy broken into separate and ideally competing parts is weaker than a united opposition. Attempts to 'divide and conquer' an enemy have been around as long as there have been wars. But, since the eighties it has been widely and very deliberately adopted by corporations and their lobbyists to counter the rise in citizen activism and social change movements.

It is just one of many tactics that lobbyists use to counter and nullify their critics. This is the shadier side of the lobbying business. In the previous chapters we looked at the 'positive' side of the industry, where lobbyists fill the media and politicians' heads with their message. This then is the 'negative' side of the industry, where they try to ensure that their voices are the *only* voices inside politicians' heads. This is about silencing the opposition.

*

When people come together, as they did at St Paul's, they do so because they see something that they think is wrong and they want to change it. In the case of Occupy what caused people to gather in public squares around the world was the immense harm caused by financial institutions that were accountable to no one, not their shareholders, their customers, not even to governments. The system was out of control, had risked too much and offloaded the damage onto ordinary people.

By meeting others who had come to the same or a similar conclusion people began to feel better about the chances of changing the order, coming up with a new contract with the finance sector, telling our politicians that they stand behind them, if only they would stand up. The camp provided the space, people came and a community was formed. There is power in this.

All over the country, people are coming together demanding change. It may be the threat to their local NHS, children's or library services, or a planned development that they see as needless or harmful. By coming together, supporting each other and realising that their concern is shared by others, that they are not alone in it, something bigger can take off.

The Tax Justice Network began just a decade ago, as a 'sad and lonely group', by its own admission, who understood the issues but had no political support or any idea how to get it.[15] Friends of the Earth was started thirty years ago by activists who saw what was being done to the environment and communities and decided to do something about it. Today 90 per cent of its support in the UK comes from individual members, who are part of a community of around two million across the world.

This is one of the central threats posed by the public to lobbyists. That people gather against them.

Lobbyists talk of the 'NGO phenomenon', non-governmental organisations like charities and church groups being very effective ways of gathering people with shared concerns. NGOs can present a major headache to corporate lobbyists. 'They play offense all the time; they take their message to the consumer; they are ingenious at building coalitions; they always have a clear agenda; they move at internet speed; they speak in the media's tone.' This is why, the agency giant Edelman said at the turn of the millennium, they are winning.[16] While this is overstating things, organised protest has the power to raise issues and dent a corporation's reputation. Lobbyists are in the business of defending it, and they have developed a great many strategies to counter and nullify their critics.

According to one PR practitioner, Ronald Duchin, activists can be divided into four distinct types: radicals, opportunists, idealists and realists. Speaking at a conference on how corporations could defeat critics, one of a growing number of events in the nineties which were focused on countering the threat of environmentalism and public interest activism, Duchin advocated that companies adopt a three-step, divide-and-conquer strategy.

Duchin told the delegates that the goal was to isolate the radicals; cultivate the idealists and educate them into becoming realists; and then co-opt the realists into agreeing with industry. It was very important to work with the realists, he argued. They should always receive the highest priority.[17]

The technique has a chequered history. In the 1970s church activists began the now famed campaign against the global food giant Nestlé and its policy of pushing baby milk formula to mothers in developing countries. The church groups thought that selling expensive milk formula to starving African mothers was, to put it mildly, unethical. Experts have long argued that breast milk is in most circumstances superior to any infant formula, nearly all mothers can breastfeed and even the slightest effort to promote infant formulas by companies such as Nestlé undermines a mother's ability to feed her child.[18] By 1980 a boycott against the company was hitting sales and the company's head-in-the-sand policy of praying the issue would go away had become untenable.

Nestlé's Vice-President wrote about the urgent need for an effective counter-propaganda operation. The food giant decided to ditch its blue chip public relations firms, Edelman and Hill & Knowlton and in their place hired two American street fighters, a former soldier, Rafael Pagan, and Jack Mongoven, an ex-hack and Republican strategist.[19]

Pagan was not an obvious choice to counter a consumer boycott. Awarded the prestigious US Bronze Star medal after being parachuted behind enemy lines in the Korean War, he had served twenty years in the US military.[20] But both he and Mongoven had studied military strategy and proposed ripping up the old, relatively genteel PR rule book. They likened the boycott movement to guerrilla warfare, fighting an international war whose roots were ideological and political. They argued that Nestlé was being used purely as a means to a political end by the boycott movement. Mongoven recalls how they planned for a major combat mission against Nestlé's critics.[21] Central to this was the strategy of divide and rule.

Their Nestlé plan was divided into four distinct phases: first, 'containment of critics', where intelligence was gathered to combat the company's opponents; next 'reaching out', where the company wanted to seize the moral initiative from the 'confrontatists'; then 'breakthrough' and 'consolidation', which led in 1984 to the campaign against the company effectively ending when the International Nestlé Boycott committee called a halt to the protest. Pagan and Nestlé claimed victory.[22]

Their success led Pagan and Mongoven to set up their own PR company, Pagan International. Its clients quickly expanded to include oil and chemical companies like Chevron, Union Carbide and Shell who faced similar opposition.[23] For the latter, it produced a three-year Neptune Strategy, designed to 'neutralise' the growing boycott against Shell for its controversial dealings with the Apartheid regime in South Africa. The main strategy was again one of divide and rule. For example, Pagan helped set up a front organisation composed largely of black clergy called the Coalition of Southern Africa, or COSA. One leader of the Shell boycott, Donna Katzin, recalled how COSA was a deliberate attempt to divide and weaken the position of the religious community.

Secrecy was central to the plan's effectiveness and so underhand were Pagan's techniques that when the 256-page Neptune Strategy was leaked in 1987, Shell very publicly pulled its account.[24] Pagan sank, but not without a trace. Mongoven and two other Pagan executives, including Ronald Duchin, resurfaced to create another PR firm, Mongoven, Biscoe and Duchin. This worked for the tobacco industry, among others, gathering intelligence on activists and implementing divide-and-conquer strategies.[25] Shell too continued on the same course.

By the mid-nineties, the oil giant, from whose London HQ you can wave to MPs across the Thames, had another major public relations battle on its hands over its operations in Nigeria. It had struck oil in the humid mangrove creeks and inlets of the Niger Delta in the late fifties and, not long after, found itself the focus of protests by the local communities. Chronic and routine oil pollution, including across farmland and into the fragile mangroves, as well as constant gas flaring increased the tensions between the community and Shell. The fact that a mere trickle of oil money made its way back to help alleviate the bone-grinding poverty of the local population added to the feeling of injustice.

Enter Ken Saro-Wiwa, the charismatic, pipe-smoking Nigerian writer, playwright and newspaper columnist. In the early nineties Saro-Wiwa started mobilising the local Ogoni population against the oil giant. The last column he wrote before being sacked from his paper talked of the 'coming war in the Delta'. The people of the region were 'faced by a company whose management policies are racist and cruelly stupid', he wrote.[26] The article was pulled from the newspaper's second edition, but Saro-Wiwa had found the oil giant's Achilles heel.

Shell stood accused of double standards: the firm would not have submitted people in the UK or US to such treatment. When Saro-Wiwa and the Ogoni signed a Bill of Rights calling for political self-determination and the right to protect Ogoniland from further degradation, it set them on a collision course with Shell, as well as the brutal Nigerian military junta. Evidence has since emerged of the deep and systematic collusion between Shell, the military and the Mobile Police Force, known locally as the 'Kill and Go'. Court documents reveal Shell's financial and logistical support to brutal military commanders, such as one colonel whose men raped pregnant women and girls and who shot and tortured at will. The colonel personally boasted of knowing over 200 ways to kill a person.[27] Shell has always dismissed the allegations saying 'there is a lack of any credible evidence' in support of them, arguing it has always spoken out against violence.[28]

Some 2,000 Ogoni were killed, 30,000 made homeless, and countless others brutally tortured and raped. The campaign would also lead to the judicial murder of Saro-Wiwa and eight others on 10 November 1995, causing international outrage.[29]

Even before Saro-Wiwa's death, Shell knew it had a major PR problem with the growing Ogoni campaign. A confidential company document from 1994 conceded that pollution, flaring, health and 'perceived double standards' were weaknesses in its campaign against its critics. Events had got so bad the company quietly conceded its 'present communication strategy could be construed as green imagery'.[30]

Crucially, Shell felt that it lacked what it termed 'influence' with western NGOs, who were now among its most prominent detractors. Its response was to begin to 'build relationships' with them in order to 'influence' them.[31] Saro-Wiwa's brutal death, however, had made front page news across the globe, turning a growing PR problem for Shell into a full-blown corporate crisis. Just two months later, a highly confidential strategy to manage the crisis was drawn up. It was finalised by the company's top brass at a secret meeting in the respectable Berkshire town of Ascot, made famous by its racecourse. Its author, Phil Watts, a Leicestershire-born Christian who had spent his career climbing up the ranks of Shell, cautioned his fellow executives of the importance of not allowing the confidential document to fall into the wrong hands.

The document came up with two strategies, one entitled 'Holding the line' and the more aggressive 'Occupying new ground'. Under the latter scenario, Shell outlined a classic divide-and-rule strategy. Headed 'Create coalitions, isolate the opposition and shift the debate', it included the proposal to 'differentiate clearly the interest groups into friends and foes'.

Shell would then 'prepare a game plan for those NGOs considered key' and work with and sway 'middle of the road' activists.[32] By the late nineties, another confidential strategy paper confirmed that Shell had cultivated active relationships with a number of NGOs and churches. The task ahead for Shell was to 'build knowledge, understanding and relationships among potentially supportive NGOs, which will enable the Group's reputation to be reinforced', while making it 'more difficult for hard-core campaigners to sustain their campaigns

Chêne. With echoes of the business lobby group the Economic League's intelligence operation of the twenties, le Chêne held a database on an astonishing 150,000 peace and environmental campaigners, and union members, in the mid nineties.

A horde of secret and deeply personal information was lifted from CAAT in the operation: from computer files to email passwords, bank account details and even personal diaries. Activists were followed home and their friends spied on. Le Chêne even had it fixed that new computers were supplied by her, so they would be accessible to her network of spooks. CAAT's correspondence with MPs, like the then Home Secretary, Jack Straw, was routinely scrutinised. So too were its celebrity supporters Helen Mirren, Prunella Scales and the Body Shop's owner, Anita Roddick. The result was that CAAT's campaign was continuously undermined. Demos at BAE sites, for example, were thwarted as protestors were served with injunctions.

When Martin Hogbin, CAAT's national coordinator, who had been involved with the organisation for six years, was exposed as a spy by the *Sunday Times* in 2003, many struggled to believe it. Here was someone who had access to almost anything that passed through CAAT's office.[44] In a bizarre twist, before Hogbin was outed, he became a target for surveillance by the Metropolitan Police surveillance unit, who were convinced he was a domestic extremist.[45]

Environmentalists, however, have remained the bread-and-butter work for the many private security firms now in the business of activist spying. Energy firm E.ON hired one to keep a 'discreet watch' on protest groups in the noughties;[46] in 2009 the private security company Vericola was employed by some of Europe's largest power companies to spy on climate activists planning a demonstration against the Ratcliffe-on-Soar power station in Nottinghamshire; the Inkerman Group security firm, which is advised by a former Met commissioner, Lord Imbert, monitored the anti-airport expansion campaigners Plane Stupid.

Plane Stupid were also infiltrated by someone calling himself Ken Tobias, who was exposed as Toby Kendall from the specialist risk company C2i International, although it claimed it never sanctioned his actions. His identity was discovered on a social networking website, Bebo, after activists became suspicious of his dreadful disguise as much as anything else.[47]

Although Kendall's amateurish sleuthing was quickly exposed, companies continue to use organisations to spy on activists on a much more systematic and sophisticated scale. A year after Kendall was outed, the controversial website WikiLeaks published what it dubbed 'The Global Intelligence Files'. This was a treasure trove of five million emails hacked from the Texas-headquartered global intelligence company Stratfor, once described as a shadow CIA.[48]

A decade before the leak, Stratfor had merged with Mongoven, Biscoe and Duchin. Jack Mongoven, who had worked on the original divide-and-rule campaign for Nestlé, had also spied on anti-tobacco activists for Philip Morris. One memo from the tobacco giant had noted: 'Mongoven has a very unique niche. At our request, he will do investigatory work on various activist groups and flag problems'.[49]

Stratfor's head of public policy is Mongoven's son, Bart, whose role it is to monitor the activities of NGOs.[50] The leaked documents showed that the firm was contracted by companies such as Coca-Cola, Dow Chemical and Union Carbide to monitor activist groups. Greenpeace, Amnesty International, as well as the spoof artists The Yes Men and the animal rights organisation PETA were all targeted.[51]

Stratfor has also been tracking the opposition to Canada's controversial tar sands, including environmental groups such as Friends of the Earth Europe.[52] For many the tar sands have become an iconic environmental struggle. When the EU sought to introduce landmark climate legislation that would have discriminated against the tar sands on environmental grounds, one Stratfor analyst circulated a press article with the quip: 'goddam euro hippies'.[53]

The leaked documents also show Stratfor using informants to provide intelligence on the anti-Shell campaign in Nigeria. The company was routinely monitoring the Ogoni, including Ken Saro-Wiwa's family's legal fight against the oil giant.[54] They had a source – codenamed NGO14 – who was an activist from the Niger Delta. This source was given a handler from the company and a credibility rating.[55] The source then started passing intelligence to Stratfor.[56] This included trying to get information on activists in the Delta and the names of those responsible for attacks on the oil industry.[57]

When the documents were released, they did not reveal the identity of NGO14, which remains a secret. One of the things they did reveal is Bart's disdain for WikiLeaks' founder, Julian Assange, who should face 'whatever trumped up charge is available to get this guy and his servers off the streets', he wrote. As for Bradley Manning, the soldier who leaked the documents to WikiLeaks, Bart added: 'I'd feed that sh*t head soldier to the first pack of wild dogs I could find.'[58] Secrecy, in this side of the lobbying business, is paramount.

*

Shell has been a pioneer of techniques to remove the threat of its critics. Besides its efforts to control opposition by divide-and-rule techniques, surveillance and spying, it was at the forefront of another tactic designed to outwit opponents.

By the late nineties, having learned from its Nigerian debacle, Shell was ready to try something new. It foresaw another PR disaster, this time in Latin America. Still bruised from its mauling over Nigeria, its reputation could not take another blow of the same magnitude. So it developed a new strategy, one that involved preemptively picking critics off before opposition gathered pace.

The company had found a huge gas reservoir, but it was deep in the remote Peruvian rainforest, which was highly ecologically and culturally sensitive. When Shell had explored the region in the eighties, it had come into contact with the remote Nahua Indians, who had up until then experienced no communication with the outside world. Subsequent bouts of whooping cough and influenza wiped out 50 per cent of the population. While its multi-billion-dollar controversial gas project was set to be one of the largest industrial developments in Latin America, it was also prime activist territory.

Shell got on the front foot. It was suddenly promising openness and transparency. It offered its opponents the chance to talk. In a process that Shell hoped would become an industry blueprint, it held workshops in London, Lima and Washington, run by a British charity called the Environment Council. Attending these were some ninety interested parties – many of them potential critics – who were formally consulted on its plans. But here is the rub. The discussions were limited to how the project should go ahead, and not whether or not Shell should go in for the gas. That option was off the table. This is the blueprint that others were to follow.

The result was that the NGOs consulted were divided: some boycotted the process, while others were so persuaded by the oil giant's plans that they were moved to lobby the Peruvian government on Shell's behalf. One veteran anti-oil campaigner, Steve Kretzmann, among those to boycott proceedings, said the consultation process appeared to be aimed at neutralising the most critical voices against the company.[59]

This is Duchin's strategy in practice: isolate the radicals, cultivate the idealists and educate them into becoming realists, then co-opt the realists into agreeing with industry.[60] It is a much-used ploy among lobbyists. The global lobbying agency Edelman even promoted the strategy in a press release touting for business. It argued that it makes sense to try and co-opt potential critics, because NGOs are twice as trusted by the public to 'do what's right' compared with corporations.[61]

Suddenly everyone wanted to talk. Dialogue was the thing and other controversial industries and companies followed Shell's lead. In the late nineties British Nuclear Fuels, the British state-owned nuclear company that ran the contaminated Sellafield site, began a process with NGOs also facilitated by the Environment Council.[62] Many of the environmental groups again pulled out, with Greenpeace concluding that there was nothing to gain from continuing in the current process. Too much was off the table.

The mining giant Rio Tinto was another to sit down and talk to its critics about its business principles, including 'what social and environmental standards' did NGOs expect the company to have. Once again the NGO community was split, with the more radical groups staying away saying that many communities affected by the company's global mining operations had been excluded. Monsanto, the controversial GM company that was caught up in a media frenzy against GM crops, initiated what it called a National Stakeholder Dialogue on genetically modified organisms. Yet again many environmental groups declined to take part, calling it a cynical PR exercise and an obvious attempt to divide and conquer opponents of genetic engineering.[63]

In the early years after the millennium, BP too developed an 'engagement strategy' to deal with the growing opposition from campaigners to its controversial pipeline from the oil city of Baku in the Caspian to the Turkish city of Ceyhan in the Mediterranean. It was another case of divide and rule to neutralise the opposition by talking to the larger, more moderate NGOs and marginalising the smaller, more radical ones.[64]

BP drew up a list: the NGOs opposed were divided into different quadrants on a page based on who was the most sympathetic to its plans. At the top, in the 'Influencers' section, were NGOs such as WWF, Greenpeace, Amnesty International, Oxfam, Save the Children and Open Society Institute. The objective was to 'engage' with them 'in a logical manner' as part of BP securing a licence to operate.

Underneath listed as 'polarisers' were organisations such as Friends of the Earth, BankWatch, the Kurdish Human Rights Project and The Corner House, which helps locally based struggles against environmental or social injustices. Here BP spelt out that there was 'no need to engage actively' as this 'would only legitimise their case'. BP would counter their arguments with a lobbying campaign to national politicians and board members of the big international financial institutions, like the World Bank.[65]

Even the tobacco industry got in on the dialogue act. In the mid-nineties, Philip Morris' covert ten-year strategy, codenamed Project Sunrise, included classic divide-and-rule tactics. One document, called 'Tipping the Scales of Justice', talked of the need to 'Drive a wedge between various anti groups' and to 'Position antis as extremists'.[66] This was familiar territory.

Approaching the millennium, tobacco was in trouble. After a fifty-year PR campaign, spent denying the link between smoking and disease, the addictiveness of nicotine and problems of secondhand smoke, and after fighting multiple lawsuits, in 1998 the four largest tobacco companies were backed into a corner. In a settlement with forty-five states in the US, they finally agreed to pay out billions of dollars in healthcare costs.[67]

The industry needed a way to retake control of the smoking and health debate. Its top brass assembled in the clean air of the watch-making Swiss city of Neuchâtel to discuss the tobacco industry's response to 'the new social and legal environment'. Industry figures, who had studied Shell's and Monsanto's handling of critics, set out to cherry-pick the best of what was out there. In order to reduce what they called 'the temperature of the whole tobacco issue', one industry veteran, John Sharkey, advised colleagues that continuous dialogue was needed. He told colleagues that dialogue with the industry's critics made outright opposition much less easy or, at least, seem much less sensible and more political.[68] Dialogue became the industry's new watchword. Philip Morris called for an era of 'constructive dialogue' on the subject of tobacco and smoking. Suddenly the companies wanted to talk 'openly' about the products they made and their role in societies in which they operated.[69]

Next up was Britain's largest tobacco company, BAT. Internal documents, released through litigation, show that the company saw dialogue as a crucial way of rebuilding its image. The accountants KPMG had written a blueprint for steering BAT out of trouble, still used today, called 'The Project: The way forward'.[70] It argued that the company's over-riding objective had to be to regain control of its own destiny by re-establishing dialogue with key groups.

In order to do this, the document argued that BAT had to be seen as a truly 'responsible global organisation, redefining itself from its present situation to the responsible company within a controversial industry'. This shift will not be easy, cautioned KPMG, noting that it would require a root-and-branch review of the whole organisation. But while KPMG explored ways in which BAT could be seen to be the one 'responsible' cigarette-maker in a disreputable business, the document conceded that there just remained a 'core problem' with the nature of the product. 'Tobacco products kill people,' they noted.[71]

Can an industry be responsible when by the very nature of its product it kills one in two of its long-term users? The idea of responsible tobacco is something of an oxymoron. This core 'product problem' lies at the heart of why so much corporate effort to engage critics fails.

It is the same with the tax avoiders. The avoidance industry of havens, bankers, accountants, lawyers, consultants and their lobbyists still had a problem that needed to be sorted out. Having hinted at a divide-and-rule strategy of picking off moderate NGOs and marginalising more radical activists, it too turned to dialogue to try and neutralise the threat. And, as with other industries, it has similarly shown little interest in addressing the central concerns of campaigners. Because, at its core, the industry has a 'product' problem. It is in the business of tax avoidance and it has no desire to stop.

For a long while corporate tax avoiders kept shtum about their tax affairs. Even with St Paul's occupied in late 2011, they were being advised not to engage with the tax justice debate. At a conference for the corporate tax community during a discussion euphemistically called 'managing tax optimisation expectations', BSkyB's tax lobbyist, Tanya Richards, reportedly warned the tax chiefs that if they put their head above the parapet, 'it's likely to get chopped off'.[72]

By early 2012 though, the issue was regularly front page news and politicians were suddenly outraged. David Cameron had a handbag fight with companies who used 'fancy corporate lawyers' to 'endlessly reduce' their tax bills (remembering that Cameron comes from an offshore dynasty: his father co-founded a Panamanian investment company and chaired an investment firm based in Jersey).[73] This was closely followed by Chancellor George Osborne's apparent and slightly worrying shock at the extent of tax avoidance in the UK.[74] This was a tipping point. The issue of corporate tax avoidance was not going away.

When the multinational tax chiefs met again in the spring of 2012, they had changed tack. They had decided to 'engage' with their critics, whom they invited along to a conference. This time the topic of the day-long discussion was 'Tax and Transparency'.[75] It was billed as an opportunity for dialogue. Sharing the platform with the heads of tax at BP and Shell were tax justice campaigners, including representatives of the large development NGOs ActionAid and Christian Aid.

The lobbyist James Henderson, head of the financial PR and lobbying agency Pelham Bell Pottinger, underlined the need for the industry to talk to its critics, both in the room and via the media. He warned the assembled tax heads against being in a 'hide' and not 'transparent' mode. He informed his audience that tax evasion had become as toxic as bankers' bonuses. But, he said, their problem was one of communication. The fact that many companies give little or no information on their tax affairs, he argued, had created an 'information void' that campaigners would readily fill.[76] With some foresight, Bell Pottinger's sister firm at the time, Corporate Citizenship, which counts Barclays and Vodafone among its longstanding clients, had already spelled out in a report on tax and corporate responsibility what companies needed to do to tackle this so-called information void. Corporations needed a new approach to communicating tax, it said. They had to identify a coherent and credible position on tax. And they had to defend their position using 'simple language'. Crucially, the report added: 'For most companies, this does not, in essence, involve paying more tax.'[77] This of course is the central motivation of citizen activism on tax avoidance. Getting corporations to pay more tax. Here is that product problem again.

Corporate producers, whether of baby milk, oil, cigarettes or tax avoidance, have all been faced with opponents that attack their core profit-making business – their product. And they have developed many techniques over decades to try and protect their reputations from criticism and NGO and activist attacks. What has changed very little throughout is their behaviour.

★

One of the problems facing the tax avoidance industry, the reason why its lobbyists do not think it is funny any more, is that the radicals are just not that radical. Sticking to the rulebook and trying to position 'the antis as extremists'[78] will not wash when it is the ordinary British public that they face. They are not 'the usual anarchists who've not worked for 20 years', said Cayman Island lobbyist Jack Irvine. The tax avoidance community needed to be extremely concerned, he warned. These were taxpaying voters. It did not help, he said, that even the normally reliable *Telegraph*, where Irvine's son is an executive, had joined the debate.[79] He is not alone in coming to this conclusion. Mark Field, Conservative MP for the City, echoed Irvine's point on the influential ConservativeHome website when he said that it was not just the usual suspects on the 'anarchistic left of politics, but increasingly a lot of middle class, Tory-voting people who feel that the rules of capitalism have become skewed against them'.[80]

This is a more pressing threat to business: that large numbers of ordinary people will lose faith in a system that serves corporations well at the expense of everyone else. It is a similar threat to that faced by business leaders a hundred years ago when the Economic League was minded to launch its Crusade for Capitalism, 'as the finest system that human ingenuity can devise'; and half a decade later when businesses on both sides of the Atlantic worried that it was not dealing with 'attacks from a relatively few extremists', but criticism from 'perfectly respectable elements of society'. As the *Financial Times* noted in 2012: 'The problem of consent in relation to capitalism is nothing new. In fact, it returns with nagging frequency.'[81]

Not only are people today still to be fully convinced, but conditions since the crisis of 2007 have led to more of the public becoming disgruntled. Many see a twin track: a fast lane for overpaid executives and the bankers who cocked things up, who through political donations and lobbying have bought themselves protection from accountability; and a stalled one with low levels of full employment, low pay, falling standards of living and fewer opportunities for everyone else. The system's failure to distribute wealth has become intolerable, again.

One of the conditions that has changed today is that people are able to connect with others in ways that were not possible before through the web and social media. This can provide a kind of optimism and feeling of agency. There are more opportunities to voice discontent. 'Ordinary people are taking the lead in defining how businesses are seen by the outside world,' says one lobbyist.[82] This is overstating the case, but it is true to say that the public has more potential now to affect the reputation of businesses and shape public conversations outside the mainstream. Which, with a depressing inevitability, has led not so much to corporate behaviour change, but to more work for lobbyists.

When James Frayne, at the time a lobbyist with Portland, revealed in 2009 that some of its clients' reputations were taking a 'near-daily hammering' in the press, his reaction was not to reflect on why, but to fight back. This is his job as he sees it. 'There are still too [many] occasions where third party organisations feel completely free to go after businesses and get coverage for themselves because they know they can't get hurt,' he said. Lobbyists needed to be more aggressive and counter-attack, he said.[83]

The threat today is coming not just from NGOs, though, but from ordinary people. Lobbyists describe today's world as a Digital Democracy.[84] They talk of a new era in politics, where decisions are no longer made by having lunch with an MP or taking a journalist out. 'Now almost everyone in the country has become a self-appointed campaigner,' says James Bethell, a lobbyist with Westbourne Communications. 'Everybody's seen the West Wing and has a Google account, and therefore has both the intelligence and the strategy, plus the technology, to put together a kitchen table campaign.'

This is the world in which commercial lobbying agency, Westbourne Communications, found itself when charged with defending the government's plans for the £43bn (and rising) proposed high-speed rail line linking London to Birmingham. HS2's opponents, armed with laptops (and lobbyists), are certainly not from the anarchistic left of politics. The proposed route cuts straight through Tory-voting counties, areas of outstanding natural beauty and ancient woodlands, and its construction would involve the demolition of listed buildings.[85] The chorus of criticism is coming from societies' 'respectable' element. Westbourne was put in charge of defeating these HS2 antis.

Westbourne's lobbyists have close ties to the top of the Tory party. It was set up by Stephen Shakespeare, founder of the polling firm YouGov and ConservativeHome, and James Bethell, or the 5th Baron Bethell,[86] a well-known Tory operator, ex-Portland lobbyist and former *Sunday Times* writer[87] who helped David Cameron's rise to the top of the Party.[88] It was also home to James Frayne, the master astroturfer and author of *Meet the People*, which promises to show businesses how to win back public support using the tactics of politicians.[89] In Chapter 3 we examined Westbourne's reframing of the HS2 debate away from the convenience of business commuters and onto its economic benefits to Northern counties. Its aim was to pit a privileged and out-of-touch elite, which in the case of HS2 was 'posh people' opposed to the new line,[90] against the needs of ordinary people, which was 'working class people getting jobs'. A pro-HS2 advertising campaign ran with the simple message: their lawns or our jobs.

Westbourne's campaign went beyond positively seeding the media with these messages though. It also involved attacking HS2's critics. Bethell referred to the campaigning efforts of these 'self-appointed' people trying to protect their homes from the noise of a 200 km/h train in their back garden as 'insurgency tactics', echoing Pagan's military talk of guerrilla warfare.

It was Westbourne's job to keep the insurgents at bay. 'You've got to fight them on every street corner,' Bethell said. 'You've got to win the ground and then hold it. You can't just sit in your fortress and then watch your opponents run around doing what they like. You've got to get out into the bush, using their tactics and being in their face.' The 'bush' in the case of HS2 presumably means Warwickshire.

One of the tactics used by Westbourne was to challenge the opposition's claims. It is of course entirely valid for lobbyists to want to rebut things that are said about the client that are wrong. However,

Westbourne's approach went further than merely correcting misinformation. It talked of 'zeroing in' on journalists who wrote 'inconsistent' articles (inconsistent, one assumes, with Westbourne's positive messages on HS2).[91] Bethell explained how it attempted to 'create a feeling among opponents that everything they say will be subject to scrutiny'. To create that mentality inside the opposition was exhausting but crucial, he said.

The strategy to silence critics appears to have gone further. Bethell explained the need to 'pick off' opponents with 'sniper-scope accuracy'.[92] One person whose detailed critical reporting on HS2 was suddenly and inexplicably cut short was the journalist Robin Stummer, although there is no evidence of Westbourne's involvement. Stummer was the founder of a specialist heritage magazine, Cornerstone, which began reporting on the families and houses at risk from the new rail line. It had started to photograph them.[93] What Stummer was managing to show were the consequences to the lives of ordinary people whose houses were at risk. Many were not in the least bit posh.[94] Soon after Stummer's anti-HS2 coverage began, the subscription-only magazine was bombarded with pro-HS2 letters. Then without reason in 2012 both Stummer and the magazine were dropped by their publisher. Stummer has since taken the magazine's owners to an employment tribunal. But he was himself then issued with what can only be described as a bizarre writ by his former employers. He returned home to find a bailiff on his doorstep who handed him the legal document that sought to prevent him from publishing online any content from previous editions of Cornerstone.[95] Then in September 2013, Stummer's former publisher suddenly dropped its legal case against him after he had spent £20,000 on legal costs. Stummer is now pursuing a contested case of wrongful dismissal and trying to recuperate some of his legal expenses.[96]

Bethell elucidated further on Westbourne's approach to tackling opponents at an HS2 event in front of a distinguished audience that included the chair of HS2, the deputy mayor of London for transport and the Tory grandee Lord Heseltine. Their tactic for diffusing the very vocal, local opposition along the proposed line was simply: 'shit them up'.[97]

When asked later to elaborate on what he meant by the words 'shit them up', Bethell replied that he 'literally' could not remember, adding that those three words could mean anything depending on the context.[98] Westbourne denied that the purpose of the campaign was in any way to intimidate or bully opponents of HS2. Then, with sudden clarity, Bethell explained that it referred to the consequences of the campaign, not its aim. Westbourne's lobbying had 'shit them up', a comment which he later regretted.[99]

An academic who had heard Bethell's presentation, however, recalled the cold, militaristic and calculated approach of the lobbyists. They came away thinking that Bethell's comments and attitude have real implications for democratic debate in Britain, particularly, they said, the element about 'scaring the living daylights out of people'.[100]

★

Intimidation campaigns are not common in lobbying, but there are cases when they have been used to try and silence critics. Individuals are targeted when they pose a threat. That is, when their voices are carrying in the media, grabbing the interest of the public, and having an impact on politicians. When what they are saying presents a threat to corporate profit-making, they may well be 'picked off'.

The moment that the food giant Dole chose to pick off the Swedish filmmaker Fredrik Gertten was when his movie *Bananas!* got into the Los Angeles Film Festival. Gertten's film was about a dozen workers from Nicaragua who had brought a lawsuit against the Dole Food Company, the largest producer of fruits and vegetables in the world, which, they claimed, used a pesticide that led banana workers to become sterile. Following the trailer's release, Dole attempted to block the film from being shown. It threatened Gertten with legal action. It then unleashed its lobbyists and PRs on the filmmaker, who did what he does best and captured it all on film. The follow-up, *Big Boys Gone Bananas!,* records the corporate bullying, scare tactics and aggressive PR campaign to shut the story down. Dole ultimately lost and we can now see both films, but at a cost to Gertten personally, as the film documents. As Dole's PR company put it, quoting Nietzsche: 'It is easier to cope with a bad conscience than a bad reputation.'[101]

Lobbyists for the private health insurance industry talked of pushing another filmmaker, Michael Moore, 'off the cliff', not literally of course, but as part of an aggressive campaign to discredit

Moore and his movie *Sicko* that damned the US healthcare system. A former insurance insider described how the lobbying firm APCO was hired to help defend the industry, in part by positioning the health insurers as the solution rather than a central problem in America's broken healthcare system. What they sought to avoid, at all costs, was for the film to reach out to ordinary people. Moore was to be portrayed as a divisive figure, loved on the left but by few others. They wanted people to see Moore as the man seeking to destroy the US's free market healthcare system and with it the American way of life. No politician was to feel comfortable talking positively about the film.[102]

Negative lobbying campaigns have similarly been launched to discredit books that seek to bring issues to the public's attention. *Diet for a Poisoned Planet* by the science writer David Steinman, which provides advice on what the author considers 'safe' to eat, contained information that the food industry objected to, such as high levels of pesticides in raisins, which offended the Californian raisin industry.[103] The lobbyists Ketchum sought to get hold of the author's promotion schedule and arrange for an industry spokesperson to follow and counteract his statements. They succeeded in getting some appearances cancelled.[104] Campaigns of this ilk can be deeply unpleasant for those on the receiving end, whether campaigning journalists or activists. They also pose an obvious threat to free speech, where the might of a multinational and its lobbyists gets to determine what we can and cannot know. But they are nothing compared to the onslaught faced by scientists whose findings threaten corporate profits.

It is apparent now that climate scientists around the world are being subjected to a vicious and hate-filled global campaign of intimidation.[105] Although there is no evidence that the threats are being orchestrated by the oil industry, think tanks funded by oil companies have participated.[106] Seasoned oil industry watchers argue that while it is difficult to connect any single email to an organised campaign, often the attack starts with paid campaigners and lobbyists.[107]

Just weeks before a major UN climate change summit in Copenhagen in 2009, thousands of emails were hacked from the University of East Anglia's Climatic Research Unit. They included correspondence between university staff, principally the Unit's head, Professor Phil Jones and many of the world's leading climate scientists, including

Michael Mann, famous for the 'hockey stick' graph. This shows temperatures holding fairly steady until the last part of the twentieth century and then suddenly shooting up.

The emails created a scandal: Climategate. They revealed what one inquiry into the affair referred to as serious shortcomings in the openness with which they worked, showing the scientists reluctant to share raw data with climate sceptics and their attempts to block legitimate Freedom of Information requests. What they did not show, however, was evidence that climate change was not happening.

In the wake of the scandal, many leading climate scientists were vilified, verbally attacked, intimidated and threatened, probably none so more than Jones. One prominent US sceptic, Marc Morano, argued that climate researchers like Jones 'deserve to be publicly flogged'.[108] Journalists joined in, the Daily Telegraph's James Delingpole calling Jones clueless and someone 'unfit to run a bath'.[109]

But it was the personal emails Jones received which delivered the truly vile attacks. Again, while they are not evidence of a coordinated effort, there was a pattern to them. 'You are a fucking scumbag, a liar and a fraud,' reads one email. 'I hope someone puts a bullet between your eyes.' Another reads: 'Fuck you for your lies and deceit. You deserve to die. And if you don't take your own life, then I fucking hope someone does it for you.' Another: 'Watch your back mother fucker. I'm on my way . . . DIEEEEEEEEEEE!!!!!!!!!!!!!!!!!!!'[110]

You get the picture. The aftermath of the leak has been described as a living nightmare by Jones, who did contemplate suicide. In its aftermath, he lost a stone in weight and had to take beta-blockers and sleeping pills.[111] Over in the US, Michael Mann was also targeted with the same level of venomous bile: 'You and your colleagues who have promoted the scandal ought to be shot, quartered and fed to the pigs along with your whole damn families,' read one email he received. Another hoped he too would commit suicide.[112] These were not isolated attacks. A leading climate scientist, Kevin Trenberth, received a nine-page document full of 'extremely foul, nasty, abusive emails'.[113] Tom Wigley, a previous director of Jones' Climatic Research Unit, now working in the US, was said to be horrified by the emails he and other colleagues received. 'They are truly stomach-turning and show what sort of venomous monsters we are up against.'[114] The evidence pointed to a concerted campaign. Mann has likened the tactic to lions on the plains of the Serengeti, where climate change deniers isolate individual scientists, and where vulnerable individuals are 'picked off from the rest of the herd'.[115]

The vilification campaign against climate scientists reached new levels after Climategate, but it was only the continuation of an often vicious and personal campaign against scientists by the denial movement over the last twenty years. The godfather of climate science is universally acknowledged to be NASA's Jim Hansen. He warned Congress a quarter of a century ago that it was time to stop waffling 'as the evidence is pretty strong that the anthropogenic greenhouse effect is here and affecting our climate now'.[116]

Hansen is no radical. He is a Republican and a life-long scientist. But, like others, he has been smeared, being called, among other things, a 'wannabe Unabomber'.[117] He has also been threatened, including having his car broken into and his house in New Jersey burned to the ground. A whole book about the Bush Administration's attempts to silence Hansen has been written, *Censoring Science*. The goal can be summed up in the words of one Bush official: 'Make him go away. Make him be quiet. Make Jim Hansen be quiet. I want you to tell him to cease and desist.'[118]

'They try and bombard you with these vexatious attacks that prevent you doing what you want to be doing with your time,' says Mann. 'Presumably they are trying to make you an example to stop other scientists speaking out.'

In Australia as well, leading climate scientists have received threatening and abusive emails.[119] So much so that in 2011 Canberra's Australian National University moved a number of its scientists into more secure accommodation after receiving emails including death threats and threats of sexual assault against their children.[120] Other researchers have had cars smeared with excrement.[121] Often these cases are sparked by media appearances, says one of Australia's leading climate scientists, David Koroly. He believes that the threats are intended to discourage scientists from speaking out on the radio and TV and presenting their evidence in public.[122]

After all that he and his family have been through, it is not the personal attacks that have got to Mann. The thing that upsets him the most, he says, 'is the larger agenda that they represent', which he describes as 'truly evil and villainous'. Pointing the finger at the fossil fuel industry, its front groups, and conservative benefactors working for them, he accuses them of poisoning public debate over 'what is perhaps the single greatest threat that we have ever collectively faced'. It is a cynical, evil campaign he says. And then pauses before calling it a crime against humanity. Mann talks passionately about what kind of world will be left for his seven-year-old daughter and her children and grandchildren.[123]

Where the oil industry goes, tobacco goes. Public health scientists have been subjected to hate campaigns similar to those faced by their climate change colleagues. Over sixty years after the first research was published linking smoking and cancer, the tobacco industry and its allies have chosen as a key tactic to smear and frighten the opposition.

Simon Chapman is a public health professor at the University of Sydney, with over 400 peer-reviewed articles and seventeen books to his name. According to tobacco lobbyists, he is 'the Worst Public Health Person in the World', who is 'responsible for the most pointless deaths of his countrymen since the guy who ordered the army to Gallipoli'. Chapman's crime is to have advised the Australian government to ban smokeless tobacco (chewing tobacco and snuff) in Australia. For this he has been targeted by the 'sewer of frothing, often anonymous, swill' that Chapman calls elements of the blogosphere. He likens the comments to today's equivalent of the threatening call from a phone box.

However, Chapman says that nothing could have prepared him for the vitriol of the UK blogger Chris Snowdon, who started the name-calling. Snowdon has described Chapman as 'simple Simon', a 'scrotum-faced head-banger' who 'has an unfortunate habit of listening to the voices in his head'.[124]

A prominent supporter of Forest, the pro-smoking lobby group, Snowdon was a speaker at Forest's 2012 Conservative Party Conference fringe event. He has also branched out to defending alcohol, tobacco, gambling, sugar, fast foods and soft drinks industries, as head of the 'lifestyle economics unit at the Institute of Economic Affairs', the oldest of Britain's free market think tanks.[125] Housed in a smart Georgian townhouse not two minutes from Parliament, the Institute is a picture of respectability.

'Gobshite', 'deranged' and a 'clueless clown' is how Snowdon has described Stan Glantz, the renowned US public health professor who has probably done more than anyone to expose the tobacco industry's deceit and deception.[126] Here in the UK Linda Bauld, another public health professor and a leading expert on smoking, who has served as the UK government's scientific adviser on tobacco control since 2007[127] is, according to Snowdon, a fantasist who promotes voodoo science.[128]

Unrelated to the attacks on her professional reputation from Snowdon, in 2010 Bauld started receiving anonymous phone calls, in the evening when she was at home with her children. 'It's an unpleasant experience,' she says. 'They don't leave their name, they just say things like "Keep taking the money" and "Who are you to try to intervene in other people's lives", using a couple of profanities.'[129]

Two days after Bauld spoke publicly of the calls, she received a letter from a pro-smoking blogger, Frank Davis:[130] he wrote that the nasty emails and phone calls she had been receiving were not going to stop. 'They're going to become more and more frequent,' the email read. 'You should start worrying when bricks start getting thrown through your window, or messages daubed on your door. They won't be planned or organised either.' Better still, Davis wrote would be to 'leave the country', because 'that way, you'll be out of the country and maybe even living under a new name when your old university department gets torched, and your old colleagues are strung up from lamp posts. Think of it as a kind of voodoo warning.'[131]

Bauld called the police, but they took no action. This contrasts with the quite proper arrest of a seventeen-year-old for threatening the Olympic diving star Tom Daley in a tweet.[132] Writing on his blog, Forest's Simon Clark linked to Davis' letter online calling it 'stunning'.[133] When asked what he meant by this, Clark said that maybe instead of calling the letter 'stunning', he should have described it as 'powerful'.[134] Other people might have called it a death threat.

Clark was never going to condemn the letter. Although Clark says he would never condone threats of any kind, in line with countless lobbyists across many industries, his job is to portray tobacco's opponents – the antis – as extremists. Public heath scientists on his blog are dismissed as fanatics, Taliban, zealots and fascists.[135] What Clark and others are trying to do is discredit and marginalise scientists and anti-smoking activists.

Most lobbyists will be horrified by intimidation campaigns like these. They may also be outraged that we have included them in a book on the influence industry. But, while these may be extreme cases, the activity of silencing critics is more common in the business than many like to admit.

There is a sliding scale of tactics to neutralise the threat from opponents. Most lobbyists will simply monitor their activities, ensuring that they are forewarned and therefore forearmed. Many will actively take critics on, attacking their arguments through the media and in government. Only some have the capacity to successfully split the opposition with divide-and-rule tactics and busy their critics with continuous dialogue. Few will spy on and infiltrate opposition groups to gain the upper hand. Fewer still will launch a coordinated intimidation campaign against those that threaten their commercial interests. But collectively this underbelly of the influence industry has a significant impact not just on those who try to challenge corporate dominance, but the information we are exposed to and what our politicians hear, how we perceive those seeking change and our sympathy for their causes. When lobbyists are successful in their fight against opponents, the chances of things changing diminishes.

7

Rig: Silencing the Public

'Businesses have to be able to predict risk and gain intelligence on potential problems. The army used to call it reconnaissance; we call it consultation.'
    Bernard Hughes, former Tesco lobbyist[1]

The offices of the 3 Monkeys PR firm sit at the northern, Crossrail end of Charing Cross Road on the edge of Soho. Its Chief Monkey, as she is known, is Angie Moxham, who according to the firm's website, with its rainforest wallpaper, maintains a middle-aged rock 'n' roll lifestyle helped by her partner, keyboard player for the eighties band Marillion.[2] The couple own a seven-bedroom Gothic rectory and an eight-bedroom French chateau. This was paid for with the money from PR – that is public relations rather than prog rock.[3]

3 Monkeys has gone from being a one-woman band 'based in an attic' to a lucrative business of sixty staff by selling PR services. This includes something called 'community consultation', a process initiated by developers and others to seek out the views of people affected by their plans. Consultation is billed as a way of giving communities a voice and an opportunity to influence developments. Supermarkets, power companies, airport operators, housing developers and waste companies are all keen advocates of community consultation. Central government has also made it a requirement for any infrastructure project or development over a certain size to consult with the public before proceeding with plans.[4]

Finding out what residents think about what gets built in their neighbourhood sounds like progress; communities participating in local decision-making; power being devolved down to ordinary people. By making community consultation compulsory, the government appears to be saying that it wants us to lobby and have influence over the decisions made about the places where we live. They are giving us a say, encouraging discussion, levelling the field with commercial lobbyists and bringing public voices into decision-making. It feels democratic. It turns out it is anything but.

Stripped bare, community consultation as seen through the eyes of developers and their lobbyists is a means of heading off local hostility and opposition from residents that might jeopardise planning consent for projects. It is a public relations exercise to secure planning permission. The job of the lobbyist is therefore to defend rather than consult. The process of finding out what local people think is a way of managing communities rather than empowering them.

Lobbyists not only dominate in national government. They are embedded in local government too, influencing the decisions made at that level. They have an insider's knowledge of the players and policies of local councils. But more than this, the process through which the views of local people are sought, the community consultation, has also been outsourced to lobbyists. Agencies like 3 Monkeys are part of a substantial niche in the influence industry that are employed by large corporations to secure local consent.

To Moxham and others in this business, the key to winning communities round lies in communications. What is needed is good PR. A lack of 'considered communications strategies', for example, lay at the heart of the government's failure to win people round to the HS2 rail line, according to 3 Monkeys. Moxham blamed the holes in the government's consultation strategy, which smacked 'somewhat of a sham', for alienating and aggravating local opposition, rather than the controversial project itself.[5]

Moxham's firm has faced similar opposition. In 2009 her troop of monkeys were drafted in to help sell a 275,000 tonne incinerator to residents in a corner of south-west Devon.[6] The waste firm Viridor, the sister company of South West Water, proposed putting it in a disused quarry just south of Ivybridge on the edge of Dartmoor. If built, the incinerator would have destroyed nearby ancient woodland, complete with nine different types of bat and threatened the river Yealm, which leads to a protected estuary and a site of special scientific interest that has supported a productive oysterage since Norman times.[7] The area is also home to one of England's more environmentally conscious communities.

3 Monkeys was hired to consult and 'engage' with the locals. It set to work in Devon, organising a meeting between Viridor and residents in the basement of a local pub, the Westward Inn. Viridor announced that it was 'committed to open and honest communication'. It would, it said, take the views of the community into account in proceeding.[8] The assembled residents were told that the company was keen to start a dialogue with the community.

This is what actually happened: Viridor was asked if it would drop its plans should the overwhelming majority of the local population say no to the incinerator. The waste company said it would press ahead anyway. There was no plan B, it admitted.[9] For all the talk of consultation and dialogue, if the community said no to the incinerator their views would simply be ignored. The consultation was an exercise in ticking boxes, allowing Viridor to claim in its public literature that the views of residents had been considered.[10] Considered and then effectively ignored.

This is typical of the consultation business, which has sucked in big-name lobbying agencies and many smaller, regional PR firms alike. Consultation is not an honest two-way conversation between developer and those affected by its plans; it is a one-way ticket for the developer to achieve what it wants. Lobbyists in the business are explicit about their role. It is, in the words of one, to 'enhance the likelihood of a favourable outcome in the planning committee'.[11] Another firm boasts that 'gaining planning committee approval is our business' and that community consultation 'helps our clients achieve planning consent'.[12]

The involvement of lobbyists in local democracy and the boom in lobbyist-directed consultation can be traced back to the point when local planning committees got political. Councils began to see a rise in the number of people leading campaigns against developments 'from their conservatories', as one lobbyist disparagingly put it.[13]

Helped by the internet, email and social networking, it has become easier for residents to organise against developments. Whether driven by threats to their well-being, their environment or indeed the value of their property, people have realised they can be heard by local politicians. Elected councillors were suddenly being forced to listen to the concerns of local residents faced with the prospect of a new runway, huge supermarket, high-speed rail link or dirty incinerator on their doorstep.

As a consequence, more and more planning committees started overturning the recommendations of their planning officers. Elected representatives began putting at risk projects worth tens of millions of pounds.[14]

Into the breach stepped the planning lobbyists, to work their magic on local politicians, dignitaries and communities to head off any threats. Community consultation, which can involve anything from running focus groups, exhibitions, planning exercises and public meetings, became one of the tricks of the trade to achieve this aim.

The techniques of community engagement were learned from the experience of Shell and others throughout the nineties, when, as we show in the previous chapter, consultation and dialogue were key to dealing with local opposition overseas and organised activists at home.

One man who helped develop these techniques is Tom Curtin, one-time head of corporate communications for Nirex, the nuclear waste body.[15] Curtin also wrote the book on it, *Managing Green Issues*. This spells out how companies can successfully push through controversial developments. The revised edition has new chapters on the benefits of community consultation.[16]

Curtin, who with his slicked-back grey hair provides the link between selling cars and flogging the UK's nuclear waste problem, describes how companies have moved from an old-fashioned DAD approach to communications – Decide, Announce and Defend – to the more progressive CHARM approach. This stands for Consult, Harmonise, Adjust, Reinforce and Maintain. 'The word adjust is important here,' writes Curtin. 'It is not change. This is an adjustment to an already existing project; change is where we start all over again.'[17]

And there is the rub and the source of so much anger among communities. Many people want more than a hearing, which at best is all consultation promises, and an ability to tweak projects. They want democratic control of the spaces in which they live. Consultation, driven by lobbyists and their clients' commercial aims, is a tool that serves to draw out community opposition and provide it with a managed channel through which to voice concerns, but with no hope of changing the outcome. The lobbyist Bernard Hughes explained: 'Businesses have to be able to predict risk and gain intelligence on potential problems. The army used to call it reconnaissance; we call it consultation.'[18]

As one lobbyist who has worked for housebuilders, infrastructure clients and supermarkets told us, key to a successful public consultation is to make sure that there is something that the local community can affect. But it will never be a yes/no to the development itself.[19] The strategy is to throw residents a bone and give people the semblance of choice 'even if it is only the colour of the bricks'.[20]

*

It is no secret that people have largely turned off from formal politics. Voter turnout at local elections is down to about one third of the electorate.[21] Surveys show that all measures – propensity to vote, satisfaction with the system of governing, contacting an elected representative, even showing an interest in politics – are at their lowest levels since surveys of such things began.[22]

The reasons for this are complex, but being routinely ignored has got to come into it. If your views, even when invited, count not a jot towards the outcome it is simply not rational to carry on contributing. Go and do something else it says to anyone sensible.

The public consultation should have provided a remedy to this and supplied a genuine process for public participation. The opportunities to contribute views to both local and national government have certainly grown. The quality of the process, however, has not. Despite being sold on the premise that by allowing people to participate in the formulation of policy, public trust increases and better, more inclusive decisions result, consultation as currently practised does the opposite. It does little to broaden the range of voices heard. Instead it is used to legitimise decisions that have already been taken behind closed doors, a place where professional lobbyists still dominate. We can put forward our views for all we are worth. Too often they cannot be heard above the quiet word in the ear from insider lobbyists to whom genuine consultation is routine.

The arrival of New Labour in 1997 marked a massive growth in public consultations both by national government and over local developments. Many were used by Tony Blair to try and secure a mandate for unpopular policies. Which meant they had to be rigged.

When Blair launched a public consultation on nuclear power in late 2005, he should have won an Oscar. He called for a much-needed debate on the future of the controversial technology, promising that the government was going to listen to the public's views. The whole thing was a charade. The decision on nuclear power was secretly taken two months before at a meeting at Chequers.[23]

The chair of Parliament's Trade and Industry Committee dubbed the consultation a rubberstamping exercise.[24] The High Court was equally unimpressed when it was dragged in to examine the process, calling the consultation seriously flawed, unfair and unlawful. Insufficient information had been made available for participants to make an intelligent response, it said.[25] The judge argued that something had 'gone clearly and radically wrong'.[26]

The government had a second stab at it two years later, launching a new consultation on the future of nuclear power.[27] It set up a consultation website encouraging people to take part, again promising that their views would contribute to the shaping of the policy on the future of nuclear power in the UK. Powerpoint presentations by officials assured participants that the government was there to listen.[28]

This consultation was also a farce. The new Prime Minister, Gordon Brown, let the cat out of the bag when he told MPs that the government had made the decision to continue with nuclear power halfway through the consultation.[29]

An academic study of this second consultation concluded that the government sought to deliberately skew the results by linking nuclear power to fears about climate change and burying the fact that it can only make a small contribution to reducing the UK's CO_2 emissions. One of those academics, Paul Dorfman, concluded that the exercise was designed to come up with a popular mandate to proceed with nuclear power by giving the public biased and incomplete information.[30]

The official trade body for the market research sector also found that the consultation was inaccurately or misleadingly presented. This, it said, posed a material risk of respondents being led towards a particular answer. That answer of course was to favour more nuclear power.

Undeterred, New Labour continued in the same vein with a 2007 consultation on the expansion of Heathrow which was so dreadful that campaigners took to wearing T-shirts at consultation events with the words 'This consultation is fixed: ask me how'. This time, however, the government was caught trying to rig the results with lobbyists inside the airport's operator, BAA, which was busy lobbying for the expansion.[31]

They too went for the hard sell on the benefits of expansion in the information given to participants. They wanted to push the pluses of Heathrow and aviation growth over its negative impacts on neighbouring residents and the environment.[32] BAA and the government agreed a common position over Heathrow's environmental impact. The government allowed BAA to supply the data for calculations on noise and pollution from expansion, data on which people were being asked to form an opinion. The BAA communications team also worked closely with the Department for Transport on the consultation's public exhibitions.

Both parties knew this level of intricate collusion was wrong. People involved were reminded of the need to be careful about circulating sensitive documents.[33] The government was also mindful of the need to be seen to be openly seeking public opinion. The Transport Secretary must deliver 'robust lines' over the consultation, said one official. They did not want it looking like the decision had already been taken to expand Heathrow.[34]

With a track record like this, it is hardly surprising that many people have become jaded about the purpose and integrity of consultations and the extent to which their views count. Regardless, governments have continued to roll them out. New Labour's approach to listening to the public appears to have rubbed off on the current Coalition government.

Take the recent consultation by the Coalition on the scrapping of subsidies for solar panels. It was deemed unlawful. The policy was enforced before the consultation had even ended. In another case, a consultation into the closure of paediatric cardiac services, a judge ruled that it was distorted to favour the saving of certain units over others.[35]

When the Health Secretary, Andrew Lansley, presented his planned changes to the NHS in 2010, he also consulted on them. Roughly 6,000 people and organisations sent him their thoughts, many of them outright hostile to the controversial proposals. The result, predictably, was that nothing much changed. The British Medical Association noted that the government did not seem to be listening. There was virtually no tangible response to the consultation at all.[36]

Lansley was not interested in compromising. The consultation was simply about explaining what the government had decided to do and how it was going to do it.[37] Perhaps, in hindsight, it was a decision that Lansley would regret.

Fast forward through a perfect storm of hostile headlines and street protests over the changes to the spring of 2011. The Prime Minister forced Lansley to pause his reforms. They needed to take the heat out of the issue, which was proving damaging to the Conservatives. The government finally said it would listen.[38] Announcing the consultation to Parliament, Lansley managed to utter that the government would 'pause, listen and engage' with people's concerns. He did not manage to say '. . . and amend' at the end, which was the official line.[39]

When announcing the expert-led consultation, David Cameron was adamant that the exercise was sincere. He told assembled NHS workers that it was a genuine chance to make a positive difference to the reforms. He promised that where there were good suggestions to improve the legislation, they would be made.[40] What was not apparent from the outset was the extent to which there was consultation with commercial lobbyists within the public consultation taking place at the same time.

Over the following eight weeks, the consultation's experts – dubbed the NHS Future Forum – travelled around the country meeting doctors, nurses, patients and communities. They heard opinions on a range of issues, including the increased role of private companies in providing healthcare, one of the most contentious aspects of the reforms. Over two hundred 'listening' events took place attended by over 6,700 people; 3,000 comments were posted online; over 25,000 individuals emailed their views. This was a 'staggering' response according to the Forum's chair, Steve Field, who one assumes never did a head count at any of the NHS anti-privatisation demonstrations.

Throughout this public consultation, however, private healthcare companies were colluding with those that were supposed to be listening. The consultation was mediated by professionals who were vulnerable to private lobbying. One expert member of the Forum, Stephen Bubb, was in charge of reporting back on the most contentious aspect of the reform: the increased role of the private sector in the NHS.

Bubb had an apparent conflict of interest. At the same time as listening, Bubb, as chair of the Association of Chief Executives of Voluntary Organisations, was leading the charge for more non-profit, but still private, healthcare organisations providing NHS services. In this role he was seen by many as a Trojan horse for more for-profit private sector involvement. On top of this, Bubb was also potentially in a conflict of interest because of his direct relationship with the for-profit lobby.

He was described as providing a 'route in' to the Forum by the head of a key private healthcare lobby group, David Worskett of the NHS Partners Network. Worskett describes how the two men had a very early, lengthy discussion at which they agreed on the approach Bubb would take on key issues and how to handle the politics of the consultation. Worskett would later write how Bubb had not deviated from this agreed line throughout the listening period.[41]

In the eyes of the private healthcare lobbyists, the public consultation presented 'considerable threats' to their ambitions in the NHS. If the results went the wrong way, Worskett argued, it would be disastrous for private health companies. 'Retrieving the position would be almost impossible,' he warned. Bubb and others were seen as vital to ensuring that the consultation proceeded in their favour.

Worskett left nothing to chance and expanded his lobbying beyond Bubb. According to a summary document of lobbying by the Network, Number 10 was also talking to the private sector lobbyists during the two-month pause. Worskett claims to have briefed Number 10's health policy adviser on the Network's line, and had several other 'stock-take' phone conversations with them. The Network's communication materials during this period were also 'cleared' with government.[42]

The health ministers, Earl Howe and Simon Burns, were also lobbied during the pause to consult the public, meeting Worskett and the Network's chair, Jill Watts, the head of the private hospital group Ramsey Health Care. Although the two ministers were 'constrained by the fact that everyone is supposed to be "listening"', wrote Worskett, they gave him 'every signal possible' that they understood and sympathised with the concerns of the private healthcare lobby. Under the circumstances, wrote the lobbyist, they could have not hoped for more from the two ministers.

The result of all this activity was that after the government's pause – to listen, engage and amend – nothing substantially changed. Greater private sector involvement in the NHS and competition between providers, remained central to the reforms. Despite opposition from the public and medical professionals to this move towards privatisation, the expert Forum's recommendations barely changed the Bill. What came out the other end, the amended legislation, was widely seen as a respray job. One commentator described it as 'a monster with lipstick'.[43] The thousands of people who participated in the consultation would have been justified in questioning why they bothered.

This is a snapshot of the chequered history of the public consult- ation at a national level. Politicians persist in this farce, all the while lamenting the declining public trust in government. 'Never has the reputation of politics sunk so low,' said David Cameron in a speech on Britain's broken politics. It was delivered just months before he became Prime Minister in the wake of yet another lobbying scandal. Britain's system, he said, concentrated too much power in the hands of an elite. He promised that he and his party – politicians relaxed about openness and trust – would be the ones to 'sort it out'. From now on he would trust local communities to know what is best for them.[44]

Yet the experience of local communities has been anything but empowering under this government. Despite Cameron's assurance to hand power to neighbourhoods to 'take control and ownership of community assets', ordinary people's wishes remain subordinate to powerful commercial interests. As we have seen nationally, lobbyists are similarly embedded in local government. They have an inside track to influencing councils. They are routinely consulted while the views of local residents are to be managed through official consultations.

Local decisions are also subject to national dictates, over which communities have no control. In these instances, local consultations can appear even more bogus. When government policy dictates a particular course, the opinions of residents count not one bit. Local developments built under the Private Finance Initiative provide one very good illustration of this.

The controversial Private Finance Initiative, or PFI, has been used

since the early nineties in Britain as a way of funding public infrastructure projects with private capital. Under PFI, instead of paying
upfront for, say, a hospital, the government agrees to pay the private
sector, often a consortium of banks and construction companies, an
annual fee to build and manage the hospital for a defined number of
years. The companies make a profit on the fee and the government
is relieved of the hassle. Part of the appeal of PFI to successive governments is that it is a neat way of keeping such public spending off the
government's books.

Many good hospitals have been built under PFI. Coventry built one
in 2002. The new hospital cost £410m,[45] but it will saddle taxpayers
with a staggering £3.3bn debt by the time it is finally paid for in 2041.[46]
It was the second most expensive PFI deal in NHS history.[47]

From 2011, if you are having a heart attack in the Warwickshire town
of Rugby you have got to go to neighbouring Coventry's A&E for
treatment. That is a thirty-minute ride away.[48] Rugby lost its Emergency
Department in a bid to cut costs and opened instead a lesser urgent-
care centre, which cannot handle heart attacks. Rugby's St Cross hospital
was not in the red though; neighbouring Coventry's PFI hospital was.
Even with the closure of services at Rugby,[49] the government was
warning that Coventry's hospital was on the list of those at risk from
the rising cost of their mortgage repayments under PFI.[50]

In 1998, the people of Coventry had been asked if they wanted a
new PFI-funded hospital. They said no, thanks. They had two hospitals, one in the city centre and one on the ring road. They preferred
that one of the hospitals be refurbished. This would have cost the
NHS around £30m. Coventry's residents thought this was a more
sensible idea. It was also the original plan of the local NHS Trust.

But suddenly the Trust changed its mind. It proposed that the two
hospitals should be closed and that a new hospital be built on the
out-of-town site. This seemed like a bad idea to the people of Coventry.
It was really difficult to get to the out-of-town hospital, especially
without a car. And surely it meant fewer beds for the people of
Coventry, at the same time as being a vastly more expensive way of
improving the city's hospitals?

A petition to save the city centre hospital gathered 120,000 signatures.
But they were overruled. But why build an expensive hospital in a
place that poorly served the city, and which the City Council and

people of Coventry clearly did not want? The answer lay in the PFI deal.

The reason why the local NHS managers chose the new PFI option over any other was because they had no choice. They were told by the government that there was no money for non-PFI schemes, like the £30m refurbishment costs of the city centre hospital. So they had to come up with a plan that was attractive to private finance, which ruled out the smaller, cheaper options that did not release any land. The scheme was tailored to fit the needs of private investors putting up the cash, not the needs of Coventry.[51]

When local officials consulted with Coventry's residents to allow them to express a view on the deal,[52] locals were denied the right to see the financial details of the PFI scheme. The amount of public money the contractors were to make was not open to scrutiny. They voted against it all the same. Some 82 per cent of residents came down in favour of retaining a city centre hospital. It did not matter. The PFI hospital was the only one the government was willing to approve and the only one that private finance would fund. 'When there is a limited amount of public-sector capital available, as there is,' the Labour Health Minister, Alan Milburn, at the time had said, 'it's PFI or bust.' PFI and bust, it now transpires.

Communities around the country are now fighting to save local health services threatened in part by mounting PFI costs. Take residents in north-west London who were faced with a massive shake-up of their local NHS and the prospect of closures, including almost half of their casualty departments.[53] Their hospitals, like Coventry's, were among the sixty or so identified as facing serious financial difficulties, which the current government blamed on hugely expensive PFI deals signed under the previous administration.[54]

Hundreds of thousands of pounds were spent on a public consultation exercise to find out what residents of north-west London thought about the changes. Adverts were placed in local newspapers and public meetings organised. Half a million leaflets were produced and distributed by community consultation lobbyists, The London Communications Agency.[55] A hundred thousand copies of an eighty-page consultation form were said to have been produced. Unsurprisingly given its complexity and length, this was filled in and returned by just 16,000 people.[56]

The consultation only told local people and health professionals part of the story. Uncomfortable details, like significant cuts to the numbers of beds in the area, were left out of the consultation, but were included in a technical and impenetrable 'pre-consultation' document. The effect was to reduce the ability of ordinary people to respond to the threat to their health services.[57] The exercise was a sales pitch to residents on what was widely seen as a done deal.

How did we get to this situation? One where local officials are forced to pursue a path that appears to so obviously contradict the public interest and goes against what its residents clearly want. Had people been genuinely consulted before decisions were made, might they have come up with suggestions that served the public interest far better? Would rational members of the public, given sight of the financials, pursue the government's favoured approach to building new hospitals under the extortionately expensive private finance deals that are now contributing to cuts in services? Given the choice, probably not.

Since PFI was pioneered by the UK in the nineties under John Major's Conservative government, business has dictated the terms through forceful lobbying. The Confederation of British Industry (CBI), Britain's main business lobby group, was at the forefront of the early campaign to make sure that PFI spread throughout government and that big business was in control of as much of the policy as possible.[58] PFI offered a huge opportunity to profit from the state. It was dubbed by one PFI advocate as the Heineken of privatisation: it was taking the private sector to the parts of the government machine not reached by previous privatisations.[59]

Twenty years later and with over 700 current PFI projects in the UK, the jury is in on PFI.[60] It has been widely damned as a way of raising money to pay for Britain's infrastructure. There has been no real transfer of risk to the private sector and the profits have been excessive.

The UK's spending watchdog, the National Audit Office, issued a stern warning to ministers in 2011. Government needed to slow down the number of deals and urgently find better ways to invest in infrastructure it said. PFI costs were increasing and the public sector's ability to pay was diminishing.[61] The Treasury was forced to respond after more damning reports, horror stories over project costs and worrying levels of public sector debt. It launched an investigation into PFI in late 2011.[62]

Chancellor George Osborne committed himself to a fundamental review of PFI. This would effectively mark the end of the initiative as we know it, according to the Treasury.[63] However, the very week that government was promising its demise, finance sector lobbyists with a clear interest in keeping PFI on track were planning its defence.

A meeting in November 2011 of TheCityUK lobby group referred to its 'work with HMG[overnment] and the response to the various campaigns against the UK model of PFI'. The meeting also included a discussion on working with government on the promotion of public–private partnerships.[64] Was this really the end of PFI, or was the review being used to rehabilitate the reputation of PFI in conjunction with the City? The answer was clear from the year-long inquiry into PFI. It was a makeover job with only minor changes made to the model. PFI had been given a new breath of life.

PFI has a history of delivering deals which are bad for taxpayers and good for business. To return to the corner of Britain in which we began this chapter, Devon, figures show the cost to the region of building new schools, hospitals and other projects under PFI will be nearly five times more than if they had been government funded: the capital costs of the new infrastructure being £530m; the total repayment cost £2.4bn.[65] Yet PFI is still being used to fund public infrastructure. Devon's new incinerator is one such project.

Viridor's incinerator in the quarry near Ivybridge was vying for a PFI contract with another proposal just down the coast in Plymouth. The contract was to burn the domestic waste from three councils across the region. Viridor eventually lost out to the German company MVV Umwelt, which meant residents near Plymouth's naval docks were faced with a 245,000 tonne a year incinerator quite literally on their doorstep.

Under the PFI deal, the company MVV would stump up some of the costs, which it would make back with a profit over the twenty-five-year lifetime of the project. The rest of the funds would come from government. It was in for £95m. This equates, with inflation, to a government subsidy of over £177m for the region's councils and MVV. The only provisos from government were that the contracts had to be signed by March 2011[66] and the public must be consulted. A necessary condition was that there had to be broad support for the project.[67]

The PFI deal was understandably seen as beneficial by both local officials and the waste company. The company made profits and, through PFI, the local councils received a welcome hand-out from government to deal with the increasingly expensive problem of what to do with their residents' rubbish [68]

The only problem was that there was no consensus. Locals were opposed to an incinerator parachuted into the middle of their community. However, by the time they were asked for their opinion, not up for discussion was whether the incinerator would go ahead, just how it would. In other words, they might get to change the colour of the bricks. The 'community consultation', conducted by MVV, did not occur until after the contract was signed. Its local liaison committee, run by lobbyists Green Issues Communiqué, held its preliminary meeting in March 2011, two months after the plans for an incinerator had been finalised and the same month that the government had given for its PFI deadline.[69] This was a done deal.

The primary driver for Plymouth's incinerator stemmed from the PFI funding, the same driver that led to Coventry's new hospital and many more projects around the country.[70] And in the same way that health officials in Coventry had initially plumped for a more suitable alternative, local officials in Devon had originally recommended small-scale, clean-tech alternatives to incineration as the way forward.[71] But if Devon's councils were to get the PFI credits, the only option on the table was a big incinerator. There was no other choice.

All that was left to do was placate the locals. MVV ploughed on with consulting Plymouth's residents after the Ministry of Defence came up with the idea of sighting the incinerator in an unused part of the city's dockyard. The incentive for the MoD was simple: they got a 20 per cent cut to their electricity and power bills from the energy produced by the incinerator. Meanwhile, the local community got next to nothing.[72]

The consultation process was run by Green Issues Communiqué, a local lobbying firm started by the ex-nuclear waste salesman Tom Curtin, the man who developed many of the techniques to win people round to controversial developments.[73] In this instance, Green Issues Communiqué was drafted in to help smooth over the small issue of a ninety-five-metre, polluting chimney being squeezed into the middle of a city. When built, it would be sixty-two metres from the nearest house in the district of Barne Barton. Usain Bolt can do that in just under seven seconds.

If you visit the area, it is clear that the local community acts as a natural amphitheatre surrounding the dockyard. The incinerator will face banks of housing which rise to the top of the local hill where there is both a primary and a secondary school. The height of this hill is exactly level with the top of the incinerator stack. Privately officials are worried about the days that the famed, local Tamar mist will hang around the city and the pollution has nowhere to go. Environmental experts believe the authorities could not have picked a worse place to site the incinerator if they had tried.

On a trip to Plymouth we visited the closest tower block overlooking the chimney's foundations. On the balcony of one local resident, we tried to work out where the top of the building would be. We realised it will block out a vast chunk of their view. Pity the lady who lives downstairs though. All she will see is the side of an incinerator. For her, it will be the building that stole the sky. Five thousand local residents petitioned against it.

Faced with this opposition, MVV and Green Issues Communiqué provided residents with an opportunity to voice their concerns. Leading the work was the lobbyist Harry Hudson who had also learnt from his experience alongside Curtin at Nirex.[74] The community was consulted, they objected and, not long after, MVV's planning application was waved through.[75]

Opponents of incineration are often depicted as Nimbys, or 'Not in My Back Yard'. But threaten a community with an incinerator and it's surprising who turns out: the community group cobbled together in Devon was made up of local green activists, but also teachers, academics, nurses, businessmen, traders, even an ex-Navy Rear Admiral. In short, the people who live there. But Nimbys they are not. Far from shirking their responsibility, and merely wanting it to be someone else's problem, many anti-incineration campaigners have sought to push for better alternatives.

Incineration is increasingly seen as yesterday's technology. Who in their right mind would burn thousands of tonnes of rubbish when it can be recycled or reused? There are also strong health concerns associated with it. Current evidence suggests that there is no safe limit for exposure to the small carcinogenic particulates of soot that will drift out of the top of the chimney in Barne Barton.[76] To add to this, there is also a strong possibility that the wave of new, publicly funded incinerators might have to be mothballed before they are even turned on because there will not be enough waste to fuel them.[77]

There are dozens of incinerators proposed in cities and rural spots across England.[78] And everywhere an incinerator is proposed, there are people opposed to it on environmental, health or economic grounds. But beyond the local press, these communities have received very little attention. Neither the problem – rubbish – nor the solution – recycling – is particularly sexy. Unlike, say, wind farms. When the then Planning Minister, Nick Boles, declared that wind turbines should be placed no closer than 1.4 miles from people's homes,[79] he was met with derision from people living just metres, not miles, from the incinerator in Plymouth.

After a year of opposing incineration, Devon's residents, including a group of engineers living in the area, came up with a detailed alternative. At a seminar attended by hundreds of local people, one of the engineers outlined how instead of just burning the lot to make energy, waste could be pre-sorted and recycled with the rest either gasified, or processed to produce a type of glass for construction. This would virtually eliminate the need for landfill, create twice as many jobs as the incinerator and conservatively save Devon an estimated £5m a year. 'This is an opportunity for Devon to take a lead,' they said.[80]

Crucially, though, such a proposal would not have needed PFI funding.[81] This is the point at which alarm bells should have rung. When residents met the official in charge of the PFI bid, Mark Turner, they were informed that their plans could not be considered because it might jeopardise the PFI funding. PFI, they were told, was 'free money'.[82] National incentives, in other words, were dictating local choices.

The people of Devon were not being allowed to make an informed decision though. The business case, detailing how much money MVV stood to make, as well as the financial costs and benefits to the council, were withheld from the public. Residents had no right to know. Just as the people opposed to Coventry's PFI hospital had no right to know the scheme's financial details. MVV's business case for the incinerator contained commercially confidential information. As a result, council officials refused to release it.[83]

Mark Turner's take on the locals and their alternative proposal is instructive. In one document released under Freedom of Information, he noted that because the population were from the very rural west of the West Country, they had 'limited daily exposure to many high-tech industrial processes and even less knowledge about waste treatment technologies'. People were concerned, he wrote, because they lacked the understanding of what an incinerator 'means in reality and what it would be actually like once such a facility is built and operating'.[84] Not only were they not allowed to scrutinise the project's finances, but they were written off as a bunch of know-nothing bumpkins.

So Plymouth's residents were consulted, but only after the decision had been made, a decision that was dictated by national PFI policy; they were denied the opportunity to properly scrutinise the deal and its value for money; and they were dismissed when they proposed alternative, cleaner technologies. In short, they had no say in the decision. The lobbyists' job was to paper over this truth.

This is a far cry from David Cameron's aspiration to trust and empower local communities. He and his minister in charge of local matters, Eric Pickles, even proposed to give us the tools to hold officials to account by opening up the government's books to provide the data on how taxpayers' money is spent. Pickles said he wanted to create an 'army of armchair auditors' around the country, to scrutinise government spending to ensure that it was used wisely.[85] But, as we have shown, any budding auditor attempting to hold local government to account will find the reality quite different.

Instead, residents are faced with developments in their neighbourhoods over which they have little or no control, particularly where PFI is involved. Opportunities to affect decisions are minimal. Worse, the process for doing so has been outsourced to lobbyists in the pay of developers seeking permission to build. Community consultation in this scenario is a tool among many used to rig local politics in their favour.

*

Winning local planning battles has long been a lucrative area for lobbying and PR companies. Today these communications firms are being joined by specialist planning companies that are establishing lobbying arms.[86] Estate agents and property consultants are also in the game.[87] As are law firms, even the multinational giants like DLA Piper. It claims an enviable track record in delivering planning permission, won in part by minimising and managing potential opposition.[88] Pity the local communities who have to face this law firm, one of the largest in the world, with earnings of nearly $2.5bn.[89]

Dundas & Wilson is another, albeit much smaller law firm that provides consultation and other services to developers seeking planning consent.[90] One recent client of theirs is the American developer Donald Trump. Dundas & Wilson was hired to help Trump secure his controversial plans to turn a stretch of wild Aberdeenshire coastline into 'the greatest golf resort in the world', as he put it.[91] The area is home to a unique dune ecosystem and a small number of people. Trump wanted the pristine land, he did not want the people. His lawyers worked to resolve the problem.

Trump's aim was to buy and demolish the homes near to his resort, but some residents were fiercely opposed to selling up. The film *You've Been Trumped* documents the alleged bullying, intimidation and harassment faced by these people to get them off the land. It shows residents' water and electricity being cut off and tonnes of earth piled up next to their houses.

Trump's people had raised the possibility of compulsory purchase orders with local Aberdeenshire Council to forcibly remove the residents. Trump's lawyers, Dundas & Wilson, had even drawn up a report justifying why compulsory purchase orders might be needed. It was drafted in the council official's name for distribution to council members, although the local authority said it was never used. It was written by Dundas & Wilson's head of planning, Ann Faulds, a former adviser to the Scottish government on the compulsory purchase of land for development.[92]

The council then discussed with Trump's lawyers the need to 'manage' the potential fallout in the media. 'Close liaison' between the two was needed to handle what was likely to be a 'difficult and emotive reaction' to the use of compulsory purchase.

What this case briefly illustrates are the advantages of having a former insider on the team. Faulds was ideally placed. Developers need someone with inside knowledge of how local decisions are taken and by whom. This need for insiders is as much a defining feature of the local lobbying industry as it is at a national government level. And as planning becomes more contentious and the stakes higher, so it seems lobbyists have become more desperate to have someone on the inside.

One lobbyist has been described as having 'the interesting habit of putting up candidates for community council elections'.[93] According to the lobbyist turned MP Thomas Docherty, early on in the planning process this lobbyist would find supporters and at the next election would try to get four or five people into key jobs, like planning secretary, to make sure clients receive favour.[94]

This practice is likely to be unusual. Much more common is the hiring of local councillors by lobbyists to secure an inside track and influence. Despite the obvious potential for a conflict of interest, councillors are not barred from offering themselves for hire to developers. They can reportedly earn fees of up to £20,000 for advice on how to get sites approved.[95]

One councillor working for a local lobbying firm, Indigo Public Affairs, was caught on film by the *Daily Telegraph* describing some of the 'tricks of the trade' for winning planning consent. These included ways to get a 'friendly face' substituted on to council committees. The Liberal Democrat councillor in Newcastle boasted that the company had 'a good chance that via our network someone will know someone who knows somebody' at every council. Indigo claimed the article 'completely misrepresented' its work and pointed to its code of conduct that bars staff who are also councillors from working on developments in their own local authority. Another councillor, unconnected to the firm, confirmed that, although he had to follow rules on planning, there were ways around the formalities, saying there was 'more than one way to skin a cat'.[96]

Indigo works on behalf of big-name house builders like Barratt and Taylor Wimpey. It boasts a planning approval success rate of over 90 per cent. Wins include permission for a fiercely opposed Tesco in a conservation area and a 100-home development on a historic site, for which Indigo drummed up a petition of support and had a ten-year-old boy present it to the council. Indigo says it achieves its success through consultation with local communities and their elected representatives.[97]

Lobbyist-councillors are a feature of councils around the country. Westminster Council in the heart of London contains upwards of ten councillors in the lobbying business and more with a financial interest in council work or developments in the borough. The minutes of Westminster's planning committee paint a picture of a tight-knit social world shared by lobbyists, developers and elected officials. There can be pages of declarations of interest before getting to the business of the committee, detailing their relationships, the hospitality and councillors withdrawing from ruling on a planning case because the applicant is a current client of the company for which they work.[98]

Hop across the Thames to the London borough of Southwark and a similar picture emerges. In 2012, just under 20 per cent of Southwark's sixty-three councillors were working as lobbyists.[99] Such a crossover of interests can have serious repercussions for local residents.

Southwark is a place of contradiction. Its riverside houses the Tate Modern and London Eye. At its southern tip is the affluent Dulwich Village. But in the middle lie some of the poorest areas in London, not least in Elephant and Castle, a place marked out by its now empty pink elephant shopping centre, lethal roundabout and Strata Tower, officially one of Britain's ugliest new buildings.

Elephant has long been earmarked for regeneration. From its centre, you can comfortably walk to the City, yet it has remained a relatively deprived area with a lot of social housing. This makes it prime development land. After several false starts, plans to reshape the area took off when the council, after years of negotiation, signed a deal with the Australian developer Lend Lease in 2010.[100] The deal centred around the sale by the council of a housing estate covering twenty-two acres of publicly owned land. The only problem was there were people living on it.[101]

The 1970s neo-brutalist Heygate estate of 1,100 homes once housed more than 3,000 people. Despite its foreboding concrete exterior, and with its hidden interior gardens, surveys showed that it was far from the hell hole that it has frequently been dubbed. It has suffered a campaign of abuse. Writing in the *Telegraph*, a second cousin of David Cameron, Harry Mount, dismissed it as 'crime-ridden and dilapidated' and an 'iconic image of hellish urban living'.[102] The Middle-England commentator Simon Heffer called it a 'sort of human dustbin', arguing if you give people sties to live in, they will live like pigs.[103]

This is not the view from the estate, which at one time housed teachers, taxi drivers, building workers, ambulance drivers, housing officers, health workers, admin assistants, office cleaners, shop workers, train and bus drivers, care assistants and youth workers. The people needed to keep London running in other words, but who increasingly find the capital impossible to afford. It was also home to a larger than average proportion of elderly people with a significant attachment to the place. This vulnerable population had an acute reluctance to relocate away from the place they called home.

Heygate's crime statistics were low.[104] It was in need of some refurbishment though, although it came way down Southwark Council's priority list, with each home needing little more than £20,000 spent on it over thirty years.[105] The best course of action, recommended by an independent study in 1998, was to demolish some of it and refurbish the rest.

The council, instead, decided to demolish the lot and bring in the developers. The plan was for managed but 'inclusive gentrification'. Local officials wanted to encourage an influx of middle-class people into the area. Existing tenants were to be rehoused in new properties nearby. But these plans fell apart as barely any of the promised new homes were built by the time the majority were evicted.

Today the Heygate lies entirely empty. The last leasehold resident to hold out against the council's plans to evict him was a teacher called Adrian Glasspool. He described how the community was broken up and all his neighbours were forced to move out of the area. Many who, like him, owned their homes were offered what they felt was inadequate compensation from the council. His neighbour and her family of five were living in a four-bedroomed property with her parents who were in their eighties. They were offered £190,000 for their home. 'Try buying a four-bed property in London for that,' he said. The move has also led to depression for some former residents forced to leave their family, friends and social networks.

For Adrian and many others from the area, the obvious driver behind the planned demolition and rebuild is the commercial value of this prime central London site. But throughout the process, the deal with Lend Lease remained obscure, with the council refusing to release the commercially sensitive financial details of the arrangement. The community was denied the right to scrutinise the deal and to know whether their council had sold them – and their homes – down the river.

Instead, they were treated to a community consultation that was summarised by one local resident as 'touchy-feely group hypnotism'. Leading the 'bottom-up and top-down' process for Lend Lease were community consultation specialists, Soundings.[106] It established a 'consultation hub' in an empty shop in the area. Inside, residents were invited to voice their dismay, frustration and concern at losing their homes with felt tips on Post-it notes in a mock play area.

One of the most pressing worries they had was the council's commitment to building replacement, affordable homes and social housing. Originally it had promised 1,000 new homes in the area with 70 per cent of these being social housing. Southwark's own policy sets a target of 35 per cent affordable homes on developments, bearing in mind that the minimum salary needed for an 'affordable rent' flat in Southwark is £47,000.[107] By the time of the consultation, this number had been reduced to 25 per cent affordable housing. No amount of Post-it notes was going to alter this.

Much, however, was made of the developers listening to community concerns about trees. The estate contained 406 mature trees in its green space. Making a tiny concession, typical of local consultations, Lend Lease removed some of its concrete and added a strip of green space, which was sold as London's biggest new public park. That it appears smaller than the Heygate's original green space, is neither here nor there. It was a concession to residents' demands.

Residents wrote a damning report on the consultation process, with its simplistic and reductive questionnaires and discussions that avoided difficult issues. The real purpose of it, they concluded, had been to get agreement on a limited and fixed set of choices. They could influence the size of the lawns.[108]

They also now feel that their homes – and public land – were sold off to Lend Lease at a knock-down price. Just days before a public inquiry opened into removing the last remaining leaseholders from the Heygate using compulsory purchase orders, the council accidentally revealed the details of its top-secret agreement with Lend Lease. It shows that the council sold the Heygate for almost what it spent on emptying the estate:[109] £50m in return for a twenty-two-acre site a mile from the City. A neighbouring 1.5 acre development site, critics point out, exchanged hands on the open market in 2011 for £40m.[110] As one commentator noted, the regeneration of the area will produce winners as well as losers.

Some of the council's officers have done well from the relationship with the developer though. Southwark Council's project manager for the Elephant & Castle regeneration project until 2011 left to work for Lend Lease. Previously, the council's communications manager for the project also quit to go and work for Lend Lease as its head of communications for the Elephant & Castle project.

Southwark Council has also spawned some of the local lobbying industry's leading lights. The former leader of Southwark, Jeremy Fraser, went on to join one of the biggest in the business, Four Communications, and its planning subsidiary, Four Local. He was later joined at Four by another Southwark councillor and the cabinet member for regeneration, Steve Lancashire.

Four Local, which has its HQ on Leicester Square,[111] helps secure planning consent for some of the country's largest developers. In total, ten of the firm's consultants are current or past councillors from across five London boroughs.[112] It also has its own 'strict' code of conduct that does not permit them to work in their own areas to avoid any conflict of interest.[113]

A current Southwark councillor and chair of its audit and governance committee, Mark Glover,[114] runs another agency in the field, Bellenden Communications. This counts many house builders and developers among its clients. Nick Stanton, another Southwark councillor and ex-leader of the council, now works for another lobbying firm, community consultation specialists Curtin & Co. This is the company that Tom Curtin, formerly of Nirex – the man who claims to have authored the 'definitive text on community relations'[115] – set up on leaving Green Issues. Alongside Curtin, the firm's staff include three current and former councillors and three former council leaders.

Developers who hire these and others with council connections are clearly advantaged when it comes to winning permission to build. Like their national counterparts, they have bought in the knowledge and contacts of insiders. But they are getting more than an inside track. These local planning lobbyists have also developed a range of techniques to win political support and deal with community opposition. The local media, for example, is a useful tool.

The precarious finances of many local newspapers in Britain means that lobbyists are often pushing at an open door. Journalist numbers have been slashed and those that remain fill pages as best they can, often with content fed to them by lobbyists. Likewise, few will find the resources necessary for investigations into local matters, including controversial developments. Deals are often left to be scrutinised by local citizen journalists.

Communities are targeted by lobbyists through their local rag. Take the media strategy crafted in 2008 by British Energy, the country's largest electricity producer, to head off any potential opposition from local residents to its new nuclear power developments. The firm was planning a number of 'community engagement programmes' around proposed new-build sites. The strategy was to position the nuclear firm and its partners as committed to open and honest communication with locals. It was at pains to avoid any sense that British Energy had 'something to hide'. It wanted to make sure that issues were addressed with the local press 'before – not after – they appear in print'. The last thing it needed was an anti-campaign in the local press.[116]

Local papers are also used to fight back against community opposition. In Aberdeenshire, the *Press and Journal* and its sister paper, the *Evening Express*, took an aggressively pro-Trump stance in covering the plans for the controversial golf course. Seven councillors who had refused Trump's application were pictured on the front page under the headline 'You Traitors'. The paper's editorial, headlined 'Betrayed by stupidity of seven', described the councillors as misfits, small-minded numpties, as well as buffoons in woolly jumpers who were traitors to the region.[117] While there is no evidence of lobbyists' influence on the coverage, the marriage in 2013 between *Press and Journal* editor, formerly of the *Evening Express*, and Trump's second-in-command in its Scottish operation, raised eyebrows.[118]

At the other end of the country, in Devon, a similar tactic was used against an elected mayor. In 2007 Sandra Semple became mayor of the seaside town of Seaton on a platform of opposition to a planned Tesco development. The local press ran what she felt amounted to a campaign against her stance. *This is Devon*, for instance, claimed she was trying to sabotage the town. At the same time it accepted a paid wraparound supplement from Tesco done in the news style of the paper.[119]

As well as attacking the town's mayor, letters started to appear in the local press in favour of Seaton's Tesco development and criticising objectors to it. A typical letter in the area's *Midweek Herald* was headlined: 'Why so much negativity in Seaton?' Anonymous comments praising the scheme also began to appear on anti-supermarket websites. Semple felt that there was a strong possibility that some of the supportive correspondence was faked.[120] Despite the majority of local people being opposed to the plans – and there already being fifteen Tescos within twenty-five miles of Seaton – the council approved the application and gave Tesco the go-ahead.[121]

Semple would not be the first supermarket opponent to spot activity of a pro-supermarket campaign. When a new Tesco was proposed in Leeds, the supermarket's representatives had 'as normal' been handing out pre-prepared letters to customers in favour of the new development, which they were asked to sign and send to the council. However, Tesco said it was appalled at the discovery that one resident had had his signature forged on a letter.[122]

Campaigners in the Norfolk seaside town of Sheringham did a bit of digging into what appeared to be a sudden groundswell of support for a new Tesco in their local *Eastern Daily Press*. In this instance, addresses were printed, which campaigners used to ask residents and postmen whether they knew the correspondents. No one did. Electoral and phone records also drew a blank, suggesting that the pro-Tesco letter writers did not actually exist. Tesco said it had nothing to do with the letters and there is no suggestion it knew of, approved or encouraged them.[123]

Tesco has also denied having a propaganda department. The supermarket simply engaged with local communities, it said. In 2013 Tesco retained six lobbying firms, four of them specialists in local lobbying, including Green Issues Communiqué. It is also known to have used Indigo Public Affairs, a firm that does not publish its clients.

The idea that support can be faked may not be so far-fetched. London's *Evening Standard* reported the case of another local lobbying firm that had been hired by a developer to help it win planning permission for a controversial housing project. The proposal had drawn hundreds of letters of objection. Then, suddenly, the council's planning committee started to get dozens of letters, apparently from local residents, praising the project and asking for it to be approved. The *Standard* suspected many of the letters were forgeries.[124] The lobbying firm vigorously refuted the accusation that they had faked them.

As well as fakery, lobbyists have also used subterfuge and

intimidation to help win planning cases. Using Parliamentary privilege, Thomas Docherty MP spelled out some of the more unseemly tactics of local lobbyists. He talked of one planning lobbyist who intimidated critics of their clients; of lobbyists pretending to be journalists to find out politicians' views towards developments; how lobbyists were planted in public meetings to distort discussions over developments in their clients' favour; and how they would try to undermine rival schemes by whipping up opposition to them in meetings.[125]

With multi-million-pound developments at stake, these tactics are unsurprising. But they are a worrying sign that local democracy is being perverted by commercial lobbyists. Tactics like sham community consultations, the hiring of council insiders and faked support suggest our local system of governance is being rigged. It is against this back-drop that decisions are being made about what gets built and where in Britain with all that this means for our towns and communities.

It does not have to be like this. But fundamental changes will be needed if people are going to meaningfully participate in decisions that affect where they live. First and most obviously, the process of consultation needs to be taken away from those with a vested interest in a particular outcome: the lobbyists and the commercial interests that hire them. The twin-track consultation, with lobbyists on the inside and the public outside must also cease.

Second, government must meet its rhetoric on trusting communi-ties with action. Ordinary people need to be listened to with as much attention as commercial lobbyists at a far earlier stage in discussions. Residents' proposals for solving an area's problems, whether housing needs or what to do with their waste, must be considered with as much seriousness as those from large, profit-driven corporations and their lobbyists. Just as locals in Devon came up with a cheaper, cleaner option for dealing with the region's waste, others too have come up with solutions that could be of greater public benefit. People who want to make a positive difference to where they live need to be treated as sensible adults.

We have barely begun to understand what genuine public involve-ment can do for public services, communities and citizens. David Cameron's Big Society project, which asked people to work hard but with little influence, was not it. Active citizens involved in campaigns to protect everything from Britain's forests to local services come closer to realising the potential. When the people who use public services help design them from the outset you get better, more efficient services and often with a more responsible attitude to the public coffers.

A recent experiment in the US brought together thousands of ordinary Americans to sit down and discuss the state of the country's finances and what to do about it. Liberals talked with conservatives, rich debated with poorer, experts with lay people, young with old. Despite the dominant media view of US society being fundamentally divided, discussions were constructive, people moderated their political views to reach consensus and common ground was found. For example, 85 per cent of participants across the nineteen city meetings came to an agreement that defence spending should be cut. Their collective views were sent to Washington. They called for politicians to treat citizen input 'as if it were coming from a powerful lobbying group'.[126]

For this to happen, the deep-seated fear of citizens in parts of government needs to radically change. Too often the public is seen as a baying mob, or just apathetic. The way that our views are solicited today through sham consultation exacerbates this, discouraging as it does any but the most determined and often angry people. Many more are just disillusioned and cynical. It is unlikely that a majority of us will be involved in helping to shape our local communities all of the time, but too many people are being put off by the current, disfunctional system.

But when we are discouraged from getting involved in decisions that affect us we leave a void. One that lobbyists have been quick to fill, leaving them to determine how our towns and communities are shaped.

8

Fight: Facing Down Threats

'Doubt is our product.'
  Brown and Williamson, subsidiary of British American
  Tobacco[1]

'At first nobody believed us,' recalled the epidemiologist Sir Richard Doll when his paper was first published on the link between smoking and cancer in 1950. 'They thought there may be other explanations.' At the time Britain had reason not to believe. The nation was addicted to nicotine. Eighty per cent of British men smoked.[2]

Doll, who would become one of the world's most famous epidemiologists due to his work on smoking and cancer, was a convivial old-style scientist with a liking for Liberty silk ties.[3] Along with Professor Bradford Hill, who was Doll's mentor and who is seen as the father of medical statistics, the two would change the debate on tobacco and disease for ever. They were investigating the alarming increase in lung cancer, which had become pronounced now the war had ended and for the first time was causing more deaths than tuberculosis. The two scientists could not have been more different: Doll was a young charismatic communist; Bradford Hill a quietly spoken conservative who would practise his lectures word-for-word on his dog.[4]

Thanks to Doll, Bradford Hill and the work of others in the US, we have known since the 1950s that smoking is a cause of lung cancer.

Despite this, over half a century later, nearly a quarter of Americans still think there is no solid evidence that smoking kills.[5] In 2010 around ten million adults in Britain still smoked.[6]

During the sixty-plus years since Doll's findings, the tobacco industry has used PR and lobbying to persuade people to continue to use its product, to get their fix, to stay hooked. To every new piece of evidence on the harm caused by smoking and the risks of second-hand smoke, to every proposed measure to protect public health, from the banning of advertising to the current plans for plain packaging or new tobacco laws from Brussels, the response from tobacco firms is always the same: deny the evidence, manufacture controversy, create doubts in people's minds and shift the blame elsewhere. Their goal? To delay any action by governments around the world to curb smoking.

Tobacco was the first, but denial campaigns to delay public health policies have been replicated in large part by other big industries facing similar threats, notably the food, alcohol and global oil companies. Learning from tobacco, they too have fought government controls on their product, using the same lobbying techniques and sometimes even the same lobbyists to defend their ground.[7] They too have set up front groups and paid scientists to undermine the science, while vilifying their critics and attacking their findings as 'junk science'. They too have pushed responsibility onto consumers, argued in favour of self-regulation and spun their ethical credentials via 'corporate responsibility' programmes. All are delaying tactics.[8]

All are a response by large corporate interests and their lobbyists to a threat. Politicians have the power to put in place measures designed to deter consumption of their products, whether it is a tax increase to challenge the increasing affordability of alcohol; restrictions on the marketing of sugary foods to children; or changes in subsidies to fossil fuel providers.

The tobacco industry is very slowly and haltingly losing its fight in Britain. The industry faces competition from burgeoning e-cigarette companies, who are marketing themselves as a safer alternative to cigarettes. The number of smokers is set to drop to below 20 per cent of the population – the first time the figure has been that low for 100 years.[9] The numbers are still significant but the market decline is clear. The same cannot be said for the alcohol, sugar and oil industries, which have all seen consumption grow. These others are all determined to avoid the trajectory of tobacco.

*

The story of the tobacco denial campaign starts in the early fifties. *Reader's Digest*, at the time the world's most widely read magazine, ran an article in 1953 called 'Cancer by the Carton'. It catapulted the issue of the harmful effects of smoking into the homes of ordinary people.

Up until that point the tobacco industry had made sure that the media ignored Doll and Bradford Hill's research, attacking the scientists and labelling their work 'unscientific'.[10] Cigarette-makers like Imperial Tobacco wielded huge financial and political influence. The company was an economic powerhouse: it commanded 80 per cent of the British cigarette market and more significantly generated over 14 per cent of the government's tax revenues.[11] So when, in early 1953, the tobacco firms argued the 'evidence is far from conclusive . . . there is no proof whatsoever of any causal connection', many in government were prepared to believe it.[12]

This line – that there is no proof of harm from smoking – was fundamental to the public relations strategy that the industry would hone to perfection over the following decades. It implies that as long as there are doubts around harm to health from cigarettes, we could continue to use its product and no government action need be taken. People just had to believe that no proof of harm from smoking existed. There was only one problem: it was a lie.

From internal tobacco documents released in the late nineties, we know that the tobacco industry conceded in 1953 that scientific studies 'tend to confirm the relationship between heavy and prolonged tobacco smoking and incidence of cancer of the lung'.[13] Instead of admitting what the growing body of evidence was showing it, the industry responded with a public relations and lobbying strategy described by the PR commentators John Stauber and Sheldon Rampton as the 'costliest, longest-running and most successful PR "crisis management" campaign in history'.[14] It was a campaign spun on both sides of the Atlantic.

On 15 December 1953, four of America's largest tobacco companies met in the opulent surroundings of New York's Plaza Hotel, which for years barred unaccompanied women from its famous Oak Room bar and where, it was once remarked, 'nothing unimportant ever happens'. It was here that the tobacco bosses were introduced to John Hill from Hill & Knowlton, one of the world's biggest PR companies.[15] Hill advised the industry that a full-blown public relations campaign was the best way to 'get the industry out of this hole'.

The PR campaign would all be about 'creating doubt about the health charge', in the industry's words.[16] It did not have to prove smoking was safe; all it had to do was keep the controversy alive by deliberately manufacturing doubt. Hill told the tobacco executives that 'scientific doubts must remain' and that they must work to convince the American public that there was 'no sound scientific basis for the charges'.[17] The industry began to change what was an emerging scientific consensus into raging scientific 'debate' to delay action.[18]

The industry's public statements from the time were peppered with phrases like 'no clinical evidence', 'no substantial evidence', 'no laboratory proof', 'unresolved' and 'still open'. Nothing has been 'statistically proven', 'scientifically proven' or 'scientifically established'. There is no 'scientific causality', 'conclusive proof' or 'scientific proof'.[19] They did it consciously and very deliberately. They knew what they were doing, as the head of research at British American Tobacco (BAT) revealed in a memo to colleagues: 'A demand for scientific proof is always a formula for inaction and delay, and usually the first reaction of the guilty.'[20]

Public denials of the science were just one strand of the campaign to cast doubt. Another very effective means was for the tobacco industry to fund and create its own science that countered health claims. At a meeting in London, just three days after the New York gathering, the tobacco industry offered to pay £250,000 – a considerable sum in those days – for 'specific research into the real cause of cancer of the lung'. There was only one caveat: 'Such research would, of course, embrace other possible factors, besides smoking'.[21]

The denials and the industry's funding of research were used to reassure the public. In 'A Frank Statement to Cigarette Smokers', a now infamous advertising campaign that reached 400 newspapers across America, the industry publicly announced the establishment of a Tobacco Institute Research Committee to oversee its work. The statement pledged 'aid and assistance' to the research effort to be led by a scientist of 'unimpeachable integrity and national repute'. It also reiterated the industry's first line of attack that there was no evidence of a link between smoking and disease; although a draft sentence that 'we will never produce and market a product shown to be the cause of any serious human ailment' was quietly deleted before publication.[22]

The industry also set about silencing its critics. In Britain, Imperial Tobacco was working on the politicians, hounding health ministers who spoke about the link between smoking and cancer.[23] In 1957 the UK tobacco lobby group the Tobacco Manufacturers Standing Committee was telling them that cigarette manufacturers were unaware of any carcinogenic substance in tobacco smoke in quantities which could cause cancer. Here it was again: there was 'no proof' that smoking caused disease.[24]

But privately it was a very different story. By the late fifties, internal industry documents show the industry knew that smoking caused cancer. BAT even had a code-word for cancer, 'ZEPHYR'. After a visit to several tobacco companies in the US, one BAT scientist wrote: 'With one exception the individuals with whom we met believed that smoking causes lung cancer: if by "causation" we mean any chain of events which leads finally to lung cancer and which involves smoking as an indispensable link.'[25]

By the sixties, the scientific evidence on causality was now getting stronger and the scientists more vocal. In 1962, a ground-breaking report by the Royal College of Physicians reaffirmed that cigarette smoking was a cause of lung cancer and bronchitis. It made front page news.[26] The government was worried about the counter-attack from tobacco companies, whose arguments it predicted would be 'as skilful as they would be insidious'.[27] It was right.[28] The industry's counter-attack was also having the desired effect: surveys showed that two-thirds of men still smoked and only a third of smokers believed their addiction caused cancer.[29]

The effect of the now overwhelming evidence served only to focus the minds of the industry. Its hired lobbyists merely upped their denial campaign. One Hill & Knowlton document from the time noted: 'The most important type of story is that which casts doubt in the cause and effect theory of disease and smoking. Eye-grabbing head-lines were needed and "should strongly call out the point – Controversy! Contradiction! Other Factors! Unknowns!"'[30] People were not to believe the evidence before them.

'Doubt is our product,' wrote one executive from BAT's subsidiary, Brown and Williamson in 1969. 'It is also the means of establishing a controversy.'[31] 'Let's face it,' wrote the head of research and development at Philip Morris a year later, 'we are interested in evidence which we believe denies the allegations that cigaret[te] smoking causes disease.'[32]

The denials continued throughout the seventies even though the industry privately conceded that the link between tobacco and cancer had long ceased to be an area for scientific controversy.[33] But by the eighties its own scientists were troubled in private that this stance was becoming untenable.

An internal BAT document worried that because the company's position on causation was no longer believed by anyone, its credibility was being undermined. It was time for plan B. The tobacco scientists argued that they should publicly acknowledge that there was a 'probability that smoking is harmful to a small percentage of heavy smokers'. It was a proposed damage limitation exercise. 'By giving a little we may gain a lot. By giving nothing we stand to lose everything,' one said.[34] The bosses ignored their advice. It would be another twenty years until they would publicly concede that smoking was bad for you. In the meantime the denials continued.

Up until this point the fight over tobacco was about whether or not cigarettes were causing harm to those who smoked them. The tobacco industry was doing everything in its power to vigorously and deceitfully dissuade smokers from believing the evidence. However, in the eighties scientists were discovering a new public health problem. Smoking was killing people who did not smoke.

In the early eighties, the *British Medical Journal* published a groundbreaking study by a Japanese scientist, Takeshi Hirayama, that non-smoking women married to smokers were more likely to develop lung cancer than non-smoking women married to non-smokers.[35]

The industry wasted no time in recognising the need to preserve what it called the 'social acceptability of smoking', the erosion of which was regarded as a serious long-term threat to profits. It was determined that smokers would not become pariahs. The next logical step, for the tobacco companies at least, was to forcefully defend people's right to smoke.

Again one of the main objectives of Philip Morris' second-hand smoke campaign was to manufacture controversy around smoking in public.[36] It set out to sabotage a major scientific study on the issue undertaken by an agency of the World Health Organisation. The study threatened to become a tool to bolster the case for regulation. The objectives of the industry's campaign were to delay the study or even get it cancelled by undermining the agency's budgets. It wanted it 'neutralised' by having the conclusions and results rewritten. It also started to fund counter-research.[37]

Philip Morris sought to create credible third parties to deliver its denial message on second-hand smoke. The tobacco giant set up something called the European Consultancy Programme, whose primary motive was to recruit scientists – 'Whitecoats' as they called them – to defend smoking and 'reverse scientific and popular misconception that [second-hand smoke] is harmful'.[38]

The tobacco giant also sought to create new, seemingly independent, front organisations to defend smoking. It enlisted two of the big PR agencies, APCO and Burson-Marsteller, to help set them up. One of these front groups in the US was called The Advancement of Sound Science Coalition, for which Philip Morris was budgeting $880,000 a year.

Philip Morris was also planning a European version, tentatively called Scientists for a Sound Public Policy.[39] Although this front group never materialised, it is believed to have formed the basis of the European Science and Environment Forum (ESEF).[40] This billed itself as an alliance of scientists concerned that government action should be founded on sound scientific principles. Like other 'sound science' front groups, its real purpose was to rubbish scientific findings that threatened commercial interests.

The Forum was headed by Roger Bate, a Cambridge-educated economist with the leading free market think tank, the Institute of Economic Affairs. Bate has since tried to deny ESEF was established by the tobacco industry,[41] but it is known that by the late 1990s the Forum was receiving significant tobacco money to assist with the campaign against second-hand smoke.[42]

Bate was out front publicly questioning the science. For example, in an article for the Wall Street Journal, he defended a Philip Morris advertising campaign, which compared breathing second-hand smoke to eating biscuits, the idea being to show that the risk of developing cancer from either activity was so small as to be meaningless.[43] He also appeared on the BBC's flagship *Today* programme to discuss passive smoking, without his tobacco backers ever being revealed.[44]

Bate's worth to the industry was obvious. One Philip Morris memo said: 'I think Bate is a very valuable resource and have strongly recommended that he play some role at UN level. I recall that we paid him up to £10,000 per month.'[45]

Alongside this denial operation ran a campaign by the tobacco companies and their front organisations to combat public concern around second-hand smoke. The industry was integral to the start of Forest, the UK's smokers' rights organisation, founded in 1979 by the pipe-smoking Battle of Britain veteran Sir Christopher Foxley-Norris, whose outrage was sparked when someone asked him to put his pipe out at Reading station.[46]

Forest was an attempt by the industry to take control of the debate. It needed to move it away from the health effects of smoking, ground on which it no longer wanted to fight. The issue was now about liberty and the 'freedom to smoke'.[47] Forest's job was to pit smokers' rights against public health 'nannies'. It moved to broaden the message beyond tobacco. Smoking, it claimed, was only the first target of the 'puritan paternalists'. Restrictions on tobacco were a step on the slippery slope to government controlling all aspects of our lives. Ralph Harris, Forest's chair, and the man widely seen as Margaret Thatcher's mentor, wrote that there was 'little likelihood that we end up being more healthy – only less free'.[48]

This tactic of associating smoking with freedom continues to this day. In 2012 a debate by Forest on tobacco regulation at the Conservative Party's annual gathering was housed in the conference's 'Freedom Zone'. It is worth remembering that this enduring association with 'freedom' began as a direct response to evidence of the harm caused to smokers' families.

And after nearly fifty years, tobacco firms continued to use denial as their defence. In the late nineties, the US Tobacco Institute was still pumping the line: it did not believe it had ever been established that smoking is the cause of disease.[49] In 1998 Geoffrey Bible, chair of Philip Morris, said: 'I'm unclear whether anyone dies of cigarette-related disease.'[50]

But in 1998 everything changed for the industry. After years of individual smokers taking tobacco firms to court, forty-six states in

America joined forces and took them on, suing for the costs of the care of sick and dying smokers. They won and the major tobacco companies were forced to pay over $200bn in damages. It was the largest civil settlement in US history.[51]

The consequences to the industry, however, extended beyond the financial payout. The legal process flushed out the companies' internal documents and revealed the extent of the deception, and the enormous lengths they had gone to, through PR and lobbying, to defend their product. There was no going back. The industry responded by under-taking a major campaign to portray itself as a socially responsible business (see Chapter 6).

Philip Morris announced the shift with a significant PR push. It finally declared: 'There is an overwhelming medical and scientific consensus that cigarette smoking causes lung cancer, heart disease, emphysema and other serious diseases in smokers. Smokers are far more likely to develop serious diseases, like lung cancer, than non-smokers. There is no "safe" cigarette.' The leopard had changed its spots, or had it? It would take the company another year to finally add: 'We agree with the overwhelming medical and scientific consensus that cigarette smoking causes various diseases.'[52]

The new 'responsible' Philip Morris was in evidence in a 2002 Californian trial, Betty Bullock versus Philip Morris. The jury awarded Bullock a mind-boggling $28bn in damages – later reduced to $28m. There to give evidence was Richard Doll. The *Los Angeles Times* described him thus: 'dignified, affable and decorated with honours, Doll is a tobacco lawyer's worst nightmare . . . By the time he has done answering questions from the plaintiff's lawyer, the Philip Morris attorney might as well have been representing Genghis Khan.'[53]

Before his death in 2004, Doll worked on a scientific paper that estimated that some six million people had died in the UK from tobacco use in the fifty-plus years since his research had been published. The industry's denial campaign continues to wreak havoc: if current trends continue, the World Health Organization calculates there will be up to one billion deaths in the twenty-first century from tobacco.[54]

Three years before his death Doll appeared on BBC Radio 4's *Desert Island Discs*. This was his advice to listeners: 'Find out what the tobacco industry supports – and don't do it; and what they object to – and do it.'[55] For the whole of his career Doll had watched the industry deny the science in the face of what it knew to be true; he had seen it mislead the public into questioning the evidence of harm from their habit; and he had waited as governments repeatedly delayed action to save lives.

A decade on from his death, we have yet to heed his advice and fully learn the lessons from the tobacco industry's denial campaign. Most recently the industry has tried to scupper plans for plain packaging in the UK. The next big fight is in Europe, where the industry employs over 100 lobbyists, and where it has spent millions of euros waging a full-blown lobbying campaign heavily targeting MEPs, to undermine and delay the introduction of a law that would further regulate tobacco.[56] A central message of the campaign has been the impact these new regulations would have on other industries such as food and alcohol.[57]

But while many lawmakers are yet to get wise to tobacco's lobbying tactics, other industries have learned from its pioneering techniques, with similar consequences for public health. One of those is the sugar business.

★

Cristin Couzens is a dentist turned muckraker on the sugar industry. She now authors a website called sugarpolitics.com that digs into the lobbying tactics of the sugar business.[58] What she and others have uncovered is that the sugar industry has been defending its product with lessons learnt from tobacco.

Couzens' journey began in 2007 at a health conference in the American coastal city of Seattle. Attendees of the conference, which was focused in part on diabetes, were advised on what to discuss with their patients. These included what to eat as part of a healthy diet. Saturated fats and salt were naturally on the list of foods to cut down on. There was no mention of sugar, to Couzens' surprise.

When a keynote speaker, a healthy-living guru and best-selling author called Steven Aldana said that there was no link between sugar and disease, Couzens felt duty-bound to challenge him. She found herself in heels, sprinting the length of a hallway outside a Seattle hotel ballroom to catch him as he left for the airport. Aldana assured her: 'There is no research to support that sugar causes chronic disease.'[59]

Couzens was so shocked by what she heard she resigned her job and set out on a quest to find signs of sugar industry involvement in the field of diabetes.[60] Fifteen months later and low on savings, she finally struck gold in a long-forgotten, dusty cardboard box buried deep in the Colorado State University archives. Just as we know about the tobacco industry tactics from millions of documents released via litigation and whistleblowers, so Couzens had stumbled on a treasure trove of 1,500 historical internal sugar industry documents.

Many of the documents had been saved to give context to a 1976 black-and-white photograph of two Sugar Association executives in bow ties standing on the podium at a Chicago ballroom to accept the prestigious Silver Anvil award. Seen as the Oscars for the PR world in America, the award from the Public Relations Society of America was for 'forging public opinion'.

'In the years before the awards ceremony, sugar was coming to be seen as a likely culprit in diabetes and obesity,' writes Couzens. 'In the years to follow, sugar was portrayed as a largely innocent victim of misguided food nannies and managed to escape regulation.' It was a public relations coup, but how did it happen?[61]

It happened by sugar learning the lessons of the tobacco industry. The internal sugar industry documents show that they used the same tactics: denying the evidence of harm and creating scientific uncertainty. The industry had the same aim in mind: to dismiss troubling health claims against its product and delay any attempts by government to curb consumption. Just as tobacco did, the sugar industry funded science to create doubt, while vilifying its critics. It framed the debate in terms of 'freedom' to consume and personal responsibility in order to prevent criticism, legislation and legal action.[62] And latterly, like tobacco, the sugar industry used distracting corporate-responsibility programmes to bolster its reputation.[63]

Since 1990, Britain's consumption of sugar has increased by over 30 per cent. Some children today receive nearly a fifth of their calories from sugar. We are less likely to buy it by the pound, but sugary drinks are now thought to be the major source of calories in the American diet and possibly the British diet too.[64] On top of this, there is the invisible sugar, added to our diets, that we do not notice, in everything from cereal, bread and smoked salmon to sausages and countless low-fat foods. This ubiquitous ingredient is addictive, makes us fat and causes disease.[65]

But despite the evidence and a public health crisis in part

attributable to our addiction to the sweet stuff, to this day the harm from excess sugar in our diets is still widely disputed by the industry.

Like the tobacco companies, all sugar companies had to do was to make sure that there was continual debate. It did not have to prove sugar was a 100 per cent 'safe' product, just that there was scientific uncertainty about its harm. And while the industry has issued its own 'frank statements' expressing public health concerns,[66] its priority has been to shed doubt on studies suggesting that too much sugar makes people sick.

Some of the similarities in the language and tactics used by the two global industries are uncanny. The documents reveal that the president of the industry's trade body in the US, the Sugar Association, reported to his board of directors in 1976 that 'in confronting our critics we try never to lose sight of the fact that no confirmed scientific evidence links sugar to the death-dealing diseases. This crucial point is the life blood of the Association.'[67]

Since the early sixties, internal Sugar Association memos show that it conceded that there were potential links between sugar and chronic diseases. In public it denied them. 'Sugar is Safe!' ran an ad campaign in the seventies which argued that sugar does not cause 'death-dealing' diseases: 'There is no substantiated scientific evidence indicating that sugar causes diabetes, heart disease or any other malady,' it proclaimed. A brochure from the sixties challenged the global 'misconceptions' around sugar's role in tooth decay and disease.[68]

Once again science – and its manipulation – was at the forefront of the PR campaign. Industry-funded research was described as 'a main prop of the industry's defence'. But rather than investigate the negative impacts of its product, the Sugar Association was concerned with making sure that 'the broadest possible audience' was convinced that sugar was a beneficial product. This was science to reassure the public and policy-makers.[69]

The sugar business similarly used friendly scientists to advocate on its behalf. It had its own 'Whitecoats'. At the time, the industry's key scientist was Frederick Stare, founder of the Department of Nutrition at the Harvard School of Public Health, which was funded by Carnation, Coca-Cola and Kellogg, among others. Stare would testify to US lawmakers about the 'wholesomeness' of sugar and appear in the media on behalf of the industry.

Internal PR documents noted that with Stare fronting the media work, they had managed to 'keep the sugar industry in the background'.[70] Which was precisely the point. As if to underline the obvious parallels, Stare also worked for tobacco, having secured funding for a study aimed at 'exonerating cigarettes as a cause of heart disease'.[71]

Sugar interests also sought to undermine research that might show the harm done by its product. As early as the mid-sixties, Britain's leading nutritionist, John Yudkin from University College London, was arguing that sugar was the main cause of atherosclerosis, or narrowing of arteries that can lead to heart disease.[72] The sugar industry lobbied hard against his findings and Yudkin complained vociferously that they were subverting some of his ideas.[73]

Another study, sponsored by the industry, was being undertaken by Walter Pover, a biochemist at the University of Birmingham. He had uncovered a possible mechanism to explain how sugar raises levels of triglycerides in the bloodstream, which have been linked to the narrowing of arteries. Pover believed he was on the verge of demonstrating this mechanism 'conclusively' and that just eighteen more weeks of work would prove it. His funding was cancelled. The sponsors said his research had 'nil' scientific value.[74]

By the late seventies, the industry was funding seventeen different scientists at some of the world's leading universities, including MIT, Harvard and Yale. Each proposal was vetted by a panel of industry-friendly scientists and a second committee made up of sugar companies and others with an interest like Coca-Cola and Hershey's.[75] Most of the cash was awarded to researchers whose studies appeared explicitly designed to exonerate sugar, according to Couzens and Gary Taubes, author of *Why We Get Fat*, who has helped Couzens analyse the documents.[76]

So successful was the PR campaign that the Sugar Association's Silver Anvil award application made the bold claim that its work made it 'unlikely that sugar will be subject to legislative restriction in coming years'.[77]

The industry did not rest on its laurels though. It started funding academic journals in a bid to dominate the science on sugar's impact on health. Nutrition journals, like the *Journal of Nutrition* and *American Journal of Clinical Nutrition*, found themselves sponsored by, among others, Coca-Cola, Nestlé, Procter & Gamble, and even the Sugar Association.[78]

Other third parties were also called on to allay the public's fears, such as medical and nutritional professionals. At a meeting of the British Nutrition Society in the late nineties, gratitude was expressed to Nestlé and Sainsbury's for funding the reception and Coca-Cola and Mars for refreshments. Meanwhile, in the US you could tuck into a Kellogg-sponsored breakfast at the American Society for Nutritional Sciences. In 2000, some thirty food and drink companies sponsored the American Dietetic Council's annual meeting.[79]

The box of documents also revealed another industry tactic to delay action. It attempted to prevent scientific advice from translating into public behaviour by blocking government dietary guidelines that would suggest limits on daily sugar consumption.[80] When a US government committee released a report in 1977, *Dietary Goals for the United States*, recommending that Americans should reduce their sugar intake by almost 40 per cent, the industry privately worried that it would 'hang sugar'. This was a major threat. The Sugar Association's plan was to 'neutralise it', because 'the consequences of losing this battle and permitting dietary goals to become a basic reference are too grave to be taken lightly'.[81]

By the eighties, independent research on sugar was effectively dead, and by the early nineties government research into sugar's health impacts had also come to a halt. So successful was the campaign that as we approached the millennium, the average American was tucking into more than double the amount of sugar which officials deemed safe.[82]

This massive over-consumption of sugar spurred some to act. Just as tobacco companies tried to 'neutralise' the World Health Organisation (WHO), so too has the sugar industry. In 1990 the WHO sought to rein in our sweet tooth, recommending that sugar be no more than 10 per cent of a healthy diet. Twenty-hour hours after the limit was decided, the industry's global lobbyists, the World Sugar Organisation, 'went into overdrive'. Subsequently, forty ambassadors from around the world wrote to the WHO insisting the report be removed The reason cited was that it would do irreparable damage to sugar-producing countries in the developing world. Professor Philip James, the British chairman of the International Obesity Taskforce, who wrote the report into nutrition, was asked not to send any more emails about the dietary aspects of health that related to sugar.[83]

Over a decade later, the World Health Organisation once again raised the issue of a 10 per cent daily limit on sugar. The industry attacked the WHO's science as flawed. It claimed that a whopping 25 per cent of what we eat and drink could safely consist of sugar.[84] But this time it threatened to bring the WHO to its knees by demanding that the US end its funding of the organisation unless the guidelines on healthy eating were scrapped. The WHO saw it as tantamount to blackmail. The sugar industry's tactics, it concluded, were worse than any pressure exerted by the tobacco lobby.[85]

Like tobacco before it, the sugar industry faces the almost inevitable prospect of its product being harmful to health. If we were to reduce our consumption to sensible levels, its profits would nosedive. As tobacco worked out many decades ago, the best way to handle this prospect is to delay action on it for as long as possible. This quote in 2012 by the president of the American Beverage Association, Susan Neely, could have come straight from the mouth of a tobacco baron: 'There's a lot of work to try to establish causality, and I don't know that I've seen any study that does that.'[86]

The undermining of science and manufacture of doubt was their answer to the crisis. When Robert Lustig, a leading authority on obesity in children, published an article in the journal *Nature* titled 'The Toxic Truth about Sugar',[87] the Sugar Association argued that the paper 'lacks scientific evidence or consensus' and is 'inconclusive at best'. Lustig is clear-eyed in his response: 'The science is in' on sugar he says, but 'the industry is going to fight tooth and nail to prevent that science from translating into public policy'. To date, it has been almost wholly successful.

By the time British children leave primary school, one in three is overweight or obese. The figures for adults are worse: 60 per cent of us are overweight or obese. 'It ain't the fat,' though, says Lustig, that is making us overweight. It is the fact that we now consume the same amount of sugar in one can of pop that adults consumed every five days less than two centuries ago.[88]

An increasing number of scientists now point to the causal link between excess sugar, obesity, diabetes and other metabolic problems. A recent study even identifies sugar as a predictor of type 2 diabetes separately from obesity, which is seen as the main driver of the disease. The study, the first large-scale, population-based one of its kind, suggested sugar has a 'direct, independent link to diabetes'. It found that the more sugar was available in a country, the more diabetes it had.[89]

British politicians, however, to date have been unmoved. They also appear not to have clocked the campaign of denial, or are choosing to ignore its function, which is to deliberately cast doubt on the evidence of sugar's harm to delay effective action. The UK government's recent response to tackling the public health crisis has been to invite the sugar lobby in to help. PepsiCo, for example, is a partner in the NHS anti-obesity Change4Life campaign.[90] It is sponsoring breakfast clubs to educate children about healthy eating.[91] The promotion of the £250m Change4Life programme was incidentally handed to a PR company, Freud Communications, which also works for PepsiCo to promote its brand.[92]

Politicians have gone further, though, and invited the sugar industry to help set public health policy. The approach of the then Health Secretary, Andrew Lansley, has been for government and companies to work together to make us well. The controversial Public Health Responsibility Deal he created was a 'critical part' of his vision for public health, he said.[93] Lansley, for his part, was familiar with the industry, having been involved until just a year before taking office, with a marketing firm whose clients have included Pepsi.

The Responsibility Deal included initiatives like a 'calorie reduction pledge', which involved firms agreeing to implement one or more of a 'menu of options', from changing recipes to reduce calories to smaller portion sizes, low-calorie options and even offering to put resealable packaging on chocolate bars. The measures were slammed for being ineffective, vague and voluntary.[94] Many in the industry simply refused to sign up to the Deal. One that did was Ribena, made by GlaxoSmithKline. Its former Director of Compliance and Regulatory Affairs was until recently a lobbyist with Imperial Tobacco.

The public health community saw the Deal and its promises for what they were. The Children's Food Campaign dubbed them 'weasel word' pledges. In early 2013 sixty health and environmental organisations, including the National Heart Forum and the Royal Society for Public Health, called on government to really act. They wanted a mandatory tax on sugary drinks of 20p per litre to tackle over-consumption.[95]

The response from the lobby to this call for regulation – the very thing that the industry had for years been seeking to avoid – was typical of the denial industries. Echoing Philip Morris' 'responsible' facelift, Coca-Cola broadcast TV ads confessing that it – possibly – had a problem with sugar: 'There's an important conversation going on about obesity out there,' it said. 'We want to be a part of the conversation.'

But the industry also continued to mislead. Gavin Partington, head of the British Soft Drinks Association, which represents, among others, Coca-Cola, PepsiCo and GlaxoSmithKline, told Channel 4 news that a tax was unnecessary and that the manufacturers were voluntarily driving the change needed. Some 61 per cent of soft drinks now contained no added sugar at all, he claimed. Partington was including the massive bottled water market to boost his figures. 'You're having a laugh,' said the Channel 4 interviewer.[96]

It is now widely recognised that obesity and diabetes are among the most serious public health crises affecting the UK. Society was finally persuaded over decades of the dangers of smoking in the face of a formidable and persistent denial campaign by the tobacco industry. Sugar has gone down the same road, seeking to delay action by government by refuting the evidence, funding its own supportive science, and sowing doubt in the public's mind.

The net result is that it has been allowed to dominate policy-making, delaying any effective action to reduce the now excessive amount of sugar in our diets. In the meantime, we likewise remain hooked.[97]

★

Soft drinks man Gavin Partington has not always defended sugar. He previously worked for the alcohol lobby.[98] At the time of his appointment, Parliament and the public health community were demanding that government got to grips with the growing harm caused by alcohol. It was finally on the political agenda. On getting the job, Partington said that he was 'delighted' to be working at a time when the alcohol industry was 'facing fresh scrutiny'.[99]

Since the fifties, English drinking habits have seen a shift. As alcohol has become more affordable and society more prosperous, so the more we drink and the more harm it causes. While there has been a slight decrease in consumption since a peak in 2004, over a third of us still drink above the recommended daily limit.[100] Another study suggests that the number could be as high as three-quarters due to underreporting.[101]

This is significant not just for us as individuals. Evidence shows that the number of really heavy drinkers is directly related to average consumption. Living in a cheap alcohol culture which encourages drinking – around £800m a year is spent on alcohol advertising and sponsorship deals in Britain[102] – leads more people to drink to excess. 'We have 30 years of academic evidence that confirms the link between alcohol price, consumption and harm,' says Dr Evelyn Gillan, who is on the front line of alcohol abuse as the head of Scotland's national alcohol charity. Put simply: 'The more a nation drinks, the more harm it will experience.'

This is not to be puritanical 'nannies'. Many millions of us have been quite seriously on the lash. And the more we all drink, the more alcoholics we create.

Were we as a nation to drink more moderately, the alcohol industry looks to lose about 40 per cent of its sales. Some put the figure higher.[103] The threat to the industry from government action and a shift in public attitudes is obvious. It is the same as the one that was faced decades ago by the tobacco industry. 'Alcohol consumption is beginning to come under attack . . . in the same way that cigarette smoking began to be attacked in the sixties,' noted British American Tobacco in 1987.

The parallels did not escape the attention of the alcohol-makers, particularly those who were also in the tobacco business. Philip Morris bought Miller Beer in 1970. Both products were coming under attack, whether in the form of constraints on advertising, tougher rules on labelling, restrictions on selling or tax increases. Ultimately, Philip Morris faced a loss of sales.

It therefore made sense for the experience of the cigarette division to be shared with their colleagues in alcohol. For example, a Miller Beer document shows how Philip Morris' alcohol division turned to a tobacco lobbying strategy to counter threats.[104] The group also pledged to defend its alcohol sales with no less gusto than it had shown tobacco. It was determined to 'fight aggressively, with all available resources, against any attempt, from any quarter', public health efforts that would curb its ability to manufacture and market its product.[105] With echoes of the New York Plaza meeting, Miller also talked of a coordinated industry response to the threat of restrictions.[106]

In Britain in the late eighties, the alcohol industry came together to form an organisation amid widespread concern that the country's drink problem was getting out of hand. One issue of concern was the targeting of young people with alcopops. The new body was called the Portman Group. It was so called because the lobbyists met in London's Portman Square, then home to Diageo,[107] makers of some of the most famous brands in the business: Guinness, Smirnoff, Johnnie Walker and Baileys to name a few. Since 2000, the man responsible for looking after Diageo's reputation, in charge of its corporate-responsibility and crisis management work, has been Guy Smith. Two decades earlier Smith was honing his skills at Philip Morris working in corporate affairs for Miller Beer, as well as the tobacco company itself.[108]

The parallels between the work of the alcohol lobby and the tactics employed by tobacco and sugar are striking. These include undermining scientific research that threatens profits, positioning themselves as responsible businesses and shifting responsibility onto individuals, rather than government intervention.

First, the Portman Group has attacked scientific evidence. In the mid-nineties, it was exposed for offering payments of £2,000 apiece to academics to anonymously rubbish a World Health Organisation report, *Alcohol Policy and the Public Good*. This was an extensive review of scientific research that unequivocally emphasised the connection between alcohol and ill-health. Professor Griffith Edwards, the report's lead author, warned that such unethical behaviour would lead the drinks industry to 'inevitably and deservedly join the tobacco industry in a pariah status'.[109]

The Portman Group has also sought to dismiss evidence showing that certain government actions would help to tackle alcohol-related harm. This included findings that suggest that a minimal rise in the cost of alcohol would reduce the number of deaths and hospital admissions in the country.[110] On this issue of 'minimum pricing', Portman stands accused of 'ignoring, misrepresenting and undermining' the scientific basis for such a policy in its conversations with government. Researchers from the London School of Hygiene and Tropical Medicine accused it of 'behaving exactly like the tobacco industry'.[111]

And like tobacco and sugar, the alcohol industry has also funded its own scientists. For example, the Portman Group paid the salaries of two prominent British academics at the University of Edinburgh.

Both were active in the industry's campaign to relax government drinking guidelines in much the same way that sugar attempted to lobby against dietary recommendations.[112]

But while alcohol has copied the tobacco industry's lobbying in many respects, it has also learned lessons from it. Cigarette-makers had responded 'too late' to threats, and in a manner that was 'passive' and 'inadequate', said one alcohol lobbyist in the mid-eighties.[113] The road ahead for alcohol was clear. It needed to get on the front foot and fast.

The strategy that it has pursued – in a manner that can only be described as both cynical and maniacal – has been to shift the blame away from the industry and its product and onto individuals, notably what it terms a minority of problem drinkers. The booze lobby seeks to paint alcohol misuse as a problem affecting a 'reckless minority' of heavy drinkers. This is clearly a false picture. The official figures put the number of people drinking more than the recommended limits at ten million adults, which is quite a significant minority. It is estimated that to reduce the consumption of this group to recommended levels would wipe £13bn off alcohol sales.[114] The incentive for the industry to argue it is only a reckless minority who are drinking too much is obvious.

The strategy by the alcohol companies has been to paint themselves as responsible corporate citizens, actively working to help change the drinking habits of a tightly defined, problematic minority. It has spent hundreds of millions on alcohol education programmes and sensible drinking messages, aggressively putting the onus on individuals, rather than seeing it as a much wider societal problem, the root of which is its product. The decade-long 'Drink Aware' campaign, initiated by the Portman Group, is a good example.[115] As is the Group's £100m social marketing 'Campaign for Smarter Drinking' targeting the young.[116]

A five-year plan from Miller Brewing in the nineties explains the rationale for such a strategy. At the time the beer company was picking up on 'anti-alcohol forces' that were seeking to impose restrictions and regulations on its product. It even noted a growing 'neo-prohibitionist legislative sentiment'. Its response was to go big on alcohol's role as a 'responsible corporate citizen', and invest in national alcohol awareness programmes, such as its 'Think When You Drink' campaign. It talked of coordinating the entire drinks industry response to proposed restrictions, which would 'stress alcohol education

programs and messages so as to develop public policy from a framework of education and responsible drinking, as opposed to one of
control'.[117]

In other words, it would position itself as a responsible industry,
then educate the public on alcohol and politicians would leave it alone.
It was a plan expressly designed to stave off effective government action.

Diageo ran its first half-a-million-pound TV advert campaign
promoting responsible drinking in 2003. It came just weeks before the
then Labour government published its strategy on alcohol.[118] In the
summer of 2007 Labour updated its plans on tackling alcohol harm.[119]
The same year, Diageo gave its £100,000 lobbying account to the
Hanover agency, which was hired to help Diageo raise awareness of
its responsible-drinking activities in government.[120] Each time, government is reminded that the industry is doing its bit, the message being
that 'controls' are not necessary, and government can just back off.

Such a strategy allows the alcohol industry to appear responsible
while at the same time defending its market. In this it is wholly
successful in that education and information campaigns tend not to
directly affect behaviour. Drinker education campaigns are consistently
found to be the least effective lever in actually reducing how much
we drink and any subsequent harm.[121] The alcohol industry's investment in such programmes – somewhere in the hundreds of millions
– is a drop in the ocean compared to the potential loss of sales, counted
in billions, from them actually working.

What is known to work to reduce alcohol consumption is its price.
For example, controls on the minimum price at which a unit of alcohol
can be sold encourage people to drink less. Just as alcohol's increasing
affordability since the 1960s had been a major driver in the rise in
consumption, so a rise in the price of alcohol is the most effective
way of reducing consumption. The efficacy of minimum pricing for
alcohol is key to why, when governments have floated the idea, the
industry has fiercely opposed it.[122]

The Scottish government was the first to propose introducing
minimum pricing, in 2009, as a way to prevent tens of thousands of
liver referrals, some 1,500 deaths and a £2.25bn annual cost in extra
services and lost productivity.[123]

The industry mobilised a massive lobbying effort – and an 'assertive
and populist' campaign – to fight it. Gavin Partington, then of the

Wine and Spirit Trade Association, weighed in, saying that minimum pricing was not the 'right answer'.[124] He was not alone. So too did Diageo and the Scottish Whisky Association, which at the time was chaired by Diageo's CEO, Paul Walsh. A quarter of its sixteen council members were also from the firm. Diageo claimed there was 'no evidence' to support minimum pricing.[125] However, the industry's real concern, according to the Association, was 'the precedent [the policy] will set for other countries',[126] suggesting it might be effective.

Part of the industry's response was to issue a legal challenge as a delaying tactic. The alcohol industry tried to argue that the measure was in breach of European competition law, just as the tobacco industry had argued previously over plain packaging. But the industry lost the first round of what is likely to be a lengthy legal battle, after Scottish judges ruled that the Scottish Parliament was within its powers to introduce Europe's first minimum pricing law, due to its protecting health.

Health campaigners were ecstatic. Dr Evelyn Gillan said there was clear evidence from Canada that the measure saved lives. The alcohol industry, said Gillan, had 'followed in the footsteps of their colleagues in the tobacco industry by seeking to delay the implementation of policies that are clearly in the public interest'.[127]

But the industry has had much better success south of the border. It set out to 'kill' the measure in England with another populist campaign. This went under the banner 'Why Should We Pay More?' which also blamed the country's alcohol problem on a 'reckless minority'. It was designed to appeal to people's pocket and the sense of being penalised for the behaviour of others.

This is itself a myth: minimum pricing is the best way to target heavy consumers without hitting moderate drinkers, the majority of whom would see their drinks bill rise by just a couple of pence. It was led by the Wine and Spirit Trade Association, supported by Diageo, SABMiller, which bought Miller Brewing and a number of supermarkets. The lobbying campaign urged customers to 'bombard the government with tweets expressing their opposition'.[128]

Days after the Scottish court's decision in May 2013, the Westminster government published its legislative plans for the following year. A minimum price on alcohol was conspicuously absent, as was another heavily lobbied health measure on the plain packaging of cigarettes. Leading the charge against the alcohol proposals was the Home

Secretary Teresa May.[129] Just a year before, May had promised that the government was committed to tackling the one million violent crimes a year that are alcohol-related.[130] The government refused to release minutes of meetings between the Home Secretary and the alcohol industry to us.[131]

The policy U-turn was a major disappointment to the public health community, but no great surprise to the alcohol lobby, which had long been inside government. Like their colleagues in sugar, alcohol lobbyists were also helping to set policy under the Public Health Responsibility Deal.[132] Diageo had been particularly keen to get to the table. Two weeks into the new government, it wrote to the Health Secretary, Andrew Lansley, saying it was looking forward to working with him to help develop 'effective and proportionate policies to tackle alcohol-related harm'.[133]

The 'dialogue' between Diageo and Lansley's team had in fact started at least eighteen months before the general election in 2010. In this knowledge, it is perhaps no surprise that the industry's focus on individual responsibility over price increases had become central to the government's public health programme. Diageo told Lansley that this was 'especially pleasing to see'. The drink giant had urged the Health Secretary to work with it to deliver an 'enhanced industry-led solution . . . before considering a legislative approach'.[134] In return, it promised to be a 'constructive and supportive' partner for as long as the government stuck to the 'contentious principles of partnership', rather than 'apportioning liability or blame'.[135]

This is the very same approach Philip Morris' Miller Beer Company advocated some twenty years earlier: focus public policy-makers on education and responsible drinking, and steer them away from seeking to 'control' the industry.[136]

The industry and government set about creating a series of 'proportionate' policies together. Leading the Deal for the alcohol industry was Gavin Partington's old boss at the Wine and Spirit Trade Association, Jeremy Beadles.[137] He was seen by some in Whitehall to have so much access in the Department of Health that he was mistaken for a civil servant, averaging fortnightly meetings with government. In total, officials and ministers had eighty-five meetings with the wider drinks industry in the first eighteen months of the new administration.[138]

What they came up with under the Deal was disappointing in the extreme. On alcohol labelling 'each company was left to use its own definition' as to how to comply with the Deal, with companies expected to 'self-certify'.[139] A study of what alcohol firms were newly required to do found that it was largely what the companies were already doing as part of their corporate-responsibility efforts. What the partnership with government did, in effect, is provide the industry with a platform to relaunch existing commitments – for which there is little or no evidence of effectiveness – and rebrand them as government approved.[140]

As delaying tactics go, the alcohol lobby's campaign has been hugely successful. It learnt from tobacco's successes, for example in attacking scientific evidence, but also from its mistakes. Alcohol gave a little ground. It painted the problem as being about a minority of 'reckless' drinkers, rather than the much wider social problem that the evidence supports.

Crucially it came forward with a solution for government to 'tackle' this smaller problem, largely through ineffective information campaigns on responsible drinking. By positioning itself as a good corporate citizen, it has been invited to help develop policies that have been shown to do little to address the problem, while simultaneously shouting down measures that would. This is time-wasting on an epic scale.

Britain is far from alone in experiencing such an assault by alcohol lobbyists to delay effective government action. In 2013, an international appeal was made to the World Health Organisation to kick the global alcohol producers out of governments. In an unprecedented move, 500 public health professionals, scientists and NGOs from sixty countries expressed their concern about: the industry's funding of science; its promotion of weak, ineffective, voluntary measures to reduce harm and its lobbying against effective, evidence-based policies; the involvement in policy-making of industry-backed bodies like Britain's Portman Group; and the obvious conflicts of interest from governments partnering with the commercial alcohol companies to try and solve the problems caused by their product.[141]

In other words, what the alcohol industry has done in Britain – lobbying to face down a threat from government – it has been doing around the world. But even this international effort is dwarfed by the recent global lobbying campaign by the oil lobby to cast doubt and delay action on perhaps the biggest public health threat of all: climate change.

★

In response to the unparalleled statement of concern about the influence of the alcohol industry, the Director General of the World Health Organisation, Dr Margaret Chan, confirmed that it was WHO's position that the alcohol industry should have no role in the formulation of alcohol policies, 'which must be protected from distortion by commercial or vested interests'.[142]

Her comments will give impetus to health campaigners who want the WHO to adopt a legally binding treaty similar to the global treaty on tobacco, which entered into force in 2005 and which quickly became one of the most widely embraced treaties in United Nations history. This treaty specifically requires governments to protect their health policies from the vested interests of the tobacco industry,[143] although there is still a cavernous gap between rhetoric and reality. In practice, the industry still exerts huge influence and continues to lobby both directly and via numerous front groups. But the treaty does represent a start in the painfully slow world of diplomatic action.

In contrast, action on climate change has almost stalled. Over twenty years after the first UN conference on climate change, a meaningful global agreement remains as far off as ever. This is despite the fact that the need for action is becoming ever more pressing.

In May 2013, a monitoring station in Hawaii recorded a first. The concentration of carbon dioxide in the atmosphere went over 400 parts of CO_2 per million molecules in the air for the first time since measuring on the Mauna Loa volcano began in 1958. The last time CO_2 was regularly above this level was three to five million years ago. This was a symbolic marker of changes to the world's atmosphere, with rising CO_2 linked to shifts in climate. 'The evidence is conclusive that the strong growth of global carbon dioxide emissions from the burning of coal, oil and natural gas is driving the acceleration,' said US senior climate scientist, Peter Tans.[144]

As if to emphasise the fact, just days later Tans' statement was backed up by new, international research examining the 12,000 scientific studies on climate change conducted in the last twenty years. Of those that asked whether climate change was man-made, there was near unanimity. Ninety seven per cent 'endorsed the consensus position that humans are causing global warming'. This showed overwhelming agreement among scientists that climate change is man-made, a consensus that has strengthened over time.[145]

And yet it is a message that is failing to reach a large proportion of the public. Nearly four out of five Americans believe that the climate is changing or probably changing.[146] But only just over half believe that this is primarily the result of human activity.[147] A third of all Americans also think that there is widespread disagreement among climate scientists.[148] The figures in the UK are similar with over 80 per cent agreeing that the planet is warming. But just a quarter of Brits attribute this to human activity mainly, with a further half of us believing that we are only partly responsible.[149]

What this shows is an obvious gap between the scientific consensus and public attitudes. A substantial number of people are clearly yet to be convinced that climate change is man-made, a view not shared by climate scientists. A proportion of the public thinks that there is controversy among scientists about the cause, again something refuted by the evidence.

This gap in understanding would matter little if governments were acting on what scientists were telling them. But few are. Politicians, without sufficient public pressure, have not taken the difficult decisions that are necessary to bring emissions down. Our economies remain dependent on fossil fuels. Weaning ourselves off oil, coal and gas will not be easy. Action is needed by governments around the world, just as the impacts will be felt across borders, although some countries will undoubtedly be harder hit than others.

This huge task has been made that much harder by a global disinformation campaign by the oil industry and its front groups designed to confuse whole populations. The aim, like the sixty-year campaign by the tobacco industry, has been to delay politicians from regulating its product.[150]

Scientists working on the issue are too few to be heard above what has been called the 'devastatingly effective' lobbying operation designed to negate their warnings.[151] The oil industry has 'literally delayed any meaningful action by decades', says one of the world's best-known climate scientists, Michael Mann, 'and for a problem where delaying action by a few years means we are committing to far worse impacts'. Mann and others in his profession have watched the campaign in disbelief: 'They have knowingly stalled action on this grave threat via a cynical campaign to confuse the public on the underlying science.'[152]

The promotion of scientific uncertainty, or the manufacture of doubt, has been at the heart of the campaign, as it was with tobacco. The effort, organisation and crucially resources put into the lobbying, however, are off the scale. At its heart is the creation of a network of scientists, think tanks, purpose-built front groups and oil-funded 'grass-roots' efforts to at once hide the oil industry's involvement while amplifying its message around the world.

Oil giant Exxon was for years central to the industry's lobbying campaign to mislead the world on the findings of climate change scientists. In the late nineties Exxon helped create a small task-force working with the American Petroleum Institute. A memo written by this Global Climate Science Team spelt out its objective: 'Victory will be achieved when average citizens understand (recognise) uncertainties in climate science' and when public 'recognition of uncertainty becomes part of "conventional wisdom"'.[153]

The man leading Exxon's climate confusion strategy was Lee Raymond, a fear-inducing oil man nicknamed 'iron ass'.[154] Exxon's influence, though, was often hidden. Through its funding of third parties, it created layers of disguise and subterfuge to form a campaign as fingerprint-free as possible. What Exxon provided, however, was the muscle – the money.

The strategy was to use the media and third parties to sell uncertainty on climate change. The communications plan by Exxon and its partners put it plainly: 'Develop and implement a national media relations program to inform the media about the uncertainties in climate science.'[155]

Exxon's methods included recruiting supposedly independent scientists who were 'new faces . . . without a long history of visibility in the debate'.[156] Again, this is reminiscent of BAT's 'Whitecoats'. But its key means of manufacturing global uncertainty on climate change was to fund a network of think tanks, seemingly independent organisations with the power to influence public debate. This network would create an 'echo chamber' that amplified and sustained scientific disinformation long after it had been debunked by climate scientists.[157]

For many of these free market, right-leaning and libertarian groups the oil industry found willing conspirators, all too eager to defend free market capitalism and to be paid to do so. 'To admit that a free economy generates a vast global external cost [CO_2] is to admit that the large-scale government regulation so often proposed by hated environmentalists is justified,' noted the *Financial Times* commentator Martin Wolf. 'For many libertarians or classical liberals, the very idea is unsupportable. It is far easier to deny the relevance of the science.'[158]

The 'echo chamber' created by climate sceptic front groups is global in reach. This is not a problem confined to the United States. The UK and Europe are equally vulnerable. Take one small example from many examples of their work in Britain over the years.

A decade ago a scientific report was published into the effects of climate change in the Arctic. It was heavyweight science, taking four years to research and drawing on the expertise of 300 climate scientists, among others. It reached some alarming conclusions, namely that the Arctic was warming much more rapidly than previously known, at nearly twice the rate as the rest of the globe. It concluded that this was projected to lead to substantial melting of the Greenland ice sheet that would contribute to a global sea-level rise at increasing rates.[159]

The science made news around the world,[160] including in Britain where the headlines were fairly sensationalist. The *Independent* ran with 'Meltdown: Arctic wildlife is on brink of catastrophe'.[161] The *Daily Mail* warned of 'The Arctic apocalypse'.[162]

The *Guardian*, normally known for its progressive stance on environmental issues, led with: 'Climate change claims flawed, says study'. Written by the paper's science editor, Tim Radford, the article attacked the Arctic study for employing 'faulty science, faulty logic and faulty economics'.[163] Radford had based his piece on a report published by a London-based think tank, the International Policy Network (IPN). What Radford failed to tell *Guardian* readers was that the IPN was receiving hundreds of thousands of dollars from Exxon to try and keep controversy about climate change alive.[164]

Exxon's long-running campaign drew the ire of the scientific community in Britain. The Royal Society, our oldest and most prestigious scientific body, issued a public rebuke in 2006. It strongly and openly criticised some thirty-nine organisations Exxon was funding, including the IPN,[165] that 'misrepresented the science of climate change, by outright denial of the evidence . . . or by overstating the amount and significance of uncertainty in knowledge'.[166]

Exxon in response withdrew funding from some think tanks, while

continuing to fund others.[167] The right-wing Competitive Enterprise
Institute that had been leading the sceptic charge in the US lost its
backing of some $2m from Exxon. The baton, however, merely passed
to the ultra-conservative Heartland Institute, which is upfront in its
claim to be 'the world's most prominent think tank promoting scepticism about man-made climate change'.[168] It no longer publishes its
donors, but it used to be funded by Philip Morris, PepsiCo and Diageo.[169]

The Heartland Institute caused outrage with a billboard campaign
in 2012 that featured pictures of the Unabomber Ted Kaczynski, insane
killer Charles Manson and the Cuban communist leader, Fidel Castro,
next to the words: 'I still believe in Global Warming. Do You?'[170] It
was an unmitigated own-goal. It had gone too far. Corporate donors
sought to distance themselves and pulled their funding.[171] The organisation lost nearly a million dollars in income, but unrepentant it went
ahead with its seventh annual international climate sceptic conference.

Heartland today is reliant on another source of funding for its ongoing
attack against climate science: the secretive multi-billionaire Koch
brothers. Kansas-based Koch Industries is a colossal petro-chemical
company with operations in nearly sixty countries and 70,000 employees.
Most of Koch's operations are invisible to the public and, for a long
time, so was its funding of the denial movement.[172]

It is now known that in little more than a decade the billionaire oil
brothers donated over $61m to front groups that attack climate
change.[173] Tracking that funding, however, is at times close to impossible. For example, a sizeable amount of the money reaching climate
denial groups today passes through two secretive American trusts: the
Donors Trust and the Donors Capital Fund. It is known that the Koch
brothers have made significant contributions to the Donors Trust.[174]
However, its other billionaire donors are untraceable. Funders are
guaranteed anonymity.

Back in 2003, these two funds were contributing to just 3 per cent
of the 'climate counter-movement', as it has been called. Six years
later the funds were supporting about a quarter of climate sceptic
think tanks. In money terms, by 2010, the Donors Trust alone had
distributed $118m to over 100 think tanks and groups that deny the
existence of a human factor in climate change, or oppose environmental regulations.[175] In other words, the Trust was helping to bankroll
a movement.

As with Exxon's funding, many of these Koch-backed organisations act as an 'echo chamber' for climate sceptic views and no opportunity is wasted to promote confusion. Take the so-called Climategate scandal in late 2009 that was created to sow doubt in people's minds by attacking the credibility of climate scientists.

The furore centred around a thousand internal emails that were hacked from one of the world's leading centres for climate change science, the Climatic Research Unit at the University of East Anglia in Norwich. The attack was timed to cause maximum damage coming just weeks before a key United Nations climate change conference. The emails revealed something of climate scientists' reluctance to share their raw data with climate sceptics. But despite the ensuing hysteria, they did not undermine the science of climate change.[176][177]

Regardless, as the story unfolded at least twenty Koch-funded organisations went about fanning the flames. They repeatedly rebroadcast and referenced the scandal and appeared in the media seeking to stoke up the controversy and bend it to promote their climate sceptic views.[178] The groups frothed with outrage, calling climate change a 'scientific fraud scandal' based on 'counterfeit assumptions' that had led to 'the biggest hoax our world has ever seen'.[179] It was a strategy designed to suck others into the game, like the BBC, which eventually apologised to the University for its misleading coverage of the pseudo-scandal.[180]

'When you look at the various outlets, organisations and individuals who immediately promoted this manufactured scandal, they are all the usual suspects,' says Michael Mann, who became embroiled in it after some of his personal emails were released.[181] 'So if you want to ask whether "Climategate" was funded by the fossil fuel industry and right-wing and conservative interests like the Koch Brothers – yes, in my view it is clear.'[182]

By far the loudest British voice in the Climategate echo-chamber was the Global Warming Policy Foundation. It was set up just before the scandal broke by the Conservative grandee Nigel (Lord) Lawson. Despite a lack of scientific credentials – Lawson was a financial journalist before becoming a politician – he has become the most high-profile and prolific climate sceptic in Britain.

The Foundation is very effective in getting its views across. A 2011 study of newspapers across six countries showed it to be particularly successful in securing media coverage. Lawson and the Foundation's director, Benny Peiser – whose education is in political science, English and sports science – were by far the two most quoted sceptics.[183]

Lawson refuses to disclose who funds him. The Foundation, which secured half a million pounds in funding in 2009–2010, does not reveal the identity of its donors, something which has drawn criticism from politicians, scientists and the media alike.[184] Lawson claims not to have taken money from 'the energy industry or from anyone with a significant interest in the energy industry.'[185] He did, however, have links to some of the world's largest energy companies.

Until 2013 Lawson was chairman of the advisory company, the Central Europe Trust, whose clients have included big names in the oil business: BP, Shell, Texaco and Total.[186] Clients of one of the Trust's subsidiaries include six fuel and oil companies, as well as ten power and energy firms, including Poland's notorious Bełchatów Power Plant, the largest point source emitter of carbon dioxide in the EU.[187] Lawson dismissed these links as historic and irrelevant.[188]

This widespread and organised denial campaign over climate change has been devastatingly effective. The scientific consensus is having little measurable impact on government action and consequently global emissions. While there is agreement that climate change is happening, widespread, manufactured uncertainty over the cause and the science remains. Politicians have been let off the hook and allowed to dither as a result.

This state has been achieved by following tobacco's lead. Doubt is the oil business' stated aim, created with a specific goal in mind: to head off the threat of government intervention and control. The shared method is clear and no more apparent than in the British think tank the Institute of Economic Affairs.

The Institute has long questioned the validity of climate change science. A decade ago, it was among those to receive Exxon money in the UK. It took $50,000 from the oil giant in 2004 through its American arm.[189] A decade earlier it had produced a book, *Global Warming: Apocalypse or Hot Air?*[190] It is a great example of the echo-chamber in action: a chapter on climate science repeatedly refers to the views of other known sceptics. It was 'hard to take seriously', as an adviser on climate change to the Prime Minister at the time put it.[191]

The book was written for the Institute by two authors, Julian Morris and Roger Bate, the latter founding the Institute's environment unit.

Both men were the initial directors of the Exxon-backed International Policy Network[192] that questioned the 'faulty science, faulty logic and faulty economics' of the 2004 Arctic report, among many other attempts at promoting public uncertainty on climate science.

Bate, currently an adviser to the Institute, was also head of the tobacco-funded European Science and Environment Forum – which, as you will remember, compared breathing second-hand smoke to eating biscuits – and was described by his backers Philip Morris as a 'very valuable resource'.

Today the Institute of Economic Affairs is heavily invested in defending industries that face government action to curb harm from their products, some of which feature in this chapter. In early 2013 it established what it called a Lifestyle Economics unit. The 'increasing focus by the government and general public on the issues surrounding alcohol, tobacco, gambling, sugar, fat and soft drinks, has made the formation of the unit timely and necessary', it says.[193]

It has already weighed in against proposals for a minimum price for alcohol.[194] It has also spoken out against a tax on sugary drinks and has played a leading part in the coalition against plain packaging of cigarettes in the UK.[195] The Lifestyle Economics unit is run by the Institute fellow Chris Snowdon, a long-term pro-smoking activist who denigrates public health scientists as 'zealots' and 'extremists', even labelling one a 'scrotum-faced head-banger', as we detailed in Chapter 5.[196]

Whether the tobacco, alcohol or sugar industries are funding the Institute is difficult to know as the IEA refuses to disclose who bankrolls it. 'We accept funding from anyone willing to give it to us,' is all its director, Mark Littlewood, says. 'We would accept any cheque that the tobacco industry or anybody else wishes to write us.'[197] However, we do know that BAT gave the IEA £11,000 in 2011 and £20,000 the following year. We know this not from the IEA, but because the tobacco giant gave in to pressure and released the figures.[198] It is no coincidence that BAT's funding for the IEA doubled just as the think tank stepped up to fight the government's plans to introduce the plain packaging of cigarettes. It is also no coincidence that BAT intends to increase funding for the IEA in 2013 and 2014.[199]

For many lobbyists today tobacco is a pariah. Its campaign of denial and misinformation, once it became public, has been widely and publicly condemned by the influence industry. A refusal to work for tobacco interests is held up by lobbyists as a sign of ethical credentials. Yet many more work for industries that have learnt from tobacco, that have adopted and adapted its tactics to defend products which similarly cause harm.

These campaigns have allowed the sugar and alcohol industries to claim a seat in government. There they are helping to set policies that will have little or no effect on public health, while scientists continue to warn of the significant and growing problems associated with their products. Their delaying tactics and obscuring of the true impact of their products have been given official approval.

But it is perhaps on climate change that the lobbyists have been most effective. They can claim victory. They have managed to derail any meaningful process at the United Nations and at the national level with many governments, particularly in the US. The fossil fuel lobby's efforts to sow doubt on the science of climate change and the causes of our warming world have succeeded in their aim. Because, if there was no uncertainty in our minds that what the climate scientists were telling us was true, surely we would all be acting differently.

9

'Reform': Creating Opportunities to Profit

'When we try to understand the world most of us have to rely on information that is profoundly unsafe.'
   Dan Hind, *Return of the Public*[1]

'We sort of quote that there's a wealth of evidence out there.'
   Elizabeth Sidwell, schools commissioner,
   Department for Education[2]

'This is GREAT Britain' shone from the enormous screen. In front stood the speaker at the government business conference held to coincide with the London Olympics. The UK's Trade Minister, Stephen Green, introduced 'One of the world's leading authorities on educational reform, Michael Barber.'[3]

While the rest of us were gripped by the Olympic triumphs of Mo Farah and Team GB, and were surprised by an opening show that celebrated the youthful, creative and slightly bonkers spirit of these islands, as well as our public-spirited inventions like the NHS and the world wide web, Barber and the British government were promoting a very different set of values to their international business audience.

Barber is a 'visionary' according to the man currently in charge of schools, the Education Secretary, Michael Gove.[4] But the vision he is promoting is far from the idiosyncratic world portrayed in Danny Boyle's opening ceremony. Barber prescribes turning whole education systems upside-down, in part, through the introduction of market competition and the greater use of technology.

The test bed for some of Barber's experiments in schools in the UK was nearly two decades earlier in Tony Blair's government. Barber was at the heart of New Labour's schools reforms. Today, though, his ambition, and those of his current employer, the textbook publisher and testing firm Pearson – dubbed the world's largest education business – extends across the globe.[5] 'Education reform used to be something that each country did individually,' Barber said. Today it is a 'global phenomenon'.[6]

It is an ambition shared by a vast, corporate-education industry. Lobbying by this industry is our focus here, but first we need to understand something of what they are seeking to do with our schools.

To imagine some of what is envisaged for schools by the education industry requires that you firmly put aside the notion that a publicly funded education will remain something delivered in a school by teachers and provided by the state.

Technology is now being used across schools to teach, test and track students' progress. The use by pupils of tablets, online textbooks, educational video and video games and digital assessments looks set to become a common feature in classrooms. Many parents of school-age children will be aware of such developments. Where this leads, however, according to school reformers, is to a revolution in schools. Technology allows learning to be done anytime, anywhere. The teaching location becomes less relevant; the teacher, more of an 'enabler' helping students as they progress through learning software. 'The learning day will spread,' says Barber. 'Some of it might be in school, some of it will be in formal settings, often it will be at home.'

Advocates of educational technology point to many benefits from the greater use of digital learning: lessons can be tailored to pupils' abilities; teachers, through their computers, can interact with more students at any one time; the performance of pupils – and teachers – can be monitored more closely to raise standards; plus it helps to hold the attention of children brought up with gadgets.

It is also cheaper. Educating students at the Florida Virtual School, the first statewide system of online teaching in the US, cited by Barber and a partner of Pearson, costs nearly $2,500 less than at a traditional school, neatly illustrating the appeal to politicians of significant levels of digital learning.[7] Computer-based approaches to learning require far fewer teachers per student, some suggest half as many teachers or even fewer than that. It is seen as a way of making schools more productive, substituting technology (cheap) for labour (expensive). To some advocates on the right, technology is a way of usurping teacher control of education.

The role of the state in providing education is also undergoing reform, something that Barber helped pioneer in the UK under Blair, and then as head of global education at the management consultants McKinsey. What we are seeing is a move away from a school system that is publicly funded and run towards one where the schools budget is shared between state schools and private operators, whether non-profit or for-profit, which are encouraged to compete with each other for pupils. In the UK this has seen the rise of state-funded, independently run academies and their subset, free schools. In the US, they are called charter schools. What they are creating is an education market.

These private providers have the potential to open schools up to more technology. As Barber points out, the public sector is resistant to 'innovation'. Advocates see new schools that are operated by people who are committed to digital learning as a way of further reforming the system. Technology interests are thus helped by and are helping to drive radical changes in education.

According to two optimistic advocates of this 'revolution', John Chubb and Terry Moe of the US conservative Hoover Institution: 'The world is in the early stages of a historic transformation in how students learn, teachers teach, and schools and school systems are organised'.[8] Their 2009 book, *Liberating Learning*, details how technology will deliver this transformation through: its 'seeping-in' to existing schools; virtual schooling; new education providers; data systems designed to monitor teacher performance; and its 'slow but inexorable undermining of the political power of the teachers unions'.[9] Michael Gove described it as an 'excellent book'.[10]

This transformation in schools paves the way for private sector companies to enter a potentially hugely profitable market. Worldwide spending on education currently tops $4tn, a figure that is predicted to rise dramatically.[11] One US investment bank was explicit in calling the privatising of America's $600bn public school system the 'final frontier'[12]: it was 'the largest market opportunity' since healthcare was privatised.[13] In profit-making terms, education was 'the big enchilada'.

It follows that the so-called education reform lobby is scaled to the size of this enchilada. England's schools budget currently stands at a mere £40bn (and falling),[14] more of a mini-taco, but still a substantial snack for the private sector.

If lobbying is employed to head off threats to corporate profits, as we explored in the previous chapter, it is equally used to drive opportunities to profit. Corporations invest in lobbying for government policies that will benefit their bottom line, with the money and effort invested often scaled to the market potential. With health systems in the UK and elsewhere fast moving into the hands of private companies, public education systems around the world are now seen by many as the next big commercial opportunity.

The mobile education market – or mEducation as Barber's former employer McKinsey calls it – is predicted to be worth $70bn worldwide by 2020. The market for devices like tablets is set to be worth $32bn. The US online learning industry is looking to nearly double in size by 2015 with revenues reaching $24bn.[15] Which is why those companies poised to benefit from these opportunities – content and assessment corporations like Pearson, firms that provide mobile networks, and companies that provide the kit, like tablets – 'have been focusing on it for years', says McKinsey.[16]

Multinational technology giants are positioned to exploit these opportunities. Microsoft's offering, for example, extends way beyond getting computers into classrooms. The tech giant today provides many of the same services that a national government would: it has its own exportable, model high-tech high school, a teacher training programme and has invested in online courses and virtual schools.[17] Its latest product, the 'school in a box', provides the technology for a whole school to learn the Microsoft way. As anticipated, early adopters in the UK include one of England's biggest academy chains and the free school led by the *Daily Telegraph* commentator Toby Young.[18]

Google is another technology firm in the school reform club. As with Apple, the internet giant is pushing hard into the world's classrooms by reaching out to governments around the globe.[19] Malaysia, for example, decided to adopt Google apps as part of its reform of its education system.[20] Alongside its apps for pupils and teachers, Google's Chromebook laptop is what it calls a 'foundation for a 100 per cent web classroom'.[21]

Another notable, but late, entry into the schools market is News Corp. In 2010, Rupert Murdoch bought an education software company for $360m.[1] Murdoch's vision for News Corp's education division, today branded Amplify, is to digitise first America's, then the world's, classrooms[23] to 'fundamentally change' the way we think about delivering education.[24] This is why. 'We see a $500billion sector in the US alone that is waiting desperately to be transformed by big breakthroughs,' Murdoch told investors.[25] He said he would be 'thrilled' if 10 per cent of News Corp's revenues came from education in the next five years,[26] bearing in mind its revenues in 2012 amounted to over $33bn.[27]

If it is not yet clear, this is one hugely profitable opportunity. It is also a market that Britain's politicians want this country to profit from. This was the reason why Barber was at the business Olympics. This is now a race between companies looking to profit, and between national education systems seeking to reform ahead of their global competitors. School 'brands' and education technology products are seen as vital exports in the years to come.[28] But it means that the UK has put itself up as a model and a laboratory for the reforms. Our school system is being used as a testbed for the reformers' ideas.

These changes in schools provide the backdrop to this chapter. It is by no means a comprehensive look at what is happening in schools. Nor is it our intention to debate the merits of such reforms.[29] That is for you to decide. But what you will struggle to find is empirical evidence on which to base your judgement. Neither the privatisation of schools nor the use of technology to teach are evidence-based policies. These reforms are, let us say, evidence-lite.

Take the handing over of schools to private operators. Claims by the UK's Education Secretary, Michael Gove, and his US counterparts that independence from state control is proving an 'unstoppable driver of excellence', which is 'solidly backed by rigorous international evidence',[30] are hard to back up. Grades at academies are 'statistically indistinguishable' from state-run schools.[31] Arguments for independence have been 'overplayed'.[32] What evidence there is on US charter schools shows a similarly mixed picture. One of the very few major studies showed a fifth of charters got higher test scores than their state-run counterparts, nearly half had gains that were no different, but over a third of charters were significantly worse.[33]

'We sort of quote that there's a wealth of evidence out there,' said the then schools commissioner and the government's own academies champion, Elizabeth Sidwell, before conceding that 'maybe' more work needed to be done to distil the case for taking schools out of public hands.[34]

Similarly, the case for the greater use of technology to teach is largely evidence-free.[35] 'The evidence on technology raising learning in a traditional setting is quite weak,' said Chris Kirk from the world's biggest privately owned school operator, GEMS.[36] This is a widely acknowledged fact, even by those who are heavily invested in it. 'The evidence on learning only using technology is quite strong,' Kirk said. 'It's not a particularly great idea.'[37] One study has shown[38] students in virtual schools perform significantly worse than pupils in regular schools, with poor test results and dropout rates.[39]

Contrast this with the evidence on what we know has an impact on standards in schools. Family income is the biggest determining factor and easiest way to predict how well a child does at school. Out-of-school factors, like income and parents' education, the neighbourhood children grow up in and the stability of their home environment, count for twice as much as all in-school factors. Discussions on poverty, though, are of little interest to education reformers.[40]

Similarly, a lack of, or conflicting, evidence on the efficacy of these changes in schools is no stop on reform. It is happening because 'the market for providing students with it will dictate it', as one lobbyist put it.[41]

It would be a mistake, however, to view reform-minded politicians bent on accelerating radical shifts in schools as merely bowing to industry demands. The UK government sees the education market as a source of economic growth. The success to date of the education reform movement, therefore, is not just a triumph of business interests. It is an illustration of both the power of business lobbying and the complex relationships between corporations and nation states.

This exposes an important characteristic of lobbying. Often it is not about changing politicians' minds, but about helping allies in government to achieve their own, coincident plans. Lobbyists promote these shared ideas and policies, helping to make them popular, or at least palatable, to the public. Lobbyists will help the government make its case.[42] This coming together of interests can, at times, feel like collusion.

Our intention, then, is to highlight some of the lobbyists helping to drive these changes, how they have organised themselves to push for reform and some of the relationships they have formed with government.

In the UK the pros and cons of these changes are not yet the subject of widespread national, public debate. Compared to discussions in the media over the albeit important changes to the school history curriculum, there has been barely a ripple. The same cannot be said of the United States, where similar reforms have caused a war.

Across the pond, the battle lines are clearly marked, the strategies of the reformers more visible, and the players – the lobbyists and their backers – more readily, although not always, disclosed. In other words, the drivers of changes in state education are much clearer to see. This is thanks, in part, to commercial lobbying in America being better resourced, more aggressive and more willing to engage in debate. It may also be because US lobbyists are subject to transparency rules. Lobbyists have to publicly declare their activities. Partly as a consequence, the reform debate is raging. It is often unhelpfully polarised but it is being had. Here, not so much.

In Britain we are experiencing fog when it comes to seeing the education reform lobby. The lines are not sharp, whole areas of activity are out of sight, the money funnelled into the lobby is hidden. But hopefully a short journey through the comparatively brightly lit streets of lobbying in America, and New York in particular, can help clear some of the British mist. And when it starts to lift, you will see that private interests – multinational corporations, city financiers and others – play a central role over here too.

*

A decade ago Barber's ideas and experience were exported to the US to assist in the reform of New York City's schools, the largest public school system in the country (in the US a public school is a state-run school, unlike in the UK where it refers to the private sector).[43] Hot-footing it from Downing Street in 2005 as a McKinsey consultant, Barber was one of a handful of advisers drafted in by the City's mayor, Michael Bloomberg, and his schools chancellor and central school reform figure, Joel Klein.[44] Together they set out to make the city a 'laboratory for educational experimentation', one that would be closely watched across the US.[45] The transformation of New York's schools was described as entire system reform.

One of the central changes undertaken by Klein was a dramatic increase in the number of independent charter schools in the city. He was, though, all too aware of the resistance such a move would face. Lined up to oppose him were America's powerful teaching unions, a sizeable proportion of New York's residents, and some vocal commentators like Diane Ravitch, a former assistant Secretary of Education under George Bush Sr. Ravitch began as a pro-reform supporter of charter schools before switching sides to become one of their fiercest critics. Klein had a fight on his hands. What follows is the abbreviated story of how he and his fellow reformers won.

In 2005 Klein put out a call to arms to corporate America. CEOs, he said, must become vocal advocates for schools reform.[46] The business community needed to step up or America's position in the world was going to be 'significantly in peril', he warned.[47] Klein's call was answered by a group of America's big-money philanthropists, dubbed the Billionaires' Boys Club. One central player was a friend of Mayor Bloomberg, Microsoft's founder and chair, Bill Gates.[48]

Gates has long been an evangelist for school reform and one of its biggest funders. He sincerely believes that business and market principles can make US schools perform better, and in technology as a means for improving standards. Through his foundation, which is worth $34bn, he has ploughed billions of dollars into US school reform programmes, or 'experiments in education,' as he puts it.[49] He has pumped money, for example, into independent charter schools, which he sees as the 'innovators' driving this revolution.[50]

Gates has also invested in education reform advocacy. He has funded PR campaigns to shift public opinion, paid for the development of policies to speed up reform and spent money on the lobbying of politicians. 'The importance of advocacy has gotten clearer,' said a Gates Foundation spokesperson. Of the $3bn-plus that the Foundation expects to pour into education in the next five or so years, up to 15 per cent of it will go on PR and lobbying.[51]

Just as New York embarked on reform, Gates declared war on the nation's school system. He claimed that US high schools had become 'obsolete', and were 'limiting – even ruining – the lives of millions of Americans every year'.[52] He pledged his support for Klein's cause. He was joined by other philanthropists in the billionaires' club, including the investor Eli Broad, the Walton family of Wal-Mart fame and the computer magnate Michael Dell. Over the next few years they collectively invested millions in filling New York with charter schools.[53]

Alongside the charter school operators looking to expand in the city, some of whom received cash from the billionaires' fund, another supportive community also pledged its commitment to reform: New York's hedge fund managers, many of whom also became charter school sponsors. These financiers were, in Klein's words, the 'army of foot soldiers for the movement'.[54] Education reform became known as the 'hot cause' for Wall Street types.[55]

This was the core of the reform lobby in the war over New York's schools: the reform-minded politicians and their officials, like Klein, the billionaires' club with their unlimited resources, the charter school operators and the financiers. Now let us turn to their lobbying.

First, they needed to win the argument. As explored in Chapter 3, the case for reform needed to be framed and crafted in such a way that large numbers of people would not just support their plans, but would be driven to organise around charter schooling and be prepared to challenge its opponents.

'We need to hit on fear and anger,' the lobbyist Rick Berman advised a gathering of wealthy philanthropists interested in school reform. 'And how you get the fear and anger is by reframing the problem,'[56] he said. Berman, who has a history of creating front groups, attacking unions and working for the tobacco industry,[57] told the reformers that rather than intellectualise the education debate, they needed to trigger an emotional reaction in people. 'Emotions will stay with people longer than concepts,' he said. So, rather than a rational debate on the merits of their plans, reformers needed to motivate supporters by tapping into their fears for their children's future and provoking anger at those opposed to reform. One evident way that this was achieved was through movies.

'Your children and future generations are on the bridge of the *Titanic* and everyone's going to drown,' says one interviewee featured in the documentary film *Waiting for 'Superman'*, which premiered in New York in 2010. 'Lives hang in the balance,' it said, echoing the reformers' dire warnings on the state of America's schools. The film, which features Gates and was supported by Broad, follows the fortunes of five aspiring students and their desperate families as they attempted to get a coveted place at a charter school, portrayed as the holy grail and central solution to the crisis. The bad guys, the ones that sank the ship in *Waiting for 'Superman'*, are the teaching unions. The finger of blame points straight at the public system, its teachers and their rights.

Waiting for 'Superman' was in fact the third in a series of films pushing the reformers' agenda. In 2009 there was *The Cartel*, which is a 'heart-breaking' (*New York Post*)[58] and 'mind-boggling' (*LA Times*)[59] documen-tary that pits charter schools (good) against public schools (bad) made by a former Bloomberg TV reporter and starring Mayor Bloomberg. That same year also saw the release of *The Lottery*, another film, featuring Klein, that highlighted the opposition from the teachers' unions to charter schools.[60]

A fourth fictional film, but one loosely 'inspired by real events', arrived in cinemas in 2012. *Won't Back Down* is the story of gritty single mum Jamie (played by Maggie Gyllenhaal) who with the help of a teacher, Nona (Viola Davis), sets about transforming their children's failing inner city school. 'Facing a powerful and entrenched bureaucracy, an estab-lishment of bad teachers, unthinking officials and a complacent teachers' union, they risk everything to make a difference to the educa-tion and future of their children.' The system does not care, but, by god, Jamie does. 'We've got to be the change we want to see,' she cries, as Gandhi didn't quite say. The choice presented in the film was obvi-ously to create an outstanding charter from the dregs of a public school.

Won't Back Down had the second-worst opening weekend of any film on wide release in thirty years. When it premiered in New York, unions and parent groups took to the red carpet to protest at its harsh portrayal of teachers and their reps as ruining the lives of children.[61] The film was also panned by critics, the *Los Angeles Times* describing it as a film 'so shamelessly manipulative and hopelessly bogus it will make you bite your tongue in regret and despair'.[62]

But as means of reinforcing the powerful messages of the reformers, the films were vital tools. All delivered a strikingly similar message:

1. America's public education system has failed, and poor students have been failed by the system more than most. This, in other words, is a moral failure.
2. Teachers, their unions and the rest of the so-called education

establishment are to blame. The system is being run for the benefit of these adults and not the children.

Here comes the jump . . .

3. The only hope is to free schools from state control through charter schools and allow competition to drive up standards.

4. The future of America is at stake. Stick with the status quo and the country will fall even further behind the global competition.

5. The need for reform is urgent, if you were in any doubt.[63]

Nobody would question that the US state education system fails an unacceptable proportion of its students, particularly minority and poorer students. Nor is there any doubt that the teachers' unions in America are formidable political players. Nor that there are some poor teachers in the system. But it is crucial to recognise that this constructed narrative – America's entire future is in peril unless schools are taken out of public hands – has been created and promoted by those whose interests are served by such reform.

Won't Back Down was seen as a powerful way to 'get the folks on the couch' with these messages, in the words of its makers, Walden Media.[64] This is a studio owned by the conservative billionaire Philip Anschutz, which also financed *Waiting for 'Superman'*, a film that was targeted at winning over a different, but equally important, audience of 'policy wonks'.

But *Won't Back Down* was not just a way of getting the reform message out to the folks at home. It was a lobbying tool. First the film asked moviegoers to become activists and spread the word of the 'pro-education' movement (as opposed to those anti-education teachers, unions and officials). It came with a 'grassroots toolkit' and materials for supporters to spread the pro-charter message virally and called on people to mobilise their communities.[65]

Second, it targeted politicians. *Won't Back Down* went on a tour of American cities, including New York, encouraging state legislators to introduce laws that would pave the way for more charter schools.[66] These so-called Parent Trigger Laws allow parents to petition to change who runs their local school. They can vote to fire staff, close the school, or convert it into a charter and hand its management over to an independent operator. Parent Trigger Laws are thus portrayed in the film as a way of empowering parents. Critics see them as a clever way to trick parents into gaining control of their schools only to hand them over to private corporations.[67]

The movie's tour was organised by the US Chamber of Commerce,[68] but the business lobby group credited with launching Parent Trigger Laws 'into hyperdrive' is an organisation called the American Legislative Exchange Council (ALEC).[69] This is a controversial network that brings together America's biggest corporations and mainly Republican politicians to craft model, state-level legislation (the level at which many decisions are taken in the US, including on schools). In other words, ALEC does not just influence laws, it literally writes them, supplying fully drafted bills that can be rolled out to state legislators.[70] [71] In this sense, it is much more than a lobby group. Until 2012 the Gates Foundation was a funder of ALEC, terminating its funding only after the network became the focus of public anger for its support of a number of highly contentious laws.[72]

The laws ALEC promotes are often designed to reduce taxes and regulations for corporations, while weakening unions.[73] The network has long had a special interest in privatisation and for almost twenty years the handing over of public schools to the private sector has been a priority.[74] Over a hundred ALEC-influenced education bills were introduced across the US in the first half of 2013, thirty-one of which became state law. Parent Trigger Laws were just one tool in their box to achieve their goal.

This leads us to the second tactic of the education reform lobby: the funding of third party groups, like ALEC, to push for change. Third party campaign groups can be essential in fronting messages, as outlined in Chapter 5. The drive to reform schools is cluttered with lobby groups supported by big-money donors. Gates leads the field in this respect. It is said to be easier to name the organisations that Gates' foundation does not support than to list all of those that it does.[75] So, we need to add a host of lobby groups funded and created by reformers to our list of reform-minded politicians and officials, the billionaires' club, the school operators and the army of financiers lobbying for reform.

These third party lobby groups – the middle managers of the reform movement – have played a dual role in the battle for America's schools. They have helped to carry the message – carefully crafted and honed with this emotional punch – to politicians, the media and the public. But some have also been key in fronting attacks on the lobby's opposition. Lobbyists need not just to push their case, but to undermine that of their opponents, something we looked at in Chapter 6. This was true in the battle over schools, with the unions bearing the brunt of attacks.

School reform lobby groups have talked openly of their underhand methods to beat their union counterparts. Tactics include employing all the best available lobbyists in a state just to prevent the unions from hiring them. They have also advised on spreading the unions thin with decoy legislation directed at teachers, allowing pro-reform laws to fly under the radar.[76] Reformers needed to 'play offense' and stop giving the opposition time to organise, advised one education reform lobbyist at a Gates-sponsored get-together of education philanthropists.[77]

Third party groups for the reformers also played a significant role in the battle over New York's schools. Three central organisations represent the core activities of the reformers' lobbying.

The campaign group, Education Reform Now, was set up to campaign for the reformers' agenda, including pushing for more charter schools, and to act as a counterforce to the state's two major teachers' unions and their combined membership of 900,000. The group is tight-lipped about its donors, but members of the billionaires' club, Walton and Broad, are among them.[78] As is typical of these lobby groups, its board includes some heavy-hitting charter school sponsors from the hedge fund world.

Education Reform Now could be seen as representing the media wing of the lobby. The advocacy group has worked hard to win New Yorkers to its side. In just two years from 2010 it spent more than $10m on campaigning, primarily attacking teachers' rights and pushing for more charters. Three-quarters of the money went on TV and internet advertising campaigns to match the media spend of the unions. The public did not see its wealthy backers though. The lobby group used selected school teachers who opposed their union's position to front their campaigns.[79]

Education Reform Now has a sibling lobby group, Democrats for Education Reform. This organisation represents the reformers' political fund. It is an entity known as a political action committee, or PAC. PACs are a significant feature of US politics. They raise and spend money to support the election of political candidates. While teaching unions are also huge spenders in US elections, their options are narrowing. Democrats for Education Reform's mission has been to win the Democratic Party over to the reformers' cause. It also lobbies for more charters.[80] In the New York State elections of 2010, it financed only pro-charter candidates.[81] Democrats for Education Reform is backed by, among others, the founders of hedge funds, and its board is again a sea of Wall Street financiers.[82]

Then there is the practical wing of the lobby, the organisations driving actual change on the ground. The New York City Charter School Center is a kind of one-stop-shop for all things charter which lobbies for and provides practical help to pro-charter supporters.[83] It was formed in 2004 by what are described as a group of philanthropists who were galvanised by Klein's reforms. Gates and the other billionaires are donors to the group and its board includes charter school operators.[84]

By 2010 these third party lobby groups were positioning themselves to go all out in their battle to reshape New York's school system. City legislators were looking to pass a new law that would more than double the amount of charter schools allowed in the city. It was the 'fight of our life', as one charter supporter put it.[85]

With a multimillion-dollar war chest, Education Reform Now embarked on a TV and radio ad campaign aimed at winning support for the new law. The funds also paid for phone banks and door-to-door canvassers to urge voters to lobby for the bill.[86] The unions hit back with a campaign attacking the hedge-funders' attack on teachers and public schools.[87]

Klein played a central role in the campaign. 'We need to mobilize,'[88] Klein wrote to a fellow reformer at the start of 2010. A tight-knit group went about the task that included Joe Williams of Democrats for Reform; a representative of Education Reform Now; James Merriman of the NYC Charter School Center, charter school operators, and Klein, the official.[89]

A cache of emails released under Freedom of Information law shows Klein and his officials coordinating the effort with the lobbyists, which included bringing in the money, although Klein denied being directly involved in fund-raising, and seeding the media with pro-charter voices. Klein was coming under pressure from the charter school operators to bear down on the opposition. One emailed that this was their 'last chance to be SUPERAGGRESSIVE in standard of excellence', advising Klein to go all out in attacking the unions: 'Blame 'em. Every hour of the day. Pr offensive,' they urged.[90]

On one occasion, Klein and several charter school lobbyists took part in a conference call with a large foundation to secure funds for Education Reform Now's campaign. After the call Klein emailed one of the lobby group's consultants: 'You were terrific,' he wrote. 'Perfect pitch, perfect message.' Another participant emailed: 'Who's the heavy breather on the call? Normally, I'd ask them to mute their phone but I don't want to alienate any donors.' 'Some overweight billionaire,' Klein replied.[91]

The emails also reveal Klein's officials collaborating with the lobbyists to place material in the media to support their campaign. This included recruiting third parties, like an influential New York pastor in Brooklyn, to write articles supporting the charter school bill. The pastor's appeared, with input from officials, in the Murdoch-owned *New York Post*.[92]

The emails reveal a shocking closeness and, as many have argued, an inappropriate alliance of interests between public officials and lobbyists. The New York City Parents Union described the arrangement as corrupt. 'The first thing I noticed was the chummy exchanges,' says Diane Ravitch,[93] who is singled out in the correspondence for her opposition to charters as 'moronic', 'idiotic' and a 'deranged crackpot'.[94] 'The public officials who are paid to protect and support the public schools of New York City are working hand-in-glove to advance the interests of the privately managed charters, not the public schools,' she said.

Klein got his bill through and the number of charter schools in New York was set to shoot up. It was a long slog and not always a pleasant one, Merriman wrote, but 'the end product . . . moves us forward and lets the chancellor [Klein] and the ed reform community continue its work'.[95] Klein quit as schools chancellor just months later. In the New Year he became chair of the lobby group Education Reform Now.[96]

In spring 2011 Klein shifted seats to chair yet another pro-reform lobby group, StudentsFirstNY, which later joined forces with Democrats for Education Reform. For its first year, StudentsFirstNY was run by the official who helped write New York's charter school law.[97] It is the state arm of a US-wide campaign group led by Klein's equivalent in Washington, its former schools chancellor and a strident education reformer, Michelle Rhee. It is known to have received funds from the billionaires' club.[98] As this illustrates, the education reform movement draws from a small but powerful well. As Chapter 3 describes, insiders make the most effective lobbyists.

Klein's standing as a successful school reformer was now beyond question. His reforms in New York were seen as a beacon. They were set to become the 'national pace car for change' that the reformers had hoped.[99] Besides Gates, Klein's work attracted the attention of others in the education technology business. Facebook founder Mark Zuckerberg donated $100m in 2010 to reforming schools in neighbouring New Jersey, part of which went on charter schools and pushing for controversial changes to teachers' contracts (introducing so-called performance-related pay).[100] An 'archetype of how this has to be done in modern America', was how Google's Eric Schmidt put Klein's achievements.[101] Schmidt describes Klein as a 'personal friend'.[102]

Schmidt shares the reformers' aims and agenda. He is a strong advocate of choice and competition and the greater use of technology in schools. He has praised Klein for his criticism of teaching unions.[103] Schmidt has come to the same conclusions that the failure of America's schools is the fault of the education establishment, whom he cites as the biggest block to reform. 'The system is run for the benefit of the adults, not the children,' he said.[104]

It was not to his friend in Google, however, that Klein turned to next in his school reform quest, nor Gates. On leaving public office, at the end of the summer of 2010, Klein was hired by Rupert Murdoch[105] and picked to lead his budding education division. The education software company that Murdoch bought, Wireless Generation, had previously held an $80m contract with Klein's department for a big data project that tracked student's test scores, which was seen by many as a failure.[106]

Since making these two acquisitions – the software firm and Klein – Murdoch has played an increasing role in pushing the reformers' agenda. We need to add him to our list of lobbyists. He and Klein had become close and reportedly talked frequently about the state of America's public schools.[107] Was he in the loop, for example, over the 2010 New York charter expansion law? Klein was advised by one of his officials: 'It may be good for you to call Murdoch and tell him why this is a good bill.'[108]

News Corporation was also involved in promoting the pro-charter film *Won't Back Down*. 20th Century Fox, a News Corp company, was the distribution partner of the film studio, Walden Media.[109] When *Won't Back Down* tanked in cinemas, an advertising campaign was launched to revive it featuring glowing quotes from the Murdoch-owned *Wall Street Journal* and *New York Post*.[110] Ahead of the movie's tour promoting its pro-charter message to politicians, Rupert Murdoch, a backer of the controversial lobby group ALEC, joined the lobby group's education wing that was pushing for pro-charter state laws.[111]

Having succeeded in his goal of making New York a 'laboratory for educational experimentation', Klein's next big task was to flog education technology on behalf of Murdoch. The 'digital revolution in education' is coming, he said in an interview in Murdoch's *Sunday Times*.[112] Klein urged the UK to 'go faster' in its adoption and predicted that in ten years' time, instead of going to school every day, children may spend more time at home, logging into virtual schools.[113] He also cited Florida's virtual schools and championed one US state that had just passed a law which mandated that every pupil receive a laptop and take courses online. He did not mention the vocal demonstrations that accompanied the unannounced reforms in Idaho. The following year, Klein's old boss, Michael Bloomberg, helped bankroll an unsuccessful campaign to stop the Idaho laws from being repealed by popular demand.[114]

This alliance of public officials and corporations and the school reforms they are introducing have been the cause of much outrage in the US. People have taken to the streets and organised in their local communities. Pearson's New York office, for example, was the target of a protest by parents, partly, as one group put it, because of 'the excessive power' it was felt to have over the City's education department. Similar parent-led campaigns have been waged around the country. Politicians' stances on reform have been probed. A lively debate has been had online, through blogs and alternative media who are intent on foregrounding the issues and what is at stake. The debate has largely been avoided, however, in the mainstream media. When Klein, Gates and others say that America's entire future rests on reforming schools, this is surprising.

A study in 2009 found that less than 1.5 per cent of US national news coverage dealt with education. This was more than in the previous two years. Most of the reporting also had nothing to do with policy. This makes it all but impossible for the public to follow the debate, the issues and the influences at work, all of which are important in making choices about their children's education.[115] But news organisations have a conflict of interest when it comes to reporting school reform. With media companies leaking money, many like News Corp see the education industry as an answer. Besides Murdoch's entry into the market, the company that owned the *Washington Post* derived more than half its 2012 income from education businesses.[116] NBC's schools offering is now available in forty-three states. Pearson, which owns the *Financial Times,* claims to have invested over $9bn in the digitisation and what it calls 'creative destruction' of education.[117] Should we expect these players to provide a forum for informed debate?

This provides a snapshot of some of the players in the education reform movement and their sustained and substantial lobbying effort in the United States. The movement has framed the debate to position its reforms as the only solution to an urgent problem. It has laid the blame on teachers and their unions and attacked them. It has created an army of third party groups and funded business lobby organisations to win the support of politicians and the public. And it has been helped in its quest by a corporate media with a vested interest in reform. The lobby is organised, well-funded and with its eye on a very big prize.

Britain's education reformers share some of these qualities. The lobby is made up of some of the same players. They have engaged in some of the same tactics – strikingly similar at times. But the changes to schools in England are also being conducted with a degree of subtlety and under a cloak of secrecy that prevents us too from having a proper, open discussion on where our children's education is heading. There is nothing sinister about this. It is just the British way.

*

When Michael Gove took the reins of England's education system in May 2010 he expressed a non-interest in technology in schools. He was all about tradition and conservative values: heads were to get more powers over discipline; he wanted a return to blazers and ties, prefects and houses; primary school children were to be taught Latin; every school in the country was getting a new, King James Bible inscribed in gold 'from the Secretary of State for Education'. That was before he started shaking up the history curriculum, damning it for its failure to teach 'one of the most inspiring stories I know – the history of our United Kingdom'.[118] He was reassuringly conservative.

Gove's enthusiasm for the rapid expansion of the schools market and the private sector's role in it, however, was apparent from the outset. He set about eagerly completing what had very tentatively begun with Thatcher and continued under Blair. More than half of secondary schools in England are now independently run academies. Over 2,000 have been created under Gove. His ambition is for all schools to be freed from local authority control. There are now also eighty new academy free schools, closely modelled on US charter schools, with over a hundred more in the pipeline.[119] These are billed as giving unhappy parents and teachers the chance to create new schools. One of the top reasons, however, for people wanting to set up a free school, 'to be honest', says Rachel Wolf, the government's free school champion, is the freedom they have over teachers' 'pay, conditions and recruitment'.[120]

Free schools also provide a structure for profit-making state schools, something that Gove supports.[121] His ambition to see all 25,000 schools in England independently run, rests on companies being able to make a return on their investment. Even today, while for-profit corporations are prohibited from taking charge of state schools, there is nothing to stop governors inviting them to help operate them. Several corporations are also looking at forming not-for-profit trusts, which would allow them to directly run schools. They would make their money selling services to the trust.

Profit-making schools raise obvious concerns: that cash will be diverted from classrooms to shareholders; more 'expensive' facilities, like science laboratories and sports amenities could be restricted; that harder to teach pupils will be kept out of schools that are judged on test scores; and that it could lead to cuts in teaching staff and the growth of cheaper, online learning.

Gove did not start this privatisation process but he is determined to finish it. In this he has been helped by a reform lobby similar to that in the US. Before looking at the players in this lobby, let us begin with the narrative they have used to justify their reforms. It is a familiar story.

Britain's schools are failing our children. This is the message at the core of the UK reformers' argument. It is one that has been used to justify education reform in this country for decades. 'We are falling further and further behind other nations,' says Gove, citing international league tables that, he claims, show an apparent and sometimes sharp decline in standards.

The figures he cites, however, have been found to be flawed. The official Statistics Authority described them as uncertain, weak and problematic and reprimanded Gove for using them. Other relatively recent international studies of test scores in maths and science showed no decline and put England near the top, beaten only by Pacific Rim countries.[122] An academic review of these contrasting test results confirmed that the government's claims that England has been 'plummeting' down international pupil performance tables could not be justified. This is not to be complacent or to make excuses. Standards need to go up, but there is scant evidence that England's schools face a crisis of the magnitude described by the reformers.[123]

We have similarly been told that this crisis is the fault of a left-leaning education establishment made up of teaching unions, bureaucrats and local officials, described by Gove as the 'enemies of promise',[124] or simply and popularly known among reformers as 'the blob' (a term first used by Reagan's education secretary).[125] Gove promised to 'put children first', not the needs of these adults.[126]

The solution presented, as in the US, is to free schools from bureaucratic control. Any problem can be solved, it seems, by Gove's reforms. Britain's recent, sluggish economic growth, according to one reformer, can be traced back to the systematic failure of its state schools.[127] A report by Unicef into Britain's youth, which highlighted the high numbers of under-age drinkers and teenage pregnancies in this country 'underlined the urgent need for [education] reforms', according to the government.[128] The need for radical education reform is, we are told 'urgent'.[129]

David Cameron has accused those who oppose the government's reforms of defending the establishment and failure.[130] Michael Gove has called teachers, critical of his reforms, 'ultra-militant' Marxists 'hell bent on destroying our schools'. The *Telegraph*'s James Delingpole describes free school opponents as 'actively evil'.

A failing school system; an urgent need to reform to keep up with the rest of the world; an education establishment as the block to improving standards. The same story is being used to sell this latest round of privatisation of state education.

Now let us come to the schools reform lobby. Like Klein, Gove has been helped by a tight-knit reform community in the UK made up of business-backed think tanks and third party lobby groups, peopled by well-connected insiders. As in New York, this lobby also appears, at times, to be working hand-in-glove with politicians and officials. What is not as apparent is the funding. In Britain we are largely in the dark on who is financing these lobbyists.

An opportunity to see them gathered in one place came towards the end of 2012. The low-key event drew fifty or so participants involved in school reform[131] to the grand surroundings of Wellington College, a fee-paying school in Berkshire, which is itself at the centre of the reform movement. It is the venue, for example, for the annual *Sunday Times* Festival of Education, a two-day event attracting thousands that has been sponsored by, among others, Microsoft, Dell, Pearson and Google.[132]

The Berkshire cast included: reform-minded policy-makers, such as Blair's Education Minister and academy champion, Andrew Adonis, and Gove's then schools commissioner, Elizabeth Sidwell; academy school operators and free school founders; and education technology lobbyists, including Microsoft. But, the select event also drew together many of the UK's think tanks and lobby groups intent on reshaping education. Collectively these groups perform much the same role as their US counterparts: coming up with policies to be fed into the political system, influencing politicians and the public through media operations and providing practical help to affect change on the ground. They also importantly provide an indirect means of financing the ambitions of politicians who share their views. Few of these groups, however, publicly reveal who their backers are.

For many years these lobbyists have helped to lay the groundwork for the changes we see today: the privatisation of schools and the greater use of technology to teach. As one central reformer, James O'Shaughnessy, host of the Berkshire gathering, said: theirs is 'a huge battle in an already very long war'.[133]

One of the youngest of the current crop of lobby groups is the New Schools Network. Its job is execution: driving the growth in free schools in England. It performs the same function as the New York

City Charter School Center: to privately lobby, publicly campaign, but also to offer practical help to new school providers. It was founded by a former Gove aide, Rachel Wolf, who, until her departure in 2013, was the country's chief free school lobbyist.

The impetus for the New Schools Network was a fact-finding trip to New York. Wolf's mission for the Conservative Party in 2008 was to study the city's charter school reforms. She took inspiration from Joel Klein and was keen to learn from his experience, asking for advice on 'convincing' arguments to persuade the public and journalists of the case for privately run schools. Klein declined an offer from Wolf to be on the Network's council. Instead James Merriman of the New York Charter School Center became an adviser to his British counterparts.

The New Schools Network was Gove's vehicle for getting free schools moving. Wolf was 'helped out' early on by another of Gove's inner circle, Dominic Cummings.[134] To get the charity off the ground, it was also controversially handed half a million pounds by Gove's department.[135] Within weeks of the Education Secretary taking the reins, Cummings was urging officials to stump up the funds without delay: 'Labour has handed hundreds of millions to leftie orgs if u guys cant navigate this thro the bureauc then not a chance of any new schools starting!!' he wrote.[136]

With the shared personnel and government support, the New Schools Network feels like an extension of Gove's department. *Spectator* editor Fraser Nelson admitted Gove uses it to further his agenda. But it also has the support of the private sector. Like its New York equivalent, its trustees are drawn from a mix of academy school operators and City figures. People like the financier Michael George and Justin Dowley, described as 'one of the wiliest foxes in finance'.[137] It is also part-financed by private donations, but unlike its New York equivalent, the New Schools Network refuses to disclose its backers: 'We have donors,' Wolf said, 'who wish to remain anonymous.'[138] Wolf remained at the helm until 2013, when she returned to New York to work with Joel Klein at the new education arm of Murdoch's News Corp.[139]

Typifying the close-knit nature of the reform lobby, Wolf was replaced at the Network by Natalie Evans, another ex-Conservative Party worker. Evans was also formerly with the UK think tank Policy Exchange.[140] Often distractingly called David Cameron's favourite think tank, Policy Exchange is one of the more vocal lobby groups in Britain's education reform movement. Michael Gove was its very first chair from 2002 to 2006, during which period it began executing its campaign to push the school reformers' agenda.

According to Wolf, Policy Exchange 'created the initial impetus', behind free schools.[141] It was a 'policy hit' for the lobby group.[142] But its lobbying – this 'impetus' – is not confined to free schools. In the past decade Policy Exchange has produced reports, hosted events and provided pages of commentary in the press on the need to reform the whole of Britain's education system on market-based principles, including advocating profit-making schools. When the former minister Andrew Adonis noted that 'the media is more balanced nowadays', compared to when he attempted change under Blair, with 'far more voices speaking up for reform', he could be referring to the PR activities of groups like Policy Exchange.[143] It could be seen as representing the media wing of the lobby.

Part of the lobby group's role has been to popularise, or at least normalise, reforms once viewed as on the fringes of what is politically acceptable and shift them to being acceptable government policy. In this it has helped Gove enormously. Radical changes promoted by the Policy Exchange and others, such as for-profit schools,[144] appear later as less radical for having been talked about. One Policy Exchange report, for example, declared that the transfer of schools to the private sector 'has now become an ambition shared by people across the political spectrum, whereas in the 1980s it was very much perceived as part of a radical market-based "Thatcherite" agenda'. This normalising of radical policies is a practice that has gone on for years and by others.

Today, Policy Exchange spends in the region of £2m a year campaigning for market-driven reforms across many policy areas, not just education.[145] It is at pains to stress, however, that its ideas are based on research that is 'strictly empirical'[146] and is adamant that the policies it advocates are free of outside influence. It does not, it says, take commissions from funders. However, like the New Schools Network, it refuses to say who is funding its work. When asked about the group's backers under his leadership, Gove's office said it was unable to help as 'he doesn't have that information'.[147]

As long as it does not disclose its sources of income, however, this independence can never be tested. From the little that is known of its funders, it is clear that a number share its interest in the privatisation of schools. As with campaign groups like Education Reform Now in the US, they include academy chain sponsors, as well as outsourcing firms and investors.

Policy Exchange was established by supporters of an agenda fronted by Michael Portillo. This was the MP who was to lead the current crop of Tory politicians, like Gove, but who failed in his bid to win over the Conservative Party. Little more is known of who put up the startup money. What is known is that Portillo's campaign attracted the support of a number of entrepreneurs with an interest in school reform:[148] Stanley (Lord) Kalms, the former chair of the Dixons Group, owners of Currys, PC World and other retailers, who sponsored the Dixons City Academy in Bradford, now part of a group of academies in Yorkshire; the property tycoon Geoffrey Leigh, sponsor of the Leigh Technology Academy, which also gave birth to a chain of academies and free schools in the Dartford area;[149] and Philip (Lord) Harris, chair of the retailers Carpetright and sponsor of a chain of nineteen primary and secondary academies in and around London.[150]

Since then, Policy Exchange's known supporters include the well-known Tory donor, Michael (Lord) Ashcroft, another academy sponsor.[151] Teachers at the Ashcroft Technology Academy in London are bound by contracts banning them from taking industrial action and union negotiation rights are not recognised by the school's leaders.[152] A Policy Exchange trustee and funder, the private equity investor Theodore Agnew, is another academy sponsor and free school founder.[153] He is also a trustee of the New Schools Network.[154] Agnew was appointed by Gove in 2013 to chair a new academies board at the Department of Education, a job that involves encouraging academy chains to be more 'innovative'.[155] Another Policy Exchange funder is John (Lord) Nash,[156] an academy sponsor and founder of the private equity firm Sovereign Capital.[157] It was named 'Education Investor of the Year' for the second year running in 2011.[158] In 2013 Nash was elevated to the Lords and made Education Minister by Gove. Nash is now responsible for free schools and academy policy. He agreed to step away from all relevant business interests while a Minister.

Policy Exchange's coffers have also been boosted by donations from Henry Pitman, founder of Tribal Group, an outsourcing firm specialising in education.[159] Among many other contracts, Tribal conducts

Ofsted inspections of schools.[160] Outsourcing giant Serco has also sponsored Policy Exchange's work. As well as running the education arms of local authorities, it is a big supplier of services to schools. It partners with academy chains, like the Harris Federation, for example, to provide IT services. It sees the direct running of whole schools as a 'natural extension' of its work.[161] BSkyB has also paid to join the think tank's 'business forum', although the hacking scandal forced Rupert Murdoch to abandon his plan to build an academy in London.[162] Whether this is the limit of his investment and how many others with an interest in reforming schools have financed Policy Exchange's campaign is not known. Since 2010, the American Friends of Policy Exchange, an independent entity, has reached out across the Atlantic in search of financial backers. It has hosted Michelle Rhee of the US lobby group StudentsFirst under this banner.[163]

As in New York, the lines between officials and groups like Policy Exchange are blurred, with people frequently moving between government and lobby groups and both drawing from a tight-knit community of reformers. Policy Exchange has become something of a feeder school for Gove's office. Besides Agnew and Nash, several ex-Policy Exchangers have followed Gove into the Department for Education. Sam Freedman, head of Policy Exchange's education unit, became an adviser to Gove. Gabriel Milland became the education department's head of news.

Another notable alumnus is James O'Shaughnessy, host of the Berkshire reform gathering, who wrote in *The Times*: 'Mr. Gove will succeed, he'd better do. I've bet my career on it.'[164] After a period under Gove at the Policy Exchange from 2004, O'Shaughnessy followed the newly appointed shadow Education Secretary to work for the Conservative Party in opposition. He then co-drafted the deal between the coalition parties in 2010, before doing a 'stint' as Cameron's Director of Policy.[165]

During this period two pieces of reform legislation were pushed through. The first, which was aimed at allowing many more schools to be independently run, was hurried through parliament, passing into law in seventy-seven days, just months after the election and 'too fast for the Liberal Democrats to marshal resistance'.[166] It was 'oven-ready' when Gove arrived. Weeks before the second piece of schools legislation became law in late 2011, O'Shaughnessy quit government to return to the private sector.[167]

Think tanks, like the Policy Exchange, are set up to promote policy agendas.[168] They shape the climate for reform, stretch debate and 'fly political kites' to test public acceptance of policies. They are ideally placed to influence public and political opinion through the media.

The value to politicians bent on radical reform in having a privately funded media and research organisation, like a think tank, should not be underestimated. 'Think tanks are places where politicians put people to work,' says one lobbying insider. 'It's outsourcing with plausible deniability.'[169] It is a trend that has emerged in recent years in the US.[170] Think tanks have become a way of funding politicians' agendas without having to directly fund their offices. Whether this applies to Gove and the Policy Exchange cannot be shown.

What is clear is that the Education Secretary is a magnet for political donors. In less than a decade he has attracted nearly half a million pounds in declared donations from outside interests, almost twice that of any of his cabinet colleagues.[171] But while this money is open to public scrutiny, the millions pouring into Policy Exchange is not. We are largely in the dark over who has funded its work to hasten the takeover of schools.

Running alongside this privatisation lobby are third party groups pushing for more technology in schools. One of the newest of these is the Education Foundation, set up in 2011. Its co-founder Ty Goddard, who gave the Berkshire gathering a lesson in ed-tech, describes the Foundation as a think tank and reform organisation. It has, however, a particular focus on technology as a driver of reform. It hosts an ed-tech incubator programme, for example, to bring classroom products to scale. Google and Facebook are both advisers to the project.[172]

The Foundation does not publish its financial backers either, although it says it is funded by charitable foundations and leading businesses through its research, sponsored events and specific projects. Those named on its website include Google, which sponsored its first birthday bash, McKinsey, for which it hosted an event,[173] and a collaboration with Facebook and the Gates Foundation on an education-centred 'hackathon', aimed at building experimental apps for schools.[174]

The group has ties with the reform lobby in the US, from whose experience it is keen to learn. Goddard was visited in London by American lobbyists to discuss strategies on 'growing the UK education reform movement'. Among those visiting was a lobbyist from the

Foundation for Excellence in Education. This is an organisation that aggressively promotes online schools. It is financed by, among others, Gates and others in the billionaires' club, as well as Pearson and Amplify, News Corp education arm.[175] Klein is also a board member. In 2013, Michael Gove, on one of his many trips to the US, delivered the keynote speech at the foundation's annual conference. Topics discussed included 'extreme choices through digital learning' and 'the art of communicating education reform'.[176] The foundation is run by Jeb Bush, brother of George. Bush is a keen advocate of virtual schooling, which has been pioneered in his home state of Florida. His foundation has come in for criticism, primarily for working with US public officials to write education laws that could benefit some of its corporate funders.[177] It has also been accused of providing 'a dating service for corporations selling educational products – including virtual schools – to school chiefs'.[178] Goddard, though, sees Bush as a 'pioneer'.[179] The US delegation spent their time visiting UK academies and meeting with senior Department for Education officials. They even had a policy discussion in Number 10.

The Education Foundation also hosted a meeting of twenty-five education reform lobby groups in Washington, part-funded by the British government.[180] Again, the purpose was to learn lessons from their US colleagues on how to secure system reform and introduce more 'innovation' to schools. It included some familiar names in the US reform lobby: Democrats for Education Reform, StudentsFirst and the Foundation for Excellence in Education. Advocacy group Education Reform Now is also on Goddard's radar. Its logo is used to promote his Foundation's 'Education Reformers of the Year' initiative.[181]

The UK's Education Foundation also has links to Britain's established think tanks. Its advisers include Anthony Seldon, head of Wellington College (an associate director of the Foundation is also Wellington's head of 'Educational Enterprises').[182] Seldon is an adviser to Gove, who, just ahead of the 2010 general election, authored *An Education Manifesto 2010–2020* for the Centre for Policy Studies. This is one of the UK's oldest think tanks, established by Margaret Thatcher to think the unthinkable' on public policy.

Seldon's report for the Centre for Policy Studies advocated every state school operating as a business, free to raise its own capital and make a profit. Seldon is steeped in this thinking. His economist father was the first research director of the oldest of the UK's free market think tanks, the Institute of Economic Affairs. It too was present at the Berkshire gathering in the form of James Croft of the Centre for Market Reform of Education. This is a lobby group financially independent of the Institute, but with whom it shares an office and has a collaborative relationship. The Centre also lobbies for profit-making schools.[183] According to Croft it provides its donors with 'private dinners' to catch up with its work at which 'a lot of deals go down'.[184] The identity of these donors, however, is also not publicly disclosed.

The Institute of Economic Affairs was where many of the ideas behind the current reforms began. The free market think tank that did much to influence Thatcher's thinking advocated not just the privatisation of the utilities – water, gas, telephones – but also health and education services. Its latest schools publication, *The Profit Motive in Education: Continuing the Revolution*, as well as the obvious, calls for more innovative, low-cost methods of education, an endorsement perhaps of more technology to teach.[185] In its sixty-year history, the Institute of Economic Affairs has never disclosed its funders.[186]

This gives us a brief snapshot of some of the third party players that have been lobbying to reform our education system, although with scant details on the money and interests behind them. Given that the academies programme is in an advanced stage, as we now turn to look at the reformers' lobbying activity, let us focus on lobbying by technology interests to disrupt schools.

The drive to embed technology in teaching in the UK began in the eighties. Thatcher's close confidant and co-founder of the Centre for Policy Studies, Keith Joseph, was noted as being particularly enthusiastic about computing in schools.[187] Joseph was Thatcher's Education Secretary. However, it was another of her education ministers, Kenneth Baker, who was explicit about using technology as a kind of blueprint for unpacking state education.

For Baker, the main attraction of a 'computer in every school' was to fundamentally reform the school system: 'By introducing a computer you make a change, there's no question about that,' he said. 'It's not just for conventional, ordinary teaching.' Baker recalled the push back from the Education Department from such a move: 'They couldn't seem to be imaginative enough to realise I was going to change everything,' he said.[188] The Thatcher government subsidised the cost of putting a computer in every school, a first for most. While the popular BBC Micro is credited with inspiring a generation of coders, Baker, however, failed in his bid to 'change everything' in schools through technology.

The second wave of government enthusiasm arrived with Tony Blair. In the mid-nineties, the New Labour shadow administration began to show a serious interest in education technology.[189] One of the first things Blair did was to commission a report into it, choosing to lead the inquiry Dennis (now Lord) Stevenson, at the time the head of Pearson. Stevenson brought McKinsey in to do the research. It concluded that if the next government did not take steps to intensify the use of technology in schools, 'a generation of children . . . will have been put at enormous disadvantage with consequences for the UK'. It wanted to see technology 'permeate the entirety of education'.[190] The following year, Bill Gates stood with Blair on the steps of No. 10 as a cheerleader for the reforms.[191]

Despite the ed-tech lobby under Blair being dominated by the big players, like Microsoft, it also included teachers, academics and a research community with an interest in what technology might do to help them teach and pupils learn. But with the arrival of Gove, this lobby of educators found itself out in the cold, we were told. It had no traction with him. Gove was not interested in technology.[192]

Despite this stated indifference, even before it came to power the government had given a strong signal to the education technology industry that it was, in fact, interested in creating a market in schools technology. Eight months ahead of the 2010 election, the Conservatives announced their intention to scrap the agency that dealt with technology in schools. It would be the first to go in their cost-cutting 'bonfire of the quangos'. The British Educational Communications and Technology Agency, or Becta, was seen as overly controlling the market. After less than a fortnight in office, Gove began winding it down.[193] Within a year it was gone. All of a sudden the market for selling technology to schools was opened up. The axing of Becta was an idea put forward by the Centre for Policy Studies just months before the Conservatives' pre-election announcement.[194]

Still, it took Gove until well into 2011 to publicly declare an interest in technology in schools. In a speech that was billed as 'at odds with his 18 months in office', he confessed to being 'behind the curve'. His department, he said, was working up new policy on using technology in the classroom. Gove was at pains to dispel the impression that his reforms would take the country's education system back to the 1950s. '[We are accused] of caring more about Tennyson than technology, Ibsen than iTunes, more about Kubla Khan than the Khan Academy,' he said. 'There was no tension', he said. 'Schools and teaching had not changed in 100 years. If we do not change this, we will betray a generation.'[195]

One catalyst of Gove's apparent conversion to technology in schools was a warning issued to Britain from Google's Eric Schmidt in the summer of 2011. Our education system was in need of urgent reform, Schmidt said. The country that invented the computer was 'throwing away' its heritage. Using the prestigious MacTaggart lecture at Edinburgh's television festival, Britain was invited to 'think back to the glory days of the Victorian era', to the 'Lyons tea shop', builders of the world's first office computer. Schmidt said he was 'flabbergasted' that today computer science was not taught as standard in UK schools.[196] Echoing Gates' warning to America, Schmidt's message was that the once great Britain was faced with the prospect of falling further behind in the global race.

Few disputed the validity of his point that Britain is going to need more computer programmers and that computer science should be taught in schools, and that this will bring benefits to individuals and the nation. It was also a point well made to have maximum impact. In a fifteen-page speech, the rest on the changing face of TV in an online world, the rebuke dominated headlines: 'Schmidt condemns British education system' (*Guardian*); 'Britain "throwing away its computer heritage"' (*Daily Telegraph*); 'UK must shun "luvvy" school subjects, says Google chief' (*Daily Mail*); 'Be a boffin, Google boss tells Brit kids' (*Sun*). Schmidt had handed them the headlines: 'The UK has stopped nurturing its polymaths . . . you're either a "luvvy" or a "boffin"', he said in the speech.[197]

It is a message that Google has taken around the world. Two years after his critique of Britain's schools, the tech giant was cautioning Australia's politicians about the state of their education system, calling for the same reforms and predicting that the country's economy would suffer unless computer science is taught in schools. Unlike our warning, which was laced with nostalgia and tethered to our anxieties about being a once great empire in decline, Google's message to Australians homed in on their national preoccupation about what happens once the mining boom ends. The local digital sector was pitched as 'crucial' to its replacement in the economy.[198] 'If we don't do it,' said Google's Australian spokesperson, 'we're going to be hosed because we can't continue to rely on the same old industries.'[199]

Google is no doubt right in both instances. School-age children tend to be consumers of technology rather than creators. Few will learn to code. Countries that produce a tech-savvy, skilled workforce will benefit. But could the timing of Google's warnings to Britain and Australia also suggest another motivation at play? By coincidence, both corresponded with the respective launches of its Chromebook laptop for schools.[200] By 2013, Chromebooks represented more than 10 per cent of notebook sales at UK retailer, Currys PC World.

Schmidt's rebuke to Britain was just one, albeit high-profile, part of a much wider campaign by a large coalition of technology interests. The push to get computer science onto the school curriculum has proceeded alongside lobbying to embed more education technology across the whole of a school. The campaign appears to comprise a number of strands, in which Microsoft and Google feature prominently alongside other tech lobbyists.[201]

In early 2011 Gove announced a review of the whole of the national curriculum. The old Information and Communication Technology, or ICT, course looked likely to be axed. This was a shake-up of technology in schools. A coalition of tech interests formed to persuade government to put computer science on the curriculum instead.[202] The IT lobby group the British Computer Society teamed up with a 'grass-roots style' organisation called Computing at School, which is funded by BCS, Microsoft and Google. Microsoft's education lobbyist, Clare Riley, 'buddied up' with these enthusiasts and, alongside Google's lobbyists, set to work.[203]

They met with ministers and officials, talked to Lords and MPs on Parliament's Education Committee and enlisted third parties to back their case, including 'captains of industry'; every head teacher was urged to support the cause; Microsoft and Google were among those who chipped in for a study by the Royal Society, the oldest and most prestigious of the science academies, to support the campaign to get computing onto the curriculum.[204] This was a concerted, well-organised effort.

At the same time, another strand of the lobbying campaign came at the issue from a different direction.[205] Government provided a second opportunity to lobby for computing in schools, commissioning a review into the future skills needed in the games and visual-effects industries. A six-month study to look into it was funded by the gaming lobby group UKIE, of which Microsoft is a member, with the support of Google, TalkTalk, Facebook, the IT lobby group Intellect, the British Computer Society, the Education Foundation and others like the Guardian Media Group.[206] Gaming was used as a poster boy for the skills review because of its status as a 'high-profile rock'n'roll industry', said the head of UKIE, Ian Livingstone. In reality the campaign was acting in the interests of this 'broad coalition'.[207] The review was run under the auspices of the National Endowment for Science, Technology and the Arts – Nesta – a body set up by the government, but now independent, for promoting innovation in the UK.

Its 'landmark' report, *Next Gen.*, made a number of recommendations. First was that computer science be included on the national schools curriculum. Next was to train a new generation of teachers to teach it. But third on the wish list was that video games be used across science, technology, engineering and maths lessons to draw pupils into these subjects. This was followed by a call for a central repository for teachers of the best video games for use in classrooms – in essence, a marketing tool – and more training for teachers in how to use them.

The central message of *Next Gen.* was unequivocal and strikingly familiar. The consequences of not reforming the UK's education system according to their recommendations would be devastating for the UK's high-tech industries. 'Unless we act quickly, we are in danger of losing out,' it said.[208] Despite an acknowledgement that Britain's gaming industry was primarily losing business to international competition because of higher costs, fewer public subsidies and a lack of investment in universities, schools reform was considered vital. We need to ape the best in the world, it said, citing Finland, whose education system consistently comes near the top of international rankings, although its schools have shown no particular enthusiasm for digital learning. The report played up the benefits of video games to teach, while ignoring the mixed results from the few trials conducted.

Next Gen. appears, therefore, as a lobbying tool for technology firms with a clear, vested interest in digitising learning, as well as enthusing a new generation of coders. As if to underline its role in kick-starting an ed-tech revolution in schools, Nesta, supported by the same coalition of technology interests,[209] followed up with a series of reports, all of which called for more technology to teach and strongly advocated the need to redesign education on digital lines.[210]

In early 2012 the campaign got what it wanted. A month after admitting to being 'behind the curve' on education technology, Gove endorsed computer science as an important academic school subject.[211] But he also went a lot further in endorsing technology to teach.[212] He praised the use of games and interactive software in classrooms. He championed online learning, and the use by charter schools of 'ubiquitous, cheap digital technology' to give pupils access to the best teachers (online). He hailed the unprecedented opportunities technology provided for testing pupils. 'Technology can be integrated and embedded across the whole curriculum,' he said, echoing many. But perhaps more importantly, in his address to the industry at a digital learning conference, Gove expressed a desire to see Britain tap into this market.

The following year saw another step forward. Gove instructed officials to help an initiative that aims for all eleven-year-olds to have access to individual tablet computers in schools.[213] Tablets for Schools is currently being trialled, with a tentative national roll-out date of the end of 2013.[214] It involves another set of players in the education industry: retailers and tech infrastructure providers. It is being led by Carphone Warehouse, a high street supplier of tablets. Its founder, Charles Dunstone – an academy school sponsor and close neighbour of David Cameron – also heads up the broadband supplier TalkTalk (a sponsor of the Policy Exchange).[215] The project team includes senior staff at both Dunstone's companies plus Dixons (now retailing as Currys and PC World), the UK's largest electronics retailer and an academy sponsor; Virgin Media, a major supplier of broadband to schools;[216] as well as Pearson and Google.[217]

Whether the technology lobby has been helped by external consultant lobbyists is not known.[218] Google's hired lobbyist is Portland. The agency has also provided lobbying services to Nesta in the run-up to the 2010 general election,[219] the IT lobby group, Intellect, and more recently the gaming lobby group UKIE (as well as BT, Virgin, Vodafone and Apple),[220] although again it is not known which areas of policy

Portland was helping these clients with. It declined to be interviewed and, unlike in the US, lobbyists here do not have to say what or whom they are seeking to influence. If, however, it was not education policy, it would have been an opportunity lost. Portland is incredibly well-connected to Gove's department.

Portland's head of campaigns in the three years to the general election was James Frayne.[221] In early 2011, Gove picked Frayne as his director of communications in an effort to 'beef up' his team with some campaigning experience.[222] Frayne's wife is Rachel Wolf, former free school champion, now at News Corp. Gove's media adviser is another from the lobbying firm. Since early 2012 Portland has also employed James O'Shaughnessy part-time, the man who has staked his career on Gove succeeding (O'Shaughnessy's other consultancy clients include Pearson and Wellington College, where Anthony Seldon is looking to set up a chain of academies).[223] Finally Portland is advised by Michael Portillo, the inspiration behind the Policy Exchange.[224] As its first chair and a committed Portillista, Gove expressed his admiration by writing his biography, *Michael Portillo: The Future of the Right*. It has long since been remaindered. The ideas, however, live on.

This revolving door between Gove's office and Portland is not evidence of anything. It is merely a structure, but one that could obviously facilitate communication between Gove and any corporation looking to reshape schools in its own interest. The potential for reform-minded politicians to work in collaboration with such lobbyists is high. They may share the same vision, many of the same personnel, as well as a twin desire to create business opportunities and economic growth through reform.

There is one other company with a direct financial stake in education reform that has yet to be mentioned in a British context: Rupert Murdoch's education division. Murdoch counts the current Education Secretary as one of his most loyal supporters. While other Parliamentarians labelled Murdoch unfit to run a multinational company amid the phone-hacking scandal, Gove vehemently defended him. In his evidence to the Leveson inquiry, Gove described him as 'one of the most impressive and significant figures of the last fifty years'.[225] We should be applauding Murdoch, not criticising him, he said.[226]

Gove has known Murdoch for many years and long enjoyed his financial support. Before turning to politics, he was a leader writer and home editor at the Murdoch-owned *The Times*. Gove's wife, Sarah Vine, has also written for the paper for many years. When Gove became an MP in 2005, *The Times* topped up his Parliamentary salary for four years with a £60,000-a-year column.[227] In 2013, the Education Secretary was also still registering income from a book deal for an undisclosed amount given to him a decade earlier by HarperCollins, a subsidiary of News Corp, for a historical biography he has yet to write.[228]

According to Gove's office 'most' of his meetings with the Murdochs 'have been about education, which is his job'.[229] And he has had many. Gove regularly dined with Murdoch and his executives. One event, for example, attended by Gove, Murdoch, Murdoch's son James and his editors celebrated a speech Murdoch had just given at the Centre for Policy Studies.[230] Echoing Gates in the US, and many CEOs in the UK, Murdoch used his address to damn the British schools system. 'There is no excuse for the way British children are being failed,' he said. He added modestly that that was why so much of News Corp's philanthropic giving was devoted to the cause of education, although he did not say who had benefited from his generosity. The speech called for a revolutionised education system in the UK.[231]

Gove is also friendly with Joel Klein, whom Gove sees as 'something of an educational superstar'.[232] Klein returned the compliment, describing Gove as a 'hero and a friend'.[233] On one occasion in early 2011 Klein was Gove's guest in Britain for three days. The trip was devoted to discussions on US education policy. Another of their meetings, accompanied by more than ten other people, occurred just before the announcement of Klein's job with Murdoch in September 2010.[234] One of those present was Fraser Nelson, editor of the *Spectator*, board member of the Centre for Policy Studies and a vocal reform lobbyist,[235] who with his fellow *Spectator* writer, free school champion Toby Young (who used his column to urge everyone in Britain to see *Waiting for 'Superman'*),[236] has doggedly stuck to the script.

But much of Gove's interaction has been with the man himself. In the spring of 2011, Murdoch and Gove had one of their breakfasts together in London. According to reports, on this occasion Murdoch flew on to address a conference of internet entrepreneurs at which he spoke in detail about News Corp's digital education plans. Classrooms had not changed since Victorian times, he said. They were the 'last holdout' from the digital revolution.[237] Just weeks later Gove delivered his first speech to teachers which called for technical innovation in the classroom. His chosen dinner partner that night was, once again, Rupert Murdoch.[238]

Giving evidence to Leveson, Gove admitted to holding discussions with Murdoch and Klein, Pearson and Microsoft on how technology will 'change the shape of education'.[239] Gove logged a meeting with Microsoft at the end of 2010 as a discussion on 'shared priorities'.[240]

*

As previously mentioned, lobbying is often not about persuading politicians to act, but about helping politicians to achieve shared aims. The tight-knit schools reform lobby surrounding the Education Secretary fits within this frame. As with its US counterparts, with whom it has ties, the lobby has helped win political support for Gove's radical agenda. It has seeded the media with supportive voices. It has defended the reform movement against opposition. It is now promoting ideas that look set to fundamentally change the way we teach children through technology.

Meanwhile, the public has been left out of the debate. We are sold policies through the press, but denied the opportunity to participate.

Trying to reach an objective view on the merits of school reform, beyond the assurances of politicians, is all but impossible. Talk to parents faced with the prospect of their child's school becoming an academy and many will point to the lack of impartial, robust information on the reforms. 'When we were consulted, the thing we needed was better information,' said Ellie, a mother of two faced with the choice. 'We wanted to know does this mean a better education for our children.' What she was looking for was a proper public discussion that could inform her decision. 'I cannot understand why there's not a lot more debate about this in the press,' she said. Any parent/teacher group wondering whether to spend funds raised on school laptops will face the same problem. Warm words, scant evidence and little debate.

These conditions favour lobbyists, who find their ability to influence diminished when the electorate is aroused.[241] The public is left to find its way in a fog created by government, corporate lobbyists and a largely complicit media.

Is the shutting down of public debate by design? Attempts by the government to restrict the flow of information to the public point to it. Gove and his advisers have engaged in practices that, if not deliberately, have inadvertently prevented public scrutiny of their activities and interactions with lobbyists. Private email accounts have been used in place of official ones, vast amounts of correspondence have been unaccountably deleted, and little information has been disclosed on meetings. The impression given by Gove and his advisers is that our right to know under Freedom of Information laws for some reason does not apply in education.

Gove, for example, was caught using an email account belonging to his wife, the 'Mrs Blurt' account, to discuss government business with his advisers. This does not break the rules. Refusing to disclose the emails under Freedom of Information laws, however, does. The practice appears to be systemic. Gove's special adviser Dominic Cummings told colleagues that he would not answer emails to his official departmental account. 'I will only answer things that come from gmail accounts from people who I know,' he wrote, suggesting that others follow suit. 'I can explain in person the reason for this,' he said.[242] Sources claim Cummings was telling party colleagues not to use his official email for political business. Another reason might be to avoid disclosure.

The systematic destruction of official government emails also appears endemic in Gove's department.[243] The department claims this is 'in line with our normal practice',[244] but there is no obvious reason for it other than to frustrate public access to information. We are similarly in the dark over who Gove's advisers are meeting, with the department giving evasive answers to Parliament.[245]

Concerns about Gove's unaccountable fiefdom are widespread. His department is described as having its 'own private and political network' and ways of working that are suggestive of 'an arrogant disregard for the established processes of government'.[246] The closer and more personal the ties are between lobbyists and government, the less we are able to see.

But only if we do see these lobbyists can we, as citizens and taxpayers footing the bill, initiate and participate in discussions about how best to educate our children.

Following Gove's election in 2005, he wrote that the reason he was in Parliament was not to see his colleagues win power, 'it is to see us at last in a position where we can give it up'.[247] Most agree that his reforms to Britain's schools will be lasting. 'Once established . . . [school] reforms are difficult to reverse,' wrote Policy Exchange.[248]

A consensus has emerged, however, that Gove is a government success story. 'In a government of disasters, unfulfilled promises and U-turns, one minister continues unflustered, unturned and largely uncriticised,' wrote the *Guardian*'s Peter Wilby: 'Gove is top of the class.'[249]

Who is teaching that class in ten years' time is anyone's guess. It could be News Corp.

10

Dominate: Lobbying to Stay in the Shadows

'Let us grow up, have a debate . . . it does not need to be as imperfect as this.'
  Graham Allen MP[1]

A 'dog's breakfast' is how one MP described the ideas the Coalition government came up with to shine a light on lobbying. To which another retorted that a lot more work goes into pet food than had ever gone into this plan.

September 2013 was the moment the government appeared to cave in to demands to allow the public to see who it is talking to behind closed doors. It published legislation that set out its proposals for a register of lobbyists. This is the mechanism that would allow scrutiny of lobbying. Done properly, it would force lobbyists to say who they are, whom they are lobbying, what they are seeking to influence and how much money they are spending in the process. It is this list, effectively, that we have been lobbying for.

With a decent register of lobbyists, the public could see who has the ear of politicians, the discussions being had and the scale of their effort. The best way of explaining the consequences of such a list of lobbying activity and how it could improve understanding of our politics is by looking at information contained on registers overseas.

In the US, for example, it is publicly known that, in the decade to 2008, Wall Street spent $3.4bn on lobbying. With that enormous investment – plus a further $1.7bn in political donations – the finance industry was, over the years, able to get rid of many rules and regulations to the point where it could operate without any effective restraints. At the point when the house of cards collapsed in 2007, a crisis caused by the finance sector not consumers, there were 3,000 officially registered lobbyists working for Wall Street, many of whom were ex-high-ranking US government officials.[2] Without the equivalent transparency in Britain, the story of the lobbying assault by their UK counterparts in the City cannot be told.

We also know that in the five years since it was taken into public hands, Royal Bank of Scotland spent more than $5m[3] of taxpayers' money trying to influence financial regulation in Washington, including consumer protection laws.[4] The British state may own most of RBS, but the British people know next to nothing of its influence in the UK. Only that it paid six UK lobbying firms in 2011 on top of its internal team of lobbyists.[5] Who and what they are seeking to influence and how much British taxpayers' money they are spending is hidden.

We can also look to the Canadian register of lobbyists for information. We can see, for example, who from Philip Morris International has been lobbying whom in the Canadian government over which specific laws, policies and taxes that they seek to influence. Detailed lobbying reports even reveal the individual meetings the tobacco giant has held, for instance, with advisers to the Canadian Prime Minister. In Britain, we are faced with an altogether more opaque situation. We know only that a key adviser to the Prime Minister, Lynton Crosby, is at the same time a lobbyist-for-hire paid by PMI. Even this information was hard to extract. What discussions have been arranged and with whom in government are secret. We Brits must make do with assurances from David Cameron that he had not been lobbied by his own election adviser on behalf of PMI.[6]

The prospect of the UK catching up with these and other countries and allowing public scrutiny of lobbying is, at the time of writing, almost nil. The Coalition government flunked its plans for a register. It is, in effect, pretending to introduce some transparency into lobbying. Its register of lobbyists is a fake.

This failure on the part of the government is all the more disheartening given the Coalition's 'clear ambition' to make the UK the 'most transparent and accountable country in the world'.[7] Much has been said by ministers on the need for greater openness so that we can hold our politicians to account for the decisions they take. 'After the scandals of recent years, people have lost faith in politics and politicians,' wrote a newly elected David Cameron. 'It is our duty to restore their trust. It is not enough simply to make a difference. We must be different.'[8]

This is a flavour of Parliament's reaction to the government's plans for a lobbying register: 'glaringly inadequate', 'deliberately evasive' and 'an intolerable way to produce bad law'. 'It opens up Parliament to ridicule and suspicion', is 'disingenuous' and 'contemptuous of the public'. The way the bill was produced, said many MPs, dragged the House of Commons into disrepute.

'The public expected that we would do something about lobbying,' a leading critic, Graham Allen MP, said. 'There was almost a contractual agreement saying very clearly that lobbying should be dealt with . . . We failed to do what we said we would do.'[9] Allen is referring to the Coalition promise to open up lobbying. As a consequence, a policy that was supposed to restore some public trust in government looks likely to have the opposite effect.

How we arrived at this position is what we will show here. It is a case study in lobbying, one that we have been in the middle of. We went into it as inexperienced campaigners, rather green but confident that rational argument, evidence of abuse and public concern would win out. We were buoyed by widespread support from MPs and tough rhetoric from party leaders that appeared to side with our cause. We were, to put it bluntly, idiots.

Instead what we have witnessed in microcosm is how lobbying corrupts the decisions that government takes. We have watched as the commercial lobbying industry has shape-shifted to defend itself against the perceived threat from greater transparency – arguing with them is like trying to wrestle a fish. We have sat on the bench as lobbyists teamed up with ministers and officials to manipulate the game – and have looked on as the government tried to keep its discussions with lobbyists secret. We have been open-mouthed as the government has gone through the rigmarole of being seen to act, even to the point of being prepared to pass legislation that is misleading, irrational and a waste of everyone's time. A dog's breakfast indeed.

MPs dubbed it the 'one per cent' lobbying Bill. That is how much lobbying activity the government's register is likely to capture. It cast a net so small and with holes so wide that the vast majority of lobbying will escape regulation. Only a handful of lobbying agencies are expected to be caught and then they have to reveal nothing more than the identities of their clients. Their dealings with government will remain off-limits. Corporate in-house lobbyists, which make up the bulk of the industry, were deliberately exempted. The government's rationale for this is genuinely nonsensical.

What was worse was that the bill, pushed through in haste, coupled the fake lobbying register with an assault on democracy in the form of a clampdown on the ability of charities and trade unions to campaign. A new law that was supposed to address public concern about the corrupting force of corporate lobbying, was turned into an opportunity to attack organisations that stand for workers and the public interest. It could have been a landmark law. Instead, what we got was a partisan apology of a bill.*

We were surprised by the crudeness of the government's approach, but not the proposals themselves. Public understanding of who is in the room making decisions with government is something that British politicians and lobbyists have long resisted. They have danced around the issue, repeating the same steps – scandal, investigation, procrastination and quietly doing nothing – for over sixty years.

In what will become a familiar pattern, it was scandal that led to the first investigation into influence-peddling in Britain. In 1947, lobbyist-for-hire Sydney Stanley was found to be trading on his political connections to solicit money from businessmen eager to circumvent post-war restrictions. Back then, however, with commercial lobbying in the UK in its infancy, MPs were sceptical that the industry even had a future. Lobbyists, they reasoned, would only attract a clientele if they were able to acquire privileged knowledge of the workings of government. 'It is difficult to see how a private intermediary can acquire this knowledge,' MPs concluded.[10] What they did not foresee was the rush of insiders into lobbying.

The first calls for some rules for lobbyists in the UK came in 1969, again prompted by scandal. The 'Greek Colonels' episode[11] saw a London-based PR firm paid £100,000 a year[12] to orchestrate a reputation-laundering media and lobbying campaign for the vicious, military

* A more detailed analysis of the lobbying bill can be found at www.lobbying transparency.org/opening-up-lobbying

government in Greece.[13] The PR firm paid for MPs to be flown to Greece to meet the Colonels, where they were courted and then encouraged on their return to give favourable reports to the British media. One of the most damning aspects was that the lobbyists employed an MP working behind the scenes to influence his colleagues in Parliament.

The scandal added to pressure for MPs to declare their outside interests, which nonetheless took another five years and another lobbying and bribery scandal involving MPs and senior officials to come into force. But it also weighed on the lobbying industry. More than simply damaging its reputation, it had alerted the public to its underhand tactics and dubious morals.

The lobbyists' response was to create an organisation that would promote and crucially defend the industry. In October 1969, ten men met in a Mayfair hotel and gave birth to the Public Relations Consultants Association.[14] This was another tactic that has been repeated over the years: the invention of organisations to protect the industry's reputation in times of crisis and defend it from government interference. The relatively young lobbying industry today has no fewer than four representative bodies.

By the mid-eighties, pressure was again mounting on the industry. Parliament, in the form of a committee set up to examine MPs' outside interests, expressed 'an uneasy feeling that the place is being perverted by commercial pressures'.[15] The feeling was by no means universal, with critics being dismissed by one MP employed by a commercial firm as 'a bunch of lefties'.[16] Parliament, though, was once more moved to investigate the influence industry.

Lobbyists sensed fresh trouble from such scrutiny, as well as from growing public concern and a more curious media. Attention was being drawn to their presence in Parliament and at party conferences 'when that elite breed of PR specialist known as the political lobbyist emerges into the sunlight'.[17] In a bid to get on the front foot and cast off their shadowy image, lobbyists proposed that they regulate themselves. They offered the most minimal system of voluntary disclosure of their activities they could get away with.[18]

This is another practice that has since been repeated: the concession of minimal transparency to head off regulation. As a second investigation by MPs in the late eighties exposed yet more dubious practices – the biggest lobbyist of the day, Ian Greer, was accused of misleading

MPs with claims that he had no Parliamentarians on retainer; when he was in fact paying them 'thank you' fees for introductions to clients – the industry was busy organising behind the scenes to pre-empt any enforced rules from government.

In 1989 a handful of the biggest lobbying agencies met alone to discuss strategy. A further 'secret gathering' of top lobbyists was reported the following year at which they discussed the possibility of regulation, the 'desirability of countering adverse publicity' and the merits of 'going on the offensive'.[19] At the top of the agenda was the need to put their house in order before Westminster forced change. 'The need to be seen to be taking action is a powerful urge felt by many lobbyists,' noted one industry commentator.[20]

There was, however, little cause for alarm. While the investigating MPs recommended that the government introduce compulsory, but severely limited, transparency rules for lobbyists – rules very similar to those proposed by the Coalition government nearly a quarter of a century later – they were roundly ignored. It took nearly two years for the proposal to be debated in the House of Commons, evidence enough that public scrutiny of lobbying was not high on the government's agenda. Procrastination has also become a common feature in the merry-go-round of lobbying transparency.

The problem, however, did not go away. Predictably, another scandal pushed the issue front-of-mind. In the early nineties, the first of a number of 'cash-for-questions' stories broke. A *Sunday Times* reporter posing as a businessman offered twenty MPs £1,000 in exchange for tabling Parliamentary questions. Two Tory MPs were fined and temporarily suspended from Parliament. The *Guardian* followed this up with allegations that Ian Greer had paid Conservative MPs for Parliamentary favours on behalf of Harrods' owner, Mohamed Al Fayed. This brought down a further two Conservative ministers.

The industry needed to respond, which it did in typical fashion. It created a new, unsullied representative body to defend itself: the Association of Professional Political Consultants. Membership was voluntary, but conditional on lobbyists having no financial relationships with MPs. The industry also needed to be seen to be acting on disclosure. To demonstrate to government that compulsory transparency was unnecessary, lobbyists proposed a minimal, voluntary system of disclosure. Lobbying firms agreed to reveal their clients on a register overseen by the industry,[21] a system latterly described as 'little better than the emperor's new clothes'.[22] As one MP noted: 'Commitment to transparency in the world of lobbying is, and always will be, a relative concept.'[23]

And so it continued. In 2007 a different set of MPs again set out to investigate the activities of lobbyists, their impact on British democracy and how to address the 'genuine issue of concern that there is an inside track, largely drawn from the corporate world, who wield privileged access and disproportionate influence'.[24] This is the point at which we joined the debate. After eighteen months of inquiry, the MPs concluded that action by government was long overdue. It recommended that a half-decent, compulsory register of lobbyists be introduced. Do nothing, it said, and public mistrust of government will increase, along with the impression that favoured groups, big business in particular, are listened to with far more attention than others.

The government did nothing and said nothing, that is until the next scandal broke. Three former cabinet ministers, Geoff Hoon, Stephen Byers and Patricia Hewitt, were suspended from the Labour Party after being secretly recorded expressing a desire to work for a lobbying firm for a fee of £5,000. Byers described himself as a 'cab for hire'.[25] All political parties bar one suddenly committed to a compulsory register of lobbyists.

The Conservatives remained opposed, despite David Cameron's prediction ahead of the 2010 election that lobbying was the 'next big scandal waiting to happen'.[26] Only when he failed to win a majority was the promise to tackle lobbying made in a concession to the Liberal Democrats. True to form, lobbyists gave birth to yet another, clean body with an untarnished name – the UK Public Affairs Council – with which to defend itself against this threat of government intervention.

★

As watchers and critics of the lobbying industry, we have been able to gain some insight into their activities to hold back regulation. The campaign they have fought against transparency has employed many of the techniques set out in previous chapters.

Let us get the personal stuff out of the way. We have been called 'conspiracy theorists',[27] 'slightly frumpy'[28] and, more puzzlingly still, 'unwashed'. We have been publicly criticised for our sources of funding, which for the sake of transparency, for the purposes of the campaign for a lobbying register, has primarily been the Joseph Rowntree Charitable Trust, a philanthropic Quaker body.* Lobbyists have disrupted our events and jabbed their finger in anger when we have been given a platform. They have repeatedly levelled the charge of hypocrisy at our door despite our clear admission that we too are lobbyists.

We have been courted, as well as criticised. It was a nice surprise to be invited to a Westminster summer party hosted by the target of our campaign, although having our presence triumphantly announced to the room of a hundred or so lobbyists was less comfortable. We are genuinely grateful to the lobbying firm that invited us into their offices to observe a day in the life of a lobbyist. That they err on the ethical side of the business, with more charitable and trade union clients than defence contractors and pharmaceutical companies, does not detract from their generosity. Commercial lobbyists have also reached out to co-opt our partners and tried to manoeuvre us into agreeing to watered-down proposals.

None of this is significant. More important is the campaign commercial lobbyists have waged on politicians, with whom they regularly and professionally interact. First, their messages for deflecting attention and winning arguments. These have developed over time. The initial case against regulation presented by lobbyists to MPs was that no problem exists that new rules would solve. 'You do not hear people in the saloon bar of the Dog & Duck talking about the lobbying industry,' lobbyist Lionel Zetter told MPs, which ignores the 'gateway' nature of lobbying as a block to reform on issues people are concerned about. The public could not give a 'rat's arse', he said.[29] Nothing to see here, this says. Move on.

This was coupled with a reluctance to reveal anything of substance about what they actually do for a living. 'Don't be coy with us,' scolded one MP. Presented with evidence of some of their tactics, the lobbyists conceded that they do 'misbehave from time to time'. They were only human. It was 'unfortunate' that some lobbyists refused to operate ethically. A case of a few bad apples. Again, no need for regulation of the whole industry.

While playing down their misdemeanours and influence, lobbyists

* A complete list of our funders can be found at Spinwatch.org

have become hysterical over the possible consequences from being forced to operate in plain sight. 'I hope we aren't going to reach the point where people need to meet by the lake in St James' Park with a rolled-up copy of the *FT* under their arm in dark glasses,' said the CBI's John Cridland in response to a court ruling that details of the business group's lobbying should be made public. The case, incidentally, was brought by campaigners concerned that the CBI had been exaggerating the costs of environmental regulation.[30]

Another commercial lobbyist warned that the industry would 'suffer the consequences' if it failed to convince government that it could regulate itself. Imposed transparency – remembering that this is simply a list of their activities – would 'change fundamentally the way all of us work on a day-to-day basis'.[31] The lobbying trade press shouted of the 'threat' and 'danger', the twin perils of 'punishment' and 'ban', as well as the mythical financial consequences to their businesses. The hyperbolic line: fight against regulation or your world will end.

Efforts also appear to have been made to alarm those who might show support for a light being shone on corporate lobbying. In the wake of the Liam Fox scandal, for example, *The Times* inexplicably led with a front page story on the threats posed to trade unions and charities from transparency rules.[32] This was to become the much repeated message surrounding the government's eventual bill, which combined a register of lobbyists with a wholly unrelated clampdown on campaigning by charities and trade unions. The headlines were inevitable: 'Lobbying bill will silence charities'. Whether or not by design, an attempt at allowing scrutiny of corporate lobbying was presented to the public as a gag on charities. A simple story became sown with confusion.

Lobbyists have also gone on the offensive with an array of initiatives to help them get on the front foot. In recent years, they have produced a reassuring number of voluntary codes of conduct, charters and 'guiding principles' as solutions to the problem as framed by lobbyists. This framing is important: the concern defined as one of ethical conduct rather than transparency. 'Stand Up For Lobbying' was another short-lived campaign aimed at defending their right to operate – without scrutiny. It 'stood up' for professionalism, accountability, fairness, ethical practice and integrity in the industry. Notably not transparency.

Yet throughout all this, lobbyists have stressed their commitment to openness. Some have positioned themselves as champions of – still very limited – transparency. To openly oppose it wholesale would be to invite more criticism and potentially worse consequences. The line has gone from this frankness in 2008 from a Bell Pottinger lobbyist to MPs: 'The public has no right to know who our clients are';[33] to this four years later when Bell Pottinger boss, Tim (Lord) Bell, was asked by Jeremy Paxman on BBC's *Newsnight* if the public were not entitled to know who is bending the ear of ministers: 'Absolutely . . . We have never said we won't publish our clients nor have we ever been untransparent about the things that we do.'[34]

Little of this activity to hoodwink MPs is very significant either. Not compared to the campaign that has been fought behind closed doors. That is, what we know of it anecdotally and through protracted freedom of information requests. While the industry was putting on its public face to remove the threat of government acting, one senior commercial lobbyist and transparency champion reportedly said: 'Why doesn't someone just take the minister out for dinner.' Lobbying, as already noted, is more effective when it is done on the quiet.

With the government in 2010 committed to introducing a register of lobbyists, we asked for a meeting with the Cabinet Office minister overseeing the policy, Mark Harper. We felt it important that some of the myths promoted by the industry were challenged with facts, chiefly:

1. That regulation is impossible because of the difficulties in defining who should be covered by the rules. This is false and lobbyists know it. There are UK lobbyists signed up to functioning registers overseas, with working definitions that could be adapted for the UK.

2. That the policy would cost the UK tens of millions of pounds to operate. This is unlikely given that Canada's sophisticated and well-resourced system costs precisely C\$4.6m (£2.6m) to operate.

3. And that the register would become a 'bureaucratic monster'. Again, judging by experience overseas, registration should take lobbyists no more than half an hour four times a year to complete.

These and other irrational arguments have recurred with surprising frequency.

Our request to meet the minister to put these and other points to him was declined. It was not 'appropriate' for him to meet us at that stage in the process, Harper said. Unbeknown to us, and by contrast, he had already granted commercial lobbyists access to influence the drafting of the register. Harper sanctioned monthly meetings between the lobbyists and his officials.[35] This is what privileged access looks like.

Harper had given the go-ahead for regular discussions to be held between his civil servants and industry representatives. At the time these lobbyists were busy resurrecting the system of voluntary self-regulation. Their goal was for government to embrace their minimal system with a 'statutory hug'.[36] The minister was kept informed of their progress and plans.

At least four 'productive and positive' discussions took place with the Cabinet Office official drafting the government's compulsory register.[37] The civil servant presented the lobbyists with the government's approach, timetable and details of who else in government was involved, all of which is vital information for those seeking to influence policy.

What the minister wanted to avoid was public knowledge of these meetings. With a surprising blind spot for the irony in trying to keep secret discussions on a policy designed to shine a light on lobbying, the government refused to disclose its dealings with these lobbyists under Freedom of Information law. The way in which it handled the information requests also reveals much about the government's willingness to open up lobbying.

Eighteen months after refusing to release details of its interaction with lobbyists, the Cabinet Office was finally instructed to hand over the information by the Information Commissioner. During this period, the department broke the rules over lengthy delays, was threatened with contempt of court proceedings by the Commissioner and was found in breach of the Freedom of Information Act for trying to use exemptions that were not valid, withdrawing them and at the last minute applying different exemptions without telling anyone. This from a government that aspires to be 'the most transparent in the world'.

One final incident served to underline the obvious disparities in access and influence, as well as the Cabinet Office's questionable commitment to the policy. The official responsible for drafting the register, who was also involved in blocking the release of information,

took to Twitter to voice her strong dislike of transparency campaigners. She wished they 'would die'. She was prepared to help them along, she tweeted. Asked why she had posted the message she said: 'I don't like them', and hung up.[38] Only after this made the papers was she moved from her role as head of constitutional policy at the Cabinet Office.

This was as much as we could see of lobbyists' interaction with the government over the new rules on lobbying. It is not known, for example, if there has been any lobbying of ministers by the CBI or the City of London Law Society, which is opposed to the inclusion of law firms on the register. We were cautioned by one commercial lobbyist that to push for disclosure of lawyers' lobbying would be foolish in the extreme. 'You will lose,' they said.

Denied the opportunity to sit down with the minister or officials we were forced to rely on the official, public consultation to voice our views. This arrived almost two years after the pledge to tackle lobbying was made. When it did, it contained false figures and misleading information. We submitted our response. A further 1,300 members of the public took the time to tell the government what they thought too. Another 74,000 people clicked a petition calling for lobbyists to be forced to operate in the open. All views were ignored. This was not the inside track.

*

This is a summary of the process that after more than three years produced the 'dog's breakfast' of a policy that the government, at the time of writing, is intent on pushing through. The manner in which it has been introduced is indeed contemptuous of Parliament and the public, as many MPs noted. But, it is merely the continuation of a process that began fifty years ago over an issue that has dogged our politics every decade since. With each lobbying scandal public trust in decision-making is eroded.

When Tony Blair was first elected, around 80 per cent of the British public thought his government to be 'honest and trustworthy'. That figure dropped to around 60 per cent the moment Blair altered policy on tobacco sponsorship of motor racing to exempt Formula One, on which he had been lobbied by its boss Bernie Ecclestone, who had given £1m to the Labour Party.[39] Fewer than a third of people today consider the government 'honest and trustworthy', only marginally higher than during the MPs' expenses saga.[40]

Distrust in government is necessary for a healthy democracy. People should doubt, probe and monitor their politicians.[41] Up to a point. Effective governing becomes impossible when too many have too little trust. Consent for tough but necessary policy decisions and compliance with the laws and taxes of the country rely on sufficient belief in the system. To a great extent this hangs on whether people experience it as fair. It matters less that people agree with government, than whether they perceive the process as rigged against them.

We began by saying that our criticism stems not from being sore because we did not get what we wanted. It comes from what we have witnessed: a rigged system that leads to bad decisions. This is by no means the only dog's breakfast produced by government. To understand why, besides ineptness, requires a knowledge of lobbying. Vested interests dominate the speaking parts in government. The access they enjoy is routine. Their expertise taken as a given. These advantages are deepened and fixed over time. The views of the public and critical outsiders are something to be managed, not actively considered. The result is too many decisions based not on evidence but on the trusted opinion of insiders with a private interest.

Many politicians do not recognise this. Some will believe it is not in their interests to expose their dealings with lobbyists. We could wait another half a century before they act. In the meantime, many policy decisions – on climate change, banking risk, public health and education, housing and wages, taxation and countless other issues of public concern – will continue to be informed by the wants and prejudices of the small number of people that enjoy privileged access and influence. That many of these decisions may not be evidence-based, centred on the wider public interest, or even rational should make us sit up.

Politics remains an insulated and exclusive club in this country, one that for a long time has had a membership fee. Inside, lobbyists are sitting down with our politicians (and much of our media), having a quiet word. Members of the public can bang on the door and shout till they are hoarse about the very many crises outside, but are rarely let in.

All that we are asking here is that the blinds be opened. Let us see inside the club. Allow us to know what is being discussed. Let us, however minimally, into our political system. This is not, as Tim Bell dismissively says, 'an obsession with wanting to look through people's windows and go through their drawers . . . because they are sure they will find some terrible conspiracy.'[42]

There is no conspiracy. Exposure would show the ordinary, everyday, professional influence industry at work. The reality, in the main, will be more mundane than is popularly imagined. What glamour lobbying has comes largely from it being secret. But disclosure would give us the window into this private world that we need if we are to be meaningfully involved in how this country operates.

If this is not granted, if we continue to be denied the right to know who has taken our seat, then we will have confirmation that we have largely been evicted from decision-making. This is why transparency forces change. It is less what is revealed that poses a danger to the establishment. It is the effort put in to denying transparency that exposes a dangerous truth. People have asked government to open up lobbying so that we might scrutinise, better understand and participate more fully in our democracy. So far, it has refused. We are still outside, only just, but they are still refusing to open the curtains. They do not want us to see in. They do not want us involved.

Notes

1 Lobby

1   Lord Chadlington at 20th Public Relations World Congress, Dubai, 13–15 March 2012, Grand Hyatt Dubai; http://www.youtube.com/ watch?v=8P_K7sqB0E0

2   Alan Rusbridger, 'The overwhelming case for plurality', *Guardian*, 24 June 2012; http://www.guardian.co.uk/media/2012/jun/24/ overwhelming-case-media-plurality

3   Leveson Inquiry Report, vol. 3, p. 1119.

4   Josh Halliday and Dugald Baird, 'Leveson Inquiry: Vince Cable and Ken Clarke appear', *Guardian*, 30 May 2012; http://www.theguardian.com/ media/2012/may/30/leveson-inquiry-cable-clarke-live

5   Leveson Inquiry Report, vol. 3, p. 1326.

6   Ibid., p. 1327.

7   James Robinson, 'James Murdoch: blocking BSkyB deal jeopardises UK jobs', *Guardian*, 17 November 2010; http://www.guardian.co.uk/ media/2010/nov/17/james-murdoch-bskyb-deal

8   Leveson Inquiry Report, vol. 3, pp. 1325, 1332.

9   Ibid., p. 1336.

10 Ibid., p. 1217.

11 James Chapman and Tim Shipman, 'Bombshell email claims Jeremy Hunt asked Murdoch empire to help him stop phone hacking inquiry', *Daily Mail*, 11 May 2012; http://www.dailymail.co.uk/news/ article-2142979/Leveson-Inquiry-Bombshell-email-reveals-Jeremy-Hunt-conspired-Murdoch-empire-prevent-inquiry-phone-hacking.html

12 Esther Addley, 'Frédéric Michel, Adam Smith and 3am texts . . . some lovers have less contact', *Guardian*, 24 May 2012; http://www.

theguardian.com/media/2012/may/24/frederic-michel-adam-smith-texts

13   Leveson Inquiry Report, vol. 3, p. 1399.

14   Ibid., pp. 1401–1402. Leveson concluded: 'It is not merely possible but probable that it was Mr Smith who had provided confidential information about Government thinking as to the appropriate form of inquiries arising from the phone hacking scandal.'

15   Ibid., p. 1327.

16   S. Thompson and S. John, *Public Affairs in Practice: A Practical Guide to Lobbying*, Kogan, 2002, pp. 4–5.

17   Policy Exchange fringe event at Lib Dem conference, September 2012: http://www.policyexchange.org.uk/modevents/item/delivering-a-pipe-dream-making-responsible-business-a-reality

18   Cited in Grant Jordon (ed.), *The Commercial Lobbyists*, Aberdeen University Press, 1991, p. 3.

19   Political and Constitutional Reform Committee, oral evidence, 2 February 2012; http://www.publications.parliament.uk/pa/cm201213/cmselect/cmpolcon/153/120202.htm

20   David Hencke, 'Tory MPs were paid to plant questions says Harrods chief', *Guardian*, 20 October 1994.

21   Claire Newell, Holly Watt, Daniel Foggo and Ben Bryant, 'Exposed: deal that sank cash for questions MP Mercer', *Telegraph*, 31 May 2013.

22   Ezra Klein, 'Our Corrupt Politics: It's Not All Money', *New York Review of Books*, 22 March 2012; http://www.nybooks.com/articles/archives/2012/mar/22/our-corrupt-politics-its-not-all-money/

23   Interview with Lord Bell, 31 October 2013.

24   Steven Strauss, 'Here's Everything You've Always Wanted To Know About Lobbying For Your Business', Business Insider, November 2011; http://www.businessinsider.com/everything-you-always-wanted-to-know-about-lobbying-2011-11#ixzz1efKUga6J

25   Self-Regulation and Regulation of the Lobbying Profession, OECD report, 2009, http://www.citizen.org/documents/Self-Regulation-and-Regulation-of-Lobbying.pdf. It notes: 'A more specific indicator of the rate of return of lobbying expenditures comes from a single lobbying firm in the United States. The Carmen Group took in $11 million in fees in 2004, and produced $1.2 billion in assistance to its clients – a ratio of about 1:100. The pay-off is large but fairly typical, noted Carmen's president David Carmen.'

26   Strauss, 'Here's Everything You've Always Wanted To Know About Lobbying For Your Business'.

27 'Ask what your country can do for you', *The Economist*, 1 October 2011; http://www.economist.com/node/21531014?fsrc=scn/tw/te/ar/money-andpolitics

28 Portland entry on the register of the Association of Professional Political Consultants, 1 March 2013 – 31 May 2013: http://www.appc.org.uk

29 Steve John, *The Persuaders: When Lobbyists Matter*, Palgrave Macmillan, 2002, p. 63.

30 Brooke Masters, George Parker and Chris Giles, 'King's parting shot at meddling UK banks', *Financial Times*, 25 June 2013; http://www.ft.com/cms/s/0/14a9d492-ddaf-11e2-892b-00144feab7de.html#axzz2XHJwOwNZ

31 ICM 'State of the Nation' poll of 2,000 people in 2004, which showed that 79 per cent of people said they felt large corporations had influence over government policies, while only 34 per cent felt they ought to enjoy such influence. A survey of 2,000 members of the public conducted by the global research agency OnePoll, published in *PR Week*, 4 July 2013, showed that 59 per cent of respondents see lobbying as an issue of growing concern; 38 per cent claimed lobbying did more harm than good to British democracy; www.prweek.com/uk/features/1188888. Transparency International's Global Corruption Barometer 2013 surveyed 114,000 people in 107 countries: 90 per cent of those polled in the UK believe that the government is run by a few big entities acting in their own interest; www.transparency.org.uk/news-room/blog/12-blog/679-global-corruption-barometer-2013

32 Lawrence Lessig on *Reclaiming Our Democracy*: http://www.youtube.com/watch?v=FK6ISk8wAio

33 Lawrence Lessig, *Republic, Lost: How Money Corrupts Congress – and a Plan to Stop It*, Twelve Books, 2011, p. 173.

34 Lawrence Lessig, 'The Moment', *Huffington Post*, 22 March 2010; http://www.huffingtonpost.com/lawrence-lessig/the-moment_b_508558.html

35 Transparency International corruption in the UK, accessed 2013: http://www.transparency.org.uk/our-work/corruption-in-the-uk

36 David Cameron's speech, 'Rebuilding trust in politics', 8 February 2010.

37 John, *Persuaders*, p. 52.

38 Klein, 'Our Corrupt Politics'.

39 Jane Howard, 'The evolution of UK PR consultancies 1970–2010', PRCA, 2011.

40 Charles Miller, *Politico's Guide to Political Lobbying*, Politico's Publishing, 2000, p. 5.

41   Lobbying at the federal level in Canada is governed by the Lobbyists Registration Act, which came into force in 1989 and established a registration system.

42   Frédéric Robert-Nicoud and Richard Baldwin, 'Industrial policy: why governments pick losers', CentrePiece, Centre for Economic Performance, London School of Economics, autumn 2009.

2 Defend

1   Lionel Zetter, *Lobbying: The Art of Political Persuasion*, Harriman House, 2008, p. 6.

2   British Library website: http://www.bl.uk/treasures/magnacarta/basics/basics.html

3   David Miller and William Dinan, *A Century of Spin: How Public Relations Became the Cutting Edge of Corporate Power*, Pluto Press, 2008, p. 43.

4   Mike Hughes, *Spies at Work*, 1 in 12 Publications, 1994.

5   Early propaganda material circulated by the Economic League, cited by Miller and Dinan in *A Century of Spin*, p. 42.

6   David Rubinstein, *The Labour Party and British Society 1880–2005*, Sussex Academic Press, 2005, p. 49.

7   1918 Labour Party General Election Manifesto.

8   Miller and Dinan, *A Century of Spin*, p. 42.

9   Hughes, *Spies at Work*.

10   Miller and Dinan, *A Century of Spin*, p. 41.

11   Corinne Souza, *So You Want to be a Lobbyist?*, Politico's Publishing, 1998.

12   Miller and Dinan, *A Century of Spin*, p. 47.

13   Ibid., p. 43.

14   Hughes, *Spies at Work*.

15   Stuart Ewen, *PR! A Social History of Spin*, Basic Books, 1996, p. 291.

16   Ibid., p. 255.

17   Ibid., pp. 300–302.

18   Ibid., p. 303.

19   Miller and Dinan, *A Century of Spin*, p. 57.

20   Edward L. Bernays, *Propaganda*, Horace Liveright, 1928.

21   Holmes Report, World PR Report 2013: http://globalpragencies.com

22   Andrew Simms, *Cancel the Apocalypse*, Little, Brown, 2013, p. 290.

23   David Kynaston, *Austerity Britain, 1945–1951*, Bloomsbury, 2010.

24   Miller and Dinan, *A Century of Spin*, p. 61.

25   Mark Hollingsworth, *MPs for Hire: The Secret World of Political Lobbying*, Bloomsbury, 1991, p. 114.

26 Grant Jordon (ed.), *The Commercial Lobbyists*, Aberdeen University Press, 1991, p. 154.

27 Aims of Industry press advert, 'The end of freedom in Britain', *The Times*, 28 December 1973. Uploaded on Powerbase: http://www.powerbase.info/index.php/File:The_End_of_Freedom_in_Britain.jpg

28 Aims of Industry, *Organised Political Pressure on Companies, Anti-Anti-Report* (Counter Counter Information Services), January 1973.

29 Lewis Powell, Confidential memorandum: 'Attack on American Free Enterprise System', 1971.

30 Andrew Denham and Mark Garnett, *British Think Tanks and the Climate of Opinion*, UCL Press, 1998, p. 97, citing Halcrow (1989).

31 Russ Bellant, *The Coors Connection: How Coors Family Philanthropy Undermines Democratic Pluralism*, South End Press, 1991; see also http://sourcewatch.org/index.php/Talk:Adolph_Coors_Foundation

32 Daniel Henninger, 'Sen. Jim DeMint to head Heritage Foundation', *Wall Street Journal*, December 2012; http://online.wsj.com/article/SB10001424127887323501404578161613763222762.html

33 Miller and Dinan, *A Century of Spin*, p. 70.

34 Ed Vaizey, 'IEA is still the oldest and biggest daddy of them all!', *Sunday Times*, 15 July 2002.

35 David McKnight, *Murdoch's Politics: How One Man's Thirst For Wealth and Power Shapes Our World*, Pluto Press, 2013, p. 123.

36 Ibid., p. 30.

37 Professor James Foreman-Peck, 'How privatisation has changed Britain', BBC News, December 2004; http://news.bbc.co.uk/1/hi/business/4061613.stm

38 Mark Hollingsworth, *MPs for Hire: The Secret World of Political Lobbying*, Bloomsbury, 1991, p. 69.

39 Mark Hollingsworth, interview with Tamasin Cave, March 2013.

40 Mark Hollingsworth, *The Ultimate Spin Doctor: The Life and Fast Times of Tim Bell*, Hodder & Stoughton, 1997, p. 147.

41 Interview with Lord Bell, 31 October 2013.

42 Hollingsworth, *MPs for Hire*, pp. 70–72.

43 Ibid., p. 72.

44 Letter from David Worskett to Bob Ricketts, 12 November 2010, received under FOI law from the Department of Health.

45 Correspondence between David Worskett and Bob Ricketts, 12 November 2010, received under FOI law from the Department of Health.

46 Randeep Ramesh, 'Private healthcare group lobbied competition body

for NHS inquiry', *Guardian*, July 2011; http://www.guardian.co.uk/society/2011/jul/29/prk. Based on documents released to Tamasin Cave under FOI law from the Department of Health and the Co-operation and Competition Panel.

47   Ibid.

48   Ibid.

49   Ibid.

50   Hollingsworth, *MPs for Hire*, p. 73.

51   Andrew Robertson, Social Investigations website: http://socialinvesti-gations.blogspot.co.uk/p/key-facts-of-lords-and-mps-connections.html

52   S. Thompson and S. John, *Public Affairs in Practice: A Practical Guide to Lobbying*, Kogan, 2002, pp. 4–5.

53   Tim Burt, *Dark Art: The Changing Face of Public Relations*, Elliot and Thompson, 2012, p. 109.

54   Tamasin Cave, contemporary note from conversation with a journalist at the Liberal Democrat conference, September 2012.

55   Ibid.

56   Burt, *Dark Art*.

57   Tamasin Cave, personal conversation with a lobbyist at the Liberal Democrat conference, September 2012.

58   Nick Davies, *Flat Earth News: An Award-Winning Reporter Exposes Falsehood, Distortion and Propaganda in the Global Media*, Vintage, 2009, p. 184.

59   Portland entry on Association of Professional Political Consultants register, 2013.

60   Andy Rowell, email; Bob Leaf, ex-Burson-Marsteller CEO, tells @UWEJournalism students only client he turned down was Gaddafi, but not Ceaușescu.

61   Andy Rowell, *Green Backlash: Global Subversion of the Environment Movement*, Routledge, 1996.

62   Peter Bingle, oral evidence to Public Administration Select Committee, 2008–09: *Lobbying: Access and Influence in Whitehall*, vol. 2.

63   Alejandro Reuss, 'Peddling miracles and amnesia', *New Internationalist*, issue 314, July 1999; http://newint.org/features/1999/07/05/peddling/

64   'What is going on in Belarus? And in its ruler's head?', *The Economist*, 3 April 2008; http://www.economist.com/node/10960124

65   Oliver Duff, Melanie Newman, 'Belarus Links: Lord Bell questions money claims of senior colleague', *Independent*, 8 December 2011: http://www.independent.co.uk/news/uk/politics/belarus-links-lord-bell-questions-money-claims-of-senior-colleague-6273821.html

66   ASDA'A Burson-Marsteller Arab Youth Survey 2010: http://www.arabyouthsurvey.com/2010/

67   Bell Pottinger Group, 'Changing perceptions of The Republic of Uzbekistan – a presentation for the Azimov Group, July 2011', http:// www.thebureauinvestigates.com/wp-content/uploads/2011/12/ BellPottpresentationtoAzimovGp1.pdf

68   'EU renews Belarus sanctions due to human rights concerns', Reuters, 15 October 2012; http://www.reuters.com/article/2012/10/15/belarus-eu-sanctions-idUSL5E8LFON820121015

69   Bell Pottinger Sans Frontières website: http://www.bellpottinger-sansfrontieres.com/person/david-richmond

70   Belarus – Çhime Communications plc: Quarterly report, Nov. 2008–Jan. 2009: http://eurocenter.by/en/news/2012/12/13/lord-bells-plan-improve-image-dictatorship

71   Arun Sudhaman, 'We become the lightning rod for mistrust', *The Holmes Report*, March 2012.

72   Foreign Agents Registration Act (FARA); http://www.fara.gov/

73   Gideon Spanier, 'Reputation launderers: the London PR firms with their own image problems', *Evening Standard*, 28 March 2011; http:// www.standard.co.uk/lifestyle/reputation-launderers-the-london-pr-firms-with-their-own-image-problems-6385745.html

74   Oliver Pauley, Portland, 'Taking on the challenge', *PR Week*, 24 May 2012; http://www.prweek.com/uk/promotional_feature/1132385/taking-challenge/

75   Miller and Dinan, *A Century of Spin*, p. 60.

76   Vaizey, Gove and Boles (eds), *A Blue Tomorrow: New Visions from Modern Conservatives*, Politico's Publishing, 2001, p. 115.

77   Andrew Mitchell, 'Ethical politics', *TLG* magazine, Summer 2013, http://tlqmedia.com/article/ethical-politics/

78   Burt, *Dark Art*, p. 14.

79   Boles, *A Blue Tomorrow*, p. 110.

80   Jonathon Carr-Brown, 'Rothschild bankrolls Mandelson think tank', *Sunday Times*, 22 September 2002.

81   Interviewed in BBC documentary series by Adam Curtis, *Century of the Self*, 2002.

82   Alex Deane, Bell Pottinger, 'A golden age for think-tanks', *PR Week UK*, 8 June 2011; http://www.brandrepublic.com/features/1072373/alex-deane-bell-pottinger-golden-age-think-tanks/

83   Tamasin Cave, personal communication with unnamed source.

84   Robert Booth, 'Who is behind the Taxpayers' Alliance?', *Guardian*, 9 October 2009; http://www.theguardian.com/politics/2009/oct/09/taxpayers-alliance-conservative-pressure-group

85   Tamasin Cave, personal communication with unnamed source.

86   The TaxPayers' Alliance website: http://www.taxpayersalliance.com

87   Robert Watts, 'Low-tax campaigner who saw off Prescott. "If you don't trust politicians, why trust them with your money?" James Frayne talks morals to Robert Watts', *Sunday Telegraph*, 15 January 2006; http://www.telegraph.co.uk/finance/2930165/Low-tax-campaigner-who-saw-off-Prescott.html

88   Myra Butterworth, 'New 50p tax rate "will stifle the economy"', *Daily Telegraph*, 28 July 2009; http://www.telegraph.co.uk/finance/personalfinance/consumertips/tax/5918979/New-50p-tax-rate-will-stifle-the-economy.html

89   Tom Clark, 'Tories retake poll lead but appear at odds with public on 50p tax', *Guardian*, 19 March 2012; http://www.theguardian.com/politics/2012/mar/19/tories-poll-lead-50p-tax-rate

90   *Encylopædia Britannica* blog, 'The Case For Alternative Vote: 5 Questions for Unlock Democracy Director Peter Facey', 14 September 2010; http://www.britannica.com/blogs/2010/09/the-case-for-alternative-vote-5-questions-for-unlock-democracy-director-peter-facey/

91   Nigel Morris, 'Nick Clegg denounces claims that AV would cost £250m', *Independent*, 5 April 2011.

92   No2AV billboard advert featured on BBC website, 'No to AV campaign reject rivals' "scare stories" claim', 24 February 2011; http://www.bbc.co.uk/news/uk-politics-12564879

93   Tim Montgomerie, 'The Story of the AV campaign', Conservative Home, 5 July 2011.

94   'Weber Shandwick lures ex-Cameron aide Alex Deane from Bell Pottinger', *Public Affairs News*, 15 September 2011.

95   John Owens, 'Prime Minister picks Jean-Christophe Gray and Susie Squire for top comms roles', *PR Week*, 31 October 2012.

96   James Frayne, 'The power of emotion in political campaigns', ConservativeHome, 27 January 2013; http://conservativehome.blogs.com/platform/2013/01/james-frayne.html#more

97   Patrick Wintour, 'Michael Gove opts for a better Frayne of mind in retelling message', *Guardian*, 25 February 2011; http://www.guardian.co.uk/politics/blog/2011/feb/25/michael-gove-james-frayne-education

98   David Singleton, 'Department for Education hires James Frayne as comms chief', Brand Republic, 24 February 2011; http://www.brandrepublic.com/news/1056837/

99   Ibid.

100   Tim Montgomerie, 'The best five new blogs on the block', ConservativeHome, 2 December 2010; http://conservativehome.blogs.com/thetorydiary/2010/12/the-best-new-blogs-on-the-block.html

101   Andy McSmith, 'Diary: Michael Gove sends a staffer stateside to

work with Republicans', *Independent*, 28 June 2012; http://www.
independent.co.uk/news/people/diary/diary-michael-gove-sends-a-
staffer-stateside-to-work-with-republicans-7893584.html

102   Publicity material for James Frayne's book, *Meet the People: Why
Businesses Must Engage with Public Opinion to Manage and Enhance Their
Reputations*, due to be published by Harriman House, 2014.

3 Access

1   Melanie Newman and Oliver Wright, 'Caught on camera: top lobbyists
boasting how they influence the PM', *Independent*, 6 December 2011.
2   Mark Hollingsworth, interview with Tamasin Cave, March 2013.
3   Mark Hollingsworth, *The Ultimate Spin Doctor: The Life and Fast Times
of Tim Bell*, Hodder & Stoughton, 1997, p. 167.
4   Ibid.
5   People Diary, *Guardian*, 30 September 1987.
6   Interview with Lord Bell, 31 October 2013.
7   Hollingsworth, *The Ultimate Spin Doctor*, p. 168.
8   Nick Robinson blog, 'Fox financial backer speaks', BBC News, 12
October 2011; http://www.bbc.co.uk/news/15283131
9   Ibid.
10   Jason Lewis, 'Fox scandal: second minister faces questions over
Werritty', *Sunday Telegraph*, 23 October 2011.
11   Rupert Neate, 'Fresh questions over company that funded Adam
Werritty's jet-set life', *Guardian*, 16 October 2011; http://www.
guardian.co.uk/uk/2011/oct/16/adam-werritty-liam-fox-pargav
12   Robert Mendick and Patrick Sawer, 'Inside the corporate intelligence
company which bankrolled Liam Fox', *Daily Telegraph*, 22 October 2011;
http://www.telegraph.co.uk/news/politics/conservative/8843810/
Inside-the-corporate-intelligence-company-which-bankrolled-
Liam-Fox.html
13   Michael Savage, Deborah Haynes and Roland Watson, 'Fox friend
'go-to-guy' for defence lobbyists', *The Times*, 10 October 2011; http://
www.thetimes.co.uk/tto/news/politics/article3189098.ece
14   Robert Booth, 'Shangri-La lifestyle of Liam Fox's friend Adam
Werritty', *Guardian*, 11 October 2011; http://www.guardian.co.uk/
politics/2011/oct/11/shangri-la-liam-fox-adam-werritty
15   Rupert Neate and Patrick Wintour, 'Revealed: how lobbyists were
paid to facilitate meeting with Liam Fox', *Guardian*, 10 October 2011;
http://www.guardian.co.uk/politics/2011/oct/09/liam-fox-
meeting-lobbyists-werritty-boulter#footnote

16   Ibid.

17   'News in Brief', *PR Week*, 4 July 2007.

18   Interview with Lord Bell, 31 October 2013.

19   Interview with Lord Bell, 31 October 2013.

20   Gordon Rayner, 'Chain of events that led to Liam Fox's resignation', *Telegraph*, 15 October 2011: http://www.telegraph.co.uk/news/politics/conservative/8828277/Chain-of-events-that-led-to-Liam-Foxs-resignation.html

21   Ibid.

22   Steve John's LinkedIn profile.

23   Steve John, *The Persuaders: When Lobbyists Matter*, Palgrave Macmillan, 2002, p. 64.

24   Oliver Wright, 'Caught on camera: top lobbyists boasting how they influence the PM', *Independent*, 6 December 2011; http://www.independent.co.uk/news/uk/politics/caught-on-camera-top-lobbyists-boasting-how-they-influence-the-pm-6272760.html

25   Caroline Davies, 'Cash for access: Sarah Southern claims to be political consultant', *Observer*, 25 March 2012; http://www.guardian.co.uk/politics/2012/mar/25/cash-for-access-sarah-southern

26   Jason Groves, 'It'll be awesome for your business: Tory treasurer told donors they could have access to PM and influence policy', *Daily Mail*, 26 March 2012.

27   'Military lobbying to be investigated by Ministry of Defence', Press Association, 14 October 2012; http://www.guardian.co.uk/uk/2012/oct/14/defence-military-lobbying-investigation

28   Insight, 'Galloping greed of the old warhorses', *Sunday Times*, 14 October 2012.

29   Gregory Palast, 'LobbyGate: "There are 17 people that count. To say that I am intimate with every one of them is the understatement of the century"', *Observer*, 5 July 1998; http://www.gregpalast.com/lobbygate-there-are-17-people-that-count-to-say-that-i-am-intimate-with-every-one-of-them-is-the-understatement-of-the-century/

30   Ibid.

31   Josie Ensor and James Kirkup, 'Adam Werritty "indulged in fantasy like a Walter Mitty figure"', *Telegraph*, 12 October 2011; http://www.telegraph.co.uk/news/uknews/defence/8822719/Adam-Werritty-indulged-in-fantasy-like-a-Walter-Mitty-figure.html

32   Ben Fenton and George Parker, 'Chummy messages put heat on Hunt', *Financial Times*, 24 April 2012; http://www.ft.com/cms/s/0/5610c57c-8e2c-11e1-bf8f-00144feab49a.html#axzz2L9zjstb3

33   Stephen Robinson, 'Of course I regret it, I need it like a hole in the head, all this s**t', *Evening Standard*, 8 December 2011; http://www.

standard.co.uk/lifestyle/of-course-i-regret-it-i-need-it-like-a-hole-in-the-head-all-this-st-6376529.html

34 'Conservatives under pressure to explain links to lobbying firms', *Telegraph*, 6 December 2011; http://www.telegraph.co.uk/news/politics/conservative/8937250/Conservatives-under-pressure-to-explain-links-to-lobbying-firms.html

35 Rory O'Neill, quoted in Lionel Zetter, *Lobbying: The Art of Political Persuasion*, Harriman House, 2008, p. 32.

36 Peter Luff's biography on the Parliament website.

37 Peter Luff, oral evidence to Public Administration Select Committee, 2008–09: *Lobbying: Access and Influence in Whitehall*, vol. 2.

38 Jordi Blanes i Vidal, Mirko Draca and Christian Fons-Rosen, 'Revolving Door Lobbyists', Centre for Economic Performance Discussion Paper No. 993, August 2010; http://cep.lse.ac.uk/pubs/download/dp0993.pdf.

39 David Singleton, 'F-H lures former Cameron adviser', *PR Week*, 17 January 2007.

40 Jim Pickard, 'Peter Bingle is Lib Dems' new best friend', *Financial Times*, 29 July 2010; http://blogs.ft.com/westminster/2010/07/peter-bingle-is-lib-dems-new-best-friend/

41 Jim Pickard, 'Lobbyists beef up links with Labour', *Financial Times*, 12 March 2013; http://www.ft.com/cms/s/0/80f31d84-880f-11e2-8e3c-00144feabdc0.html

42 'Bill Morgan appointed as Special Adviser to Andrew Lansley', MHP blog, 4 June 2010; http://www.mhpc.com/blog/bill-morgan-appointed-special-adviser-andrew-lansley/

43 Hannah Crown, 'Former NHS reform adviser Bill Morgan returns to MHP', *PR Week*, 6 December 2012; http://www.prweek.com/uk/news/1162988/Former-NHS-reform-adviser-Bill-Morgan-returns-MHP/

44 Holly Watt, Rosa Prince and Robert Winnett, 'Wife of Health Secretary Andrew Lansley gave lobbying advice', *Telegraph*, 5 February 2011; http://www.telegraph.co.uk/news/politics/8305506/Wife-of-Health-Secretary-Andrew-Lansley-gave-lobbying-advice.html

45 Matt Cartmell, 'Edelman MD James Lundie moves to risk advisory role', *PR Week*, 27 September 2012.

46 Claire Newell and Holly Watt, 'John Hutton faces calls for inquiry over Whitehall lobbying by wife's firm', *Sunday Times*, 23 September 2007.

47 John (Lord) Hutton's biography on Parliament website.

48 Global Political Strategies website: http://globalpoliticalstrategies.com/bios/john_hutton.html

Hyatt Dubai on youtube: http://www.youtube.com/watch?v=8P_K7sqBoEo

78   Richard Cookson, Rob Evans and Tony Levene, 'Ultra-rich lobby group with influence at No 10', *Guardian*, 12 February 2008; http://www.guardian.co.uk/business/2008/feb/12/economy.gordonbrown

79   Rob Evans, David Leigh and Kevin Maguire, 'Tobacco firm gained secret access to Blair', *Guardian*, 27 October 2004; http://www.theguardian.com/uk/2004/oct/27/freedomofinformation.politics

80   'Dave's Buller buddy is Brown's bailout adviser', 'Who knows who', Channel 4 website, undated; http://whoknowswho.channel4.com/clubs/Bullingdon_Club/stories/Dave's_Buller_buddy_is_Brown's_bailout_adviser

81   Chris Blackhurst, 'Goldman's big hitter on the credit crunch – and his passion for a small London charity', *Evening Standard*, 10 December 2008; http://www.standard.co.uk/news/goldmans-big-hitter-on-the-credit-crunch-and-his-passion-for-a-small-london-charity-6859497.html

82   'SEC charges Goldman Sachs with fraud in structuring and marketing of CDO tied to subprime mortgages', SEC press release, 16 April 2010; http://www.sec.gov/news/press/2010/2010-59.htm

83   Letter from Boris Johnson to Lloyd C. Blankfein, 15 January 2010, released under FOI law by the Greater London Authority.

84   Letter from Boris Johnson to Michael Sherwood, 31 December 2009, released under FOI law by the Greater London Authority.

85   'Alastair Campbell Joins Portland To Work For His Old Deputy', *Huffington Post*, 23 May 2012.

86   Andrew Orlowski, 'Why DOES Google lobby so much?', The Register, 23 July 2012; http://www.theregister.co.uk/2012/07/23/google_lobby_why/page2.html

87   Nicole Perlroth, 'Under Scrutiny, Google Spends Record Amount on Lobbying', *New York Times*, 23 April 2012; http://bits.blogs.nytimes.com/2012/04/23/under-scrutiny-google-spends-record-amount-on-lobbying/

88   Tony Romm, 'How Google beat the Feds', Politico, 3 January 2013; http://www.politico.com/story/2013/01/how-google-beat-the-feds-85743.html

89   Bobbie Johnson, 'A brief guide to tech lobbyists in Europe', Gigaom, 28 January 2013; http://gigaom.com/2013/01/28/a-brief-guide-to-tech-lobbyists-in-europe/

90   'Crowdsourced lobby exposé shows Internet giants have footprints on our data privacy laws', Corporate Europe Observatory, 18 February 2013; http://corporateeurope.org/blog/crowdsourced-lobby-expos-shows-internet-giants-have-footprints-our-data-privacy-laws

91 Felix Salmon, 'Davos: Google grows up', *Reuters*, 8 January 2013; http://blogs.reuters.com/felix-salmon/2013/01/08/davos-google-grows-up/

92 Claire Ellicott, 'From the internet giant obsessed with openness the two-day "Zeitgeist" that's completely private', *Daily Mail*, 22 May 2012; http://www.dailymail.co.uk/news/article-2147863/Google-conference-From-internet-giant-obsessed-openness-2-day-Zeitgeist-thats-completely-private.html#ixzz2LGzxNbvq

93 Gideon Spanier, 'The Google guestlist: Who's heading to the Zeitgeist?', *Evening Standard*, 18 May 2012; http://www.thisislondon.co.uk/lifestyle/london-life/the-google-guestlist-whos-heading-to-the-zeitgeist-7766021.html

94 Linda Whetstone, Companies House records, accessed March 2013.

95 David Singleton, 'Google snares top No. 10 aide Tim Chatwin to take top comms role', *PR Week*, 8 September 2011.

96 John Owens, 'Clegg adviser Verity Harding joins Google in policy role', *PR Week*, 19 June 2013.

97 Jack Doyle, 'Happy families . . . but for how long?', *Daily Mail*, 27 May 2012; http://www.dailymail.co.uk/news/article-2150619/Cameron-Hunt-attend-aristocrats-posh-wedding-Ministers-career-line.html

98 'London's 1000 most influential people 2011: Gatekeepers & Fixers', *Evening Standard*, 7 November 2011; http://www.standard.co.uk/standard-home/londons-1000-most-influential-people-2011-gatekeepers-fixers-6365559.html

99 Ibid.

100 'City Spy: Blair babe is quitting for Tesco role', *Evening Standard*, 23 September 2011; http://www.standard.co.uk/business/city-spy-blair-babe-is-quitting-for-tesco-role-6446428.html

101 Letter from Simon Walker, CEO BVCA, to Boris Johnson, 7 May 2008; letter from Simon Walker, CEO BVCA, to Boris Johnson, 20 October 2008; letter from Simon Walker, CEO BVCA, to Boris Johnson, 5 December 2008; all received under FOI law from Greater London Authority.

102 Quentin Letts, 'This lobbying stinks like a decapitated, ageing trout', *Daily Mail*, 20 June 2008; http://www.dailymail.co.uk/news/article-1027852/This-lobbying-stinks-like-decapitated-ageing-trout.html

103 Rob Brown, 'The worst job in Britain', *Independent*, 17 March 1997; http://www.independent.co.uk/news/media/the-worst-job-in-britain-1273405.html

104 Tamasin Cave, personal communication with a lobbyist, Liberal Democrat conference, September 2012.

105 Christopher Hope, 'Whitehall's most wined and dined civil servant

is HMRC's Dave Hartnett', *Telegraph*, 17 June 2010; http://www.telegraph.co.uk/news/politics/7833886/Whitehalls-most-wined-and-dined-civil-servant-is-HMRCs-Dave-Hartnett.html

106 Vanessa Houlder, 'Did light touch tax become soft touch?', *Financial Times*, 31 May 2012; http://www.ft.com/cms/s/0/f5b698c0-aa8f-11e1-899d-00144feabdc0.html

107 Andy Rowell and Richard Cookson, 'Civil servants lived the high life courtesy of nuclear lobby', *Independent on Sunday*, 24 February 2008.

108 Andy Rowell and Rich Cookson, 'Nuclear Hospitality of Key Officials Exposed', Spinwatch, 28 November 2012.

109 Savoy Hotel website.

110 Melanie Newman, 'Gaping hole in rules lets Eric Pickles keep five-star business dinner private', Bureau of Investigative Journalism, 22 October 2011; http://www.thebureauinvestigates.com/2011/10/22/gaping-hole-in-rules-lets-eric-pickles-keep-business-dinner-private/

111 Nick Cohen, 'Tony Blair's moral decline and fall is now complete', *Observer*, 27 May 2012; http://www.guardian.co.uk/commentisfree/2012/may/27/nick-cohen-tony-blair-kazakhstan

112 TheCityUK, 'Agenda for dinner with Andrew Bailey, 6 March 2012: Institution profiles', received under FOI law from the Bank of England.

113 Invitation from Chris Cummings to Andrew Bailey to TheCityUK Summer Reception, 23 January 2012, received under FOI law from the Bank of England.

114 Lucy Kellaway, 'The networker', *Financial Times*, 12 August 2011; http://www.ft.com/cms/s/2/32df3c52-c2f1-11e0-8cc7-00144feabdc0.html#axzz2ei2mHvKc

115 Finsbury entry on the PRCA register, various dates, e.g. March 2013.

116 Tim Burt, *Dark Art: The Changing Face of Public Relations*, Elliot and Thompson, 2012, p. ix.

117 Chris Blackhurst, 'The MT interview: Roland Rudd', *Management Today*, 1 August 2007.

118 Ibid.

119 Burt, *Dark Art*, pp. 59–60.

120 Letter to Boris Johnson from Roland Rudd, senior partner, Finsbury, 12 May 2008, received under FOI law from Greater London Authority.

121 Boris Johnson's speaking notes for dinner on 26 February 2009 at Roland Rudd's house, received under FOI law from Greater London Authority.

122 Stephen Castle, 'Rise and fall of the greed generation's lobbyist', *Independent*, 6 October 1996; http://www.independent.co.uk/lifestyle/rise-and-fall-of-the-greed-generations-lobbyist-1356986.html

123   David Cameron's speech, 'Rebuilding trust in politics', 8 February 2010.

124   Nick Hopkins, Rob Evans and Richard Norton-Taylor, 'MoD staff and thousands of military officers join arms firms', *Guardian*, 15 October 2012; http://www.guardian.co.uk/uk/2012/oct/15/mod-military-arms-firms

125   Advisory Committee on Business Appointments, Sixth Report, 2004.

126   Ibid.

127   Letter from Kevin Tebbit to Des Browne, 30 July 2007, released under FOI law from the Ministry of Defence.

128   Manuela Mesco and Andy Rowell, 'Revolving doors revealed', Spinwatch, 26 July 2011.

129   'Ian Dalton leaves NHS to lead health services at BT', PMLive, 4 February 2013; http://www.pmlive.com/appointments/healthcare/2013/february/ian_dalton_leaves_nhs_to_lead_health_services_at_bt

130   Ibid.

131   Marina Soteriou, 'Exodus of senior NHS managers to private sector continues', *GP*, 1 February 2013; http://www.gponline.com/News/article/1169261/Exodus-senior-NHS-managers-private-sector-continues/

132   Julian O'Halloran, 'Revolving doors', BBC Radio 4, *File on 4*, 31 July 2011; http://www.bbc.co.uk/programmes/b012qtvw

133   'David Cameron's health adviser says the NHS will be "shown no mercy" by the Government', *Mirror*, 14 May 2011.

134   Patrick Wintour, 'Michael Gove appoints Tory donor John Nash as education minister', *Guardian*, 10 January 2013; http://www.theguardian.com/education/2013/jan/10/gove-appoints-john-nash-education-minister

135   'HSBC money laundering – what did Lord Green know?', Channel 4 News, 18 July 2012; http://www.channel4.com/news/what-did-lord-green-know-about-hsbc-money-laundering

136   Email from MM at McKinsey to David Bennett and Adrian Masters of Monitor, 31 May 2010, released under FOI law by Monitor.

137   Randeep Ramesh, 'German company involved in talks to take over NHS hospitals', *Guardian*, 4 September 2011, based on documents released under FOI law to Tamasin Cave by the Department of Health; http://www.guardian.co.uk/society/2011/sep/04/german-company-takeover-nhs-hospitals

138   The Big Four accountancy firms are PwC, Deloitte, Ernst & Young and KPMG.

139   PwC speaking at 'Free Thinking: Using Independence to Transform Schools' conference, Wellington College, 30 November 2012.

140   Ibid.

141   Austin Mitchell and Prem Sikka, *The Pin-Stripe Mafia: How Accountancy Firms Destroy Societies*, Association for Accountancy and Business Affairs, 2011, p. 5; http://visar.csustan.edu/aaba/PINSTRIPEMAFIA.pdf

142   Committee of Public Accounts, *Tax Avoidance: The Role of Large Accountancy Firms*, Forty-Fourth Report of Session 2012–13; Report, together with formal minutes, oral and written evidence, House of Commons, 26 April 2013.

143   Rajeev Syal, Simon Bowers and Patrick Wintour, '"Big four" accountants "use knowledge of Treasury to help rich avoid tax"', *Guardian*, 26 April 2013, http://www.guardian.co.uk/business/2013/apr/26/accountancy-firms-knowledge-treasury-avoid-tax

144   Ernst & Young, 'Ernst & Young partners join Treasury's tax forum', 21 July 2010, http://www.ey.com/UK/en/Newsroom/News-releases/Tax---10-07-21---EY-partners-join-Treasurys-tax-forum

145   Ernst & Young, 'About tax policy and controversy', website, undated, accessed June 2103; http://www.ey.com/UK/en/Services/Tax/Tax-Policy-and-Controversy/Tax---TPD---About

146   Elizabeth Rigby, 'Lord Green's matchmaking finally revealed', *Financial Times*, 2 November 2011; http://blogs.ft.com/westminster/2011/11/lord-greens-matchmaking-finally-revealed/

147   Richard Brooks, written evidence to the Treasury Select Committee, 21 January 2011; http://www.publications.parliament.uk/pa/cm201011/cmselect/cmtreasy/memo/taxpolicy/m46.htm

148   From *Panorama*, 'The Truth about Tax', 17 May 2012; http://www.bbc.co.uk/programmes/b01hzg7y

149   Damian Carrington, 'Energy companies have lent more than 50 staff to government departments', *Guardian*, 5 December 2011; http://www.guardian.co.uk/business/2011/dec/05/energy-companies-lend-staff-government

150   Ibid.

151   Letter to Maurice Frankel from FCO, 18 June 2002; http://www.cfoi.org.uk/fco.html

152   Email to Spinwatch from the Department for Energy and Climate Change, 15 February 2013.

153   Paul Hutcheon, 'Concerns at Diageo executive's role on alcohol misuse panel', *Scottish Herald*, 13 December 2008.

154   Mark Baird, interview with Claire Harkins, August 2007; http://www.powerbase.info/index.php/Mark_Baird

155   Spinwatch, *Who Really Runs This Place? A short report on the Big 4 accountancy firms and their ties to government*, June 2013.

4 Distort

1   James Frayne, 'How public affairs agencies need to up their game', *PR Week*, 19 June 2009.
2   Peter Oborne, *The Triumph of the Political Class*, Simon and Schuster, 2007, p. 249.
3   Lionel Zetter, *Lobbying: The Art of Political Persuasion*, Harriman House, 2008, p. 93.
4   Case study drawn from the CIPR Excellence Awards 2002.
5   Ibid.
6   Zetter, *Lobbying*, p. 94.
7   'Rebutting the myths about 50p tax from its supporters on Budget Day 21 March 2012'.
8   Bell Pottinger presentation: 'Changing perceptions of The Republic of Uzbekistan', July 2011.
9   Simon Goldsworthy, interview with Tamasin Cave, 19 November 2012.
10 Ibid.
11 Nick Davies, *Flat Earth News*, Vintage, 2009, p. 87.
12 Trevor Morris and Simon Goldsworthy, *PR: A Persuasive Industry*, Palgrave Macmillan, 2008, p. 31.
13 John Owens, 'BAA hires *Sunday Telegraph*'s Robert Watts', *PR Week* 24 September 2013.
14 Email from TheCityUK to UK Trade and Industry (Department for Business), 3 January 2012.
15 Email from TheCityUK, 23 April 2012, received under FOI law from Greater London Authority.
16 Tim Burt, *Dark Art: The Changing Face of Public Relations*, Elliot and Thompson, 2012, p. 33.
17 'Insider' reveals: 'PR men would think up a story and Rebekah's *Sun* and *News of the World* would run it, word for word. Some were complete fiction', *Daily Mail*, 9 July 2011, http://www.dailymail.co.uk/news/article-2013046/Rebekah-Brooks-Sun-News-World-run-fictional-stories-insider-claims.html#ixzz2FhqmoKIr
18 Frayne, 'How public affairs agencies need to up their game'.
19 Heather Stewart, 'Fears of mass UK banking exodus prove unfounded', *Guardian*, 18 February 2010; http://www.guardian.co.uk/business/2010/feb/18/uk-banker-exodus-exaggerated
20 Richard Brooks, *The Great Tax Robbery*, Oneworld Publications, 2013.
21 Leo Cendowicz, 'Is E.U. crackdown on hedge funds bad for business?', *Time*, May 19, 2010.

22 AIMA press release, 'AIMA warns of wider impact of AIFM Directive', 14 May 2010.

23 Patrick Jenkins and Megan Murphy, 'Goldman warns Europe on regulation, *Financial Times*, 30 September 2010.

24 'Diageo "could leave UK" if 50p tax rate remains', *Telegraph*, 23 October 2011; http://www.telegraph.co.uk/news/politics/8844284/Diageo-could-leave-UK-if-50p-tax-rate-remains.html

25 'Diageo threatens to leave UK over high taxes', CIPD, 12 February 2010.

26 Martin Wolf, 'Taxation, productivity and prosperity', *Financial Times*, 31 May 2012; http://www.neweconomics.org/blog/entry/mythbusters-a-competitive-tax-system-is-a-better-tax-system

27 Morris and Goldsworthy, *PR: A Persuasive Industry*, p. 34.

28 Jonathan Tilley, 'Greenpeace Shard stunt attracts global coverage', *PR Week*, 12 July 2013.

29 Associated Press, 'Davos activists occupy Shell station to protest Arctic drilling, warn of environmental danger', 25 January 2013.

30 Hilde Øvrebekk Lewis, 'Greenpeace boards Statoil rig in Arctic drilling protest', *Aftenbladet*, no. 10, April 2013.

31 Ros Donald and Chris Peters, 'Statoil's UK PR campaign: a quiet power play', Carbon Brief, 19 September 2012; http://www.carbonbrief.org/blog/2012/09/statoils-pr-campagin-a-quiet-power-play

32 Statement for Social Investigations from the NHS Partners Network, 3 August 2012; http://socialinvestigations.blogspot.co.uk/2012/08/nhs-partners-network-response-to.html

33 Mark Hollingsworth interview with Tamasin Cave, 13 March 2013.

34 Ibid.

35 Further written evidence from Alan Rusbridger, *Guardian*, to the Culture, Media and Sport Committee inquiry into Press standards, privacy and libel, September 2009; http://www.publications.parliament.uk/pa/cm200910/cmselect/cmcumeds/362/9071417.htm

36 Alan Rusbridger, 'The Trafigura fiasco tears up the textbook', *Guardian*, 14 October 2009; http://www.guardian.co.uk/commentisfree/libertycentral/2009/oct/14/trafigura-fiasco-tears-up-textbook

37 Further written evidence from Alan Rusbridger.

38 Ibid.

39 Alan Rusbridger, 'The Trafigura fiasco tears up the textbook'.

40 Interview with Lord Bell, 31 October 2013.

41 David Leigh and Owen Bowcott, 'Injunction publicity backfires on celebrity law firm – After Ryan Giggs' lawyers tried to sue Twitter for the initial internet leaks, thousands more tweets followed in retaliation', *Guardian*, Tuesday, 24 May 2011.

42   Schillings website accessed on Internet Archive: http://web.archive.
     org/web/20120407015522/http://www.schillings.co.uk/services/
     business-and-entrepreneurs/corporate-reputation-protection/

43   Schillings website accessed on Internet Archive: http://web.archive.
     org/web/20120407015527/http://www.schillings.co.uk/services/
     business-and-entrepreneurs/media-protection/

44   Michael Hayman, *Face Value: A Coutts & Co Report*.

45   Ibid.

46   Of Simons Muirhead & Burton.

47   Louis Charalambous, email to Andy Rowell, March 2013.

48   Oral evidence to House of Lords Communications Committee
     inquiry: 'The future of investigative journalism', 18 October 2011;
     http://www.parliamentlive.tv/Main/Player.aspx?meetingId=9198

49   Ibid.

50   Quiller Consultants website: http://www.quillerconsultants.com/

51   Email from Tony Halmos to Quiller Consultants, 9 November 2011,
     received under FOI law from City of London Corporation.

52   The Square Mile is split into twenty-five electoral wards, in only
     four of which are residents allowed to vote. Votes are given to
     corporations, mainly banks and financial firms, in the remainder.
     The number of votes is determined by the size of the company,
     with corporate chiefs deciding on who within these firms can cast
     a vote. http://www.theguardian.com/commentisfree/2011/oct/31/
     corporation-london-city-medieval

53   Alexandra Topping and Shiv Malik, 'Students marching against
     tuition fees met with "total policing" tactics', *Guardian*, 9 November
     2011; http://www.guardian.co.uk/uk/2011/nov/09/student-tuition-
     fees-protest-policing

54   Quiller Consultants website: www.quillerconsultants.com/Our-People

55   Email from City of London Corporation to Quiller Consultants, 11
     November 2011, received under FOI law from City of London
     Corporation.

56   Burt, *Dark Art*, p. 94.

57   Lord Chadlington at 20th PRWC, Dubai, 13–15 March 2012, Grand
     Hyatt Dubai.

58   Anthony Hilton, 'Financial PR needs to widen horizons', *PR Week*,
     21 November 2012.

59   Kevin Murray, chairman of Bell Pottinger, 'Engaging Stakeholders'
     conference, November 2011.

60   Burt, *Dark Art*, p. 101.

61   Rupert Neate and Mark Sweney, 'Phone hacking: Rupert Murdoch
     calls in PR firm Edelman', *Guardian*, 14 July 2011; http://www.

guardian.co.uk/media/2011/jul/14/phone-hacking-rupert-murdoch

62 Peter Gummer at 20th PRWC, Dubai, 13–15 March 2012, Grand Hyatt Dubai.

63 Oliver Wright, 'Lobbying company tried to wipe out "wife beater" beer references, *Independent*, 4 January 2012, http://www.independent.co.uk/news/uk/politics/lobbying-company-tried-to-wipe-out-wife-beater-beer-references-6284622.html

64 Harry Glass and Sean Poulter, 'Controversial payday lender Wonga makes a mint out of cash-strapped consumers as number of loans last year rose nearly 300%', *Daily Mail*, 17 September 2012; http://www.dailymail.co.uk/news/article-2204489/Wonga-makes-mint-cash-strapped-consumers-number-loans-year-rose-nearly-300.html

65 Mark King, 'Wonga apologises to Stella Creasy over abusive Twitter messages, *Guardian*, 21 November 2012, http://www.guardian.co.uk/business/2012/nov/21/wonga-apologises-stella-creasy-abusive-twitter-messages?intcmp=239

66 Billy Kenber and Murad Ahmed, 'Wiki wipes of multinational companies exposed', *The Times*, 17 November 2012.

67 Wikipedia page statistics.

68 Violet Blue, 'BP accused of rewriting environmental record on Wikipedia', CNET, 20 March 2013; http://news.cnet.com/8301-1023_3-57575460-93/bp-accused-of-rewriting-environmental-record-on-wikipedia/

69 Melanie Newman, 'PR uncovered: Top lobbyists boast of how they influence the PM', The Bureau of Investigative Journalism, 5 December 2011; http://www.thebureauinvestigates.com/2011/12/05/pr-uncovered-top-lobbyists-boast-of-how-they-influence-the-pm/

70 Melanie Newman and David Pegg, 'Bell Pottinger targeted campaigner on Wikipedia', The Bureau of Investigative Journalism, 8 December 2011, http://www.thebureauinvestigates.com/2011/12/08/bell-pottinger-targeted-environmental-campaigners-website/

71 'Deforestation in Sarawak', *The Economist*, 3 November 2012.

72 User contributions for Biggleswiki.

73 Melanie Newman and David Pegg, 'Bell Pottinger targeted campaigner on Wikipedia'.

74 Burt, *Dark Art*, p. 108.

75 Interview with Lord Bell, 31 October 2013.

76 Burt, *Dark Art*, p. 110.

77 Reputation Changer website: http://www.reputationchanger.com

78 Billy Kenber, 'How celebrities keep their secrets safe from Google', *The Times*, 1 June 2011.

79   Jacqueline Leo, 'BP using Google to manipulate public opinion', *Huffington Post*, 3 June 2010, http://www.huffingtonpost.com/jacqueline-leo/bp-using-google-to-manipu_b_598677.html

80   Bell Pottinger, 'Changing perceptions of the Republic of Uzbekistan – A presentation for the Azimov Group', July 2011, p. 25.

81   Alec Mattinson, 'Bahrain passes brief on to Bell Pottinger', *PR Week*, 14 January 2009; http://www.brandrepublic.com/news/873574/Bahrain-passes-brief-Bell-Pottinger

82   Matt Cartmell, 'Bell Pottinger's work for Bahrain Government under the spotlight', *PR Week*, 25 February 2011; http://www.prweek.com/uk/news/1057005/Bell-Pottingers-work-Bahrain-Government-spotlight/

83   Marcus Baram, 'Lobbyists Jump Ship In Wake Of Mideast Unrest', *Huffington Post*, 25 March 2011; http://www.huffingtonpost.com/2011/03/24/lobbyist-mideast-unrest-departures_n_840231.html

84   US Dept of Justice: Qorvis FARA Exhibit AB to Registration Statement for Kingdom of Bahrain (Aug 4, 2011) http://www.fara.gov/docs/5483-Exhibit-AB-20110804-32.pdf

85   Qorvis FARA filing: http://www.scribd.com/doc/51333212/Qorvis-Bahrain-Statement-11-1-10

86   Marcus Baram, 'Lobbyists Jump Ship In Wake Of Mideast Unrest'.

87   Ibid.

88   Andrew Quinn, 'Bahrain violence presents U.S. with fresh dilemma', *Reuters*, 16 March 2011; http://www.reuters.com/article/2011/03/16/us-bahrain-usa-idUSTRE72F8CE20110316

89   Martin Chulov, 'America rebukes Bahrain after violent crackdown on demonstrators', *Guardian*, 16 March 2011; http://www.guardian.co.uk/world/2011/mar/16/five-die-bahrain-crackdown

90   Press release: 'Bahraini Ambassador Welcomes Secretary of State's Positive Remarks Regarding The U.S. Friendship with Bahrain and Calls for National Dialogue', featured on *Reuters*, 19 March 2011; http://www.reuters.com/article/2011/03/20/idUS19086+20-Mar-2011+PRN20110320

91   Paul Blumenthal, 'Bahrain's PR team', Sunlight Foundation, 22 March 2011; http://sunlightfoundation.com/blog/taxonomy/term/bahrain/

92   Ken Silverstein, 'How Bahrain works Washington', Salon, 8 December 2011.

93   Interview with Lord Bell, 31 October 2013.

94   Masterclass guide to campaigning, Ellwood Atfield: http://www.ellwoodatfield.com/pdf/Masterclass_guide_to_campaigning.pdf

95   Mark Leftly, 'The wrong side of the tracks: Lobbyists for HS2 rail line

funded by the taxpayer', *Independent*, 25 August 2013; http://www.independent.co.uk/news/uk/politics/the-wrong-side-of-the-tracks-lobbyists-for-hs2-rail-line-funded-by-the-taxpayer-8783673.html

96   Matt Rumble, 'Campaigns Showcase: Public Affairs – Westbourne Communications   HS2 supporters put their case on the line', *PR Week*, 14 December 2012; http://www.prweek.com/uk/news/1164032/Campaigns-Showcase-Public-Affairs---Westbourne-Communications--HS2-supporters-put-case-line/?DCMP=ILC-SEARCH

97   Anna Minton, *Scaring the Living Daylights Out of People: The local lobby and the failure of democracy*, Spinwatch publication, 2013; http://www.spinwatch.org/index.php/issues/lobbying/item/5458-the-local-lobby-and-the-failure-of-democracy

98   Jamie Carpenter, '"Little" evidence HS2 will rebalance economy, says watchdog', *Planning Resource*, 16 May 2013; http://www.planningresource.co.uk/go/breakingnews/article/1182583/little-evidence-hs2-will-rebalance-economy-says-watchdog/

99   Mark Odell, 'Watchdog rejects strategic case for building HS2 link', *Financial Times*, 16 May 2013; http://www.ft.com/cms/s/0/a014324c-bd7b-11e2-a735-00144feab7de.html

100   Department of Trade and Industry, 'Our energy future – creating a low carbon economy', White Paper, February 2003; http://webarchive.nationalarchives.gov.uk/+/http://www.berr.gov.uk/files/file10719.pdf

101   NIA website from 2003, accessed on Internet Archive: http://web.archive.org/web/20030625110414/http://www.niauk.org/

102   Email from Weber Shandwick to BNFL, 15 December 2004, received under FOI law.

103   'Nuclear power "must be on agenda"', BBC News, 24 May 2007.

104   Special report: 'The fallout from Fukushima', *New Scientist*, September 2013; http://www.newscientist.com/special/fukushima-crisis

105   John McNamara, LinkedIn profile.

106   'UK government and nuclear industry email correspondence after the Fukushima accident', *Guardian*, 30 June 2011; http://www.theguardian.com/environment/interactive/2011/jun/30/email-nuclear-uk-government-fukushima

107   Ibid.

108   Ibid.

109   John McNamara, 'Facing up to the Fukushima Challenge', *Insight*, Issue 6, 2011.

110   HM Government, 'The UK's Nuclear Future', March 2013.

111   Jason Groves, 'Nuclear somersault: New Energy Secretary changes his tune and says he won't block reactor plans', *Daily Mail*, 6 February

2012; http://www.dailymail.co.uk/news/article-2097481/Ed-Davey-performs-U-turn-nuclear-power.html#ixzz2OfmjVvfH

112   HM Government, 'The UK's Nuclear Future'.

113   Fiona Harvey, 'Fossil fuel firms use "biased" study in massive gas lobbying push', *Guardian*, 20 April 2011; http://www.guardian.co.uk/environment/2011/apr/20/fossil-fuel-lobbying-shale-gas

114   Fiona Harvey, 'Gas rebranded as green energy by EU', *Guardian*, 29 May 2012; http://www.guardian.co.uk/environment/2012/may/29/gas-rebranded-green-energy-eu

115   Matt Ridley, *The Shale Gas Shock*, Global Warming Policy Foundation, May 2011.

116   Fiona Harvey, 'Anti-fracking campaigners target Cuadrilla HQ', *Guardian*, 19 August 2013; http://www.theguardian.com/environment/2013/aug/19/anti-fracking-campaigners-cuadrilla-hq

117   Boris Johnson, 'Ignore the doom merchants, Britain should get fracking', *Daily Telegraph*, 9 December 2012; http://www.telegraph.co.uk/comment/columnists/borisjohnson/9733518/Ignore-the-doom-merchants-Britain-should-get-fracking.html

118   Tim Steer, 'Fracking has the power to transform, so all hail to the shale', *Daily Telegraph*, 29 December 2012; http://www.telegraph.co.uk/finance/comment/9770894/Fracking-has-the-power-to-transform-so-all-hail-to-the-shale.html

119   Earthworks, 'Gas Patch Roulette – How Shale Gas Development Risks Public Health in Pennsylvania', October 2012; http://www.earthworksaction.org/files/publications/Health-Report-Summary-FINAL.pdf

120   Tim Webb, 'Fracking will cut energy bills, says poverty chief', *The Times*, 21 August 2013; http://www.thetimes.co.uk/tto/news/uk/article3848589.ece

121   David Morris, 'Fracking could reduce bills and create jobs', *The Visitor*, 16 August 2013; http://www.thevisitor.co.uk/news/columnists/david-morris-column-fracking-could-reduce-bills-and-create-jobs-1-5948274

122   Pembina Institute, Climate Impacts: http://www.pembina.org/oil-sands/os101/climate

123   Ian Austen, 'Oil sands industry in Canada tied to higher carcinogen level', *New York Times*, 7 January 2013.

124   Oil Sands: the Facts, 2010 – fax sent to Mission Canada on 2 September 2010.

125   Andy Rowell, 'Canada's dirty lobby diary – Undermining the EU Fuel Quality Directive', Friends of the Earth Europe, July 2011.

126   Joris Luyendijk, 'Our banks are not merely out of control. They're beyond control', *Guardian*, 19 June 2013; http://www.guardian.co.uk/profile/joris-luyendijk

127   Bischoff Report, 2009: http://webarchive.nationalarchives.gov.
       uk/20100407010852/http://www.hm-treasury.gov.uk/d/uk_
       internationalfinancialservices070509.pdf

128   Wigley Report, 2010: http://legacy.london.gov.uk/mayor/economy/
       docs/london-winning-changing-world.pdf

129   Nick Anstee, *EN* magazine, undated; http://www.enforbusiness.
       com/interview/nick-anstee

130   TheCityUK Annual report 2011.

131   Email from Cicero to Lord Green, 31 May 2011, received under FOI
       law from UK Trade and Industry (Department of Business).

132   Centre for Research on Socio-Cultural Change, University of
       Manchester, *An Alternative Report on UK Banking Reform*; http://
       www.cresc.ac.uk/publications/an-alternative-report-on-uk-banking-
       reform

133   'Job losses in London and NY', *Financial Times*, 15 October 2008; http://
       www.ft.com/cms/s/2/f7dbccac-9a93-11dd-bfd8-000077b07658.html-
       #axzz2HCKxDrF8

134   Ian Hall, 'Bundle of lobbying energy puts Cicero at heart of City',
       Public Affairs News, April 2011.

135   Ibid.

136   Speech given by Robert Jenkins at the third Gordon Midgley Memorial
       Debate, London, 22 November 2011; http://www.bankofengland.
       co.uk/publications/Documents/speeches/2011/speech533.pdf

137   Speech given by Robert Jenkins at the International Centre for
       Financial Regulation's 3rd Annual Regulatory Summit, London, 25
       September 2012; http://www.bankofengland.co.uk/publications/
       Documents/speeches/2012/speech603.pdf

138   Ibid.

139   Centre for Research on Socio-Cultural Change, *An Alternative Report
       on UK Banking Reform*.

140   Press release, 'Annual results for the year ending 30 Sept 2010', General
       Healthcare Group.

141   Tribal press release, 'The NHS cannot be protected from economic
       reality any longer', 13 July 2010.

142   'Opportunities Post Global Healthcare Reforms', Apax Global
       Healthcare Services Conference, October 2010; http://www.powerbase.
       info/images/f/fe/Apax_Healthcare_conference_2010.pdf

143   James Bremner, 'Straight Talk. New Approaches in Healthcare.
       Capital Financing. Beyond the Shores of Your Typical Transaction,
       Modern Healthcare, 24 November 2003.

144   NHS Partners Network: Director's update on the NHS Reforms – 20
       May 2011.

145 Oliver Huitson, 'How the BBC betrayed the NHS: an exclusive report on two years of censorship and distortion', Open Democracy, September 2012; http://www.opendemocracy.net/ourbeeb/oliver-huitson/how-bbc-betrayed-nhs-exclusive-report-on-two-years-of-censorship-and-distortion

146 Bonnie Gardiner, 'The Health and Social Care Bill', YouGov, 6 March 2011; http://yougov.co.uk/news/2012/03/06/health-social-care-bill/

147 Patrick Butler, NHS reforms live blog, Guardian, 7 February 2012; http://www.theguardian.com/society/blog/2012/feb/07/nhs-reforms-bill-live-blog-lansley-lords

5 Conceal

1   Merrill Rose, 'Activism in the 90s: Changing Roles for Public Relations', Public Relations Quarterly, vol. 36, no. 3, 1991, pp. 28–32.

2   BBC News, 'Ban on tobacco displays announced', 9 December 2008.

3   Rose, 'Activism in the 90s'.

4   Phil Chamberlain, 'Independence of nutritional information?' British Medical Journal, 22 March 2010.

5   Amanda Little, 'A green corporate image – more than a logo', presentation to Green Marketing Conference, 25–26 June 1990.

6   Also see Report of the Committee of Experts on Tobacco Industry Documents, Tobacco Company Strategies to Undermine Tobacco Control Activities at the World Health Organization, July 2000.

7   PMI documents leaked to the SmokingGate website (no longer active), published in part by the Tobacco Control Research Group, University of Bath, at http://www.tobaccotactics.org/index.php/Philip_Morris%27_PR_Campaign_Against_the_Display_Ban

8   Ibid.

9   Richard Kay, 'How an Earl crashed the King's party', Daily Mail, 16 December 2011; http://www.dailymail.co.uk/news/article-2074873/How-Earl-crashed-Kings-party.html

10 Ibid.

11 iNHouse Communications website, 'About Us'; http://www.inhousecomms.com/index.php/new_site/about/ About

12 SmokingGate, 'PMI in secret cooperation with a British health minister', 20 December 2011; http://www.smokingate.com/2011/12/20/philip-morris-in-secret-cooperation-with-a-british-health-minister-earl-howe/

13 For more information on smuggling see analysis by the Tobacco

Control Research Group, University of Bath, 'Tobacco smuggling', published on the Tobacco Tactics website: http://www.tobaccotactics.org/index.php/Tobacco_Smuggling

14   'European Commission and PMI International sign 12-year Agreement to combat contraband and counterfeit cigarettes', 9 July 2004: http://ec.europa.eu/anti_fraud/documents/cigarette-smugg-2004/pr_en.pdf

15   Nick Goodway, 'Tories back industry appeal against cigarette display law', *Evening Standard*, 26 April 2010.

16   PMI, UK POSD Action Plan, undated.

17   SmokingGate, 'PMI in secret cooperation with a British health minister'.

18   PMI, UK POSD Action Plan, undated.

19   Denis Campbell, 'BAT denies allegations that it funded anti-tobacco ban lobby', *Guardian*, 27 April 2011; http://www.guardian.co.uk/business/2011/apr/27/retail-newsagents-tobacco-ban

20   Denis Campbell, 'BAT admits bankrolling newsagents' tobacco campaign – Health Secretary Andrew Lansley will be asked whether he was aware of cigarette firm's role in fight', *Guardian*, 28 April 2011; http://www.guardian.co.uk/business/2011/apr/28/bat-admits-backing-newsagents-campaign%20BAT%20admits%20bankrolling%20newsagents%27%20tobacco%20campaign

21   Jamie Doward and Alex Ascherson, 'Tobacco firms accused of funding campaign to keep cigarettes on display', *Guardian*, 26 February 2011; http://www.guardian.co.uk/business/2011/feb/26/tobacco-firms-campaign-cigarettes-display

22   Nick Corrin, letter to Trading Standards Officer, 2012.

23   Nick Corrin, email, November 2012.

24   Nicholas S. Hopkinson, John Moxham, Hugh Montgomery, Robert West, Gabriel Scally, Martin McKee, Stephen Spiro, Andrew Bush, John Stradling, Athol Wells, Kian Fan Chung, Stephen R. Durham, Finbarr C. Martin, Jo Congleton, Elin Roddy, Mark Dayer, Patrick White, Philip W. Ind, Joanna L. Brown, Irem Patel, Keir Lewis, Nicholas Hart, Samuel Kemp, Jack Barker, Matthew Hind, David Nicholl, Myra Stern and Sarah Elkin, 'Tobacco industry lobbyists and their health-care clients', *The Lancet*, vol. 381, issue 9865, 9 February 2013, p. 445; http://www.thelancet.com/journals/lancet/article/PIIS0140-6736%2813%2960236-6/fulltext

25   Loulla-Mae Eleftheriou-Smith and Daniel Farey-Jones, 'Luther Pendragon dropped by ABPI over tobacco client', *PR Week*, 7 February 2013; http://www.prweek.com/uk/bulletin/prweekukdaily/article/1170082/luther-pendragon-dropped-abpi-tobacco-client/

26   Lynsey Barber, 'Luther Pendragon no longer working with PMI', *PR Week*, 11 February 2013.

27 Alex Ralph, 'Illicit cigarettes burn €12.5bn in unpaid taxes, claims report', *The Times*, 18 April 2013.

28 'Leeds: Illicit tobacco rates are real problem', *Yorkshire Evening Post*, 12 November, 2012. 'Illicit cigarette problem worsens', *Sunderland Echo*, 19 September 2012.

29 Luk Joosens, 'Smuggling and the Tobacco Industry and Plain Packs', Cancer Research UK, November 2012.

30 University of Bath, Tobacco Tactics website: http://www.tobacco-tactics.org/index.php/The_Common_Sense_Alliance

31 Jamie Doward, 'Revealed: tobacco giant's secret plans to see off plain cigarette packets', *Observer*, 27 July 2012.

32 Leaked PMI documents, 2012.

33 Ben Quinn and Mark Sweney, 'Tobacco firm begins "stealth-marketing" campaign against plain packaging – Messages in packs of Marlboro cigarettes invite buyers to visit campaigning website', *Guardian*, 7 June 2013.

34 Ibid.

35 Simon Clark, 'Get the Party Started', Taking Liberties blog, 8 May 2103; http://taking-liberties.squarespace.com/

36 Leaked PMI documents, 2012.

37 'Lynton Crosby "didn't intervene" on tobacco packaging decision', BBC News, 21 July 2013; http://www.bbc.co.uk/news/uk-politics-23394471

38 Toby Helm and Jamie Doward, 'Lynton Crosby must go, urges former Lib Dem health minister, as cross-party anger grows over U-turn on cigarettes – David Cameron told to sack strategy chief over link to tobacco giants', *Observer*, 14 July 2013.

39 'Cigarette packaging: a retreat on public health that shames No. 10', *Observer*, 14 July 2013.

40 Gabriella Griffith, 'Plain cigarette packaging stubbed out for now', *Management Today*, 12 July 2013.

41 More information on US astroturf campaigns can be found at www.sourcewatch.org/index.php/Astroturf

42 Matthew Elliott and James Frayne on David Cameron's first 100 days: 'Tax', ConservativeHome, 17 March 2006; http://conservative-home.blogs.com/platform/2006/03/over_the_last_w.html

43 Robert Booth, 'Big money alliance at heart of the low tax campaign: Taxpayers' Alliance portrays itself as voice of the people, but where does its £1m funding come from?', *Guardian*, 10 October 2009.

44 TaxPayers' Alliance, 'Changing policy through powerful campaigns . . . and how you can help', Annual Review 2011; http://www.taxpay-ersalliance.com/annualreview2011.pdf

45   Suzanne Goldenberg, 'Republicans attack Obama's environmental protection from all sides', *Guardian*, 4 March 2011 http://www. theguardian.com/world/2011/mar/04/republicans-attack-obamas-environmental-protection; http://www.sourcewatch.org/index. php?title=Americans_for_Prosperity

46   James Frayne, 'Why should we lift the ban on political advertising on UK TV', *Portland Quarterly*, 12 October 2012; http://www.port-land-communications.com/publications/the-quarterly-issue-8/why-should-we-lift-the-ban-on-political-advertising-on-uk-tv/

47   Westbourne Communications website: http://changeopinion.com/ services/

48   James Frayne biography, Westbourne Communications website, 2010.

49   Matt Rumble, 'Campaigns Showcase: Public Affairs – Westbourne Communications – HS2 supporters put their case on the line', *PR Week*, 14 December 2012; http://www.prweek.com/uk/news/1164032/ Campaigns-Showcase-Public-Affairs---Westbourne-Communications--HS2-supporters-put-case-line/?DCMP=ILC-SEARCH

50   Westbourne Communications website: http://changeopinion.com/ services/

51   Letter to the editor, 'Cut the 50p tax rate to help boost business and encourage entrepreneurs', *Telegraph*, 29 February 2012; http://www. telegraph.co.uk/comment/letters/9114040/Cut-the-50p-tax-rate-to-help-boost-business-and-encourage-entrepreneurs.html

52   Robert Winnett, '50p tax rate is damaging economy and delaying recovery from recession, warn 500 business leaders', *Daily Telegraph*, 29 February 2012.

53   Westbourne Communications website: http://changeopinion.com/ services/

54   'Budget 2012: 50p tax should remain, say majority of voters in ComRes poll', *Huffington Post*, 18 March 2012; http://www.huffing-tonpost.co.uk/2012/03/18/50p-tax-should-remain-poll-budget-comres_n_1356195.html

55   Policy Exchange, 'Why the Tories must shed their "party of the rich" image', 11 January 2012; http://www.policyexchange.org.uk/ media-centre/blogs/category/item/why-the-tories-must-shed-their-party-of-the-rich-image

56   Jason Groves, 'Osborne "will axe the 50p tax": Chancellor in "last ditch battle" with Lib Dems before Budget', *Daily Mail*, 16 March 2012; http://www.dailymail.co.uk/news/article-2115707/George-Osborne-axe-50p-tax-rate-ditch-battle-Lib-Dems-UK-Budget-2012. html#ixzz1zfToT9Ub

57   John Stauber and Sheldon Rampton, *Toxic Sludge is Good for You!*

Lies, Damn Lies and the Public Relations Industry, Common Courage Press, 1995, p. 141.

58 Andy Rowell, *Green Backlash: Global Subversion of the Environment Movement*, Routledge, 1996.

59 Stauber and Rampton, *Toxic Sludge is Good for You!*, p. 141.

60 Open Secrets, 'Total Lobbying Spending', Centre for Responsive Politics, accessed August 2013; http://www.opensecrets.org/lobby/

61 Timothy Karr, 'Washington's astroturf economy', Freepress (US), 18 November 2009; http://www.freepress.net/blog/09/11/18/washington%E2%80%99s-astroturf-economy

62 Rowell, *Green Backlash*, pp. 84–5.

63 'Philip Hilts coalition opposing health plan is called a front group for insurers', *New York Times*, 20 October 1993; http://www.nytimes.com/1993/10/20/us/coalition-opposing-health-plan-is-called-front-group-for-insurers.html

64 Public Citizen, 'Organizing astroturf: evidence shows bogus grass-roots groups hijack the political debate; need for grassroots lobbying disclosure requirements', January 2007.

65 Ibid.; Americans for Tax Reform, Sourcewatch profile, accessed July 2013; www.sourcewatch.org/index.php/Americans_for_Tax_Reform

66 *Lobbying: Access and Influence*, Public Administration Select Committee Report, Oral and Written Evidence (vol. 2), January 2009.

67 Phillip Inman, 'US Tea Party in London to spread low tax message – In an event organised by the Taxpayers' Alliance and sponsored by US lobbyists, the group will also promote small government', *Guardian*, 7 September 2010.

68 Amanda Fallin, Rachel Grana and Stanton A. Glantz, 'To quarter-back behind the scenes, third-party efforts: the tobacco industry and the Tea Party', *Tobacco Control* doi:10.1136/tobaccocontrol-2012-050815; Ben Quinn and Mark Sweney, 'Tobacco firm begins "stealth-marketing" campaign against plain packaging', *Guardian*, 7 June 2013.

69 Sharon Bender, *Global Spin – The Corporate Assault on Environmentalism*, Green Books, 1997, p. 33; Peter Stone, 'Green, Green Grass', *The National Journal*, 27 March 1993, vol. 25, no. 13; p. 754.

70 Brian McNeill, 'Forged letters to congressman anger local groups', *Daily Progress*, 31 July 2009, http://www2.dailyprogress.com/news/cdp-news-local/2009/jul/31/letters_sent_to_perriello_called_fakes_area_advoc-ar-78413/; Zachary Roth, 'Lobby firm sent forged climate change letter to Congressman', TPMMuckraker, 31 July 2009, http://tpmmuckraker.talkingpointsmemo.com/2009/07/lobby_firm_sent_forged_climate_change_letter_to_c.php

71   Brendan DeMelle, 'Bonner & Associates coached employees to lie to generate letters to Congress – Will Congress rein in such astro-turf?' Desmogblog, 28 August 2009; http://www.desmogblog.com/bonner-associates-coached-employees-lie-generate-letters-congress-will-congress rein-such-astroturf

72   Justin Elliott, Astroturf Firm Bonner Institutes New No-Forgery Quality Control Policy, *TPM Muckraker*, 28 August, 2009 http://talkingpointsmemo.com/muckraker/astroturf-firm-bonner-institutes-new-no-forgery-quality-control-policy?ref=fpa

73   Hands Off Our Packs, 'Half a million oppose plain packaging', 16 August 2012, accessed June 2013; http://www.handsoffourpacks.com/newsroom/half-a-million-oppose-plain-packaging/

74   Department of Health, letter to Simon Clark, Forest, 14 June 2012, accessed June 2013; https://www.wp.dh.gov.uk/transparency/files/2012/09/FOIreply719739attachment2.pdf

75   Tobacco Control Manager, email to Simon Clark, 16 July 2012, accessed June 2013; https://www.wp.dh.gov.uk/transparency/files/2012/09/FOIreply719739attachment3.pdf

76   Ibid.

77   Ibid.

78   Simon Clark, letter to the Department of Health, 30 August 2012, accessed June 2013; https://www.wp.dh.gov.uk/transparency/files/2012/12/7.8-Forest_30.8.12.pdf

79   Ibid.

80   Simon Clark, Smear test: how the plain packaging consultation turned ugly, Taking Liberties blog, 19 November 2012; http://taking-liberties.squarespace.com/blog/2012/11/19/smear-test-how-the-plain-packaging-consultation-turned-ugly.html

81   Richard Berman, letter to Barbara Trach from PMI, 5 September 1995; http://legacy.library.ucsf.edu/tid/ewko6coo/pdf

82   Paul Staines, 'You want policy? In cash?' *The Times*, 20 December 2005.

83   Reform website: http://www.reform.co.uk/content/3279/about_us/our_people/executive_team/andrew_haldenby

84   Reform website: http://www.reform.co.uk/content/2984/reform/directors_introduction/directors_introduction

85   Roundtable debate: 'Future of Healthcare; Health Insurance & Protection', November 2005, p. 6.

86   Ibid.

87   'The Future of Health', Reform conference and publication, 2009.

88   Dr Paul Charlson, speaking on a 'NHS shake-up debate', *Jeremy Vine Show*, BBC Radio 2, 16 March 2011; http://www.bbc.co.uk/programm555

89   Tamasin Cave, 'Lobby Watch: Nurses for Reform', *British Medical*

Journal, 10 March 2010; http://www.spinwatch.org/reviews-mainmenu-24/48-lobbying/5351-nurses-for-reform

90   Tom Harris MP, 'Nurses for Reform and David Cameron: the unanswered questions', Labour List, 8 January 2010; http://labourlist.org/2010/01/nurses-for-reform-and-david-cameron-the-unanswered-questions/; Helen Evans, 'Nurses' group welcomes review to usher in private top-ups', 19 June 2008; http://www.nursesforreformblog.com/2008/06/19/nurses-group-welcomes-review-to-usher-in-private-top-ups-2/

91   Martin Salter, 'David Cameron's Health Supremo has some embarrassing questions to answer', *Telegraph*, 3 February 2010. http://blogs.telegraph.co.uk/news/msalter/100024735/david-camerons-health-supremo-has-some-embarrassing-questions-to-answer/

92   Cave, 'Lobby Watch: Nurses for Reform'.

93   Shane Frith profile on EzyOrder website: http://ezyorder.com/about-us.php; Shane Frith profile on LinkedIn: http://uk.linkedin.com/in/shanefrith

94   Stockholm Network, press release, 22 August 2007; http://www.stockholm-network.org/downloads/press/SN_press_release_staff.pdf

95   Cave, 'Lobby Watch: Nurses for Reform'.

96   Ibid.

97   James Frayne biog., Westbourne Communications, undated; accessed May 2012.

98   Doctors for Reform, 'Free at the point of delivery – reality or political mirage?', April 2007; http://www.reform.co.uk/client_files/www.reform.co.uk/files/free_at_the_point_of_delivery.pdf

99   'Annual results for the year ended 30 September 2010', General Healthcare Group; http://www.generalhealthcare.co.uk/GHG-PLC/PDFs/Annual-Results2010.pdf

100 Michael Gillard, 'MPs "conned" over obesity charity that was front for diet firm', *Independent on Sunday*, 20 January 2008.

101 Nick Mathiason, 'Microsoft in row over lobby tactics', *Observer*, 23 September 2007; http://money.guardian.co.uk/print/0,,330793003-110144,00.html

102 'Complaint forces European Privacy Association to confirm Facebook, Google, Microsoft and Yahoo are corporate backers', Corporate Europe Observatory, 18 June, 2013.

103 Sarah Boseley, 'Concern over cancer group's link to drug firm', *Guardian*, 18 October 2006; http://www.theguardian.com/society/2006/oct/18/cancercare.health

104 James Lyons, 'Drug firms cash in on David Cameron's £650 million cancer fund sparking new lobbying row', *Mirror*, 29 April 2013;

http://www.mirror.co.uk/news/uk-news/drug-firms-cash-david-camerons-1859000

105 Dan Bilefsky, 'Lobbying Brussels: It's getting crowded', *New York Times*, 29 October 2005; http://www.nytimes.com/2005/10/28/business/worldbusiness/28iht-wblobby.html?pagewanted=all&_r=0

106 Tom Curtin, *Managing Green Issues*, Palgrave Macmillan, 2000, p. 132.

107 Ibid., p. 133.

108 Andy Rowell, 'Power struggles – how the unions took the nuclear shilling', Spinwatch, 18 July 2006; http://www.spinwatch.org/index.php/andy-rowell/item/425-power-struggles-how-the-unions-took-the-nuclear-shilling

109 Andy Rowell, 'Plugging the gap', *Guardian*, 3 May 2006.

110 Ibid.

111 Andy Rowell, 'Hard rockers – The views of the green lobby should be challenged, according to a new alliance', *Guardian*, 11 July 2001; http://www.powerbase.info/index.php/Scientific_Alliance

112 Scientific Alliance website: www.scientific-alliance.com

113 'An analysis of trends in aggregates markets since 1990', prepared for the British Aggregates Association, February 2005.

114 See Scientific Alliance website for examples: http://www.scientific-alliance.org/energy-climate-change

115 Andy Rowell, 'Revealed: The Hidden Agenda Behind Al Gore Attack', Spinwatch, 11 October 2007.

116 Andy Rowell, 'BBC Messes Up Again on Gore Story', Spinwatch, 12 October 2007.

117 Alex Black, 'Issues management: how nuclear power got its groove back', *PR Week*, 2 March 2006.

6 Attack

1   Anna Minton, *Scaring the Living Daylights Out of People: The local lobby and the failure of democracy*, Spinwatch, March 2013; comment by James Bethell from Westbourne Communications, working for High Speed 2 Campaign, on what to do with opponents.

2   Commonwealth Secretariat and IFC Forum Conference (podcasts and contemporary notes), 20 October 2011; http://www.cicero-forum.com/conf_overview.php?eid=66

3   'Occupy LSX cite tax justice as a key demand', Tax Justice Network blog, 23 October 2011; http://taxjustice.blogspot.co.uk/2011/10/occupy-lsx-cite-tax-justice-as-key.html

4   Matt Cartmell, 'Jack Irvine – The combative crusader', *PR Week*, 7 July 2011; http://www.prweek.com/uk/features/1078626/Jack Irvine---combative-crusader/

5   'Launch of the International Financial Centres Forum', Ogier, 4 December 2009; http://www.ogier.com/News/Pages/LaunchofIFC Forum%E2%80%93NewVoiceforInternationalFinancialCentres.aspx

6   International Financial Centres Forum website: http://www. ifcforum.org/about.php

7   Cicero Group website: http://www.cicero-group.com/leadership-team/mark-twigg/

8   Mark Twigg, 'Cicero Consulting: No longer just the dark arts', *PR Week*, 8 June 2011; http://www.prweek.com/uk/news/1072374/ Mark-Twigg-Cicero-Consulting-No-longer-just-dark-arts/?DCMP= ILC-SEARCH

9   Felicity Lawrence, 'Tax havens: G20 has failed to crack down, says campaign group', *Guardian*, 4 October 2011; http://www.guardian. co.uk/business/2011/oct/04/taxavoidance-corporate-governance

10 Commonwealth Secretariat and IFC Forum Conference (podcasts and contemporary notes), 20 October 2011; http://www.cicero-forum.com/conf_overview.php?eid=66

11 David Wilkes, 'Portrait of a very middle class protest', *Daily Mail*, 18 October 2011; http://www.dailymail.co.uk/news/article-2049722/ Occupy-London-St-Pauls-protest-camp-includes-extra-Downton-Abbey.html

12 Amy Wilkes, 'The *Sun* goes undercover at St Paul's anti-capitalism demo', *Sun*, 5 November 2011; http://www.thesun.co.uk/sol/home-page/features/3916139/The-Sun-goes-undercover-at-St-Pauls-anti-capitalism-demo.html

13 Have I Got News For You, BBC1, October 2011 http://www.youtube. com/watch?v=8WvAkhW-XNI

14 Michael Klein, 'Q&A with Richard Hay', *Cayman Financial Review*, 5 October 2011; http://compasscayman.com/cfr/2011/10/05/Q-A-with-Richard-Hay/

15 Bibi van der Zee, 'Holy cow, taxman! Featherweight activist battles the dodgers', *Guardian*, 7 July 2011; http://www.guardian.co.uk/busi-ness/2011/jul/07/interview-john-christensen-tax-justice-network

16 Edelman presentation, February 2001; http://www.sourcewatch. org/images/f/ff/EdelmanNGOPresentation_-_2-28-01.pdf

17 *PR Watch*, 'MBD's Divide-and-Conquer Strategy to Defeat Activists', October–December 1993, vol. 1, no. 1, p. 5.

18 Marion Nestle, *Food Politics: How the Food Industry Influences Nutrition and Health*, University of California Press, 2002, p. 145.

19   Eveline Lubbers, *Secret Manoeuvres in the Dark: Corporate and Police Spying on Activists*, Pluto Press, 2012, pp. 47–8.

20   Ibid., pp. 76–8.

21   Ibid., p. 76.

22   Ibid., pp. 45–58.

23   John Stauber and Sheldon Rampton, *Toxic Sludge is Good for You: Lies, Damn Lies and the Public Relations Industry*, Common Courage Press, 1995, pp. 52–3.

24   Ibid., p. 53.

25   Stacy M. Carter, 'Mongoven, Biscoe & Duchin: Destroying Tobacco Control Activism from the Inside, *Tobacco Control*, 2002, vol. 11, issue 2, pp. 112–18.

26   Andy Rowell, James Marriott and Lorne Stockman, *The Next Gulf: London, Washington and Oil Conflict in Nigeria*, Constable, 2005, pp. 2–3.

27   Andy Rowell, 'Shell's secret collusion documents', 15 June 2009, the priceofoil.org; http://priceofoil.org/2009/06/15/shells-secret-collusion-documents/

28   Andy Rowell and Eveline Lubbers, 'Ken Saro-Wiwa was framed, secret evidence shows', *Independent on Sunday*, 5 December 2010.

29   Rowell, Marriott and Stockman, *The Next Gulf*, p. 89.

30   Eveline Lubbers and Andy Rowell, 'NGOs and BBC targeted by Shell PR machine in wake of Saro-Wiwa death', *Guardian*, 9 November 2010.

31   Shell, 'Background to the Nigeria issue. Confidential', c.1994.

32   Shell, 'Nigeria crisis management strategy and plan. Most confidential', 24 January 1996.

33   Pagan International, *Greenpeace: A Special Report*, October 1985.

34   Jeremy Page, 'Mystery deepens in death of Briton in China', *Wall Street Journal*, 27 March 2012; http://online.wsj.com/article/SB10001424052702304177104577305532056722676.html

35   Tania Branigan, Luke Harding and Dom Gilchrist, 'Dead British businessman in China had links to ex-MI6 officers' firm. Mystery deepens over in Chongquing death of Neil Heywood, occasional consultant to business intelligence firm Hakluyt & Co', *Guardian*, 27 March 2012.

36   Lubbers, *Secret Manoeuvres in the Dark*, p. 140.

37   Ibid., p. 144.

38   Ibid., pp. 145–7.

39   Baby Milk Action website: http://info.babymilkaction.org/nestle-free

40   Lubbers, *Secret Manoeuvres in the Dark*, pp. 58–9.

41   ATTAC Switzerland, Nestlé /Attac / Securitas: legal complaint against X, 13 June 2008, http://www.suisse.attac.org/Nestle-Attac-Securitas-legal; Pratap Chatterjee, 'Nestlé found guilty of spying on Swiss activists', 30 January 2013, http://www.corpwatch.org/article.php?id=15812

42   ATTAC Switzerland, 'Nestlegate: successful civil lawsuit against Nestlé and Securitas', 26 January 2013; translation and article, *Le Courrier*, 26 January 2013, entitled 'Nestlé loses spying case – Swiss media report', on Baby Milk Action website, http://info.babymilkaction.org/news/campaignblog260113

43   Baby Milk Action website: http://info.babymilkaction.org/nestlefree

44   For more information see Lubbers, *Secret Manoeuvres in the Dark*, pp. 159–94.

45   Paul Lewis and Rob Evans, 'Green groups targeted polluters as corporate agents hid in their ranks. Special report: After revelations of police spying, the focus turns to firms paid to infiltrate protesters', *Guardian*, 14 February 2011.

46   Rob Evans, Amelia Hill, Paul Lewis and Patrick Kingsley, 'Mark Kennedy: secret policeman's sideline as corporate spy; former under-cover officer apparently also worked privately as a corporate spy using the same false identity', *Guardian*, 13 January 2011.

47   Lewis and Evans, 'Green groups targeted polluters as corporate agents hid in their ranks'.

48   Jonathan R. Laing, 'The shadow CIA – A private intelligence service predicts more terror attacks – and victory for the U.S., Barron's, 15 October 2001.

49   Philip Morris, *Corporate Affairs Corporate Cost Review*, 1993; http://legacy.library.ucsf.edu/tid/wqq02a00/pdf

50   Sourcewatch Profile of Mongoven: http://www.sourcewatch.org/index.php?title=Bart_Mongoven

51   WikiLeaks, The Global Intelligence Files; Jeb Boone, 'WikiLeaks emails allege "Stratfor spied on activists"', *Global Post*, 27 February 2012.

52   WikiLeaks, 'Oil industry accused of undermining emissions reduction efforts', 30 April 2008; http://search.wikileaks.org/gifiles/?viewemailid=1212803

53   WikiLeaks, 'CANADA/EU – Canada warns EU to not rank oil sands as dirty energy', 24 October 2011; http://search.wikileaks.org/gifiles/?viewemailid=130223

54   WikiLeaks, 'NIGERIA/US/ENERGY – Ogoni leader welcomes U.S. Supreme Court decision on Shell case', 18 October 2011; http://search.wikileaks.org/gifiles/?viewemailid=149265

55   WikiLeaks, 'INSIGHT – NIGERIA – on the Joint Revolutionary

Council', 12 February 2010; http://search.wikileaks.org/gifiles/? view-emailid=1104164

56   WikiLeaks: http://search.wikileaks.org/gifiles/?viewemailid=5094274
57   WikiLeaks, 'INSIGHT – NIGERIA – on the Joint Revolutionary Council', 12 February 2010; http://search.wikileaks.org/gifiles/? viewe-mailid=1107427
58   Wikileaks, email from 10 December 2010; http://search.wikileaks.org/gifiles/?viewemailid=389793
59   Andy Rowell, 'Dialogue: Divide and Rule', in Eveline Lubbers, *Battling Big Business: Countering Greenwash, Infiltration and Other Forms of Corporate Bullying*, Green Books, 2002, pp. 35–6.
60   *PR Watch*, 'MBD's Divide-and-Conquer Strategy to Defeat Activists', p. 5.
61   Edelman presentation, February 2001; http://www.sourcewatch.org/images/f/ff/EdelmanNGOPresentation_-_2-28-01.pdf
62   The Environment Council, *BNFL National Stakeholder Dialogue – Discharges Working Group, Interim Report*.
63   Rowell, 'Dialogue: Divide and Rule', pp. 35–9.
64   James Marriott and Mika Minio-Paluello, *The Oil Road: Journeys from the Caspian Sea to the City of London*, Verso, 2012, pp. 172–3 185.
65   Ibid.
66   Philip Morris, 'Tipping The Scales of Justice', 1996; http://legacy.library.ucsf.edu/tid/ndf37c00/pdf
67   Graham Kelder and Patricia Davidson, *The Multistate Master Settlement Agreement and the Future of State and Local Tobacco Control: An Analysis of Selected Topics and Provisions of the Multistate Master Settlement Agreement of November 23, 1998*, prepared by The Tobacco Control Resource Center, Inc., at Northeastern University School of Law, http://www.tobacco.neu.edu/tobacco_control/resources/msa/; Master Settlement Agreement, http://web.archive.org/web/20080625084126/http://www.naag.org/back-pages/naag/tobacco/msa/msa-pdf/11109185724_1032468605_cigmsa.pdf
68   John Sharkey, 'Tobacco industry's response to the new social and legal environment', 28th IKK Meeting, 26 August 2000; http://legacy.library.ucsf.edu/tid/zwm10c00/pdf
69   Philip Morris, 'Philip Morris calls for constructive dialogue – 'It's time to talk', 13 October 1999; http://legacy.library.ucsf.edu/tid/dbh60a99/pdf
70   KPMG, 'BAT. The Project: The way forward', 15 November 1999; http://legacy.library.ucsf.edu/tid/eyb04a99/pdf
71   Ibid.

72   'An insider's view on the Tax Journal Conference 2011', UK Uncut, 17 November 2011; http://ukuncut.org.uk/blog/an-insiders-view-tax-conference

73   Gavin Allen, '"Wealthy elite" should pay more tax, say Cameron and Clegg as they push for law against tax-avoidance', *Daily Mail*, 5 January 2012; http://www.dailymail.co.uk/news/article-2082506/Wealthy-elite-pay-tax-says-Clegg-calls-law-tax-avoidance.html#ixzz202TcFpbl

74   Larry Elliott, 'Osborne will regret tax "shock" – maybe not today, maybe not tomorrow', *Guardian*, 10 April 2012; http://www.guardian.co.uk/business/economics-blog/2012/apr/10/george-osborne-regret-tax-shock-casablanca

75   Tax and Transparency Forum 2012, London, International Tax Review conference, 2 May 2012; http://www.internationaltaxreview.com/pdfs/TaxTransparency.pdf

76   Ibid.

77   Richard Hardyment, Peter Truesdale and Mike Tuffrey, 'Tax as a Corporate Responsibility Issue', Corporate Citizenship Insights, May 2011.

78   Philip Morris, 'Tipping The Scales of Justice', 1996; http://legacy.library.ucsf.edu/tid/ndf37c00/pdf

79   Commonwealth Secretariat and IFC Forum Conference (podcasts and contemporary notes), 20 October 2011 http://www.ciceroforum.com/conf_overview.php?eid=66

80   Mark Field MP, 'How CEOs should adapt to the collapse of trust in the rules of capitalism', ConservativeHome, 19 July 2012; http://conservativehome.blogs.com/platform/2012/07/the-role-and-changing-powers-of-ceos-in-the-spotlight-when-historians-look-back-upon-the-first-decade-or-so-of-the-twenty-fi.html

81   John Plender, 'Capitalism in crisis: the code that forms a bar to harmony', *Financial Times*, 8 January 2012; http://www.ft.com/cms/s/0/fb95b4fe-3863-11e1-9d07-00144feabdc0.html

82   Publicity material for James Frayne's book, *Meet the People*, due to be published by Harriman House, 2014; http://www.harriman-house.com/book/view/475/business/james-frayne/meet-the-people/

83   James Frayne, 'How public affairs agencies need to up their game', *PR Week*, 19 June 2009; http://www.prweek.com/uk/news/914492/James-Frayne-public-affairs-agencies-need-game/?DCMP=ILC-SEARCH

84   Westbourne Communications website: http://changeopinion.com/practices/

85   Gerri Peev, 'The HS2 rail link IS going happen says George Osborne', *Daily Mail*, 1 September 2013, http://www.dailymail.co.uk/news/

article-2408420/George-Osborne-HS2-rail-link-IS-going-happen.
html#ixzz2en5ASupW; Harry Mount, 'Hundreds of historic houses
will be flattened or ruined by new high speed train link', *Daily Mail*,
14 January 2012; http://www.dailymail.co.uk/news/article-2086518/
HS2-rail-link-Hundreds-historic-houses-ruined-new-high-speed-line.
html

86   James Bethell's profile: http://www.lukearcherphotography.co.uk/
inheritance/?cat=33

87   David Singleton, 'Senior Tories join forces to form new lobbying
agency called Westbourne', *PR Week*, 13 May 2009; http://www.
prweek.com/uk/news/905738/

88   Ibid.

89   Publicity material for James Frayne's book, *Meet the People*, due to be
published by Harriman House, 2014; http://www.harriman-house.
com/book/view/475/business/james-frayne/meet-the-people/

90   Jamie Doward, 'High-speed rail opponents 'portrayed as posh
nimbys' by peer's lobbying firm', *Observer*, 6 April 2013;
http://www.theguardian.com/uk/2013/apr/06/high-speed-
rail-hs2-nimbys

91   University of Pennsylvania, 'Early Actions for High Speed Rail:
Final Report, Spring 2012'; http://issuu.com/penndesign/docs/
highspeedrail2012

92   James Bethell, Yes2highspeedrail video presentation, 15 February
2012; http://www.youtube.com/watch?v=kGM58gDQBxw

93   Mount, 'Hundreds of historic houses will be flattened or ruined by
new high speed train link'.

94   Robin Stummer, phone conversation with Andy Rowell, April 2013.

95   William Turvill, 'Axed magazine editor issued with "bizarre"
writ by former employers', *Press Gazette*, 26 November 2012; http://
www.pressgazette.co.uk/axed-magazine-editor-issued-bizarre-writ-
former-employers

96   Gavriel Hollander, 'Charity publisher drops passing off claim against
former editor', *Press Gazette*, 27 September 2013; R. Stummer, Email
to Andy Rowell, October 2013.

97   Minton, *Scaring the Living Daylights Out of People*.

98   Ibid.; comments by James Bethell from Westbourne Communications
working for High Speed 2 Campaign, on what to do with opponents.

99   Anna Minton on Westbourne's response to Spinwatch local lobbying
and planning abuses report, Spinwatch.org, 8 April 2013.

100 Minton, *Scaring the Living Daylights Out of People*.

101 *Big Boys Gone Bananas!* website: http://dogwoof.com/films/big-
boys-gone-bananas

102   Wendell Potter, *Deadly Spin: An Insurance Company Insider Speaks Out on How Corporate PR is Killing Health Care and Deceiving Americans*, Bloomsbury Press, 2011.

103   John Stauber, 'Burning books before they're printed', PR Watch, fourth quarter, 1994.

104   Ibid.

105   Graham Readfearn, 'Who Is Filling Climate Scientists' Inboxes With Abuse, Intimidation And Hate?', DeSmogBlog, 14 June 2012; http://www.desmogblog.com/who-filling-climate-scientists-inboxes-abuse-intimidation-and-hate

106   Union of Concerned Scientists, 'Scientists Who Had Emails Stolen Ask Heartland Institute to End Attack on Climate Science', 17 February 2012; http://www.ucsusa.org/news/press_release/scientists-emails-stolen-heartland-institute-1372.html

107   Michael E. Mann, *The Hockey Stick and the Climate Wars: Dispatches from the Front Line*, Columbia University Press, 2012, pp. 226–7; Douglas Fischer, 'Cyber bullying rises as climate data are questioned', The Daily Climate, 1 March 2010; http://wwwp.dailyclimate.org/tdc-newsroom/2010/03/cyber-bullying-rises-as-climate-data-are

108   Mann, *The Hockey Stick and the Climate Wars*, p. 225.

109   James Delingpole, 'Climategate 2.0: the not nice and clueless Phil Jones', *Daily Telegraph*, 24 November 2011.

110   Emails from unnamed source to Phil Jones, various dates 2009–10, released under FOI law by the University of East Anglia; http://www.whatdotheyknow.com/request/116404/response/288373/attach/4/Appendix%20A%20Data%20file%20072.pdf

111   Richard Girling, 'The leak was bad. Then came the death threats', *Sunday Times*, 7 February 2010.

112   Mann, *The Hockey Stick and the Climate Wars*, pp. 226–8.

113   Ibid.

114   Kate Ravilious, 'Hacked email climate scientists receive death threats', *Guardian*, 8 December 2009.

115   Mann, *The Hockey Stick and the Climate Wars*, pp. 4–5.

116   Mark Bowen, *Censoring Science: Inside the Political Attack on Dr James Hansen and the Truth of Global Warming*, Plume, 2009, p. 1.

117   Mann, *The Hockey Stick and the Climate Wars*, pp. 73, 77.

118   Bowen, *Censoring Science*, pp. 61, 132.

119   Graham Readfearn, 'Emails reveal nature of attacks on climate scientists', 7 June 2011; http://www.readfearn.com/2011/06/emails-reveal-nature-of-attacks-on-climate-scientists/

120   Rick Piltz, 'Australian climate scientists targeted by death threats', Climate Science Watch, 6 June 2011; http://www.climatescience-

watch.org/2011/06/06/australian-climate-scientists-targeted-by-death-threats/

121   Readfearn, 'Who Is Filling Climate Scientists' Inboxes With Abuse, Intimidation And Hate?'

122   Oliver Milman, 'Australian climate scientists receive death threats – Universities move staff into safer accommodation after a large number of threatening emails and phone calls', *Guardian*, 6 June 2011.

123   Michael Mann, interview with Andy Rowell, 30 November 2012.

124   Simon Chapman, 'Hate mail and cyber trolls: the view from inside public health', The Conversation, 6 September 2012; http://theconversation. edu.au/hate-mail-and-cyber-trolls-the-view-from-inside-public-health-9329. Chris Snowdon, 'Prohibitionist accidentally tells the truth', Velvetgloveironfist, 4 April 2012; http://velvetgloveironfist.blogspot. co.uk/2012/04/prohibitionist-accidentally-tells-truth.html

125   Institute of Economic Affairs website: http://www.iea.org.uk/about/people;   http://www.iea.org.uk/events/iea-lifestyle-economics-%E2%80%A8official-launch-event

126   Chris Snowdon, '2011: The ten best bits', 31 December 2011; Chris Snowdon, 'Standon Glantz: Clueless clown', 6 October 2011.

127   Linda Bauld's profile on the Stirling University website: http://www. stir.ac.uk/management/staff-directory/institute-for-socio-management/linda-bauld/

128   Chris Snowdon, 'A real scientist speaks', Velvetgloveironfist, 5 March 2012; http://velvetgloveironfist.blogspot.co.uk/2012/03/real-scientist-speaks.html

129   Steve Connor, 'Exclusive: Smoked out: tobacco giant's war on science – Philip Morris seeks to force university to hand over confidential health research into teenage smokers', *Independent*, 1 September 2011; http://www.independent.co.uk/news/science/exclusive-smoked-out-tobacco-giants-war-on-science-2347254.html

130   Frank Davis, 'Letter to Linda', 3 September 2011; http://cfrankdavis. wordpress.com/2011/09/03/letter-to-linda/

131   Ibid.

132   Chris Greenwood . . . , 'We can't control Twitter, insist police', *Daily Mail*, 1 August 2012 http://www.dailymail.co.uk/news/article-2181851/We-control-Twitter-insist-police-Storm-arrest-17-year-old-offensive-tweets-Tom-Daley.html#ixzz2Hyou2f93

133   Simon Clark, 'Hold the front page!', Taking Liberties, 3 September 2011; http://taking-liberties.squarespace.com/blog/2011/9/3/hold-the-front-page.html

134   Denis Campbell, James Meikle, 'Pro-smoking activists threaten and harass health campaigners', *Guardian*, 1 June 2012.

135   Tobacco Control Research Group, research into Simon Clark, published on the TobaccoTactics website, University of Bath, 2013; http://tobaccotactics.org/index.php/Simon_Clark

7 Rig

1   Chris Scott, 'Public Affairs: The boom in consultation', *PR Week*, 8 November 2002, accessed June 2012; http://www.prweek.com/uk/news/163376/

2   Angie Moxham's profile on 3 Monkeys website: http://3-monkeys.co.uk/angie-moxham/, accessed June 2013.

3   Alison Smith-Squire, 'The women earning double their husband's wage', *Daily Mail*, 16 November 2006, accessed June 2013; http://www.dailymail.co.uk/femail/article-416697/The-women-earning-double-husbands-wage.html

4   See for example the Environmental Impact Assessment Directive: http://ec.europa.eu/environment/eia/eia-legalcontext.htm

5   3 Monkeys website, 'The importance of being properly consulted', undated; http://www.3-monkeys.co.uk/the-importance-of-being-properly-consulted/

6   Gemma O'Reilly, '3 Monkeys picks up brief with waste management firm Viridor', *PR Week*, 16 October 2009.

7   Kate Wilson, response to Planning Application Reference DCC/2975/2010, New England Quarry, Lee Hill, Lee Mill, Development of the New England Resources Recovery Centre, Friends of the Earth, 19 April 2010; http://www.devon.gov.uk/neqconsresponses1-14.pdf. Robin Hogg, New England Quarry Resource Centre, Near Lee Mill, CPRE Devon, 16 April 2010; http://www.devon.gov.uk/neqconsresponses20-27.pdf

8   Howard Ellard, Proposed New Resource Recovery Centre at New England Quarry – Community Consultation Group, 8 September 2011.

9   Andy Rowell, notes of the meeting held at Westward Inn, Lee Mill, 8 September 2009.

10   Viridor, New England Resource Recovery Centre Proposal – Project Update, undated.

11   Terence Fane-Saunders, 'My take on the PR industry', Chelgate website, undated, accessed June 2013; http://www.chelgate.com/featured/my-take-on-the-industry/

12   Indigo website listing on OnGreen website, undated, accessed June 2013; http://www.ongreen.com/companies/Indigo-Public-Affairs-Ltd?tab=news

13   Scott, 'Public Affairs'.

14   Fane-Saunders, 'My take on the PR industry'.

15   Kate Magee, 'Green Issues founder launches Curtin&Co', *PR Week*, 1 April 2009.

16   Tom Curtin, *Managing Green Issues*, Palgrave Macmillan, 2000.

17   Ibid., pp. 79–82, 92–93.

18   Scott, 'Public Affairs'.

19   Tamasin Cave, personal conversation with lobbyist.

20   Richard Patient, 'Developers vs democracy', *PR Week*, 8 May 2009, accessed June 2013; http://www.prweek.com/uk/news/904465/Developers-vs-democracy/?DCMP=ILC-SEARCH

21   Tim Hughes, 'Elections but no democracy', Involve website, 24 May 2012; accessed June 2013; http://www.involve.org.uk/elections-but-no-democracy/

22   Ibid.

23   Andy Rowell, 'Plugging the gap – Nuclear energy is back on the agenda. But how has it risen from its pariah status to become today's favoured "green" option?' *Guardian*, 3 May 2006, accessed June 2013; http://www.guardian.co.uk/environment/2006/may/03/energy.society?INTCMP=SRCH

24   Nuclear Consultation Working Group, *Nuclear Consultation: Public Trust in Government* (ed. Paul Dorfman), 2008, accessed June 2013; http://www.nuclearconsult.com/docs/NUCLEAR_REPORT_COMPLETE_HIGH.pdf

25   Mr Justice Sullivan, *Greenpeace Limited vs Secretary of State for Trade and Industry*, 15 February 2007, accessed June 2013; http://www.greenpeace.org.uk/MultimediaFiles/Live/FullReport/ERJRSullivanJudgement.pdf

26   BBC News, 'Blair defiant over nuclear plans', 15 February 2007, accessed June 2013; http://news.bbc.co.uk/1/hi/uk_politics/6366725.stm

27   Department of Trade and Industry, *Meeting the Energy Challenge: A White Paper on Energy*, May 2007, accessed June 2013; http://www.berr.gov.uk/files/file39387.pdf

28   Department for Business Enterprise and Regulatory Reform, *The Future of Nuclear Power*, undated, accessed June 2013; http://webarchive.nationalarchives.gov.uk/+/http://www.berr.gov.uk/files/file53508.pdf

29   Nuclear Consultation Working Group, *Nuclear Consultation*.

30   Julian Rush, 'Spinning a nuclear consultation', Channel 4 News, 19 September 2007. Nuclear Consultation Working Group, *Nuclear Consultation*.

31   Jon Ungoed-Thomas and Marie Woolf, 'Revealed: the plot to expand Heathrow', *Sunday Times*, 9 March 2008. 'Greenpeace, Airfixed! Why

the government's consultation on Heathrow is a sham', 25 January 2008; http://www.greenpeace.org.uk/blog/climate/airfixed-the-governments-sham-consultation-on-heathrow-20080125

32 Heathrow Project Board Meeting Note, Item 5, Item 8, 12 September 2006, released under FOI law from the Department for Transport.

33 Heathrow Project Board Meeting Note, Item 1, 12 March 2007, released under FOI law from the Department for Transport.

34 Heathrow Project Board Meeting Note, Item 4, December 2006, released under FOI law from the Department for Transport.

35 Edward Andersson, Sam McLean, Metin Parlak and Gabrielle Melvin, 'From Fairy Tale to Reality: Dispelling the Myths around Citizen Engagement', Involve, February 2013; http://www.involve.org.uk/wp-content/uploads/2013/02/From-Fairy-Tale-to-Reality.pdf

36 Nicholas Timmins, *Never Again: The Story of the Health and Social Care Act 2012*, Institute for Government and Kings Fund, 2012.

37 Ibid., p. 77.

38 Hélène Mulholland, 'Government to "pause, listen, reflect and improve" NHS reform plans', *Guardian*, 6 April 2011, accessed June 2013; http://www.guardian.co.uk/society/2011/apr/06/government-pause-listen-reflect-improve-nhs-reform

39 Timmins, *Never Again*, p. 95.

40 Mulholland, 'Government to "pause, listen, reflect and improve" NHS reform plans'.

41 NHS Partners Network, 'Director's update on the NHS Reforms', 20 May 2011, released by the NHS Partners Network.

42 Ibid.

43 Timmins, *Never Again*, p. 102.

44 David Cameron's speech 'Rebuilding trust in politics', Conservatives website, 8 February 2010; http://www.conservatives.com/News/Speeches/2010/02/David_Cameron_Rebuilding_trust_in_politics.aspx

45 George Monbiot, 'This great free-market experiment is more like a corporate welfare scheme', *Guardian*, 4 September 2007; http://www.theguardian.com/commentisfree/2007/sep/04/comment.politics

46 'Coventry University Hospital will cost £3.3 billion – eight times its worth', *Coventry Telegraph*, 10 February 2010, accessed June 2013; http://www.coventrytelegraph.net/news/coventry-news/coventry-university-hospital-cost-33billion-3068423

47 'Coventry University Hospital "being put at risk by PFI"', *Coventry Telegraph*, 23 September 2011, accessed June 2013; http://www.coventrytelegraph.net/news/coventry-news/coventry-university-hospital-being-put-3037963

48 David Rose, 'Revealed: Shocking truth of axed A&E wards (and where it will now take you an hour to reach casualty)', *Daily Mail*, 14 July 2012; http://www.dailymail.co.uk/news/article-2173704/Closed-casualty-units-Shocking-truth-axed-A-E-wards-hour-reach-casualty.html

49 'Casualty units shut to pay for private finance hospital contracts', *Daily Telegraph*, 27 January 2011, accessed June 2013; http://www.telegraph.co.uk/health/healthnews/8285150/Casualty-units-shut-to-pay-for-private-finance-hospital-contracts.html

50 'Coventry University Hospital "being put at risk by PFI"', *Coventry Telegraph*.

51 George Monbiot, *Captive State: The Corporate Takeover of Britain*, Macmillan, 2000, p. 70.

52 Ibid.

53 NHS North West London, *Shaping a healthier future – consultation document*, webpage, undated, accessed June 2013; http://www.healthiernorthwestlondon.nhs.uk/document/shaping-healthier-future-consultation-document

54 Nicholas Cecil and Michael Pooler, 'Ten NHS trusts in debt crisis', *Evening Standard*, 26 June 2012; http://www.standard.co.uk/news/health/ten-nhs-trusts-in-debt-crisis-7887787.html

55 London Communications Agency, Services, Website, accessed June 2013; http://www.londoncommunications.co.uk/why/services/

56 Jo Macfarlane, 'NHS wastes £7 million on "sham" consultation over A&E closures . . . as we reveal SIX more casualty units to be cut', *Daily Mail*, 28 October 2012, accessed June 2013; http://www.dailymail.co.uk/news/article-2224150/NHS-wastes-7million-sham-consultation-A-E-closures--reveal-SIX-casualty-units-cut.html

57 Lewisham Keep Our NHS Public, 'London Health Emergency: Hidden plans revealed to axe a quarter of West London hospital beds', press release, 23 October 2012, accessed June 2013; http://www.lewishamkonp.org/pressreleasehealthemergency

58 Monbiot, *Captive State*, pp. 86–8.

59 Ibid., p. 86.

60 Public Accounts Committee, 'Forty-Fourth Report: Lessons from PFI and other projects', 18 July 2011; http://www.parliament.uk/business/committees/committees-a-z/commons-select/public-accounts-committee/news/pfi-report-publication/

61 Polly Curtis, 'PFI projects not best value for money, says watchdog', *Guardian*, 28 April 2011, accessed June 2013; http://www.guardian.co.uk/politics/2011/apr/28/pfi-not-best-value-money

62 'Government plans to reform PFI model', HM Treasury press release,

15 November 2011; https://www.gov.uk/government/news/government-plans-to-reform-pfi-model

63   Stephen Adams, 'NHS PFI debts rising by 5pc a year', *Daily Telegraph*, 28 November 2011, accessed June 2013; http://www.telegraph.co.uk/health/healthnews/8918662/NHS-PFI-debts-rising-by-5pc-a-year.html

64   Email from TheCityUK to unnamed official at UK Trade and Industry, 23 November 2011, received under FOI law from the Department for Business.

65   Simon Hall, 'Private finance initiative: PFI projects cost £2.4bn', BBC, 1 May 2013; http://www.bbc.co.uk/news/uk-england-devon-22355993

66   South West Devon Waste Partnership, 'Final Business Case for the Procurement of Waste Treatment Services: Report of the Executive Director of Environment, Economy and Culture, County Solicitor and Director of Finance', 7 February 2011.

67   South West Devon Waste Partnership, Defra Criteria Checklist, Appendix 1A; http://www.plymouth.gov.uk/swdwp_waste_pfi_outline_business_case_appendix1.pdf

68   South West Devon Waste Partnership, 'Energy from Waste', undated, accessed June 2013; http://www.plymouth.gov.uk/swdwpproposed-scheme.html

69   MVV, 'MVV Devonport Update', undated, accessed June 2013; https://www.mvv-energie.de/media/media/downloads/mvv_energie_gruppe_1/geschaeftsfelder_1/umwelt_1/environment_2/environment_1/plymouth/linksanddownloads/newsletter/2011_04_MVV_Devonport_Update.pdf

70   South West Devon Waste Partnership, Joint Working Agreement (JWA), Appendix 6B, 28 April 2008; http://www.plymouth.gov.uk/swdwp_waste_pfi_outline_business_case_appendix6b.pdf

71   Devon County Council, *Municipal Waste Management Strategy for Devon*, 2005, accessed June 2013; http://www.devon.gov.uk/index/environment/waste_disposal/waste_management_strategy_for_devon.htm:

72   Neil Shaw, 'Plymouth incinerator approved for Devonport Dockyard', *Plymouth Herald*, 23 December 2011.

73   Curtin, *Managing Green Issues*.

74   Green Issues Communiqué website, profile of Harry Hudson, undated, accessed June 2013; http://www.greenissuescommunique.com/index.php/team/harry_hudson

75   Paul Barnard, letter to URS Scott Wilson Limited, 3 February 2012, accessed June 2013; http://www.plymouth.gov.uk/11-00750-ful_-_decision_notice_1_-2.pdf; Shaw, 'Plymouth incinerator approved for Devonport Dockyard'.

76   World Health Organisation Office for Europe, 'Review of evidence on health aspects of air pollution – REVIHAAP Project, Technical Report', 2013.

77   Heather Saul, 'UK incinerator plans? They're just rubbish – As garbage-burning plants proliferate, Britain could end up with too little waste to put in them', *Independent*, 10 March 2013, accessed June 2013; http://www.independent.co.uk/environment/green-living/uk-incinerator-plans-theyre-just-rubbish-8527830.html

78   United Kingdom Without Incineration Network, 'Table of Potential, Existing and Prevented Incinerators', undated, accessed June 2013; http://ukwin.org.uk/resources/table/

79   Christopher Hope, 'Wind farms should not be less than 1.4 miles from people's homes, Nick Boles suggests', *Daily Telegraph*, 17 December 2012, accessed June 2013; http://www.telegraph.co.uk/news/politics/9751195/Wind-farms-should-not-be-less-than-1.4-miles-from-peoples-homes-Nick-Boles-suggests.html

80   Andy Rowell, notes of a meeting in Ivybridge organised by Devon Alliance Against Incineration, November 2010.

81   Keith Rossiter, 'Incinerator to go ahead', *Plymouth Herald*, 5 November 2010, p. 13. Keith Rossiter, 'Waste plant cost will save taxpayers £560m', *Plymouth Herald*, 5 April 2011, p. 2.

82   Andy Rowell, interviews with campaigners who attended meeting, January 2013.

83   South West Devon Waste Partnership (SWDWP), Torbay Council Cabinet approval of Final Business Case, 7 February 2011.

84   Mark Turner, 'Possible visit to Sheffield EfW facility', email to Keith Riley, 17 August 2011.

85   Cabinet Office, Ministerial Code, Foreword by the Prime Minister, May 2010; https://www.gov.uk/government/uploads/system/uploads/attachment_data/file/61402/ministerial-code-may-2010.pdf

86   Thomas Docherty, second reading of Commercial Lobbyists (Registration and Code of Conduct) Bill, Hansard, 1 February 2013; http://www.publications.parliament.uk/pa/cm201213/cmhansrd/cm130201/debtext/130201-0001.htm

87   Knight Frank, 'Healthcare: Property advisory and consultancy services for the healthcare sector', undated, accessed June 2013.

88   DLA Piper, Global Government Relations, 'Property and planning communications' brochure, October 2010.

89   Drew Combs, 'DLA Piper's Gross Revenue Rises 8.6 Percent to $2.44 Billion', *Am Law Daily*, 1 February 2013.

90   Dundas & Wilson, Planning section of website, accessed June 2013;

http://www.dundas-wilson.com/Expertise/planning/dw_cms_1474.asp

91 Joanna Foster, 'Golf Course vs. Dunes: A Rebellion That Failed', *The New York Times*, 3 August 2012, accessed June 2013; http://green.blogs.nytimes.com/2012/08/03/golf-course-vs-dunes-a-rebellion-that-failed/

92 Anna Minton, *Scaring the Living Daylights Out of People: The local lobby and the failure of democracy*, Spinwatch, March 2013, accessed June 2013, based on documents released under FOI law by Aberdeenshire Council; http://www.spinwatch.org/images/Reports/Scaring_the_living_daylight_final_27_March_13.pdf

93 Docherty, second reading of Commercial Lobbyists (Registration and Code of Conduct) Bill.

94 Ibid.

95 Holly Watt, Claire Newell and Ben Bryant, 'Councillors for hire who give firms planning advice', *Daily Telegraph*, 10 March 2013; http://www.telegraph.co.uk/news/uknews/9921344/Councillors-for-hire-who-give-firms-planning-advice.html

96 Ibid.

97 Indigo Public Affairs website, accessed June 2013: http://indigopa.com/

98 For example, see: Planning applications sub-committee No. 1, 16 February 2012, Minutes of Proceedings.

99 According to Southwark Council's register of members' interests, out of Southwark's sixty-three councillors twelve work as lobbyists.

100 Elephant and Castle, 'Background to the Regeneration Programme', undated, accessed June 2103; http://www.elephantandcastle.org.uk/pages/regeneration_change/130/background_to_the_regeneration_programme.html

101 Minton, *Scaring the Living Daylights Out of People*.

102 Harry Mount, 'Tower blocks haven't only scarred city skylines – they've ruined lives', *Daily Telegraph*, 24 January 2013; http://www.telegraph.co.uk/culture/art/architecture/9824432/Tower-blocks-havent-only-scarred-city-skylines-theyve-ruined-lives.html

103 Simon Heffer, 'Brilliant architecture can rescue even Basingstoke', *Daily Telegraph*, 18 September 2010; http://www.telegraph.co.uk/comment/columnists/simonheffer/8010830/Brilliant-architecture-can-rescue-even-Basingstoke.html

104 Minton, *Scaring the Living Daylights Out of People*.

105 In January 1998, Southwark Housing commissioned NBA Consortium Services to provide a comprehensive stock condition survey of its housing stock. The Consortium delivered its report in May 1999. You

can download a summary here: http://betterelephant.org/blog/

106   Soundings website, accessed June 2013: http://www.soundingsoffice.com/about-us

107   35 Percent campaign website, Towering Disgrace, 10 August 2013: http://affordable.heroku.com/blog/2013/08/10/towering-disgrace/

108   'Soundings: The Consultation Industry in the Elephant & Castle', Corporate Watch, 10 January 2013; http://www.corporatewatch.org.uk/?lid=4635. Minton, *Scaring the Living Daylights Out of People*.

109   'Elephant & Castle: council accidentally publishes details of Lend Lease deal', London SE1, 4 February 2013; http://www.london-se1.co.uk/news/view/6595

110   Better Elephant Blog, Creating a More Equitable Elephant, website, accessed June 2013: http://betterelephant.org/blog/

111   Four Local, Contact, website, undated, accessed June 2013: http://www.fourcommunications.com/four-local/contact/

112   'A hung parliament, but local election results sees [sic] Labour surge to take control of key councils', Four Communications website, May 2010; http://www.fourcommunications.com/mailers/election results/index.html

113   Four Local website, undated, accessed June 2013: http://www.four-communications.com/four-local/

114   Councillor Mark Glover's profile on Southwark Council website, accessed June 2013; http://moderngov.southwark.gov.uk/mgUserInfo.aspx?UID=183

115   Curtin and Co website: http://www.curtinandco.com/community-politics/methodology/book/

116   Athene Communications, 'Nuclear New Build Programme: Draft Framework Plan for Site Engagement Programmes 2008, Draft for Discussion', April 2008.

117   'Betrayed by stupidity of seven', *Evening Express*, 30 November 2007, p. 6.

118   Private Eye, No. 1334, February 2013.

119   Minton, *Scaring the Living Daylights Out of People*.

120   Ibid.

121   Ibid.

122   James Hall, 'Tesco "appalled" by forged letter of support for new store development', *Daily Telegraph*, 28 July 2009; http://www.telegraph.co.uk/finance/newsbysector/retailandconsumer/5926269/Tesco-appalled-by-forged-letter-of-support-for-new-store-development.html

123   Martin Hickman, 'Tesco, dirty tricks, and the battle over a new store

in rural Norfolk', *Independent*, 10 July 2010; http://www.independent.co.uk/news/uk/home-news/tesco-dirty-tricks-and-the-battle-over-a-new-store-in-rural-norfolk-2023130.html

124   Andrew Gilligan, 'Trickery, Deceit, Manipulation: Revealed: the story behind one of London's most controversial new developments. The company that lobbies planners for leading housebuilders and big retailers such as Sainsbury's stands accused of these underhand tactics over the gigantic Imperial Wharf scheme: Forging letters of support from local people. Infiltrating residents' protest groups. Obtaining tapes of private meetings. Using undercover operatives', *The Evening Standard*, 30 July 2007, p. 18.

125   Docherty, second reading of Commercial Lobbyists (Registration and Code of Conduct) Bill.

126   Anderson et al., 'From Fairy Tale to Reality'.

8 Fight

1   Brown and Williamson, 'Smoking and Health Proposal', 1969; http://legacy.library.ucsf.edu/tid/zqy56b00

2   BBC News, 'Sir Richard Doll: A life's research', 22 June 2004; http://news.bbc.co.uk/1/hi/health/3826939.stm

3   David Simpson, interview with Andy Rowell, 23 August 2012; David Simpson, 'Sir Richard Doll, 1912–2005', *Tobacco Control*, 2005, 14, pp. 289–90.

4   Conrad Keating, *Smoking Kills: The Revolutionary Life of Richard Doll*, Signal Books, 2009, pp. 63, 66, 77.

5   Naomi Oreskes and Erik Conway, *Merchants of Doubt: How a Handful of Scientists Obscured the Truth on Issues from Tobacco Smoke to Global Warming*, Bloomsbury, 2010, p. 241.

6   Cancer Research UK, 'Smoking statistics': http://info.cancerresearchuk.org/cancerstats/types/lung/smoking/lung-cancer-and-smoking-statistics#source6

7   Union of Concerned Scientists, *Smoke, Mirrors and Hot Air: How ExxonMobil Uses Big Tobacco's Tactic to Manufacture Uncertainty on Climate Science*, January 2007; http://www.ucsusa.org/assets/documents/global_warming/exxon_report.pdf

8   Kelly Brownell and Kenneth Warner, 'The Perils of Ignoring History: Big Tobacco Played Dirty and Millions Died. How Similar is Big Food?', *The Milbank Quarterly*, vol. 87, no. 1, 2009, pp. 259–94. Anna Gilmore, Emily Savell and Jeff Collin, 'Public Health, Corporations and the New Responsibility Deal: Promoting Partnerships with

Vectors of Disease?', *Journal of Public Health*, 2 February 2011. Oreskes and Conway, *Merchants of Doubt*.

9   Emma Innes, 'Number of smokers in the UK set to fall below 20% for the first time in a century', *Mail on Sunday*, 20 July 2013; http://www.dailymail.co.uk/health/article-2370456/Number-smokers-UK-set-fall-20-time-century.html?ns_mchannel=rss&ns_campaign=1490

10   Keating, *Smoking Kills*, pp. 105, 182.

11   David Pollack, *Denial and Delay*, Action on Smoking and Health, 1999, p. 15.

12   Ibid., pp. 16–17.

13   Claude Teague, 'Survey of Cancer Research with Emphasis upon Possible Carcinogens from Tobacco', 2 February 1953; http://legacy.library.ucsf.edu/tid/dda50i00/pdf

14   John Stauber and Sheldon Rampton, *Toxic Sludge is Good for You: Lies, Damn Lies and the Public Relations Industry*, Common Courage Press, 1995, p. 27.

15   Oreskes and Conway, *Merchants of Doubt*, pp. 14–15.

16   Stauber and Rampton, *Toxic Sludge is Good for You*, p. 27.

17   Oreskes and Conway, *Merchants of Doubt*, pp. 14–15.

18   Ibid., pp. 18, 19.

19   Action on Smoking and Health, *Tobacco Explained: The Truth about the Tobacco Industry in Its Own Words*, 1998, p. 2.

20   S. J. Green, 'Smoking, Associated Diseases and Causality', 1980; http://legacy.library.ucsf.edu/tid/cjv80a99

21   Pollack, *Denial and Delay*, p. 25.

22   Action on Smoking and Health, *Tobacco Explained*, p. 4.

23   Pollack, *Denial and Delay*, p. 40.

24   Ibid., p. 52.

25   H. R. Bentley, D. G. I. Felton and W. W. Reid, 'Report on Visit to USA and Canada, by H. R. Bentley, D. G. I. Felton, W. W. Reid', 17 April, 1958; http://legacy.library.ucsf.edu/tid/zja50i00

26   Royal College of Physicians, *Smoking and Health: A Report of the Royal College of Physicians on Smoking in Relation to Cancer of the Lung and Other Diseases*, Pitman Medical Publishing, 1962, p. 43.

27   Pollack, *Denial and Delay*, pp. 83–4.

28   Ibid., pp. 87–8.

29   Ibid., p. 132.

30   R. Kluger, *Ashes to Ashes: America's Hundred-Year Cigarette War, the Public Health, and the Unabashed Triumph of Philip Morris*, Alfred A. Knopf, 1996, p. 324, quoting C. Thompson, Memo to Kloepfer, 18 October 1968.

31   Brown and Williamson, 'Smoking and Health Proposal'.

32   Helmut Wakeham, '"Best" Program for C.T.R.', 8 December 1970; http://legacy.library.ucsf.edu/tid/khd76boo

33   Stanton A. Glantz et al., *The Cigarette Papers*, University of California Press, 1996; quoted in Oreskes and Conway, *Merchants of Doubt*, p. 24.

34   BAT, 'Secret – Appreciation', 6 May 1980, quoted in Action on Smoking and Health, *Tobacco Explained*, p. 10.

35   Takeshi Hirayama, 'Non-Smoking Wives of Heavy Smokers Have a Higher Risk of Lung Cancer: A Study from Japan', *British Medical Journal*, 1981, 282 (6259), pp. 183–5.

36   Oreskes and Conway, *Merchants of Doubt*, p. 140.

37   Report of the Committee of Experts on Tobacco Industry Documents, *Tobacco Company Strategies to Undermine Tobacco Control Activities at the World Health Organization*, July 2000; http://www.who.int/tobacco/en/who_inquiry.pdf

38   Action on Smoking and Health, *Tobacco Explained*, p. 63.

39   Philip Morris, 1994 Communication Plan: http://legacy.library.ucsf.edu/tid/hnf34eoo. Tom Hockaday and Neal Cohen, 'Thoughts on TASSC Europe', APCO Associates, 25 March 1994; http://legacy.library.ucsf.edu/tid/pqa35eoo/pdf. David Greenberg and Matt Winokur, Burson-Marsteller, 'Scientist Group in Europe', 18 April 1994; http://legacy.library.ucsf.edu/tid/ywy88eoo/pdf

40   Elisa Ong and Stanton A. Glantz, 'Tobacco Industry Efforts Subverting International Agency for Research on Cancer's Second-Hand Smoke Study', *The Lancet*, vol. 355, issue 9211, 8 April 2000, pp. 1253–9.

41   Roger Bate, 'DDT Works', *Prospect Magazine*, 24 May 2008; http://www.prospectmagazine.co.uk/magazine/ddtworks/

42   BAT, 'CORA Centre Plan 1998', 26 September 1997; http://legacy.library.ucsf.edu/tid/mnx71a99/pdf. BAT, 'Science and Regulation Forecast', 16 September 1999; http://legacy.library.ucsf.edu/tid/mwg61a99/pdf. Robert Matthews, 'Facts versus Factions: The Use and Abuse of Subjectivity in Scientific Research', Working Paper, ESEF, September 1998; http://legacy.library.ucsf.edu/tid/ryoo3coo/pdf. Robert Nilsson, 'Environmental Tobacco Smoke Revisited: The Reliability of the Evidence for Risk of Lung Cancer and Cardiovascular Disease', ESEF, March 1988; http://legacy.library.ucsf.edu/tid/wdt55coo/pdf

43   Roger Bate, 'Is Nothing Worse Than Tobacco?', *Wall Street Journal Europe*, 24 July 1996; http://web.archive.org/web/19970212030536/http://www.esef.org/wsjtobac.htm

44   Broadcast report of the Today Programme, BBC, 19 August 1998: http://legacy.library.ucsf.edu/tid/das62a99/pdf

45 John Roberts, 'RE: Bate', 21 October 1998; http://legacy.library.ucsf. edu/tid/svp83c00/pdf

46 House of Commons, Select Committee on Health, Minutes of Evidence, 20 January 2000; http://www.parliament.the-stationery-office.co.uk/pa/cm199900/cmselect/cmhealth/27/0012006.htm

47 BAT, 'Public Affairs Presentation, 1981', 6 February 1981; http:// legacy.library.ucsf.edu/tid/rkm45a99Notes

48 Oreskes and Conway, *Merchants of Doubt*, p. 164.

49 Murray Walker, testimony at Minnesota trial, 1998; quoted in Action on Smoking and Health, *Tobacco Explained*, p. 12.

50 D. Shaffer, 'No proof that smoking causes disease, tobacco chief says', *Pioneer Press*, 3 March 1998; quoted in Action on Smoking and Health, *Tobacco Explained*, p. 12.

51 State of California, Office of the Attorney General: http://oag. ca.gov/tobacco/msa. Keating, *Smoking Kills*, p. 446.

52 Lissy C. Friedman, 'Philip Morris's website and television commercials use new language to mislead the public into believing it has changed its stance on smoking and disease', *Tobacco Control*, 16 (6), December 2007.

53 Keating, *Smoking Kills*, p. 447.

54 World Health Organisation website, Tobacco facts http://www.who. int/tobacco/mpower/tobacco_facts/en/

55 Keating, *Smoking Kills*, pp. 445–8.

56 David Cronin, 'The muscle and money of Big Tobacco', EU Observer, 13 September 2013; http://blogs.euobserver.com/cronin/2013/09/13/ the-muscle-and-money-of-big-tobacco/#comment-14. Jamie Doward, 'Tobacco giant Philip Morris "spent millions in bid to delay EU legislation" – Leaked documents show scale of Philip Morris efforts against anti-smoking directive', *Observer*, 8 September 2013.

57 Hubert van Breemen, notes from meeting on December 14, on EU Tobacco Product Directive, VNO NCW Brussels, 14 December 2011.

58 Kelly Crowe, 'Sugar industry's secret documents echo tobacco tactics', CBC News, 8 March 2013; http://www.cbc.ca/news/health/ story/2013/03/08/f-vp-crowe-big-sugar.html

59 Cristin Kearns Couzens, 'How a Former Dentist Drilled the Sugar Industry', *Mother Jones*, 31 October 2012; http://www.motherjones. com/environment/2012/10/former-dentist-sugar-industry-lies

60 Ibid.

61 Ibid.

62 Brownell and Warner, 'The Perils of Ignoring History', pp. 259–94.

63 Lori Dorfman, Andrew Cheyne, Lissy Friedman, Asiya Wadud and Mark Gottlieb, 'Soda and Tobacco Industry Corporate Social

Responsibility Campaigns: How Do They Compare?', *PLOS Medicine*, vol. 9, issue 6, June 2012.

64 'Preliminary data suggest that soda and *sweet drinks* are the main source of calories in American diet', *Science Daily*, 27 May 2005; http://www.sciencedaily.com/releases/2005/05/050527111920.htm

65 William Leith, 'The bitter truth about sugar', *Telegraph*, 27 March 2012; http://www.telegraph.co.uk/health/dietandfitness/9160114/The-bitter-truth-about-sugar.html

66 Brownell and Warner, 'The Perils of Ignoring History', pp. 259–94.

67 Gary Taubes and Cristin Kearns Couzens, 'Big Sugar's Sweet Little Lies', *Mother Jones*, November/December 2012; http://www.mother-jones.com/environment/2012/10/sugar-industry-lies-campaign

68 Ibid.

69 Ibid.

70 Excerpt of Minutes of a Public Communications Committee Meeting, April 1975, (accessed from the *Mother Jones* website); http://www.motherjones.com/documents/486093-comms-committee

71 Document accessed from Legacy Tobacco Documents Library: http://legacy.library.ucsf.edu/tid/qhn96b00

72 'Sugar May be Cardiac Culprit', *Medical World News*, 27 August 1965.

73 Jacques Peretti, 'Why our food is making us fat', *Guardian*, 11 June 2012; http://www.guardian.co.uk/business/2012/jun/11/why-our-food-is-making-us-fat?INTCMP=SRCH

74 Taubes and Couzens, 'Big Sugar's Sweet Little Lies'.

75 Kelly Crowe, 'Sugar Industry's secret documents echo tobacco tactics', CBC News, 8 March 2013.

76 Taubes and Couzens, 'Big Sugar's Sweet Little Lies'.

77 Ibid.

78 Marion Nestle, *Food Politics: How the Food Industry Influences Nutrition and Health*, University of California Press, 2002, p. 113.

79 Ibid., p. 115.

80 Kelly Crowe, 'Sugar industry's secret documents echo tobacco tactics', CBC News, 8 March 2013; http://www.cbc.ca/news/health/story/2013/03/08/f-vp-crowe-big-sugar.html

81 Ibid.

82 Taubes and Couzens, 'Big Sugar's Sweet Little Lies'.

83 Sarah Boseley, 'Sugar industry threatens to scupper WHO', *Guardian*, 21 April 2003; http://www.guardian.co.uk/society/2003/apr/21/usnews.food?INTCMP=SRCH

84 Ibid.

85 Ibid.

86 Jacques Peretti, 'Why our food is making us fat', *Guardian*, 11 June

2012; http://www.theguardian.com/business/2012/jun/11/why-our-food-is-making-us-fat

87   Robert H. Lustig, Laura A. Schmidt and Claire D. Brindis, 'Public Health: The Toxic Truth about Sugar', *Nature*, 2 February 2012; http://www.nature.com/nature/journal/v482/n7383/full/482027a. html?WT.mc_id=TWT_NatureRevEndo

88   Alex Renton, 'Coca-Cola's sugar problem', *Guardian*, 18 January 2013; http://www.guardian.co.uk/lifeandstyle/wordofmouth/2013/jan/18/coca-cola-sugar-problem

89   Leith, 'The bitter truth about sugar'.

90   National Health Service, partners of Change4Life: http://www.nhs.uk/change4life/Pages/national-partners-pepsico.aspx

91   Daniel Boffey, 'PR guru Matthew Freud is criticised for a conflict of interests regarding the government's healthy eating campaign', *Observer*, 20 March 2011; http://www.guardian.co.uk/media/2011/mar/20/matthew-freud-change4life-healthy-eating

92   Ibid.

93   Department of Health, 'A Public Health Responsibility Deal', 14 September 2010.

94   'Responsibility Deal: One Year On', *Which?*, March 2012 http://www.which.co.uk/documents/pdf/responsibility-deal-one-year-on-which-briefing-281519.pdf

95   '61 organisations call for a sugary drinks duty in Budget 2013', Sustain, 29 January 2013; http://www.sustainweb.org/news/jan13_childrens_future_fund/

96   'Charity calls for new tax on sugary drinks', Channel 4 News, 29 January 2013; http://www.channel4.com/news/drink-up-as-charity-calls-for-new-tax-on-sugary-drinks

97   David Stuckler and Marion Nestle, 'Big Food, Food Systems and Global Health', *PLOS Medicine*, vol. 8, issue 9, June 2012.

98   Gavin Partington's LinkedIn profile: http://uk.linkedin.com/pub/gavin-partington/24/a24/111

99   just-drinks global news, UK: WSTA appoints communications head, 16 January 2008.

100   President of the Royal College of Physicians, quoted in House of Commons Health Committee, Alcohol, First Report of Session 2009–10.

101   BBC News 'Health: Level of excess drinking of alcohol "is underestimated"', 27 February 2013; http://www.bbc.co.uk/news/health-21586566

102   Data from the Office for National Statistics General Household Survey 2007: http://news.bbc.co.uk/1/hi/health/7844449.stm

103 House of Commons Health Committee, Alcohol, First Report of Session 2009–10.

104 JGR, Philip Morris document, 1995, document accessed from Legacy Tobacco Documents Library; http://legacy.library.ucsf.edu/tid/pwl27a00/pdf

105 Miller Brewing Company, Five Year Plan 1992–1996: 1992, document accessed from Legacy Tobacco Documents Library; http://legacy.library.ucsf.edu/tid/kwn09e00/pdf

106 Miller Beer, 'Environmental Assessment', 1998: http://legacy.library.ucsf.edu/tid/ehe36c00/pdf

107 Portman Group website: http://www.portmangroup.org.uk/?pid=14&level=2

108 Guy Smith's Forbes profile: http://www.forbes.com/profile/guy-smith/. David Jernigan, 'Global Alcohol Producers, Science and Policy: The Case of the International Centre for Alcohol Policies', *American Journal of Public Health*, 17 November 2011.

109 'Alcohol strategy questioned', *Alcohol Alert*, Institute of Alcohol Studies, issue 3, 2003; http://www.ias.org.uk/What-we-do/Publication-archive/Alcohol-Alert/Issue-3-2003/Alcohol-strategy-questioned.aspx

110 Claire Harkins, 'Lobby Watch: The Portman Group', *British Medical Journal*, 340: b5659, 2010.

111 BBC News Scotland, 'Minimum pricing: Drinks industry "distorted evidence"', 24 April 2013; http://www.bbc.co.uk/news/uk-scotland-22250584

112 Leonard Doyle, 'Pro-alcohol academics paid by drinks lobby', *Independent*, 5 December 1994; http://www.independent.co.uk/news/proalcohol-academics-paid-by-drinks-lobby-1389050.html

113 P. Anderson, 'The Beverage Alcohol Industry and Alcohol Policy', in *Proceedings of The International Conference, Thinking Drinking: Achieving Cultural Change by 2020*, hosted by The Australian Drug Foundation, Melbourne, from 21 to 23 February 2005.

114 'Level of excess drinking of alcohol "is underestimated"', BBC News, 27 February 2013; http://www.bbc.co.uk/news/health-21586566

115 House of Commons Health Committee, Alcohol, First Report of Session 2009–10.

116 Portman Group, 'Biggest ever campaign to encourage responsible drinking announced', 16 July 2009.

117 Miller Brewing Company, Five Year Plan 1992–1996: 1992.

118 Maxine Frith, 'Vodka-makers are screening TV commercials telling US to drink less', *Independent*, 20 July 2003.

119 David Singleton, 'Diageo hires Hanover as alcohol concerns grow', *PR Week*, 20 September 2007.

120   Ibid.

121   David Miller and Claire Harkins, 'Corporate Strategy, Corporate Capture: Food and Alcohol Industry Lobbying and Public Health', *Critical Social Policy*, vol. 30 (4), pp. 564–89; 376805 10.1177/ 0261018310376805http

122   Louise Lucas, 'Minimum alcohol pricing poses problems', *Financial Times*, 8 March 2012; http://www.ft.com/cms/s/0/d94f3538-6936-11e1-9618-00144feabdco.html#ixzz1pg3hYMoo

123   Scottish Government, 'Tackling alcohol misuse', 2 March 2009; http://www.scotland.gov.uk/News/Releases/2009/03/02085300

124   Eddie Barnes, 'Minimum price for alcohol set at 40p per unit', *Scotland on Sunday*, 5 July 2009, p. 2.

125   Paul Hutcheon and Tom Gordon, 'Anger over spirits giant's link to drunk, fire-raising lord', *Sunday Herald*, 8 February 2009, p. 7.

126   Paul Hutcheon, 'Minimum pricing fightback by whisky industry – Plans for "populist" campaign', *Herald*, 10 November 2009, p. 4.

127   Severin Carrell and Denis Campbell, 'Scottish ministers win court battle over minimum alcohol pricing', *Guardian*, 3 May 2013.

128   Ian Quinn, 'Big Hitters Join Forces to "Kill" Minimum Pricing Proposals', *The Grocer*, 26 January 2013.

129   ITV News, 'Theresa May "hiding" from minimum drink prices debate', 14 March 2013.

130   BBC News, 'Minimum alcohol price planned for England and Wales', 23 March 2012.

131   Stephen Donaghy, email to Andy Rowell, 2 July 2013.

132   Felicity Lawrence, 'Do Andrew Lansley's "responsibility deals" mean food firms' dream of writing public health policy has come true?', *Guardian*, 12 November 2010; http://www.guardian.co.uk/politics/2010/nov/12/government-health-deal-business

133   Diageo, letter to Andrew Lansley, 21 May 2010, received under FOI law from the Department of Health.

134   Ibid.

135   Diageo, Alcohol Responsibility Deal, 19 July 2010 received under FOI law from the Department of Health.

136   Miller Brewing Company, Five Year Plan 1992–1996: 1992.

137   A Public Health Responsibility Deal, Overview and Action Points, 22 September 2010.

138   Marie Woolf, 'Drink firms "call shots" on health policy', *Sunday Times*, 27 November 2011, p. 16.

139   Email to Chris Heffer, Labelling – The Portman Group Offer, 1 November 2010.

140   Gary Fooks, Eleanor Rogers and Anna Gilmore, 'Evidence Based Policy

and Voluntary Regulation: A Brief Examination of the Public Health Responsibility Deal', submitted to *European Journal of Public Health*.

141   European Alcohol Policy Alliance, 'WHO confirms that the alcohol industry has no role in the formulation of alcohol policies', 15 April 2013; http://www.eurocare.org/library/updates/alcohol_industry_conflict_of_interest

142   Ibid.

143   About the WHO Framework Convention on Tobacco Control, see the WHO website: http://www.who.int/fctc/about/en/index.html

144   National Oceanic and Atmospheric Administration, 'Carbon dioxide at NOAA's Mauna Loa Observatory reaches new milestone: Tops 400 ppm', 10 May 2013.

145   John Cook, Dana Nuccitelli, Sarah A. Green, Mark Richardson, Bärbel Winkler, Rob Painting, Robert Way, Peter Jacobs, Andrew Skuce, 'Quantifying the consensus on anthropogenic global warming in the scientific literature', *Environmental Research Letters*, 2013, 8 024024 doi:10.1088/1748-9326/8/2/024024

146   Allison Winter, 'Poll Reveals American Attitude Towards Climate Change, Support for Clean Energy', ENN, 13 February 2013; http://www.enn.com/pollution/article/45590

147   Ibid.

148   'Climate Change in the American Mind: Americans' Global Warming Beliefs and Attitudes in April 2013', Yale project on climate change communication; http://environment.yale.edu/climate-communication/article/Climate-Beliefs-April-2013/

149   Dr Joel Faulkner Rogers, 'Talking trust on climate science', YouGov, 15 April 2013; http://yougov.co.uk/news/2013/04/15/talking-trust-climate-science/

150   Union of Concerned Scientists, *Smoke, Mirrors and Hot Air*, p. 10. Greenpeace, Factsheet on The Advancement of Sound Science Coalition; http://www.exxonsecrets.org/html/orgfactsheet.php?id=6

151   Michael Mann, interview with Andy Rowell, 30 November 2012.

152   Ibid.

153   Joe Walker, 'Draft Global Climate Science Communications Plan', April 1998.

154   Steve Coll, *Private Empire: Exxon Mobil and American Power*, Allen Lane, 2012, pp. 47, 57.

155   Joe Walker, 'Draft Global Climate Science Communications Plan', April 1998.

156   Union of Concerned Scientists, *Smoke, Mirrors and Hot Air*, p. 14.

157   Ibid., p. 11.

158   Martin Wolf, 'Why the world faces climate chaos', *The Financial Times*, 15 May 2013, p. 13.

159   *Arctic Climate Impact Assessment*, New Scientific Consensus: Arctic Is Warming Rapidly, Much larger changes are projected, affecting global climate, 8 November 2004; http://amap.no/workdocs/index.cfm?action=getfile&dirsub=%2FACIA%2Fmediakits&filename=ACIAinternationalPR%2Edoc

160   Usha Lee McFarling, 'Climate Change Accelerating, Report Warns', *Los Angeles Times*, 8 November 2004; http://articles.latimes.com/2004/nov/09/science/sci-arctic9. 'Report says Arctic rapidly warming', *Seattle Times*, 9 November 2004; http://seattletimes.nwsource.com/html/nationworld/2002085775_arctic09.html

161   Steve Connor, 'Meltdown: Arctic wildlife is on the brink of a catastrophe', *Independent*, 11 November 2004.

162   'The Arctic Apocalypse', *Daily Mail*, 9 November 2004, p. 35.

163   Tim Radford, 'Climate change study flawed, says study', *Guardian*, 9 November 2004.

164   Andrew Rowell, 'Exxon's Foot-Soldiers', in William Dinan and David Miller, *Thinker, Faker, Spinner, Spy*, Pluto Press, 2007, pp. 94–116.

165   David Adam, 'Royal Society tells Exxon: stop funding climate change denial', *Guardian*, 20 September 2006; http://www.guardian.co.uk/environment/2006/sep/20/oilandpetrol.business?INTCMP=SRCH

166   Bob Ward, letter to Nick Thomas, Royal Society, 4 September 2006; http://image.guardian.co.uk/sys-files/Guardian/documents/2006/09/19/LettertoNick.pdf

167   Exxon Mobil Corporation, 2011 Worldwide Contributions and Community Investments; http://www.exxonmobil.com/Corporate/Files/gcr_contributions_pubpolicy11.pdf

168   Heartland Institute website, accessed August 2012: http://heartland.org/sites/all/themes/heartland_org/images/QuoteBarGraphic.png

169   James Hoggan with Richard Littlemore, *Climate Cover-Up: The Crusade to Deny Global Warming*, Greystone Books, 2009, p. 78; Josh Israel and Brad Johnson, 'Exposed: The 19 Public Corporations Funding The Climate Denier Think Tank Heartland Institute', ThinkProgress, 17 February 2012.

170   Jesse Coleman, 'Heartland Institute Compares Climate Advocates to Mass Murderers', PolluterWatch blog, 5 May 2012; http://www.polluterwatch.com/blog/heartland-institute-compares-climate-advocates-mass-murderers. Brian Vastag, 'Group pulls plug on billboard linking global warming believers to terrorists', *The Washington Post*, 4 May 2012; http://www.washingtonpost.com/national/health-

science/group-pulls-plug-on-billboard-linking-global-warming-be-lievers-to-terrorists/2012/05/04/gIQAU2q51T_story.html

171 'Eli Lilly, BB&T, and Pepsi Confirm They Will No Longer Fund the Heartland Institute, Bringing the Total Number of Defections to Eleven', Forecast the Facts, 14 May, 2012; http://forecastthefacts.org/press/releases/2012/5/14/eli-lilly-bbt-and-pepsi-confirm-they-will-no-longe/

172 Greenpeace, 'Koch Industries: Secretly Funding the Climate Denial Machine', 30 March 2010; http://www.greenpeace.org/usa/Global/usa/report/2010/3/koch-industries-secretly-fund.pdf

173 Greenpeace, 'The Koch Brothers: Funding $61,485,781 to Groups Denying Climate Change Science since 1997', undated; http://www.greenpeace.org/usa/en/campaigns/global-warming-and-energy/polluterwatch/koch-industries/. Greenpeace, 'Koch Brothers Exposed: Fueling Climate Denial and Privatizing Democracy', Update, 20 June 2012; http://greenpeaceblogs.com/2012/04/02/koch-brothers-exposed-fueling-climate-denial-and-privatizing-democracy

174 Frontline, 'Robert Brulle: Inside the Climate Change "Countermovement"', PBS, 23 October 2012; http://www.pbs.org/wgbh/pages/frontline/environment/climate-of-doubt/robert-brulle-inside-the-climate-change-countermovement/

175 Suzanne Goldenberg, 'How Donors Trust distributed millions to anti-climate groups', Guardian, 14 February 2013.

176 House of Commons Science and Technology Committee, 'The Disclosure of Climate Data from the Climatic Research Unit at the University of East Anglia', Eighth Report of Session 2009–10, Report, 24 March 2010, p. 46.

177 'What do the "Climategate" hacked CRU emails tell us?', Skeptical Science, undated; http://www.skepticalscience.com/Climategate-CRU-emails-hacked.htm

178 Greenpeace, 'Koch Industries: Secretly Funding the Climate Denial Machine'.

179 Quotes taken from Greenpeace, 'Koch Industries: Secretly Funding the Climate Denial Machine'. And http://www.globalwarming.org/

180 University of East Anglia, 'BBC apologises to University of East Anglia for "incorrect" remark', press release, 7 August 2010.

181 Michael Mann, interview with Andy Rowell, 30 November 2012.

182 Ibid.

183 James Painter, Poles Apart: The International Reporting of Climate Scepticism, Reuters Institute for the Study of Journalism, November 2011; http://reutersinstitute.politics.ox.ac.uk/fileadmin/documents/Publications/Other_publications/Poles_Apart_Executive_Summary.pdf

184   Damian Carrington, 'Chris Huhne blasts Lord Lawson's climate sceptic think tank – Huhne says influential Global Warming Policy Foundation is "misinformed", "wrong" and "perverse" following GWPF report', *Guardian*, 22 November 2011. Editorial: 'All interests must be declared', *Independent*, 24 January 2013; http://www.guardian.co.uk/environment/2011/nov/22/chris-huhne-lawson-think-tank?intcmp=239

185   The Global Warming Policy Foundation, Financial Statements, Period 15 July 2009 to 31 July 2010.

186   CET website, 'Our Clients': http://www.cet.co.uk/clients.htm

187   Data provided by sandbag, January 2011; http://www.cet.com.pl/en/list-selected-clients. Damian Carrington, 'Lord Lawson's links to Europe's colossal coal polluter', *Guardian*, 6 March 2012; http://www.guardian.co.uk/environment/damian-carrington-blog/2012/mar/06/climate-change-sceptic-lawson-coal?INTCMP=SRCH

188   Carrington, 'Lord Lawson's links to Europe's colossal coal polluter'.

189   ExxonMobil, Worldwide Giving Report 2004, Worldwide Contributions and Community Investments, Public Information and Policy Research; http://www.exxonsecrets.org/html/orgfactsheet.php?id=126

190   Roger Bate and Julian Morris, *Global Warming: Apocalypse or Hot Air?*, IEA Environment Unit, 1994.

191   Andrew Rowell, *Green Backlash: Global Subversion of the Environment Movement*, Routledge, 1995, p. 328.

192   Atlas Economic Research Foundation working as the International Policy Network, Report and Financial Statements, 31 December 2001.

193   Institute of Economic Affairs website: http://www.iea.org.uk/life-style-economics

194   Institute of Economic Affairs website: http://www.iea.org.uk/in-the-media/press-release/minimum-alcohol-pricing-makes-minimum-sense

195   Institute of Economic Affairs website: http://www.iea.org.uk/life-style-economics/about

196   Institute of Economic Affairs website: http://www.iea.org.uk/lifestyle-economics. Tobacco Control Research Group, research into Chris Snowdon, published on the TobaccoTactics website, University of Bath, 2013; http://tobaccotactics.org/index.php/Christopher_Snowdon

197   Mark Littlewood, *PM* programme, BBC Radio 4, 27 February 2012.

198   Simon Millson, British American Tobacco, letter to Deborah Arnott, 20 May 2013.

199   Simon Millson, British American Tobacco, letter to Deborah Arnott, 18 June 2013.

9 Reform

1   Dan Hind, *The Return of the Public*, Verso, 2010, p. 107.

2   Taped at Wellington College conference: 'Free Thinking: Using Independence to Transform Schools', 30 November 2012.

3   Sir Michael Barber, Chief Education Adviser, Pearson, UK Trade & Investment Education Summit, August 2011; http://www.youtube.com/watch?v=T3ErTaP8rTA&feature=youtu.be

4   Michael Gove, speech to the Education World Forum Organisation, Department for Education, 11 January 2012; https://www.gov.uk/government/speeches/michael-gove-to-the-education-world-forum

5   Peter Wilby, 'Mad professor goes global', *Guardian*, 14 June 2011; http://www.guardian.co.uk/education/2011/jun/14/michael-barber-education-guru

6   Barber, UK Trade & Investment Education Summit.

7   Lee Fang, 'How Online Learning Companies Bought America's Schools', *The Nation*, 16 November 2011; http://www.thenation.com/article/164651/how-online-learning-companies-bought-americas-schools

8   John Chubb and Terry Moe: 'Higher Education's Online Revolution', *Wall Street Journal*, 30 May 2012.

9   John Chubb and Terry Moe, *Liberating Learning*, Jossey-Bass, 2009, p. 150.

10   Michael Gove speech to the Schools Network, Birmingham, 11 January 2012: https://www.gov.uk/government/speeches/michael-gove-speaks-to-the-schools-network

11   Valerie Strauss, 'Global education market reaches $4.4 trillion – and is growing', *The Washington Post*, 9 February 2013; http://www.washingtonpost.com/blogs/answer-sheet/wp/2013/02/09/global-education-market-reaches-4-4-trillion-and-is-growing/

12   Jonathan Kozol, 'The big enchilada', *Harper's Magazine*, August 2007; http://harpers.org/archive/2007/08/the-big-enchilada

13   Ibid.

14   Department for Education, Statistical Release, September 2013.

15   Fang, 'How Online Learning Companies Bought America's Schools'.

16   McKinsey and Company, 'Transforming learning through mEducation', April 2012; http://mckinseyonsociety.com/transforming-learning-through-meducation/

17   Anthony G. Picciano and Joel Spring, *The Great American Education-Industrial Complex: Ideology, Technology, and Profit*, Routledge, 2013, p. 98.

18   Microsoft Education UK 'Microsoft School in a Box', BETT 2012 presentation, 16 January 2012; http://www.slideshare.net/Microsoft-eduk/bett-2012-microsoft-school-in-a-box-you-teach-we-deliver

19   Rip Empson, 'With Google Play For Education, Google Looks To Challenge Apple's Dominance In The Classroom', Techcrunch, 15 May 2013; http://techcrunch.com/2013/05/15/with-google-play-for-education-google-looks-to-challenge-apples-dominance-in-the-class-room/

20   'For Malaysia: Bringing Google Apps and Chromebooks to the class-room', GoogleBlog, 10 April 2013; http://googleblog.blogspot.co.uk/2013/04/for-malaysia-bringing-google-apps-and.html

21   'Google steps up help for schools looking for savings', Merlin John Online, 9 January 2012; http://www.agent4change.net/bett-week/news/1426-google-steps-up-help-for-schools-looking-for-savings.html

22   Claire Atkinson, 'News Corp. acquires Wireless Generation', *New York Post*, 23 November 2010; http://www.nypost.com/p/news/business/news_corp_acquires_wireless_generation_3uZF9uEJu09Kekc6wYEggK

23   Sian Griffiths, 'Log on and learn', *Sunday Times*, 29 May 2011; http://www.thesundaytimes.co.uk/sto/newsreview/education/article636272.ece

24   Gregory Ferenstein, 'News Corp Announces Business Plans To Disrupt Education', Techcrunch, 23 July 2012; http://techcrunch.com/2012/07/23/news-corp-announces-business-plans-to-disrupt-education-amplify-mobile-technology-and-assessment/

25   David Leigh, 'The schools crusade that links Michael Gove to Rupert Murdoch', *Guardian*, 27 February 2012; http://www.guardian.co.uk/politics/2012/feb/26/schools-crusade-gove-murdoch

26   Ibid.

27   News Corporation, Annual Report, 2012.

28   Department for Business, Innovation and Skills press release, 'New Push to grow UK's £17.5 billion education exports industry', 29 July 2013.

29   For a critical discussion of the reforms read Stephen Ball, *Education plc: Understanding Private Sector Participation in Public Sector Education*, Routledge, 2007, or Melissa Benn, *School Wars: The Battle for Britain's Education*, Verso, 2012.

30   Michael Gove, speech on academies, Department for Education, 4 January 2012; http://www.education.gov.uk/inthenews/speeches/a00201425/michael-gove-speech-on-academies

31   Jessica Shepherd, 'Academy and comprehensive exam results "indistinguishable"', *Guardian*, 4 June 2009; http://www.theguardian.

com / education / 2009 / jun / 04 / academy-comprehensive-results-indistinguishable

32   Ron Glatter, 'Academy schools: a flawed system that cannot be sustained', *Guardian*, 24 January 2013; http:// www.guardian.co.uk/ teacher-network/ teacher-blog/ 2013/ jan/ 24/ academy-school-system-heading-rocks

33   Diane Ravitch, 'Why I Changed My Mind About School Reform', *Wall Street Journal*, 9 March 2010; http:// online.wsj.com/ article/ SB10 001424052748704869304575109443305343962.html

34   Taped at Wellington College conference: 'Free Thinking: Using Independence to Transform Schools'.

35   Matt Richtel, 'In Classroom of Future, Stagnant Scores', *New York Times*, 3 September 2011; http:// www.nytimes.com/ 2011/ 09/ 04/ technology/ technology-in-schools-faces-questions-on-value. html?pagewanted=all&_r=o

36   Taped at Wellington College conference: 'Free Thinking: Using Independence to Transform Schools'.

37   Ibid.

38   Searching for the reality of virtual schools, Center for Public Education, May 2012; http:// www.centerforpubliceducation.org/ Main-Menu/ Organizing-a-school/ Searching-for-the-reality-of-virtual-schools-at-a-glance

39   Chris Kirk, taped at Wellington College conference: 'Free Thinking: Using Independence to Transform Schools'.

40   David Sirota, 'New data shows school "reformers" are full of it', Salon, 3 June 2013; http:// www.salon.com/ 2013/ 06/ 03/ instead_of_a_war_on_teachers_how_about_one_on_poverty/

41   Chris Kirk, taped at Wellington College conference: 'Free Thinking: Using Independence to Transform Schools'.

42   VMA Group, UK Public Affairs Survey 2012/ 13: http:// www. vmagroup.com/ brochures/ public-affairs-survey-2012/ files/ assets/ downloads/ VMA%20Group%20UK%20Public%20Affairs%20 Survey%202012.pdf

43   Sam Dillon, 'Imported From Britain: Ideas to Improve Schools', *New York Times*, 15 August 2007; http:// www.nytimes.com/ 2007/ 08/ 15/ education/ 15face.html?pagewanted=all

44   Ibid.

45   David M. Herszenhorn, 'New York Rethinks Its Remaking of the Schools', *New York Times*, 9 April 2006; http:// www.nytimes. com/ 2006/ 04/ 09/ nyregion/ 09Klein.html?pagewanted=all

46   'The K-12 Dilemma: What Can Be Done?', Chief Executive, 1 January 2005; http:// chiefexecutive.net/ the-k-12-dilemma-what-can-be-done

47   Ibid.

48   Carl Campanile, 'Gates' $4 Mil Lesson', *New York Post*, 17 August 2009; http://www.nypost.com/p/news/regional/item_ekjA6OeX-IrxZjDATHPbkuJ

49   Lawrence Harmon, 'Bill Gates's risky adventure', *Boston Globe*, 27 April 2010; http://www.boston.com/bostonglobe/editorial_opinion/oped/articles/2010/04/27/bill_gatess_risky_adventure/

50   Bill Gates, keynote speech, SXSWEdu Conference 2013: http://sxswedu.com/news/watch-bill-gates-sxswedu-keynote-video-now

51   Sam Dillon, 'Behind Grass-Roots School Advocacy, Bill Gates', *New York Times*, 21 May 2011; http://www.nytimes.com/2011/05/22/education/22gates.html?_r=1

52   Rita Beamish, 'Back to school for the billionaires', The Centre for Public Integrity, 1 May 2011.

53   Gates Foundation press release, 'Expanded Investment in New High Schools Aims to Increase Graduation, College-Going Rates of New York City Public School Students', 15 February 2005; http://www.gatesfoundation.org/Media-Center/Press-Releases/2005/02/New-High-Schools-Aims-to-Increase-Graduation-Rates

54   Nancy Hass, 'Scholarly Investments', *New York Times*, 4 December 2009; http://www.nytimes.com/2009/12/06/fashion/06charter.html?pagewanted=all

55   Ibid.

56   Fang, 'How Online Learning Companies Bought America's Schools'.

57   J. Patrick Coolican and Michael Mishak, 'Teachers: Watch out, Berman is coming!', *Las Vegas Sun*, 3 November 2007; http://www.lasvegassun.com/news/2007/nov/03/teachers-watch-out-berman-is-coming/#axzz2TlabMA23

58   Kyle Smith. 'NJ paradox: Piles of cash, failing schools', *New York Post*, 6 August 2012; http://nypost.com/2010/04/16/nj-paradox-piles-of-cash-failing-schools/

59   Kevin Thomas, 'Capsule Movie Reviews: "The Cartel" examines a state falling down on the job in educating its children', *Los Angeles Times*, 16 April 2010; http://articles.latimes.com/2010/apr/16/entertainment/la-et-capsules-20100416

60   Diane Ravitch, 'The Myth of Charter Schools', *New York Review of Books*, 11 November 2010; http://www.nybooks.com/articles/archives/2010/nov/11/myth-charter-schools/?pagination=false

61   Kay Shackleton, 'Union protest greets cast and crew at premiere of "Won't Back Down" in NY', examiner.com, 23 September 2012; http://www.examiner.com/article/union-protest-greets-cast-and-crew-at-premiere-of-won-t-back-down-ny

62   Valerie Strauss, '"Won't Back Down": Film critics pan parent-trigger movie', *The Washington Post*, 27 September 2012; http://www.washingtonpost.com/blogs/answer-sheet/post/wont-back-down-what-actual-film-critics-think/2012/09/27/ac057088-08cd-11e2-afff-d6c7f20a83bf_blog.html

63   Ravitch, 'The Myth of Charter Schools'.

64   'Filmmakers hope "Won't Back Down" inspires reform', *USA Today*, 16 February 2013; http://www.usatoday.com/story/news/nation/2013/02/16/wont-back-down-reform/1924753/

65   *Won't Back Down* website (retrieved from Archive): http://web.archive.org/web/20130204114001/http://wbdtoolkit.com/tools-to-help/

66   'Filmmakers hope "Won't Back Down" inspires reform', *USA Today*.

67   Mary Bottari, '"Won't Back Down" Film Pushes ALEC Parent Trigger Proposal', PR Watch, 19 September 2012; http://www.prwatch.org/node/11763

68   'Filmmakers hope "Won't Back Down" inspires reform', *USA Today*.

69   Valerie Strauss, 'Real consequences of "school choice"', *The Washington Post*, 12 March 2013; http://www.washingtonpost.com/blogs/answer-sheet/wp/2013/03/12/real-consequences-of-school-choice/

70   Paul Krugman, 'Lobbyists, Guns and Money', *New York Times*, 25 March 2012; http://www.nytimes.com/2012/03/26/opinion/krugman-lobbyists-guns-and-money.html?_r=1

71   Ed Pilkington, 'Alec dismantles controversial taskforce after big firms cut ties', *Guardian*, 17 April 2012; http://www.guardian.co.uk/world/2012/apr/17/alec-dismantles-controversial-taskforce

72   Andy Kroll, 'The Gates Foundation Is Done Funding ALEC', *Mother Jones*, 10 April 2012; http://www.motherjones.com/mojo/2012/04/alec-gates-foundation-pepsi-kraft

73   Mike McIntire, 'Conservative Nonprofit Acts as a Stealth Business Lobbyist', *New York Times*, 21 April 2012; http://www.nytimes.com/2012/04/22/us/alec-a-tax-exempt-group-mixes-legislators-and-lobbyists.html?_r=2&

74   The Center for Media and Democracy, 'ALEC Exposed' project: http://www.alecexposed.org/wiki/Privatizing_Public_Education,_Higher_Ed_Policy,_and_Teachers

75   Dillon, 'Behind Grass-Roots School Advocacy, Bill Gates'.

76   Fang, 'How Online Learning Companies Bought America's Schools'.

77   Ibid.

78   Alice Brennan and Curtis Skinner, 'Schools fight dominates record spending on lobbying', *New York World*, 16 April 2012; http://www.thenewyorkworld.com/2012/04/16/schools-fight-dominates-record-spending-on-lobbying/

79   Ibid.

80   Michael Hirsch, 'Who are Democrats for Education Reform?', United Federation of Teachers, 16 December 2010.

81   Ibid.

82   Education Reform Now website: http://www.edreformnow.org/about/board/

83   New York City Charter School Center: website: http://www.nyccharterschools.org/about-us

84   Ibid.

85   Anna M. Phillips, 'E-Mails Provide Inside Look at Mayor's Charter School Battle', New York Times, 11 May 2012; http://www.nytimes.com/2012/05/12/nyregion/bloombergs-charter-school-battle-detailed-in-e-mails.html?_r=1

86   Trip Gabriel and Jennifer Medina, 'Charter Schools' New Cheerleaders: Financiers', New York Times, 9 May 2010; http://www.nytimes.com/2010/05/10/nyregion/10charter.html?pagewanted=all

87   Ibid.

88   Phillips, 'E-Mails Provide Inside Look at Mayor's Charter School Battle'.

89   Sharon Otterman, 'The Commercial War on Teacher Layoffs', New York Times, 15 February 2011; http://cityroom.blogs.nytimes.com/2011/02/15/the-commercial-war-on-teacher-layoffs/

90   Email from Eva Moskowitz to Joel Klein, 20 December 2009, released by the NY Education Department under FOI law.

91   Phillips, 'E-Mails Provide Inside Look at Mayor's Charter School Battle'.

92   Ibid.

93   Diane Ravitch, 'Something Scary Happened Last Night', blog post, 12 May 2012; http://dianeravitch.net/2012/05/12/something-scary-happened-last-night/

94   Ibid.

95   Email from James Merriman to Lasher Micah and others, 28 May 2010, released by the NY Education Department under FOI law.

96   Celeste Katz, 'Ex-Schools Chancellor Joel Klein Named Chair Of Education Reform Now', NY Daily News, 24 January 2011; http://www.nydailynews.com/blogs/dailypolitics/2011/01/ex-schools-chancellor-joel-klein-named-chair-of-education-reform-now

97   Javier C. Hernandez, 'Bloomberg's Man in Albany Is Young but Seasoned', New York Times, 6 June 2010; http://www.nytimes.com/2010/06/07/nyregion/07lasher.html

98   Valerie Strauss, 'Walton Foundation giving $8 million to Rhee's StudentsFirst — plus 2012 donations', The Washington Post, 1 May

2013; http://www.washingtonpost.com/blogs/answer-sheet/ wp/2013/05/01/walton-foundation-giving-8-million-to-rhees-studentsfirst-plus-2012-donations/

99   David M. Herszenhorn, 'New York Rethinks Its Remaking of the Schools'.

100   Maggie Severns, 'Whatever Happened to the $100 Million Mark Zuckerberg Gave to Newark Schools?' *Mother Jones*, 28 March 2013; http://www.motherjones.com/mojo/2013/03/zuckerberg-advocacy-group-100-million-donation-newark-schools

101   Transcript, Menlo Park Meeting: U.S. Education Reform and National Security, Council on Foreign Relations, 14 May 2012; http://www.cfr.org/education/menlo-park-meeting-us-education-reform-national-security/p28335

102   Ibid.

103   Ibid.

104   Ibid.

105   David Leigh, 'The schools crusade that links Michael Gove to Rupert Murdoch', *Guardian*, 27 February 2012; http://www.guardian.co.uk/politics/2012/feb/26/schools-crusade-gove-murdoch

106   Picciano and Spring, *The Great American Education-Industrial Complex*, pp. 59–60.

107   Amy Chozick, 'Steering Murdoch in Scandal, Klein Put School Goals Aside', *New York Times*, 7 May 2012; http://www.nytimes.com/2012/05/08/business/media/scandal-distracts-klein-from-his-education-goals-at-news-corp.html?pagewanted=all

108   Email from Bradley Tusk to Joel Klein, 28 May 2010, released by the NY Education Department under FOI law.

109   Alexander Zaitchik, 'School reform's propaganda flick', Salon, 27 September 2012; http://www.salon.com/2012/09/27/the_corporate_education_agenda_behind_wont_back_down/

110   noplot, '(Updated) Won't Back Down: Back despite popular demand', Daily Kos, 13 October 2012; http://m.dailykos.com/story/2012/10/13/1144241/-Won-t-Back-Down-Back-despite-popular-demand

111   Jason Tomassini, 'News Corp., Not Wireless Generation, Is ALEC Education Member', *Education Week*, 25 May 2012; http://blogs.edweek.org/edweek/marketplacek12/2012/05/news%20corp_wireless_alec.html

112   Sian Griffiths, 'Log on and learn', *Sunday Times*, 29 May 2011 http://www.thesundaytimes.co.uk/sto/newsreview/education/article636272.ece

113   Ibid.

114   Jessie L. Bonner, 'Tom Luna's Controversial Education Reform
      Sparks Attempt At Repeal In Idaho', *Huffington Post*, 6 August 2011;
      http://www.huffingtonpost.com/2011/06/08/tom-luna-idaho-
      education-reform_n_873339.html; 'Michael Bloomberg Gives $200,000
      To Support Idaho's Education Reform Laws', *Huffington Post*, 11
      February 2012; http://www.huffingtonpost.com/2012/11/01/
      michael-bloomberg-gives-2_n_2059504.html

115   Picciano and Spring, *The Great American Education-Industrial Complex*,
      p. 162.

116   John Hechinger, 'Washington Post Co.'s Future Tied to For-Profit
      Kaplan Business', *Bloomberg*, 7 August 2013; http://www.bloomberg.
      com/news/2013-08-07/washington-post-co-s-future-tied-to-for-
      profit-kaplan-business.html

117   Brooks Barnes and Amy Chozick, 'Media Companies, Seeing
      Profit Slip, Push Into Education', *New York Times*, 19 August
      2012; http://www.nytimes.com/2012/08/20/technology/discovery-
      invests-in-digital-textbooks-in-hopes-of-growth.html? pagewanted
      =all&_r=0

118   Tristram Hunt, 'If we have no history, we have no future', *Observer*,
      28 August 2011; http://www.theguardian.com/commentisfree/2011/
      aug/28/tristram-hunt-history-teaching-schools%20

119   Department for Education press release, 'More than 100 free schools
      applications approved', 22 May 2013; https://www.gov.uk/govern-
      ment/news/more-than-100-free-schools-applications-approved

120   Taped at Wellington College conference: 'Free Thinking: Using
      Independence to Transform Schools'.

121   Estelle Morris, 'Profit-making schools threaten the moral purpose
      of education', *Guardian*, 25 June 2012; http://www.theguardian.
      com/education/2012/jun/25/profit-making-threatens-moral-
      purpose-education

122   Anna Bawden, 'Should schools be more like Tesco?', *Guardian*, 14
      October 2009; http://www.theguardian.com/education/mortar-
      board/2009/oct/14/schools-like-tesco

123   John Jerrim, 'England's "plummeting PISA test scores between 2000
      and 2009": Is the performance of our secondary school pupils really
      in relative decline?', Institute of Education, December 2011.

124   Michael Gove, 'I refuse to surrender to the Marxist teachers hell-bent
      on destroying our schools', *Daily Mail,* 23 March 2013.

125   Dennis Sewell, 'Michael Gove vs the Blob', *Spectator*, 13 January 2010;
      http://www.spectator.co.uk/features/5704478/michael-gove-vs-the-
      blob/

126   Michael Gove speech, 'How are the children?', 27 June 2012.

127   Fraser Nelson, 'The economic case for sacking bad teachers', *Spectator*, 18 June 2013; http://blogs.spectator.co.uk/coffeehouse/2013/06/the-economic-case-for-sacking-bad-teachers/

128   Josie Ensor, 'British children facing bleaker future than rest of Europe, warns Unicef', *Telegraph*, 10 April 2013; http://www.telegraph.co.uk/education/educationnews/9982175/British-children-facing-bleaker-future-than-rest-of-Europe-warns-Unicef.html

129   James Forsyth, 'The urgent need for school reform', *Spectator*, 13 March 2009.

130   Nicholas Watt, 'Free school opponents "defending failure", says David Cameron', *Guardian*, 9 September 2011; http://www.theguardian.com/education/2011/sep/09/free-school-opponents-defending-failure-says-cameron

131   Wellington College conference: 'Free Thinking: Using Independence to Transform Schools'.

132   Festival of Education brochure: http://www.festivalofeducation2013.org.uk/mint-project/uploads/400755205.pdf

133   Ben Duckworth, 'In conversation with . . . Neil O'Brien', *Total Politics*, 8 February 2012; http://www.totalpolitics.com/print/294267/in-conversation-with-neil-oand39brien.thtml

134   Tom Clark, 'New Schools Network lacks transparency', *Guardian*, 6 July 2010; http://www.guardian.co.uk/education/2010/jul/06/michael-gove-new-schools-transparency

135   *New Statesman*, 'The shadow power list', 11 February 2013; http://www.newstatesman.com/2013/02/shadow-power-list

136   Ibid.

137   New Schools Network website: http://www.newschoolsnetwork.org/about/team

138   Clark, 'New Schools Network lacks transparency'.

139   *New Statesman*, 'The shadow power list'.

140   Ibid.

141   Policy Exchange, 'A discussion with StudentsFirst founder Michelle Rhee', 26 June 2012; http://www.policyexchange.org.uk/modevents/item/michelle-rhee

142   Policy Exchange, 'Politics? Nothing that a bit of thinking can't cure', 30 January 2011; http://www.policyexchange.org.uk/media-centre/in-the-news/category/item/politics-nothing-that-a-bit-of-thinking-can-t-cure

143   Andrew Adonis, *Education, Education, Education: Reforming England's Schools*, Biteback Publishing, 2012, p. 60.

144   Patrick Wintour, 'Michael Gove under pressure to allow profit-making

in schools', *Guardian*, 17 October 2012; http://www.guardian.co.uk/education/2012/oct/17/michael-gove-pressure-profit- schools

145   Tom Mills, Tom Griffin and David Miller, *The Cold War on British Muslims*, Spinwatch, 2011; http://www.middleeastmonitor.com/downloads/documents/the-cold-war-on-british-muslims.pdf

146   Policy Exchange website: http://www.policyexchange.org.uk/about-us

147   George Monbiot, 'Think of a Tank', Monbiot.com, 12 September 2011; http://www.monbiot.com/2011/09/12/think-of-a-tank/

148   Michael Portillo, Register of Members Interests, 2001: http://www.publications.parliament.uk/pa/cm200102/cmregmem/memi22.htm

149   Leigh Academies Trust website: http://www.leighacademiestrust.org.uk/aboutus/chief-executive-statement.php

150   Harris Federation website: http://www.harrisfederation.org.uk/142/our-sponsor

151   Mills, Griffin and Miller, *The Cold War on British Muslims*.

152   Kerra Maddern, 'No industrial action, no negotiations and no reply', *Times Educational Supplement*, 30 September 2011; http://www.tes.co.uk/article.aspx?storycode=6114412

153   Somerton Capital website: http://www.somertoncap.com

154   Education Committee, Third Report: 'Governance and leadership of the Department for Education' (part 2: 'Changes to the Departmental Board'), October 2012; http://www.publications.parliament.uk/pa/cm201213/cmselect/cmeduc/700/70004.htm

155   'Academies board', Department for Education, 26 April 2013; http://www.education.gov.uk/schools/leadership/typesofschools/academies/sponsors/a00221975/academies-board

156   Mills, Griffin and Miller, *The Cold War on British Muslims*.

157   Centre for Policy Studies website: http://www.cps.org.uk/about/board/john-nash/

158   'Sovereign Capital named Education Investor for second year running', Sovereign Capital website, 18 November, 2011; http://www.sovereigncapital.co.uk/media-centre/press-releases/2011/sovereign-capital-named-education-investor-for-second-year-running/

159   Mills, Griffin and Miller, *The Cold War on British Muslims*.

160   Oliver Burkeman, 'Next stop, schools', *Guardian*, 26 June 2001; http://www.guardian.co.uk/education/2001/jun/26/schools.uk

161   Greg Hurst, 'Business will seek to run state schools after shift in political attitudes', *Times*, 31 March 2010

162   David Leigh, 'The schools crusade that links Michael Gove to Rupert Murdoch', *Guardian*, 27 February 2012; http://www.guardian.co.uk/politics/2012/feb/26/schools-crusade-gove-murdoch

163   American Friends of Policy Exchange, Policy Exchange website: http://www.policyexchange.org.uk/support-us/afpx

164   James O'Shaughnessy, 'Change in schools has to start at the bottom', *Times*, 3 January 2012; http://www.thetimes.co.uk/tto/opinion/columnists/article3274191.ece

165   Richard Vaughan, 'Former No 10 adviser sets his sights on failing schools', *Times Educational Supplement*, 16 November, 2012; http://www.tes.co.uk/article.aspx?storycode=6301748

166   Francis Beckett, 'The NS Profile: Michael Gove', *New Statesman*, 6 September 2010.

167   James O'Shaughnessy's profile, Policy Exchange website: http://www.policyexchange.org.uk/people/alumni/item/james-o-shaughnessy

168   Tara Hamilton-Miller, 'A new background noise', *New Statesman*, 13 September 2007; http://www.newstatesman.com/uk-politics/2007/09/quality-life-dave-cameron

169   Tamasin Cave personal communication with lobbyist, 2012.

170   Public Citizen, 'Organizing Astroturf' briefing, January 2007; http://www.citizen.org/documents/Organizing-Astroturf.pdf

171   Vincent Moss, 'Michael Gove banks £500,000 in donations sparking rumours of leadership plot', *Mirror*, 21 July 2013; http://www.mirror.co.uk/news/uk-news/michael-gove-banks-500000-donations-2070503

172   Education Foundation, EdTech Incubator website: http://www.edtechincubator.com/people/

173   The Education Foundation, 'Facebook Guide for Educators', June 2013; http://www.ednfoundation.org/2013/06/21/facebook-guide-for-educators/

174   EdTech Incubator, 'Facebook & Gates Foundation hackathon for social learning': http://www.edtechincubator.com/facebook-gates-foundation-host-hackathon-for-social-learning/

175   Valerie Strauss, 'E-mails link Bush foundation, corporations and education officials', *The Washington Post*, 30 January 2013; http://www.washingtonpost.com/blogs/answer-sheet/wp/2013/01/30/e-mails-link-bush-foundation-corporations-and-education-officials/

176   Foundation for Excellence in Education, National Summit on Education Reform, October 2013: http://excelined.org/national-summit/2013-agenda/

177   Strauss, 'Emails link a Bush Foundation, corporations and education officials'.

178   Josh Eidelson, 'Jeb Bush ed reform group accused of abusing nonprofit status to help corporations', *Salon*, 21 October 2013: http://

www.salon.com/2013/10/21/jeb_bush_ed_reform_group_accused_of_abusing_non_profit_status_to_help_corporations/

179   Education Foundation, 'Growing the UK education reform movement – part 2': http://www.ednfoundation.org/2012/12/14/growing-the-uk-education-reform-movement-part-2/

180   Education Foundation website: http://www.ednfoundation.org/our-events/

181   Education Foundation website: http://www.ednfoundation.org/category/media/

182   Education Foundation website: http://www.ednfoundation.org/about/people/david-james/

183   Centre for Market Reform of Education website: http://www.cmre.org.uk/who-we-are/

184   Tamasin Cave, contemporary note at Wellington College conference, November 2012.

185   James B. Stanfield, 'The Profit Motive in Education: Continuing the Revolution', IEA, 19 Jul 2012; http://www.iea.org.uk/publications/research/the-profit-motive-in-education-continuing-the-revolution

186   Institute of Economic Affairs website: http://www.iea.org.uk/about/what-we-do

187   Neil Selwyn, '"Micro" politics: mapping the origins of schools computing as a field of education policy', *History of Education*, 2014; http://newmediaresearch.educ.monash.edu.au/lnmrg/selwyn

188   Ibid.

189   Tamasin Cave, interview with Neil Selwyn, August 2013.

190   The Independent ICT in School Commission 1996/7, 'Information and Communications Technology in UK Schools', 1997; http://rubble.heppell.net/stevenson/vision.html

191   Tamasin Cave, interview with Neil Selwyn, August 2013.

192   Ibid.

193   Emma Simpson, 'Becta, the first quango to be cut, closes its doors', BBC News, 1 April 2011; http://www.bbc.co.uk/news/business-12932140

194   Tom Burkard and Sam Talbot Rice, 'School quangos: A blueprint for abolition and reform', Centre for Policy Studies, August 2009; http://www.cps.org.uk/files/reports/original/111027120256-20090813PublicSerivesSchoolQuangos.pdf

195   Richard Vaughan, 'Mr Gove is finally turned on to technology', *Times Educational Supplement*, 9 December 2011; http://www.tes.co.uk/article.aspx?storycode=6149504

196   James Robinson, 'Eric Schmidt, chairman of Google, condemns British education system', *Guardian*, 26 August 2011; http://www.

guardian.co.uk/technology/2011/aug/26/eric-schmidt-chairman-google-education

197   Full text of Eric Schmidt's MacTaggart lecture in the *Guardian*, 26 August 2011; http://www.guardian.co.uk/media/interactive/2011/aug/26/eric-schmidt-mactaggart-lecture-full-text?INTCMP=SRCH

198   Miles Godfrey, 'Google calls for education reforms', AAP Newsfeed, 13 March 2013.

199   Ibid.

200   Schmidt speech: August 2011; US/UK Chromebook announcement May 2011; http://phys.org/news/2011-05-google-powered-laptops-sale-june.html. Google Oz warning, 13 March 2013; Chromebook Oz release, March 2013; http://www.news.com.au/technology/tech spert-the-google-chromebook/story-e6frfro0-1226607504743

201   'Thanks to the hard work of Ian Livingstone and Next Gen Skills Computer Science is being introduced into the English Baccalaureate', UKIE website: http://ukie.info/content/thanks-hard-work-ian-living stone-and-next-gen-skills-computer-science-being-introduced-engli

202   'Detailed background on what's been happening', BCS website: http://academy.bcs.org/content/detailed-background-whats-been-happening

203   Computing at School website: http://www.computingatschool.org.uk/index.php?id=about-us

204   'Detailed background on what's been happening', BCS website.

205   Katie Scott, 'MP Ed Vaizey admits Livingstone gaming report initally ignored', *Wired*, 26 January 2012.

206   Nick Cowen, 'London Game Conference: Ian Livingstone Interview', *Guardian*, 7 November 2011.

207   Ibid.

208   Ian Livingstone and Alex Hope, *Next Gen.*, Nesta, February 2011; http://www.nesta.org.uk/library/documents/NextGenv32.pdf

209   *Next Gen. Next Steps*, Nesta; http://www.nesta.org.uk/library/docu ments/NextGenNextSteps.pdf

210   Ibid.

211   Department for Education press release, '"Harmful" ICT curriculum set to be dropped to make way for rigorous computer science', 11 January 2012; http://www.education.gov.uk/inthenews/inthenews/a00201864/harmful-ict-curriculum-set-to-be-dropped-this-september-to-make-way-for-rigorous-computer-science

212   Michael Gove speech at the BETT show 2012, 13 January 2012.

213   Matthew Chapman, 'Govt approves Carphone Warehouse Tablets for Schools drive', *Marketing*, 12 March 2013; http://www.market ingmagazine.co.uk/article/1174153/govt-approves-carphone-ware house-tablets-schools-drive

214   'DfE supporting "Tablets for" research findings', Merlin John Online, 15 July 2013; http://www.agent4change.net/policy/ict-provision/2058-dfe-supporting-tablets-for-schools-research-findings.html

215   Policy Exchange, 'Britain's Broadband Future' (Conservative Conference), 9 October 2012; http://www.policyexchange.org.uk/events/pastevents/item/conservative-conference-britain s-broadband-future?category_id=37

216   Jennifer Scott, 'Virgin Media Business to power London school network', ITPro, 26 January 2011; http://www.itpro.co.uk/630370/virgin-media-business-to-power-london-school-network

217   Tablets for Schools website: http://www.tabletsforschools.co.uk/about/

218   Many lobbying agencies, like Portland, sign up to voluntary registers operated by the industry, but only declare their clients.

219   Portland entry on the Public Relations Consultants Association public affairs register Dec–Feb 2010.

220   Ibid.

221   James Frayne, 'Why should we [sic] lift the ban on political advertising on UK TV', Portland website; http://www.portland-communications.com/publications/the-quarterly-issue-8/why-should-we-lift-the-ban-on-political-advertising-on-uk-tv/

222   Patrick Wintour, 'Michael Gove opts for a better Frayne of mind in retelling message', Guardian, 25 February 2011; http://www.guardian.co.uk/politics/blog/2011/feb/25/michael-gove-james-frayne-education

223   Policy Exchange, 'A chain reaction that would fix Britain's failing schools', 16 October 2012; http://www.policyexchange.org.uk/media-centre/blogs/category/item/a-chain-reaction-that-would-fix-britain-s-failing-schools

224   David Singleton, 'Portland signs up Conservative Party heavyweight Michael Portillo', PR Week, 24 September 2009; http://www.prweek.com/uk/news/940934/

225   Michael Gove, evidence to the Leveson Inquiry, Transcript of Afternoon Hearing, 29 May 2012.

226   David Leigh, 'The schools crusade that links Michael Gove to Rupert Murdoch', Guardian, 27 February 2012; http://www.guardian.co.uk/politics/2012/feb/26/schools-crusade-gove-murdoch

227   Ibid.

228   Ibid.

229   Watson, Dial M for Murdoch, p. 258.

230   Rupert Murdoch, The Inaugural Margaret Thatcher Lecture, Centre for Policy Studies, 21 October 2010; http://www.cps.org.uk/events/q/date/2010/10/21/rupert-murdoch-lecture-21-october-2010/

231   Leigh, 'The schools crusade that links Michael Gove to Rupert Murdoch'.

232   Gove, evidence to the Leveson Inquiry.

233   Speech by Joel Klein, Free Schools Conference, Department for Education, 29 January 2011; http://www.youtube.com/watch?v=S-YaFQdh_tw

234   'Michael Gove – Meetings with Media Organisations – 6 May 2010–15 July 2011; https://www.gov.uk/government/uploads/system/uploads/attachment_data/file/190803/michael_gove_media_meetings_may_2010___july_2011.pdf

235   Fraser Nelson, Centre for Policy Studies website; www.cps.org.uk/about/board/fraser-nelson/

236   Toby Young, 'Status Anxiety: I can't wait for Superman', *Spectator*, 27 November 2010; http://www.spectator.co.uk/life/status-anxiety/6489258/status-anxiety-i-cant-wait-for-superman/

237   Leigh, 'The schools crusade that links Michael Gove to Rupert Murdoch'.

238   Ibid.

239   Gove, evidence to the Leveson Inquiry.

240   Michael Gove, ministerial meeting log, October to December 2010 https://www.gov.uk/government/uploads/system/uploads/attachment_data/file/190783/quarterly_information_for_ministers_1_october_to_31_december_2010.pdf

241   Steve John, *The Persuaders*, Palgrave Macmillan, 2002, p. 54.

242   Josie Ensor, 'Michael Gove faces questions over use of private email', *Telegraph*, 20 September 2011; http://www.telegraph.co.uk/news/politics/8775646/Michael-Gove-faces-questions-over-use-of-private-email.html

243   Chris Cook, 'Gove staff destroyed government emails', *Financial Times*, 2 March 2012; http://www.ft.com/cms/s/0/f70db1e0-6458-11e1-b50e-00144feabdc0.html

244   Email to Tamasin Cave from the Department of Education, 21 February 2013.

245   Question from John Mann MP to Tim Loughton MP, 11 June 2012: http://www.theyworkforyou.com/wrans/?id=2012-06-11b.109229.h&s=special+adviser+speaker%3A11093#g109229.qo

246   'Michael Gove under pressure over use of private emails', BBC News, 20 September 2011; http://www.bbc.co.uk/news/education-14987075

247   Decca Aitkenhead, 'Michael Gove: the next Tory leader?', *Guardian*, 5 October 2012; http://www.theguardian.com/politics/2012/oct/05/michael-gove-next-tory-leader

248   Policy Exchange report, 'A Guide to School Choice Reforms',
      2009.
249   Peter Wilby, 'Michael Gove is hailed as a rising star. He does not
      deserve it', *Guardian*, 7 December 2012; http://www.theguardian.
      com/commentisfree/2012/dec/07/gove-myth-educational-standards-
      private-providers

10 Dominate

1   Graham Allen, Committee Stage Debate of Transparency of
     Lobbying, Non-party Campaigning and Trade Union Administration
     Bill 2013-14, House of Commons, 9 September 2013.
2   Wall Street Watch, 'Sold Out: How Wall Street and Washington
     Betrayed America', March 2009.
3   Open Secrets, RBS Lobbying Spending 2008–2013, Center for
     Responsive Politics; http://www.opensecrets.org/lobby/clientsum.
     php?id=D000028825&year=2013
4   Rajeev Syal and Solomon Hughes, 'Bailed-out RBS spends millions
     on Washington lobbyists', *Guardian*, 27 January 2012; http://www.
     theguardian.com/business/2012/jan/27/royal-bank-scotland-wash-
     ington-lobbyists
5   Ibid.
6   Nicholas Watt, 'Lynton Crosby "would have discussed" cigarette pack-
     aging with PM', *Guardian*, 22 July 2013; http://www.theguardian.com/
     politics/2013/jul/22/lynton-crosby-cigarette-packaging-pm
7   Francis Maude, 'This will be the most transparent and accountable
     government in the world', *Guardian*, 19 November 2010; http://
     www.theguardian.com/commentisfree/2010/nov/19/francis-
     maude-government-data-published
8   Prime Minister's foreword to the Ministerial Code, Cabinet Office,
     May 2010; https://www.gov.uk/government/uploads/system/
     uploads/attachment_data/file/61402/ministerial-code-may-2010.
     pdf
9   Committee Stage Debate of Transparency of Lobbying, Non-Party
     Campaigning and Trade Union Administration Bill, Hansard, 9
     September 2013; http://www.publications.parliament.uk/pa/
     cm201314/cmhansrd/cm130909/debtext/130909-0002.htm
10   Grant Jordan, *The Commercial Lobbyists*, Aberdeen University Press,
     1991, p. 153.
11   John Warden, 'Axe grinding: The fast approaching party conference
     season heralds the time when that elite breed of PR specialist known

as the political lobbyist emerges into the sunlight', *Marketing*, 24 September 1987.

12 Mark Hollingsworth, *MPs for Hire*, Bloomsbury, 1991, p. 114.

13 Richard Clogg, 'The colonel, the PR man and the MP', *Times Educational Supplement*, 21 November 1994; http://www.timeshigher-education.co.uk/story.asp?storycode=154290

14 Jane Howard, 'The evolution of UK PR consultancies 1970–2010', PRCA, 2011.

15 Jordan, *The Commercial Lobbyists*, p. vii.

16 Ibid., pp. 23–4.

17 Warden, 'Axe grinding'.

18 Ibid.

19 Tom O'Sullivan, 'Lobbyists to clean up act', *PR Week*, 5 July 1990.

20 Tom O'Sullivan, 'Judgment day looms for the lobbyists', *PR Week*, 19 July 1990.

21 David Hencke, 'Lobbyists split over registers', *Guardian*, 28 September 1994.

22 Public Administration Select Committee, 'Lobbying: Access and Influence in Whitehall', vol. 2, 2008–9.

23 Ibid.

24 Ibid.

25 *Dispatches*, 'Politicians for Hire', Channel 4, 22 March 2010.

26 David Cameron's speech, 'Rebuilding Trust in Politics', 8 February 2010.

27 Public Administration Select Committee, 'Lobbying: Access and Influence in Whitehall', vol. 2, 2008–09.

28 Jonathan McLeod, chairman of public affairs at the lobbying giant Weber Shandwick, *PR Week*, February 2008.

29 Public Administration Select Committee, 'Lobbying: Access and Influence in Whitehall', vol. 2, 2008–9, p. 45.

30 Jim Pickard, 'Data freedom ruling to affect lobbying', *Financial Times*, 1 May 2008; http://www.ft.com/cms/s/0/ad73c760-1716-11dd-bbfc-0000779fd2ac.html#axzz2gKLLgDBq

31 Mark Adams, 'The Choice is Yours', *Public Affairs News*, September 2009, p. 24.

32 Sam Coates, Roland Watson and Deborah Haynes, 'Clamp on lobby-ists will hit charities and unions', *The Times*, 19 October 2011; http://www.thetimes.co.uk/tto/news/politics/article3199098.ece

33 Public Administration Select Committee, 'Lobbying: Access and Influence in Whitehall', vol. 2, 2008–09.

34 Lord Bell interviewed on the BBC's *Newsnight*, April 2012; http://www.youtube.com/watch?v=DvTQLlo4sgM

35   UK Public Affairs Council board meeting minutes, 16 September 2010; http://www.publicaffairscouncil.org.uk/en/utilities/document-summary.cfm?docid=5EB4517D-2E8C-49CE-9A217C6F7A0BC43A

36   Elizabeth France interviewed on CIPR TV, 16 January 2011.

37   Michael Gillard, '"Abusive" lobbying reform chief quits over tweets', *Sunday Times*, 29 January 2012; http://www.thesundaytimes.co.uk/sto/news/uk_news/Tech/article864434.ece

38   Oliver Wright, 'Lobbying official turned down reform meetings', *Independent*, 30 January 2012; http://www.independent.co.uk/news/uk/politics/lobbying-official-turned-down-reform-meet-ings-6296562.html

39   John Rentoul, 'The Long Decline of Trust in Government', *Independent*, 29 September 2013; http://blogs.independent.co.uk/2013/09/28/the-long-decline-of-trust-in-government

40   Ibid.

41   Paul Whiteley, 'Why Do Voters Lose Trust in Governments? Public Perceptions of Government Honesty and Trustworthiness 1997–2013', paper presented at the Conference on 'Citizens and Politics in Britain Today: Still a Civic Culture?', London School of Economics, 26 September 2013; http://www.kent.ac.uk/politics/research/comparativegroup/Whiteley-paper.pdf

42   Interview with Tim Bell, 31 October 2013.

Further Reading

There are many excellent books and online resources we have drawn on in the research and writing of this book, many of which we reference in the text. These are just a number that we feel may be a particularly useful starting point for anyone interested in reading more on the subject.

Spinwatch's (www.spinwatch.org) online encyclopedia, Powerbase (www.powerbase.info), is a resource that can be invaluable for researchers and citizens wanting to make sense of the various lobbies out there. Focused on the networks of individuals and institutions shaping the public agenda, its 13,000 or so articles cover topics including food, alcohol, finance, nuclear and health lobbies, with information on think tanks, front groups and lobbyists.

A Century of Spin by David Miller and Will Dinan (Pluto Press, 2007) is, as far as we are aware, the only history of PR and lobbying that looks in detail at the UK. Chapter 1 owes much to their book (although any mistakes belong to us). *Thinker, Faker, Spinner, Spy* edited by Miller and Dinan (Pluto Press, 2007) adds weight to their case.

Nick Davies' *Flat Earth News* (Vintage, 2009) is as complete a picture as you will get about the state of the UK media and how unreliable it has become as a source of accurate information. For a thorough account of corporate approaches to dealing with 'antis' turn to Eveline Lubbers' *Battling Big Business, Countering Greenwash, Infiltration and Other Forms of Corporate Bullying* (Green Books, 2002) and *Secret Manoeuvres in the Dark* (Pluto Press, 2012). She has also, usefully, set out many tools to help activists and citizens recognise corporate PR strategies and how they can be countered.

The UK lobbying scene is small in comparison to the two big centres of power: Washington and Brussels. Lobbyists over here, however, are involved over there and have clearly learnt from their US counterparts in particular. The excellently-named *Toxic Sludge is Good for You: Lies, Damn Lies and the Public Relations Industry* by John Stauber and Sheldon Rampton (Common Courage Press, 1995) is a one-off, fascinating account of PR and lobbying tactics in the US. Stauber and Rampton were co-editors of PR Watch (www.prwatch.org), a publication of the Center for Media and Democracy, who were described by lobbyist Rick Berman, as 'self-anointed watchdogs', a charge that has been levelled at us. We like them.

Lawrence Lessig, author of *Republic, Lost: How Money Corrupts Congress – and a Plan to Stop It* (Twelve, 2011) is nothing like them. A Professor of Law at Harvard Law School and a Republican, his book is an equally urgent call for reform of American politics, which, he convincingly argues, has been co-opted by outside interests. To see the extent to which money corrupts US politics, visit the Centre for Responsive Politics' Open Secrets website (www.open-secrets.org).

For a troubling and often hidden view of lobbying in Brussels, journalist David Cronin's *Corporate Europe: How Big Business Sets Policies on Food, Climate and War* (Pluto Press, 2013) tells you what you need to know. Campaigning researchers in Corporate Europe Observatory are also leading work to expose the influence of the thousands of corporate lobbyists resident in the EU capital (www.corporateeurope.org).

There are a great many excellent books that expose the power of specific lobbies. Among those that we have found most useful are: *Merchants of Doubt: How a Handful of Scientists Obscured the Truth on Issues from Tobacco Smoke to Global Warming* by Naomi Oreskes and Erik Conway (Bloomsbury, 2010); Michael Mann's *The Hockey Stick and the Climate Wars: Dispatches from the Front Lines*, Columbia University Press, 2012; *Climate Cover-Up: The Crusade to Deny Global Warming* by James Hoggan with Richard Littlemore (Greystone Books, 2009); Marion Nestle's *Food Politics: How the Food*

Industry Influences Nutrition and Health (University of California Press, 2002) and Stewart Player and Colin Leys' timely *The Plot Against the NHS* (Merlin Press, 2011).

Acknowledgements

This book would not have been possible without the work of David Miller and Will Dinan, co-founders (with Andy) of Spinwatch, who have looked extensively at the PR and lobbying industries for many decades. Their understanding has been invaluable. We owe a debt to journalist Melissa Jones who also oversees Spinwatch's wiki, Powerbase.info, which provides a more thorough guide to these issues than we could ever include in a book. Eveline Lubbers, Clare Harkins and others who have greatly contributed to this work also deserve much thanks.

We have, as well, drawn on the expertise of many other researchers in different fields. Thanks to Anna Gilmore, Gary Fookes, Cathy Flower, Eveline Lubbers, Karen Evans-Reeves and Silvy Peeters at the Tobacco Control Research Group at the University of Bath. Deborah Arnott from Action on Smoking and Health and Andy Lloyd from FRESH who have also been tracking the tobacco industry's tactics; Richard Cookson and Pete Roche for helping investigate the nuclear industry; Darek Urbaniak who has worked on the anti-tar sands campaign in Europe; Steve Kretzmann and Lorne Stockman from Oil Change International, who have worked on oil industry tactics and lobbying; Colin Leys, Caroline Molloy and Andy Robertson for their expertise on NHS privatisation.

Great thanks go to those who have campaigned with us for transparency regulations. Chiefly Alexandra Runswick, James Graham and Peter Facey of Unlock Democracy, as well as Owen Espley, formerly of Friends of the Earth, Barry White of the Campaign for Press and

Broadcasting Freedom and many others over the years. The Joseph Rowntree Charitable Trust has shown tremendous support, thank you. We are grateful too for the contribution of many campaigners, in particular those opposed to incineration in Devon and Plymouth.

The work of a number of journalists has also been invaluable, in particular Melanie Newman and Nick Mathiason of The Bureau of Investigative Journalists. Thanks too to Mark Hollingsworth, whose books have greatly informed this one. We are grateful too to Michael Gillard and Dave Connett for advice and to those reporters, academics and lobbyists who have talked openly to us. Thanks is also due to the many journalists, particularly those outside of the mainstream, and researchers who have done much to shine a light on lobbying and whose work we reference.

Kay Peddle from Bodley Head, you have been a steadying hand throughout for which we are sincerely grateful. Thanks also to Stuart Williams and Katherine Ailes who helped see the book through its final stages. Thanks too to Dan Hind and Anna Minton for sound guidance. To AB for support and understanding. And to JB for patience and a lot more.

Index